689
11
306
322

Locker 605
32-7-19

THE NEW

Building
Better
English .... 11 ..

MELLIE JOHN

PAULENE M. YATES

Illustrations by Muriel and Jim Collins

ROW, PETERSON AND COMPANY

Evanston, Illinois   White Plains, New York

PREFACE

The authors and publishers of "The New Building Better English" series have a firm conviction that instruction in English, to be effective, must be based upon a recognition of the fact that it is a basic-skills subject.

What qualities, then, should distinguish a good English series?

1. The content must show careful, logical organization; and that organization must be clearly apparent. Piecemeal, hit-or-miss instruction should have no place in English texts. Further, the content must show an orderly, definite progression from one book of the series to the next. Finally, the arrangement of material must be such as to make it readily adaptable to varied types of curricula.

2. Each of the large areas of communication—speaking, listening, reading, and writing—must receive ample treatment, not merely token recognition.

3. Instruction must be clear and specific, with rules, definitions, and guides easily distinguishable from introductions and exercises. The practice material must be useful, varied, and appealing; and there must be consistent maintenance of skills throughout. In addition, there should be available a thorough testing program that covers the mechanics of expression.

4. An integral part of the texts should be concrete provision for applying English skills to the work in all subjects as well as to life outside school.

5. The content must "make sense" to the students who use the books. It is the belief of the makers of this series that boys and girls do not object to hard work if they understand what they are to do and how they are to go about it.

Even a cursory examination of "The New Building Better English" will reveal how thoroughly these books measure up to the preceding criteria. A careful examination should bring the conviction that pupils and teachers who use this series will find the study of English a productive and pleasurable experience, not a dreary chore.

The Publishers

CONTENTS

SECTION II   *Read and Grow!*

SECTION III *Write and Refine!*

SECTION IV   *Know the Structure!*

SPEAK AND Listen

Thinking and Speaking

1. GETTING ACQUAINTED WITH KINDS OF THINKING

"I KNOW IT'S A STUDY NIGHT, BUT THIS MOVIE IS EDUCATIONAL. IT'S LAID IN A JUNGLE."

READ AND THINK ABOUT

If you were to ask Arbee,* in any of the three situations pictured above, "What are you doing?" his reply probably would be, "I'm thinking!"

What differences are there in the kinds of thinking illustrated?

---

* Arbee (real name, Rouncivelt Berwilliger Frimble), the red-headed young hero of *The New Building Better English, Grade Nine,* is growing up physically, as you can see. He is growing up mentally, too, though the process is not always so apparent.

3

What do *you* mean when you say, "I've been thinking"? Have you merely been indulging in dreams of what you would like to do or be; that is, have you been doing "wishful thinking"? Or have you been "rationalizing" about something—developing reasons and excuses for yourself?

Neither of the kinds of thinking described in the preceding paragraph calls for much serious mental activity on your part. There is, however, a kind of thinking that develops and trains the mind. It is the type of thinking that analyzes an idea by questioning it, finds reasons that are not influenced by the questioner's own feelings, and arrives at logical conclusions. It is the kind of thinking that Columbus did when he discarded old theories about the shape of the world and formed a new idea. It is the kind of thinking that the Wright brothers did when they conceived the idea of the airplane. It is the type of thinking that makes the world a better place to live in, but unfortunately it is too rare a type. To do creative thinking, you must clear your mind of hand-me-down ideas, of prejudices, of excuses for yourself; then go on to attack an idea by study and analysis. Such procedure is not easy, you will find. Try yourself out by analyzing why you argue hotly for one political party; why you belong to this church or that social organization; why you like a particular style of clothing; why you have a certain attitude toward some other person or group of persons.

Be word-wise! *

Skim the preceding paragraphs for these words: *reply, serious, rare, attack*. Your dictionary lists varied synonyms for them and explains the fine shades of meaning that they express. Decide which of the synonyms would not be good substitutes for the words as they are used in this lesson. Which synonym for *attack* does the drawing illustrate?

LEARNING ACTIVITIES IN ANALYZING YOUR THINKING

A. Which type of thinking is revealed by each of the following remarks? Compare your answers in class.

1. Why don't I make better marks in my classes? There must be something that I can do to improve.
2. I'm as good as half the players on the team. Coach is just down on me.
3. I wish I'd been born back in Daniel Boone's day. Life was exciting then.

---

*This heading, wherever you find it in your text, indicates a vocabulary-building exercise based upon words in the lesson. Doing these vocabulary exercises will help to make you aware of the importance of choosing the *right* word. If "skim" is a new word to you, see the guides on page 113.

4. What practical improvements need to be made in this machine?
5. Life on a South Sea island! I can just see myself there!
6. It isn't that I'm prejudiced; I just don't care to associate with such people.
7. I could make them all sit up and take notice if I really wanted to. I'm just not the show-off type, or I'd do it!
8. What makes Johnny act the way that he does? There must be something I can do to help him.

B. Choose one of the statements that follow or some other one that appeals to your group. Conduct a question-and-answer forum that will bring out your ideas on the statement chosen. Set a definite time limit.

1. The schools should replace interschool athletic contests with an intramural sports program for all students.
2. High school education should be extended two years beyond the usual twelfth grade.
3. Military discipline should be enforced in the public schools.

After your discussion, analyze yourselves by the following statements.

1. I (do, do not) take part readily in a question-and-answer forum.
2. I (am, am not) quick at reacting to ideas.
3. I (am, am not) hasty at stating opinions.
4. I (forget, remember) to call by name persons whom I question or answer.
5. I (am, am not) able to listen to the development of the main idea and to follow it as it progresses.
6. I (am, am not) able to speak so that I aid in keeping the discussion on the main idea when there is a tendency to get sidetracked.
7. I (can, cannot) listen courteously until the chance comes for me to speak.
8. When I speak, the audience is (interested, bored, politely tolerant).

2. Following an Idea to a Climax or a Conclusion

When you get into your car, you usually go by the shortest and most direct route to a fixed destination. Thinking should be as directed as driving a car. To ramble along, talking aimlessly, is to be mentally lazy.

To aid the reader in following ideas, written composition is broken into *paragraphs*. Each paragraph contains only one main idea, either stated specifically in a *topic sentence* or implied clearly. The topic sentence is also called the *topic statement*.

In oral composition, the need for a division into main ideas or paragraphs is just as great. Each central idea should be clear and definite. The grouping of thoughts around that central idea should be orderly. All confusing or unrelated thoughts should be discarded.

GUIDES FOR DEVELOPING THE ORAL PARAGRAPH

1. Plan a forceful beginning for every paragraph.
2. Make sure to have only one central idea and to make it stand out clearly.
3. Use only sentences that contribute to the main idea.
4. Plan a closing sentence that will be a climax to the paragraph, a summary of it, or a conclusion drawn from it. If you draw a conclusion, the closing sentence can be your topic sentence.

LEARNING ACTIVITIES IN FOLLOWING AN IDEA

A. Use one of these topic statements as the first sentence of an oral paragraph. Conclude with a sentence that will clinch the idea of the paragraph.

1. In war even the victor loses.
2. Baseball is our national sport.
3. The things that we get for nothing cost the most.
4. This community needs a new high school building.

B. The following paragraph shows poor development. Restate the paragraph to eliminate the faults. Compare work in class or in your small groups.

> The rooms in this building are too small. All the classes are large and we are crowded into small spaces so that we cannot do good work. We need outdoor facilities for sports. We need an auditorium for our assemblies. There are so many reasons for building a new high school building that any one of them ought to convince the public that there is a necessity for one. Elmwood has a new school; and we have a larger enrollment than Elmwood, so we can afford a new building, too. The north entrance is really unsafe, and the fourth floor is a fire hazard.

C. "The only way to be sure of becoming the kind of person that you want to be is to begin and continue being that sort of person." Use this sentence as the final sentence of an oral paragraph. Form a careful beginning sentence that will attract interest; perhaps a rhetorical question (see page 411) will be effective. Make your last sentence a climax, a summary, or a general conclusion.

3. USING YOUR MIND TO SELECT SUBJECTS FOR SPEECH

READ AND THINK ABOUT

In your experience are vast numbers of subjects on which you can speak because your mind has done something with them. Perhaps some of them involve only the simplest form of mental activity, undirected dreaming.

Others call for a simple decision. Still others find your mind offering excuses and explanations. But if you are examining a subject, questioning its meaning and use, you are approaching worth-while mental activity.

What do you talk about? Well, you talk about yourself, for example. You talk about people, machines, animals, plants, leisure, life, death, birth, love, hate. You talk about inventions, government, discoveries, events, books, magazines, drama, art, music. You talk about what others have said.

In any of these subjects, you can be a parrotlike repeater of what has been said before. You can be a wishful dreamer on each subject. You can justify yourself and your existence through each topic. But as soon as you begin to ask *Why? How? What? Where? When?* and to seek out the answers for yourself, you become a creative thinker and speaker.

LEARNING ACTIVITY IN FINDING SUBJECTS FOR SPEECH

What can you talk about? Prepare a list of all the topics on which you can talk as individuals; compare lists and find the total number of subjects available in class. As you make your lists, group them under (1) subjects from experiences that you have had, (2) subjects from the knowledge that you possess, and (3) subjects on which you must use sources of information other than your own experience or knowledge. The general outline that follows may assist you in giving specific titles to your subjects.

    I. Finding subjects of speech from one's own experiences
        A. Work: description of, how done, why enjoyed or disliked
            1. Favorite school subjects; difficult ones
            2. Home tasks and contributions to general family welfare
            3. Vocational interests and special abilities
            4. Tools for work: use, nature, . . .
        B. Leisure activities: when? how? descriptions of, . . .
            1. Sports and games
            2. Favorite books, magazines, news articles, . . .
            3. Hobbies
            4. Social activities
            5. Artistic interests: music, drama, drawing, . . .
            6. Travel: where, how, incidents, why, . . .
        C. Health: achieving, maintaining, restoring, preventing accidents
        D. Home
            1. Family: members, characteristics, employment, ancestors, interests
            2. Dwelling: how built, type, value for home, . . .
        E. Social activities
            1. Friends: standards of choice, characteristics, value, . . .
            2. Entertainment: kinds, methods, values
        F. Clothes: importance, relation to personality, ways of making
        G. Food: favorite kinds, preparation, . . .

II. Finding subjects from one's own knowledge or thoughts

    A. Things: machines, instruments and tools, buildings, . . .

    B. Ideals and desires
        1. Changes desired in life about one
        2. Type of government admired
        3. Country or locality most attractive
        4. Kind of man or woman most admired
        5. Kind of work desired
        6. The greatest work in the world

    C. The world about you
        1. Nature: plants, animals, rocks, birds, . . .
        2. Inventions: sciences, trades, arts
        3. Discoveries: nature, science, medicine
        4. People: deeds and achievements
        5. Natural formations: streams, mountains, canyons, caves, . . .
        6. Works of man: buildings, dams, bridges, tunnels, canals, . . .
        7. Religions
        8. Governments

III. Finding subjects in sources of information

    A. Reading: in general books, periodicals, textbooks, . . .

    B. Listening to those who know

    C. Observation: using eyes, ears, and nose

4. Thinking Your Way through Debatable Questions

"JUST DON'T ASK ME TO ASSOCIATE WITH HIM!"

"TO THINK THAT I WAS ONCE AS PREJUDICED AS THAT!"

READ AND THINK ABOUT

Is Arbee's friend being guided by his feelings, or by his mind?

How do *you* react when someone expresses opinions that differ from yours?

Suppose that you find yourself confronted with an idea that is debatable. For example, you may be asked this question: *Should all physically qualified American boys be required to take military training?* If your emotions

8

or your prejudices rule, you are likely to give a quick, emphatic *yes* or *no*. But that instant reply is not an evidence of thinking. First of all, you must be open-minded on so controversial a matter. Consider these questions:

What evils may grow out of such a procedure?
Would these evils be greater than those under present conditions?
Would there be valuable financial and emotional gains?
Who might be authorities on such a question? What do they say?
Does history reveal evidence that supports either side of the question?
What in your own experience gives proof on one side or the other?

If you are to have something worth while to say on a debatable subject, you must have these qualities:

1. A genuine desire to express your ideas
2. An open and questioning mind that seeks for conclusions and answers
3. The ability to do co-operative thinking by evaluating the ideas of others and modifying your own in accordance with them
4. The ability to organize ideas logically in written notes and outlines

Be word-wise!

Skim the preceding paragraphs for these words: *consider, valuable, reveal*. Which synonyms for these words, as explained in the dictionary, would not be suitable substitutes for the words as used in this lesson? Which synonym for *reveal* does the drawing illustrate?

GUIDES FOR IMPROVING THINKING

1. As the first step in improving your thinking, jot down the ideas that you already have on a subject.

2. Examine those ideas. Discover whether they are merely an expression of dreams and wishes, of prejudices, or of the opinions of others. Ask yourself: *Why is this thing true? How is this idea used? What are the causes? What are the results? What else can I learn about this matter? What truths can I establish from this idea? What sources of authority could I use to check this conclusion?*

3. Go to sources of authority. Formulate a series of questions that will lead to authoritative conclusions. Interview people who are authorities; consult reference books and articles.

4. Organize the information collected so that your idea is developed to a definite conclusion. Weigh and compare all the ideas that you have gathered, asking always of each idea, "Is it true?"

A. Use this exercise for class discussion. In the statement of the question: "Should all physically qualified American boys be required to take military training?" there are expressions that are open to various interpretations. Such expressions make it difficult to answer the question intelligently. Exactly what is meant by "physically qualified"? Does the expression apply only to those fit to engage in actual combat, or does it include those able to perform limited service? Who shall be the final authority in deciding an individual's physical fitness? Does the term "all" include members of religious denominations whose beliefs forbid them to participate in military activities? Can "American" be interpreted in more than one way? What age limits are covered by the term "boys"? At what age should training begin? Exactly what is meant by "military training"? How long shall the training course be?

Restate the question so that its meaning is no longer doubtful.

B. Write three good discussion statements. Make every word count. Be sure that each statement includes the entire idea that you want to develop. Exchange papers with a classmate. Correct any faulty word usage; revise to correct any omission of ideas. Consult the dictionary for good synonyms.

FOLLOW-UP ACTIVITY

Study again the list of guides that you should follow in developing a subject (page 9). Check those in which you need most practice; then take every opportunity to develop skill in applying them.

5. Developing Ideas through Deductive and Inductive Reasoning

"INDUCTIVE REASONING? THAT'S WHAT THE DRAFT BOARD USED WHEN THEY PUT MY COUSIN ERNIE INTO THE ARMY!"

THINK IT OVER...

Do you agree with Arbee's explanation?

What is the difference between *inductive* and *deductive* reasoning?

In this chapter you have been learning to find subjects for the expression of ideas. Having ideas to express is important, but just as important is the ability to think so clearly that you can make your ideas easily understandable by others.

There are two chief methods of developing a subject logically. These are the *inductive* method and the *deductive* method.

1. The inductive method begins with a series of observations that lead to a definite conclusion. James Watt, as he sat in the kitchen watching how steam from the boiling water lifted the lid of the kettle on the hearth, used inductive reasoning to reach the conclusion that steam could be harnessed and made to work for man. To put it another way, the inductive method works from the *particular* (observing a steaming teakettle) to the *general* (reaching the conclusion that steam is a great force that can be put to work).

2. The deductive method of reasoning begins with the statement of a known law or fact and then applies that statement to certain observations, or finds evidence to support the statement. For example, the doctor, as he applies his medical knowledge to the analysis of a patient's symptoms, makes use of deductive reasoning. In other words, the deductive method is the opposite of the inductive method: it works from the *general* (the doctor's medical knowledge of disease) to the *particular* (his conclusions about an individual patient).

LEARNING ACTIVITIES IN DEDUCTIVE AND INDUCTIVE THINKING

A. Discuss the following questions in class or in your small groups.

1. What kind of reasoning led Columbus to seek a new route to India?
2. What kind of thinking does an architect do as he plans a new building?
3. What kind of thinking was demonstrated by Edison? by Pasteur?
4. Which kind of reasoning is a person using when he says, "From these circumstances I infer that . . ."?

B. Which of the following paragraphs is developed deductively, and which inductively? How do you know? Discuss those questions.

Because Mary T. is interested in the high school science courses and has real sympathy for sick people, she has decided to be a nurse. What Mary T. does not realize is that nursing, particularly the training of a student nurse, involves the heaviest kind of work. She does not think of the tension of the operating room, where cool nerves are needed for efficient work despite the sight of blood and the fumes of ether. Her nerves would be overstrained by one night in an emergency ward handling the broken bodies of accident cases. Because she does not know the work, Mary is planning on a career in which she would undoubtedly fail.*

* E. W. Andrews, *Looking Ahead,* pages 20–21 (adapted). "Basic Social Education Series." Evanston, Illinois: Row, Peterson and Company, 1941.

By every means at their command, soil experts are trying to solve the problems of the plains farmers. Wherever they can get the interest and co-operation of the farmers, these experts are introducing practices like terracing, strip cropping, and the use of cover crops. To aid farmers still further, these men have developed new machinery that lists the land into ridges, and blocks the action of the wind on the land surface. One new method, called "basin listing," sets up a series of counter-ridges along the main ridges, forming hollows which provide for water storage on the field. In many places where the rainfall is under twenty inches a year, the experts are advising a combination of cattle raising and farming.*

C. Here is a list of topic sentences. In a class discussion, decide which method of development would suit each of them. Could most of them be developed either deductively or inductively?

1. I think that I was born four hundred years too late.
2. If man ever develops a feeling of security, progress will cease.
3. Traveling by air has fewer hazards than traveling by highway.
4. Winter (*or some other season*) has really arrived.
5. Many people seem to want not to grow up.

D. Choose two of the topic sentences and make a brief outline to show how you would develop each of them. Use deductive reasoning in one and inductive reasoning in the other. Check your outlines by these questions:

1. In the outline worked out inductively, does each point build up evidence leading to the topic sentence?
2. In the outline worked out deductively, does each point offer proof of the topic sentence?

USING ENGLISH IN ALL CLASSES

In a science, history, mathematics, or some other text, find paragraphs that show deductive and inductive thinking. Read these aloud in class; ask classmates to identify the type of reasoning illustrated. Be sure to apply the Guides to Effective Oral Reading, page 41.

6. LEARNING TO ANALYZE PROPAGANDA

READ AND THINK ABOUT

What does the word "propaganda" mean to you? Contrary to what many people think, propaganda is not necessarily bad. Any organized attempt, whether by a group or by an individual, to influence others by the expression of ideas is propaganda. Whether or not the actual word is used

---

* Murl Deusing, *Soil, Water, and Man,* page 38. "Basic Social Education Series." Evanston, Illinois: Row, Peterson and Company, 1941.

to name the act, propaganda has always been an influence that has led men and nations into war as well as into ways of peace; it is the way by which sales of many material goods, as well as those of necessities and luxuries, are made; it is the power that is used to move men to take any action at the polls, in civic movements, in moral issues, . . .

In its specialized meaning, however, propaganda involves a systematic campaign of spreading ideas, such as when one nation tries to affect the thinking of another people by carefully planned campaigns of thought distribution. In such uses, the aim is to influence thought or action for the benefit of those who are spreading the propaganda. Everyone should learn to judge and analyze all forms of propaganda so that he may differentiate between the good and the bad.

GUIDES FOR RECOGNIZING DISHONEST PROPAGANDA

1. Unscrupulous propagandists get in some of their most telling blows by appealing to the emotions in such ways as the following:
   a) Covering up selfish interests under a pretense of patriotism
   b) Emphasizing points that will arouse or strengthen race, class, religious, or party prejudice
   c) Fostering the idea that what they advocate will bring fulfillment of one's dreams and desires
   d) Playing upon fears of the future, of the new and untried, of being thought queer or different, of being unpopular
   e) Whitewashing individuals, actions, or policies with names that denote desirable qualities: "this unselfish patriot," "deep love for the common man," "acting from purest motives only"
   f) Implying that to be happy one must "keep up with the Joneses"

2. Dishonest propagandists conceal truth by such means as these:
   a) Pointing out only the good points of what they advocate
   b) Twisting facts so as to give entirely wrong impressions
   c) Dealing in vague generalities instead of in specific facts
   d) Omitting any news unfavorable to their policies
   e) Quoting an authority incompletely to give the impression that he favors something which he actually opposes

3. Unscrupulous propagandists frequently accomplish their ends by trying to make opponents look ridiculous. They imply that support for those opponents comes only from the weak and the unintelligent.

LEARNING ACTIVITIES IN ANALYZING PROPAGANDA

A. Discuss the devices listed in "How to Recognize Dishonest Propaganda." Then search your newspapers and magazines carefully to see how many of those devices you can detect. How effective do you think that these devices are?

B. Listen to radio and television programs (including the commercials) and judge which ones have as their aim to influence thought or action of the listeners. Judge whether such action or thought is for the real benefit of those at whom it is directed. Decide for yourself whether you are listening to "good" or "bad" propaganda.

C. Study leading advertisements in newspapers and magazines. Note the means used to influence thinking and action. On what do the advertisers base their appeal? Is it on *pride? property ownership? romance? security? health? fear? egoism? personal appearance? intelligence? adventure?* How many of these advertisements seem to promise more than they can fulfill?

D. If you can, give instances in which propaganda has led you to biased thinking or hasty action; to careful, thoughtful action.

E. Which form of misleading or dishonest propaganda is illustrated by each of the following statements? Jot down your answers; then compare notes.

1. Everyone knows that he is a radical.
2. My opponent has insulted the intelligence of you fine people.
3. Will you invest a small sum with us, or will you pass up this glorious opportunity?
4. I haven't anything against him, but if he gets to be class president, you can bet that the whole class will be in trouble.
5. It was that referee who lost us the game. He's down on us!
6. I ask you to go to the polls tomorrow and cast your vote for this man who stands above his opponents like a knight in shining armor.
7. Here is the lotion that will make you irresistible!
8. Can you afford to risk what your neighbors will say?

7. Reviewing the Use of the Mind in Speech

The following review offers an excellent opportunity to master what you have been studying about how to use the mind in speech. Work out this review in a class discussion period, a question-and-answer forum, or a written lesson.

1. What are the three sources of ideas for expression? Illustrate them.
2. What are the various kinds of thinking in which one usually engages? Which type contributes most to the service of the world?
3. Name several subjects on which every normal person should be able to express himself orally.
4. Give the steps to follow in developing any idea for expression.
5. What attitudes must one have on debatable questions?
6. How important is the ability to recognize dishonest propaganda? What are the various methods of using such propaganda?

Are You Listening?

"You say something, dear?" *

READ AND DO

An old proverb says, "Speech is silver; silence is golden." You may conclude from that quotation that it is always wiser to keep quiet than to talk, but what it really means is that there are times when listening is better than speaking.

You have been learning about the importance of using your mind to improve your speech. Just as important but probably even more neglected is your listening ability. To demonstrate that fact, perform the following experiment.

Read and think about the questions that follow. Then number a sheet of paper from 1 to 11. Beside each number write *yes* or *no* to the corresponding question. Be honest with yourself. Hand in your paper without signing your name to it.

---

* J. Whiting cartoon. Reprinted from the *Saturday Evening Post*.

Take time in class to tabulate the results. If you answer truthfully, doubtless most of you will realize that your listening habits need improving.

1. Do you ever do poor work in your classes because you only half listen to assignments? Do you ever find yourself saying, "But, Mr. Blank, I thought you said . . ."?
2. Are you ever embarrassed by having to say to a companion, "I'm sorry, but I didn't hear what you said. I'm afraid I wasn't listening."
3. Have you ever become lost in a strange place because you failed to listen carefully to directions?
4. Have you ever tried to repeat a story told you, only to find yourself confused because you could not recall parts of it accurately?
5. Has the failure to listen carefully to instructions ever led to your having an accident? to your losing money?
6. Do you make a real effort to hear yourself speak, so that you can analyze the impression that you make on others?
7. Do you know someone who seems to get far more than you do out of music, drama, speeches, sermons, . . . ?
8. Have you ever found yourself in trouble because you repeated inaccurately a piece of news told you?
9. Do you ever close your ears and mind to opinions with which you disagree?
10. As you listen to public addresses, assembly talks, sermons, or radio speeches, can you keep your mind on what the speaker is saying?
11. Have you ever listened to a joke and then tried to tell it later, only to have it fall flat because you failed to use the exact wording in giving the "punch line"? For example, there is the old story about the Englishman who asked his American-farmer host what he did with the quantities of sweet corn raised on his farm. The farmer told him, "We eat what we can, and what we can't, we can." Back home, the Englishman told his friends, "This farmer grows enormous quantities of corn. He says that they eat what they can, and what they can't, they preserve." Then he wondered why no one laughed.

No trick is involved in learning to be a good listener, but it does require conscious effort and an alert mind. The following suggestions will help only if you make a habit of applying them every day.

Be word-wise!

Skim the preceding questions for these words: *embarrassed, afraid, strange, accurately*. Which synonyms that the dictionary lists for these words would not be good substitutes for them as used in the questions? Which synonym for *afraid* is illustrated by the drawing?

GUIDES TO GOOD LISTENING

1. As you listen to a speaker, either in person or over the air, ask yourself: "Exactly what ideas is he stating? Do I agree? If not, what are my reasons? Are any of those reasons based upon prejudices, not upon facts or logic?"

2. In listening to explanations or directions, repeat each step to yourself as it is given. Ask questions about anything not clear to you. Then go over the steps in order.

3. In conversational situations, keep in mind that later you may want to repeat something said by a companion. Be sure to get it straight; people resent being misquoted. Ask yourself, "Does he really mean that? Does he know what he's talking about? Do I agree?"

4. Make the speaker feel that you are really listening. Show by your expression that you are reacting to his words. Ask questions or make comments that will indicate your interest.

5. Do not attempt to listen and do something else at the same time. It is neither a polite nor a profitable habit.

6. Listen for *transitional* expressions; that is, those that carry the speaker's thought along or that give a clue to his attitude or point of view. *Next, however, unfortunately, on the contrary, in addition, therefore* are examples of such expressions.

7. Pay attention to the speaker's tone of voice. Often it may convey an entirely different meaning from that given by the words themselves. "You are a real friend," for example, if spoken in a sarcastic tone, means the very opposite.

8. If you can see the speaker, note facial expressions and gestures. They help to carry his message.

9. Summarize mentally what the speaker is saying.

LEARNING ACTIVITIES IN LISTENING

Directions: The activities that follow are intended to start you on the road to better listening habits. Perform them thoughtfully.

A. After dark tonight take a fifteen-minute walk in the streets near your home. See how many different sounds you can hear and identify. Later, list them. Compare notes in class the following day. You will be amazed at the number of sounds that you ordinarily fail to hear.

B. Think back over the conversations that you had yesterday. Choose one of them and try to write down everything that you can remember the other person's having said.

C. Make a survey to discover how many in the class have the radio or television set turned on while studying at home. For those of you who do, is the quality of your work affected? Do you find yourself working more slowly? Discuss these questions.

D. The next time that you are in a social group, see how long you can keep someone talking to you while you simply make brief, interested comments or ask encouraging questions. If this exercise proves difficult, you can be sure that you need to improve as a listener.

E. Listen to a five-minute summary of the news on radio or TV. See how accurately you can repeat the news to some member of your family.

RELATED ACTIVITY

For a good study of how tone affects meaning, bring copies of Shakespeare's *Julius Caesar* to class. Turn to Antony's oration over Caesar's dead body (Act III, Scene 2). When he begins his speech, Antony faces a mob with hatred for Caesar in their hearts; when he concludes, Caesar has become to them a noble patriot. Antony has played upon their feelings largely by a change of tone as he speaks two words: "ambitious" and "honorable." Analyze his speech to decide how he must have spoken the lines containing them. Take turns reading those lines. Listen to one another critically.

FOLLOW-UP ACTIVITY

This book offers you many chances to improve as a listener. Work hard at them, but do not forget that everyday life presents the best opportunities to practice good listening. Do not waste them. Someone has said, "A good listener is not only popular, but eventually he learns something." Remember and apply that remark.

What Does Your Speech Reflect?

1. ANALYZING YOUR SPEECH

READ AND DO

Have you ever stopped to think that your way of speaking reflects the kind of person that you are? The idea may be new to you, but your speech is truly a mirror—a mirror of your personality and your character.

With that idea in mind, it is worth while to look honestly at what the mirror of your speech reflects.

1. Does the mirror show that you are word-poor? Do you describe every experience as "swell," "lousy," . . . ?
2. Is your image blurred? Do your words run together so that people often fail to understand what you say?
3. Is the reflection of the real *you* distorted by serious errors in pronunciation and grammatical usage?
4. Does your speech reflect a mind that is actually thinking, or a mind that echoes only the ideas of others?
5. Does your voice or bodily action create an image that annoys or bores those who see and hear you?

Although oral expression is the most important composition skill that you need to master, every direction in this field applies equally well to the writing that you do. This text offers you concrete help if you are dissatisfied with what the mirror of your own language shows.

Begin by doing the following things:

1. In a class discussion, name the abilities in oral and written expression that you think high school juniors and seniors should have. List these upon the blackboard.
2. Copy the list. Underline those skills that you need to practice.
3. Check any of the skills that you feel that you have really mastered. Be strict with yourself.
4. File the list in your notebook. Use it as a guide in the practice work that you do in your classes this year.

2. Finding the Way to Better Speech

READ AND THINK ABOUT

Now that you have taken a good look at yourself, you are ready for the next step, beginning a course of improvement. Because you must use speech so often, learning to speak effectively is the most important English activity that you can practice. Except in school, you use speech from one hundred to one or two thousand times as often as any other kind of communication. From a material standpoint, analyzing the ways in which men make a living will show the importance of knowing what to say and how to say it. Therefore, even if you think of schooling only as a means to financial success, skill in speech is your most useful tool. Still more valuable is the feeling of satisfaction that comes with the ability to express ideas well.

If you want to speak well, you must be willing to work. You must learn to concentrate on one phase of improvement until you have mastered it. The first step is to stop excusing yourself with the self-centered words, "I'm afraid to talk."

Most often the things that men fear are the things which they do not know or do not understand. That statement is true of your being afraid to speak before others. If you are ignorant of how to use body, mind, and emotions in holding an audience and of how to find and develop a subject, of course you are afraid to speak.

On the other hand, your dislike of speaking may be due to fear of being criticized. You should understand that real criticism is far more than a matter of finding fault; it points the way to improvement. You are childish if you are too sensitive; learning to take criticism gracefully is a sign that you are growing up mentally.

GUIDES FOR THE IMPROVEMENT OF ORAL WORK

1. Be your own critic of all your oral work. If you can catch your errors before others catch them, you are beginning to improve.
2. Organize your class into groups of helpful critics who will point out improvement and suggest methods of attacking individual difficulties.
3. Use notes from teacher or classmates to help you to realize your errors and to guide you in correcting them.
4. Do not try to overcome all your difficulties at once. Attack your greatest difficulty first.
5. Do not depend for improvement upon the little time spent in practice within the English classroom. *Practice everywhere.*

LEARNING ACTIVITY

In class, go over the guides. Why should applying any or all of these guides make you (1) a better listener, (2) a better speaker, and (3) a more popular person than you now are?

3. ACQUIRING BODILY EASE

Some critic has said that graduates of American high schools cannot *walk, sit, stand, talk,* or *think.* Is your posture so poor that such criticism might include you? Do you slump, slouch, sprawl? Bodily posture often reflects mental and emotional reactions. The boy who drapes one leg around the other as he waits on the stage to receive his athletic award and the girl who twists her ankles and hands as she is being introduced show a lack of poise that will be reflected in their speech. This same lack of poise exhibits itself in what its victims do with their eyes. They look down at the floor, up at the ceiling, over the heads of the audience, out the window, anywhere but into the faces before them.

Be word-wise!

Skim the preceding paragraph for these words: *include, posture, exhibits.* What synonyms do you find for them in the dictionary? Which synonyms would be poor substitutes for the words as used in this lesson? Which synonym for *posture* does the drawing illustrate?

GUIDES FOR ACQUIRING BODILY EASE

1. Stand with feet fairly close together, with the toe of one shoe somewhat in advance of the other toe, and with the forward foot at a slight angle to the rear foot. As a general rule, if your weight is on the *forward* foot, the *ball* of that foot should carry the weight; if on the *rear* foot, the *heel* should carry the weight. The foot and limb not bearing the weight should be relaxed but should never be allowed to droop. The relaxed foot should act as a steering gear when you move to a different position. If you follow the preceding instructions, you will have no tendency to sway back and forth, and you will both look and feel comfortable. The important thing to remember is to keep one foot ahead of the other, no matter on which one you place your weight.

2. Look at your audience. To make sure that you look at all persons in your audience, make mental notes about them as you stand there. For example, estimate the number of people in the room; note how many are wearing glasses, neckties, or necklaces; . . .

3. Keep your abdomen flat. This action will aid automatically in straightening your shoulders and avoiding a dropped chin.

4. Let hands and arms hang naturally at your sides; when you use them, swing them freely from the shoulders; swing them freely from the wrists.

5. Use face and body to emphasize what you say or how you feel about it. *Pantomime,* the expression of ideas by actions without words, will help to make face and body effective aids to your words.

LEARNING ACTIVITIES IN USING THE BODY

A. Stand in the following easy position based upon all the preceding guides: *weight chiefly on one foot, hands hanging naturally at sides, abdomen flat, shoulders straight, eyes on the class, chin up.* Keep practicing such posture until you take it naturally in class, at home, on the street, or anywhere.

B. Place a chair at the front of the room and practice sitting. Relax, but let the spine serve its real purpose of supporting the back. Sit with one foot slightly in advance of the other. Let the hands rest quietly in the lap. When you rise, as when you sit down, the back foot should assume the chief part of your weight. Since you are not an elderly person, do not raise or lower yourself by grasping the chair. (Notice how gracefully professional actors or public speakers sit and rise.) Practice rising, advancing a few steps, and taking a speaking position.

C. At home, practice to improve your breathing habits. Place the hands at the sides of the waist. Inhale slowly and deeply until the muscles of the diaphragm are fully expanded; exhale slowly. Do this exercise frequently and naturally. Do not be rapid or explosive. Perhaps your music teacher or your physical education instructor will suggest other good breathing exercises.

D. Use pantomime to convey any of the following ideas or emotions. Let the class interpret what you are expressing.

1. Walk across the room in a manner that shows anger, timidity, confusion, eagerness, . . .
2. Use the hands to show grief, worry, joy, satisfaction, exasperation, . . .
3. Use the feet to show perplexity, suspense, annoyance, weariness, . . .
4. Use the shoulders to show scorn, doubt, despair, . . .

E. Pantomime a story or portray a scene. *Do not use the voice at all.* Practice at home before a mirror; then try your pantomime on someone there. You may use a chair but no other properties. Plan your pantomime so that your actions and facial expressions are at all times visible to your audience. In other words, face them. Several ideas are suggested here; you may think of others.

1. You are wearing a pair of new shoes at a dance. They grow increasingly uncomfortable. The best dancer at the party asks you to dance.
2. Communicate to a friend in study hall an invitation to have lunch with you. He does not sit very near you.
3. You suddenly awaken to see the clock hands pointing to the hour at which the train leaves for the week-end trip that you were to take.
4. You are in a boat, fishing. The fish are biting, but so are the mosquitoes.
5. You arrive late at school and must get a tardy slip from the principal.

F. In your small groups, plan and carry out a story suggested by the preceding activity. Practice carefully before presenting the pantomimes for the class. Make sure that you have a definite beginning and a definite ending.

4. MAKING THE MOST OF YOUR VOICE

READ AND THINK ABOUT

Americans often have been criticized as having harsh, nasal voices, accompanied by the defect of poor enunciation. Do you agree that the criticism is a justifiable one?

Whether or not the charge is true, probably you can improve the use of your voice. The voice is like a fine violin; anyone can make noises with it, but only careful study and practice can bring out the best in it.

● **WHAT YOU SHOULD KNOW ABOUT YOUR VOICE**

1. The sound effect of the voice depends largely upon five factors.

   a) *Pitch* refers to highness or lowness of tone. For ordinary speech, medium-pitched voices are best. Monotones, whether shrill or rumbling, should be avoided. In general, low pitch is best suited to expressing deep or sorrowful emotions and ideas of grandeur or majesty; a higher pitch, to lighter emotions and those of fear or anger.

   b) *Volume* refers to loudness of tone. Volume alone will not make certain that you are heard. However, few students speaking in class or before an assembly speak loudly enough.

   c) *Inflection* refers to the variation in pitch within the words spoken. Inflection has much to do with meaning. Notice the different meanings that are suggested by varying the inflection in one simple sentence.

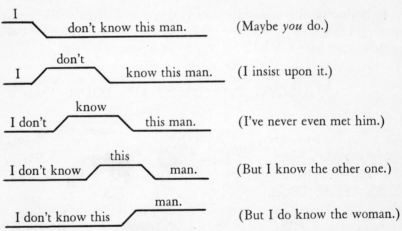

I don't know this man.	(Maybe *you* do.)
I don't know this man.	(I insist upon it.)
I don't know this man.	(I've never even met him.)
I don't know this man.	(But I know the other one.)
I don't know this man.	(But I do know the woman.)

   d) *Rate* refers to the speed with which words are spoken.

   e) *Quality* refers to that characteristic of a tone which distinguishes it from another tone of the same pitch and loudness. For example, a soprano voice will not sound the same as a bass voice even when given the same pitch and the same degree of loudness. In telling a story, an effective speaker changes the quality of his voice to suggest each type of character.

2. The better you can control the five vocal factors, the more pleasing your voice will be to those who hear it, and the better will be its projection (literally, a "throwing forward") to your audience.

24

Skim pages 23–24 for the following words: *defect, avoided, type.* Which of their synonyms, as given in the dictionary, would not be suitable substitutes for the words as used in this lesson? Which synonym of *defect* is suggested by the drawing?

LEARNING ACTIVITIES IN USING THE VOICE

Directions: Do as many as you can of these exercises. Work by yourselves, with a partner, in your small groups, or as a class.

A. If your school has recording equipment, make a record of each voice in the class. Each of you should give his name and then read or speak a few lines. The sound of your own voice may surprise or dismay you. If possible, make other later records to check whether you have improved.

B. Carry out the following activities in varying vocal pitch.

1. If your pitch needs exercises for giving it range, try running the vocal scale of speech by saying *ah* as low as you can and running it on an ascending scale as high as you can carry it. Do not sing. Try this exercise often when you are alone. Do all the other vowels the same way. Run the scale, saying all the long vowel sounds: $\bar{a}, \bar{e}, \bar{\imath}, \bar{o}, \bar{u}$.

2. Emotion affects pitch. Read the following lines aloud. Use the pitch that you think fits the emotion suggested. Discuss the interpretations.

   a) I've come to the end of my rope.
   b) I could not love thee, dear, so much,
   Loved I not honor more.—LOVELACE
   c) Light breezes blew across the meadows.
   d) The bell boomed the midnight hour.
   e) Get out! Do you hear me? Get out!
   f) There it is again! Don't you hear it? I'm frightened!

C. Here is a simple sentence: *Give me that apple.* Read that line with varying inflection to express these meanings:

1. Don't expect me to *pay* for it.
2. Give it to *me*, not to Mary.
3. I don't want the one next to it.
4. I want the *apple*, not the orange.

D. Read the following sentences with varied pitch and inflection to demonstrate different emotions. The class should listen carefully to decide what emotion you are trying to convey.

1. Oh, I never could believe that! (*shock, scorn, . . .*)
2. I left my purse right here, and it's gone! (*anger, shock, anxiety, . . .*)

3. Come here, Towser. (*friendliness, sternness, anger, . . .*)

4. You should have heard what he said! (*anger, sorrow, joy, . . .*)

5. Here they come! (*fear, anticipation, regret, . . .*)

6. Now, Sue, you can do better! (*exasperation, sympathy, doubt, . . .*)

E. To demonstrate how inflection influences the effect of what is said, carry out this little activity. With a partner, plan and then demonstrate a "gossipy" conversation in which you use numbers or the letters of the alphabet instead of words. The class will enjoy trying to "translate" the conversation.

F. Inhale deeply. As you exhale, pronounce slowly the word *sigh*. Note how the sound of the word gives its meaning.

As a group and then as individuals, pronounce the following words slowly, so that you give the sounds the significance of the words: *moan, groan, woe, low, creep, splash, buzz, hiss, purr, boom, swish*. Keep a natural pitch.

G. "You will do this in our way; I am sure of that."

1. Say the above sentence persuasively.
2. Say it sternly.
3. Say it doubtfully.
4. Say it aggressively.
5. Say it sneeringly.
6. Say it pleadingly.

H. How rapidly do you talk? The average rate of normal, unhurried speech is 160 words a minute. To determine your approximate rate, have a classmate check the number of words that you say in a minute of ordinary conversation.

If one were excited, would the rate be faster or slower than the normal rate? How does emotion help to determine the rate?

Perhaps you can find some interesting facts about the fast rate used by certain noted individuals. What radio speakers can you name whose success is partially due to the use of a rapid rate of speech?

I. Behind a screen, present a short radio play, original or otherwise. Let pitch, inflection, volume, and quality of voice aid interpretation.

RELATED ACTIVITY

Find in a science or a speech textbook or in a book in the library an illustration and explanation of the organs of speech. Reproduce the drawings on the blackboard and explain them to the class. (See page 35 for help in explaining.)

5. IMPROVING ENUNCIATION AND PRONUNCIATION HABITS

READ AND DISCUSS

Shakespeare has a line in the play *Hamlet* in which instructions are being given to actors. Hamlet says, "If you mouth it [the lines] as many of your players do, I had as lief the town crier spoke my lines."

What did Hamlet mean by "mouthing" lines? What kind of enunciation evidently characterized the messages of the town crier? What modern vocations call for much repetition of the same lines? The drawings suggest such occupations. Name others.

In addition to their work in pitch, volume, inflection, and quality, the vocal organs control two other factors essential to effective speaking. These factors are *enunciation* and *pronunciation*. Enunciation refers to the *distinctness* of sound of spoken words, while pronunciation has to do with the *correctness* of the sounds spoken and with accented and unaccented syllables. Clear enunciation depends upon careful habits of using lips, tongue, and jaws. Correct pronunciation depends largely upon good use of the dictionary.

LEARNING ACTIVITIES IN ENUNCIATION AND PRONUNCIATION

A. Practice the following exercises. You may want to score your work on a record similar to that on page 31. Listen closely; criticize helpfully.

1. Do you run your words together? Speak these words aloud: "What are you going to give me?" Did you say, "Watcha gonna gimmee?" If you did, repeat the line until each word is clear.

2. Do you slur the sounds of certain letters or syllables? Look at these sentences: "He finly reconize me. I spose he was suprise to fine me in the libary steada in the labatory." Decide what the speaker is trying to say; then take turns reading his words correctly. Take advantage of class criticism.

3. Here is another sentence showing poor enunciation: "I'm gonna begin writin an readin better senences an studyin better litachoor." Treat this sentence as you treated the ones in 2.

4. Do you substitute the incorrect sound of a letter for the right one? Speak this sentence: "This is the way that those boys hit the ball." Did you say, "Dis is de way dat dose boys hit de ball"? If so, you need to sound *th* more carefully in all your speech.

B. Perhaps the reason for some difficulties in enunciation and pronunciation lies in lazy use of the vocal organs. Practice these exercises before a mirror.

1. Relax the jaws by letting the lower jaw drop as if you are asleep; as if you are suddenly amazed or shocked; as a baby does when crying.

2. Use lips and jaws in giving the full range of the sounds of each of these vowel or vowel-consonant combinations: ā, ē, ī, ō, ū, ă, ĕ, ĭ, ŏ, ŭ, o͞o, o͝o, ow (as in *how*).

3. Practice these tongue twisters:
   a) What water was washing the White Webton ways?
   b) Safe kept, the child slept where wild the waves leapt.
   c) Three thousand thistles that thickly throw prickles
      Thus thicken the thicket that thwarts Theseus' thrusts.
   d) Pick plenty of pears; pare perfect the plums;
      Pack package and pan; pass peas in the pod;
      Peddle a peck; be pesky, persistent.
   e) Booth Brewster brought better butter than Bruce Booth's big brother Buster brought.
   f) "She shall certainly sell me some shellfish!" selfish Sharon Shaw shrieks.

C. This exercise is one commonly used in dramatic schools. Read it aloud slowly, separating the words and exaggerating the mouth-and-tongue movements necessary to produce the sounds.

Once there was a young rat named Arthur, who could never make up his mind. Whenever his friends asked him whether he would like to go out with them, he would only answer, "I don't know." He wouldn't say *yes* or *no*, either. He would always shirk making a choice. His Aunt Helen at last said to him, "Now, look here. No one is going to care for you if you carry on like this. You have no more mind than a blade of grass." That night there was a big crash. In the foggy morning, some men, with some boys and girls, rode up and looked at the barn. One of them moved a board and saw a young rat, quite dead, half in and half out of his hole. Thus the shirker got his due.*

* Marian Robertson, *One in a Thousand: The Way of Life on the Road to Hollywood,* page 8. "The Way of Life Series." Evanston, Illinois: Row, Peterson and Company, 1942.

D. Here is a list of other words often mispronounced. Form the class into two groups. Each group should divide the one hundred words in the list among its members. Someone on the team opposite yours will thus be responsible for the same words as you. If he is called upon to read his words, it will be your duty to check any mispronunciation. *You will need to listen carefully.* Do not depend upon your own judgment; check each word in your list by the dictionary before you read your words in class. After a word has been said correctly by a student, the class should repeat the word. From this list, make a special list of words that *you* need to watch; then practice saying them correctly.

1. address	26. idea	51. cement	76. government
2. perform	27. heroine	52. February	77. umbrella
3. recognize	28. probably	53. Italian	78. apparatus
4. geography	29. column	54. juvenile	79. arctic
5. municipal	30. hygiene	55. corps	80. mischievous
6. coupon	31. library	56. finance	81. different
7. due	32. partner	57. adult	82. temperament
8. deaf	33. gesture	58. quantity	83. accidentally
9. surprise	34. radio	59. really	84. perspiration
10. influence	35. picture	60. finally	85. poem
11. rinse	36. industry	61. radish	86. considerable
12. wrestle	37. aviation	62. data	87. trousseau
13. permanent	38. film	63. whether	88. contradict
14. athletics	39. theater	64. piano	89. formerly
15. interested	40. larynx	65. salmon	90. envelope
16. discharge	41. hundred	66. realize	91. maintenance
17. literature	42. children	67. entire	92. absolutely
18. evidently	43. detour	68. inquiry	93. favorite
19. restaurant	44. eczema	69. bouquet	94. laboratory
20. secretary	45. aviator	70. directly	95. sandwich
21. percolator	46. elm	71. figure	96. experiment
22. genuine	47. several	72. program	97. because
23. positively	48. status	73. suite	98. boundary
24. attacked	49. used	74. athlete	99. preferable
25. radiator	50. zoology	75. garage	100. remembrance

E. How accurately do you pronounce the words that you use every day? Test yourself by the words in this list. The rhyming word in parentheses after each word indicates the correct pronunciation.

1. just (*dust*)	8. than (*pan*)	15. height (*might*)
2. are (*car*)	9. can (*pan*)	16. catch (*latch*)
3. our (*tower*)	10. was (*ah's*)	17. mince (*since*)
4. for (*more*)	11. roof (*proof*)	18. often (*soften*)
5. get (*wet*)	12. such (*much*)	19. toward (*lowered*)
6. men (*Ben*)	13. root (*shoot*)	20. address (*unless*)
7. wash (*squash*)	14. new (*few*)	21. pretty (*witty*)

F. Write a nonsense paragraph using the twenty-one words in *E*. Read your work aloud. Your classmates will listen carefully for accurate pronunciation.

6. ANALYZING YOUR PROGRESS

"Practice makes perfect" is a familiar saying, but practice is wasted if one keeps on making the same mistakes. A businesslike method of checking your progress and your needs is to use a score card similar to the one on page 31. Make such a record now. File it in your notebook; then check it following each speech assignment that you complete. You may wish to use the following symbols to mark your progress.

G—good   F—fair   P—poor   I—improving

In judging speech performance, rate each speaker on a slip of paper numbered to correspond with the chart. Note also on the slip any special fault or improvement. For the time being, concentrate on checking the items under *A* and *B*. As you become more proficient speakers, rate one another also on the items under *C*, as shown on the slip below. To be of real help to the speaker, you will need to listen and observe carefully. Be honest in your criticism, but be fair also. Take time at the close of the period to discuss individual progress frankly but courteously.

Speaker			
1.		10.	
2.		11.	
3.		12.	
4.		13.	
5.		14.	
6.		15.	
7.		16.	
8.		17.	
9.			

Speaker	Ted C.		
1. F		10. F	
2. G		11. G	
3. F		12. F	
4. G		13. G	
5. F		14. F	
6. F		15. F	
7. G		16. I	
8. G		17. P	
9. I			

You are pitching your voice lower. Fine!

You still place your feet too far apart.

N. M.

Speech Score Card

Name *Myron Ferris*

	Date	10/3						
A. Use of body								
1. Balance		F						
2. Hands		P						
3. Feet		F						
4. Eyes		I						
B. Use of voice								
5. Volume		I						
6. Pitch		F						
7. Inflection		F						
8. Quality		F						
9. Rate		P						
10. Breath control		F						
11. Enunciation		F						
12. Pronunciation		G						
C. Content								
13. Choice of topic		G						
14. Coherence (sticking to topic)		F						
15. Organization		P						
16. Grammatical usage		I						
17. Vocabulary		F						

Gaining Skill in Speech

1. Asking and Answering Questions

"NOT KNOW HOW TO ASK QUESTIONS? THAT'S SILLY! IT'S WHAT WE DO IN SCHOOL ALL THE TIME!"

READ AND DISCUSS

At first thought, you may be inclined to agree with Doretta. Stop to think, however.

Have you ever failed a test, oral or written, because you could not figure out what a question meant? How many times have you sat in a class and found yourself confused, yet unable to tell what it was that you did not understand? How often have you been silent during the discussion of a problem on which you desired information? Were you silent because you did not know how to word the question that would bring the response that you wanted?

It is not only in school that difficulties with questions are common. Listen to radio programs or to public forums. Observe how often a question is poorly worded and as poorly answered. Think of the uses to which questions and answers are put in the business world. What is the duty of the floorwalker in a large store? What is one of the chief duties of the attendant at a gas station? How important are complete questions and answers in applying for a position or in carrying on an interview?

Be word-wise!

Skim the preceding paragraphs for these words: *stop, confused, silent, complete.* Which of the synonyms given in the dictionary would not be good substitutes? Which synonym for *stop* does the drawing illustrate?

GUIDES FOR ASKING AND ANSWERING QUESTIONS

1. Examine all parts of a question carefully. If it is a fact question, you may be able to answer quickly. Discussion questions, on the other hand, require you to analyze and interpret facts.
2. Make questions clear, concise, and exact.
3. In conversational or discussion groups, ask tactful questions that will lead shy members to talk.
4. Use the name of the person addressed, both in questions and in answers.
5. If you fail to understand a question, do not try to answer until you have asked the questioner to explain.
6. Listen closely so that you will not need to ask for questions or answers to be repeated.

LEARNING ACTIVITIES IN ASKING AND ANSWERING QUESTIONS

A. Bring to class questions from letter forums in magazines and newspapers, or questions asked by an inquiring reporter. Analyze these questions and the answers for defects and values.

B. Carry out one or more of the following question-and-answer dramatizations. The class will judge your performance.

1. Conduct an imitation radio or television quiz program, making all questions and answers conform to the guides.
2. As a reporter for the school paper, you are sent to interview the mayor about a plan to build playgrounds next to each school building in town. (See the Guides for Taking Part in Interviews, page 54.) Do not forget the courteous address, "Mr. Mayor, . . ."

C. Why is each of the following questions and answers poor? In class, find the faults and revise the sentences to eliminate them.

1. Is there a river called the Columbia in Oregon?
2. A race is where there is competition in speed.
3. John wants to know what is the assignment today.
4. You can't tell us how to get to Gayville, can you?
5. Well, it's kind of square and not very big and there is a thingamajig on top.
6. What is the location of Singapore and its climate and people?

USING ENGLISH IN ALL CLASSES

Prepare a lesson in social science, natural science, mathematics, or language by framing questions that cover the important points. Submit your questions to the class or to your small group for analysis and criticism.

2. MAKING CLEAR EXPLANATIONS

"IT'S LIKE THIS — YOU TAKE THE LITTLE WHAT-YOU-CALL-IT AND HOOK IT TO THE TOP OF THE —— OH, NO — I FORGOT! HERE'S THE WAY IT GOES......"

READ AND DISCUSS

How would you account for Arbee's poor showing as he tries to explain whatever it is that he is holding? Is it possible to understand something and yet be unable to explain it clearly? Why or why not?

Just as important as skill in asking and answering questions is the ability to explain. In fact, an explanation is usually the answer to a question: *How do you do that dance step? Why did you change your mind? How can birds tell when spring comes? What makes the tide come in? How do you prove this theorem?* Much inability to solve the problems of life lies in the failure to explain clearly or to understand an explanation.

What subjects in school depend wholly upon clear explanations? In which of these subjects is the use of drawings, graphs, and charts an aid to making clear explanations?

GUIDES TO CLEAR EXPLANATIONS

1. Understand completely whatever you wish to explain.
2. Begin by stating definitely what you plan to explain.
3. Proceed step by step or point by point, repeating or amplifying any details not clear to your audience.
4. Be careful to include all necessary details, but omit any that do not bear directly on your explanation.
5. Use a vocabulary that your hearers will understand. Explain clearly any technical terms necessary to your explanation.
6. To avoid confusing your listeners, stick to one point of view. For example, if you begin your explanation in the second person: "First *you* take ...," do not shift to first or third person: "Then *I* ..." or "Next, the two *pieces* are ..."
7. Make all possible use of illustrations, charts, graphs, or comparisons.
8. Allow time for questions, either during the explanation or afterwards.
9. Conclude by summarizing your explanation briefly.

LEARNING ACTIVITIES IN GIVING EXPLANATIONS

Directions: Select from the following activities in giving explanations any that offer you useful practice. As the talks are given, listen thoughtfully so that you can rate each speaker fairly by the first twelve items on the Speech Score Card, page 31.

A. Explain some process or mechanism.

1. How one of these operates: dial telephone, mimeograph, camera, electric eye, fluorescent lighting, helicopter, teletype machine, radar, FM radio, TV receiver, ...
2. How to carry out an experiment in chemistry, physics, ...
3. How to hold a baseball in throwing *a curve, a knuckle ball, an inshoot, a drop, a slow ball, a floater,* ...
4. How to repair a leaky faucet, a barbed-wire fence, a window latch, an extension cord, ...
5. How to understand football (or some other sport). With the help of classmates, demonstrate certain plays or techniques.

B. Explain certain technical terms. Tell how, when, and why they might be used. Where possible, give examples.

1. Sports expressions: *hit and run, squeeze, sacrifice, balk, mouse trap, press, lay-up, zone defense, Statue of Liberty, pitchout*
2. Cookbook terms: *moderate oven, sauté, marinate, deep fry, parboil, simmer, au gratin*
3. Sewing terms: *hemstitch, felled seam, shirr, pinking, French seam, running stitch, blanket stitch, gore, tack*

C. Explain clearly the differences between the following:

1. Two makes of automobiles, TV sets, tractors, airplanes, boats, . . .
2. Two breeds of cattle, horses, hogs, chickens, dogs, . . .
3. Two methods of swimming, mining, planting corn, mixing cake, . . .
4. Two different styles of play in football or basketball

D. Explain some printed material.

1. Bring to class a cartoon based upon a current social, political, or economic question. Explain its significance and its purpose.
2. In a textbook, a magazine, or a newspaper, find a chart, a graph, or a diagram and explain it fully to the class.

3. Giving and Following Directions

". . . then y' go on 'bout 5 more miles 'til y' come to Carter's Junction . . .
Don't take this road t' the left—goes to Watkins Glen . . .
y' wanna keep straight on 'bout 10 miles to . . . !" *

On the way home from school, Arbee remarked to a friend, "Dad said something the other night that really set me to thinking. I'd told him that I could hardly wait to grow up so that I could begin telling people what to do and how to do it—instead of having someone always telling *me!* He laughed and said, 'Son, the older you grow, the more you will realize that it is twice as hard to tell someone else how to follow orders or directions as it is to follow them yourself.' You know something, Pete? I think that maybe Dad is right! I've been trying to teach my little sister how to play checkers—and believe me, I'm stumped!"

* Used by permission of Charles Sharman and the *Saturday Evening Post*.

As Arbee's father says, learning to direct others is harder than learning to follow directions. Even the directions that you are called upon to give in everyday life will be poor until you learn how to give them. If you feel like Arbee, probably you need to study and practice the guides that follow.

GUIDES FOR GIVING AND FOLLOWING DIRECTIONS

1. Suit directions to the knowledge and the ability of the listener.
2. Keep all directions clear and simple.
3. Proceed step by step in an orderly fashion.
4. Give any necessary illustrations, names, markings (as on highway routes), or drawings. In telling how to reach a certain destination, remember that many people become confused on points of the compass. Say, "Turn *left* . . ." in preference to saying, "Turn *north* . . ."
5. Be courteous throughout.
6. Answer all questions fully and clearly.
7. In listening to or reading directions, be sure that you understand clearly how you are to proceed. If possible, repeat the directions to the giver so that he can check your understanding.
8. As you carry out each step, check back to see that you have overlooked nothing.

LEARNING ACTIVITIES

A. In a class discussion, carry out the exercises in this activity.
1. List situations in which it is important to be able to give directions well.
2. List the qualities that you want in directions given you.
3. List occasions in your own life that call for giving directions.
4. List situations in your daily life that call for following directions.
5. List situations in the life that you expect to lead as an adult in which you will need to take or give directions.

B. Apply the guides as you plan, prepare, and practice the directions called for in the following activities. Give the directions in your small groups. Listen carefully; then rate each speaker by your Speech Score Card, page 31.

1. From the list that you made in *A 3,* choose one situation and give directions to fit it. Be sure to use the guides.
2. Give directions for a lesson preparation in one of your classes.
3. Give a committee clear directions on time, place, and subject for a meeting.
4. You are employed in a local store. A customer is interested in a certain machine or article but knows nothing about its operation. Give the necessary directions and a demonstration.

C. Prepare carefully and give directions to fit one of the following situations. Use your Speech Score Card.

1. You are the attendant at an oil station. Direct a traveler to the nearest scenic attraction in or near your town.
2. You are chairman of a committee that has planned a picnic. Give directions for reaching the destination on foot, by car, and by bus. Draw a plan of each route.
3. Your principal has asked you to assist in getting new students acquainted with the school building. Draw a plan of the building, locating classrooms, study halls, offices, and all other places with which they need to be familiar. If your school has a printed plan, use that. Your listeners can help you by asking questions.
4. An out-of-town friend telephones to say that he has just arrived in town and will come out to see you. No taxicab is available, and you are unable to meet the guest. Give clear directions for getting to your home by bus, streetcar, or walking.

RELATED ACTIVITY

Tell the class about an incident that you have experienced in which inability to follow directions led to serious or embarrassing results. Apply the Guides for Developing the Oral Paragraph, page 6.

4. REPORTING EXPERIENCES AND OBSERVATIONS

How good are you at giving others information about what you see and hear? How accurately can you report your observations? The conflict in the testimony that witnesses give during a trial shows how poorly most people observe and listen. To train your mind to do its work well, you should practice taking notes, either mental or written, of the things that you see and hear.

Be word-wise!

Skim the preceding paragraph for these words: *information, conflict, trial, mental.* Which synonyms that the dictionary gives would not be good substitutes for the words as used in this lesson? Which synonym for *conflict* does the drawing illustrate?

GUIDES FOR REPORTING EXPERIENCES AND OBSERVATIONS

1. If you know that you will be asked for a report, take careful written notes. Make sure that you cover these points.
   a) Persons, places, and time involved
   b) Important ideas (in a speech, an interview, a discussion)
   c) Important features (of an exhibit, a contest, a demonstration)
2. Go over your notes thoughtfully. Organize the items in what seems to you their most effective order.
3. Practice the report, preferably for a listener, until you are sure of your facts. Use the Speech Score Card, page 31.
4. Even when you do not know that you will be asked for a report, form the habit of taking mental notes. Ask yourself, "What will be worth telling someone about this experience?"

LEARNING ACTIVITIES IN REPORTING EXPERIENCES AND OBSERVATIONS

Directions: Carry out the following activities in pairs, in groups, or as a class, whichever arrangement fits your needs best. Plan an interest-catching first sentence and a final summarizing statement. Review the Guides to Good Listening, page 17. Check the reports by your Speech Score Card and record the results.

A. Make a report based upon one of these listening experiences.

1. Listen to a talk or lecture by an assembly speaker, a minister, any public speaker. Listen thoughtfully to class or group criticism of your report. Make notes of ways in which you need to improve.
2. Try to arrange for all the group to listen to the same address in a public forum or over the radio. Take notes separately and make your outlines. (See page 118 for help in outlining.) Discuss the best features of each report as given.
3. Conduct an interview on a controversial question with someone whose opinion you respect. (Be sure that you apply the Guides for Taking Part in Interviews, page 54.) Suppose that you do not agree at all with the one interviewed. Conduct the interview, take notes, ask questions, and make the report to your group without at any time revealing your own difference of opinion or your reaction to the ideas that you are reporting. This activity is excellent practice in making you broad-minded and tolerant. Perhaps you may want to use one of these topics.
   a) Pupils should have social engagements only on week ends.
   b) All pupils in public schools should wear uniform clothes.
   c) Boys and girls over eighteen years old should pay board at home.
   d) High school education should be on a tuition basis.
   e) No student should be permitted to participate in more than two extra-curricular activities.

B. Choose one of these activities; prepare the report called for.

1. Your principal has asked each home room to discuss the plan of beginning school at seven-thirty. You are selected to report for your group, which wants the principal to understand that its ideas have been developed through reasoning and not through personal bias. This exercise will give you practice in developing an idea, in being courteous, and in planning an effective beginning and a suitable ending.

2. You are going to the hospital to visit a friend who has been shut in for some time but is eager to keep up on school activities and is well enough to hear about them. Plan and practice before the class a report that you can make to him. Think of the point of view of your listener.

3. If you have the opportunity, visit an exhibit or watch a demonstration or a contest. Plan and give an oral report which will show that you really were an intelligent listener or observer.

4. You have witnessed an accident on the street. You know that you will be called to appear in court as a witness. Organize your observations in consecutive and logical notes. Dramatize the situation so that you withstand the cross-examination of the opposing lawyer.

FOLLOW-UP ACTIVITY

As a member of any group (such as another class, a church group, the student council, or a club) in which you will need to make an oral report soon, practice the report in your English class. Profit by their suggestions.

5. READING ALOUD

READ AND DISCUSS

How important is the ability to read well orally?

If you are interested in choosing any one of certain vocations, you must be able to read effectively. For example, successful teachers, preachers, lawyers, actors, radio or television announcers, commentators, or entertainers must be fluent and pleasing readers.

You may not be interested, however, in any of the vocations named above. That circumstance does not mean that you can forget about acquiring skill in oral reading. Just how often do you read aloud, anyway? Not very often, you may think. As a matter of fact, your daily life is full of oral reading situations. Examine those that follow.

1. Wanting to share a letter or parts of it
2. Finding a news item that you think will interest someone

3. Reading a joke you want to share
4. Wanting to prove a point by a quotation from an authority
5. Taking part in church, club, or lodge rituals
6. Reading the minutes of a meeting
7. Reading a report
8. Reading a set of resolutions
9. Reading aloud to help yourself get the meaning
10. Entertaining a small child or an invalid
11. Memorizing or trying to fix facts in mind
12. Reading an announcement

How many others can you add?

Careful listening will convince you that the average person needs to improve his reading aloud. Here are some helpful guides.

GUIDES TO EFFECTIVE ORAL READING

1. Before trying to read anything orally, be sure that you understand the material. If you fail to understand, you will be unable to interpret to others what the author has to say.
2. Apply all that you have learned about effective use of pitch, volume, inflection, and quality.
3. Enunciate distinctly.
4. Be sure of your pronunciation.
5. Group words into phrases that make clear the thought or that add rhythm. The larger your audience, the fewer should be the number of words in the phrases. In reading to a small group, the phrases can be much longer.

(For a large audience)
Careful / listening / will convince / you / that the average / person / needs / to improve / his reading / aloud.

(For a small group)
Careful listening / will convince you / that the average person / needs to improve / his reading aloud.

Practice your phrasing to be sure that you read smoothly.
6. In poetry, the thought often carries over from line to line. Do not, therefore, automatically drop your voice at the end of a line. Concentrate instead on reading to bring out the meaning.
7. Practice much when you are alone. The oftener that you hear and criticize yourself, the faster your reading will improve.
8. Take every opportunity to read for others. There is no substitute for actual practice.

A. Do at least one of the following exercises in reading aloud to give information. Watch your pronunciation and your enunciation. Be sure that your voice and body convey the author's idea and mood. Score these exercises by points 1–12 on your Speech Score Card, page 31.

1. Select a passage of several paragraphs from a textbook and read it to the class so effectively that they can take clear notes.
2. Listen to a classmate or the teacher read a selection that presents an idea for discussion. After hearing the selection only once, write the main idea and the steps in its development. Compare your results and decide which ideas are best. This exercise tests skill in reading, but it also tests how well you listen.
3. Read to the group a news item of ten or more lines. Judge your performance by the ability of the group to tell what you have read.
4. Read to the group a newspaper editorial, perhaps one from your school paper. Judge your reading ability by the exactness with which the group analyzes the editorial.

B. Study the following paragraph until you understand the thought and feel the mood. Take turns reading the paragraph in your small groups; then choose one member to read it to the class, who should listen carefully to evaluate the effectiveness of phrasing, inflection, and rate.

Roll back the tide of eighteen hundred years. At the foot of the vine-clad Vesuvius stands a royal city. The stately Roman walks its lordly streets, or banquets in the palaces of its splendors. The bustle of busied thousands is there; you may hear it along the thronged quays; it rises from the amphitheater and the forum. It is the home of luxury, of gaiety, and of joy. There togaed royalty drowns itself in dissipation; the lion roars over the martyred Christian; and the bleeding body of the gladiator dies to the shouts of applauding spectators. It is a careless, a dreaming, a devoted city. But look! There is blackness about the horizon, and an earthquake is rioting in the depths of the mountains! Hark! a roar! a crash! and the very foundations of the eternal hills are belched forth in a sea of fire! Woe for that fated city! The torrent comes surging like the mad ocean! It boils above wall and tower, palace and fountain, and Pompeii is a city of tombs!

—Anonymous

C. Many times in your reading you will not have an opportunity to practice the material beforehand. The better you have learned to group words into phrases, the better will be your sight reading. To give you stimulating practice, read the following paragraph as a group exercise in sight phrasing. Whoever begins, reads only a phrase; the one next to him reads the next phrase; and so on around the group. This exercise calls for you to be alert, since you cannot be sure on which word the reader just before you will stop.

I went to Washington the other day and I stood on Capitol Hill; my heart beat quick as I looked at the towering marble of my country's Capitol; and the mist gathered in my eyes as I thought of its tremendous significance, of the armies and the Treasury, of the judges and the President, of the Congress and the courts, and of all that was gathered there. And I felt that the sun in all its course could not look down on a better sight than that majestic home of a republic that had taught the world its best lessons of liberty. And I felt that if honor and wisdom and justice abided therein, the world would at last owe that great house in which the ark of the covenant of my country is lodged, its final uplifting and its regeneration.

—HENRY W. GRADY

D. Each of you should choose and carry out one of the following exercises in reading to entertain the listener. Follow the guides on page 41. Rate one another's performance by points 1–12 on your Speech Score Card.

1. From a book that contains one of your favorite book people, choose several lines spoken by that person.
2. Find a humorous anecdote, and read it to bring out the humor.
3. Let each of your small groups find and prepare for reading in class a "short short" story. One person in the group should read until he reaches a change in action; then he should pass the book.
4. From a short story that you like, read a conversation. Indicate characters by changes in the pitch, quality, inflection, and volume of your voice.
5. From one of Poe's tales, read to the class a paragraph that expresses horror.
6. Read a paragraph that shows some other definite emotion or mood.

FOLLOW-UP ACTIVITIES

A. Do some oral reading every day, either by yourself or for an audience.

B. At least once a week, take time for group practice in phrasing. Read a paragraph or more from your literature book, proceeding as in *C,* page 42.

6. Enjoying Choral Reading

Oral reading usually is an individual activity. More and more, however, school classes in literature, music, and speech are learning to enjoy literature through choral reading.

If you are guided by the directions that follow, you, too, will find increasing pleasure in oral group interpretation.

DIRECTIONS FOR CHORAL READING

1. Before you attempt to read a selection together, study it carefully in class. *What is the author trying to express?*
2. Remember, the aim is not merely to speak in unison. The thought, the mood, the spirit of a passage should guide your reading.
3. Apply what you have learned about enunciating consonant sounds crisply, clearly, and correctly.
4. Keep vowel sounds full and open.
5. Vary the pitch of the voices to fit the ideas and emotions. If necessary, review page 24.
6. Assign the parts of a selection carefully. Certain passages demand solo interpretations; others, only a few voices; some, a large chorus; certain selections need special voices, such as sopranos, altos, or basses. Group together voices of similar tone and pitch. Sometimes, like an old chorus, you may have responsive parts, or *antiphonal* reading, as the Greeks called it. Here deep and light voices alternate in expressing the ideas.
7. Plan the phrasing of each passage so that thought and mood units get complete expression. Plan the rate for each phrase unit so that slow or fast tempo may aid the idea. Choose the words that need most emphasis and then enunciate them so that they carry the idea.
8. Keep bodies and voices relaxed; speak naturally.
9. Work under a leader, preferably your teacher or a member of the class who has had experience in leading musical numbers. Try leading if you feel the rhythm and spirit of a selection. The aim should never be primarily to achieve perfection; rather, it should be to bring pleasure and satisfaction to those who participate in reading aloud together.

LEARNING ACTIVITIES IN CHORAL READING

A. For your first activity, the poem on page 45 has been marked for choral reading. Study it carefully for the thought and the mood; then assign parts and practice reading the poem.

WANDER-THIRST *

Girls || *Boys*
Beyond the East the sunrise, || beyond the West the sea,

Duet || *All*
And East and West || the wander-thirst that will not let me be;

Boys || *Solo 1*
It works in me like madness, || to bid me say goodbye;

Row 1 || *Row 2* || *All*
For the seas call || and the stars call, || and oh! the call of the sky.

Girl 1 || *Girls*
I know not where the white road runs, || nor what the blue hills are,

Boy 1 || *Boys*
But a man can have the sun for friend, || and for his guide a star;

All
Ah, there's no end of voyaging when once the voice is heard,

Rows 3 & 4 || *Rows 5 & 6* || *Solo 2*
For the river calls || and the road calls, || and oh! the call of a bird!

All || *Boys*
Yonder the long horizon lies, || and there by night and day

Girls
The old ships draw to home again, || the young ships sail away;

Girl 2 || *Boy 2* || *Boys*
And come I may, || but go I must; || and, if men ask you why,

Rows 1 & 2 || *Rows 3 & 4*
You may put the blame on the stars || and the sun

Rows 5 & 6 || *All*
And the white road || and the sky.

—GERALD GOULD

B. Choose one or more of the following exercises. All offer enjoyable practice in choral reading. Be sure to follow the directions on page 44.

1. Edgar Allan Poe was a master in the use of vowels and consonants and rhythms; try to express the full force of his art as you read "The Bells," "Annabel Lee," "Ulalume," "The Haunted Palace," "The Raven."

2. Since choral reading really originated with the ancient Greeks, perhaps you can find and enjoy reading one of the choruses in an old Greek play.

3. Select an old folk ballad like "The Wife of Usher's Well," "The Twa Sisters," "Edward," "Get Up and Bar the Door," or "Robin Hood and the Widow's Three Sons."

4. Many of the Old Testament Psalms are beautiful and inspiring in their ideas and moods. Try one of them or some other Bible passage.

* Used by special arrangement with Mr. Michael Ayrton, of London. Choral arrangement as found in *Let's-Read-Together Poems*, Book 7, by Helen A. Brown and Harry J. Heltman. Copyright, 1954, by Row, Peterson and Company.

C. Much light or humorous verse is well adapted to choral reading. *The Book of Humorous Verse* compiled by Carolyn Wells contains many usable selections. Several that you will enjoy doing are listed below. Consult the card catalogue (see page 127) to find whether the book is in your library. If not, use the card catalogue to see whether you can locate some of these poems elsewhere.

"Some Little Bug" by Roy Atwell
"Hiram Hover" by Bayard Taylor
"The Sorrows of Werther" by W. M. Thackeray
"The Usual Way" by Frederic E. Weatherly
"The Kitchen Clock" by John Vance Cheney
"The V-A-S-E" by James Jeffrey Roche
"The Meeting of the Clabberhuses" by Sam W. Foss
"Here Is the Tale" by Anthony C. Deane
"The Modern Hiawatha" (Author unknown)
"Nursery Song in Pidgin English" (Author unknown)
"The Village Choir" (Author unknown)
"Nightmare" by W. S. Gilbert

D. The following selections are expressive of various dramatic moods and effects. Most of them you can find in anthologies of American and British poetry.

"The Barrel Organ" by Alfred Noyes
"Grass" by Carl Sandburg
"The Sands of Dee" by Charles Kingsley
"Southern Ships and Settlers" by Rosemary and Stephen V. Benét
"Lepanto" by Gilbert K. Chesterton
"Boots" by Rudyard Kipling
"The Oregon Trail" by Arthur Guiterman
"American Names" by Stephen Vincent Benét
"Forty Singing Seamen" by Alfred Noyes
"The West Wind" by John Masefield
"Up-Hill" by Christina Rossetti
"Abraham Lincoln Walks at Midnight" by Vachel Lindsay
"The Creation" by James Weldon Johnson

E. Bring into class a selection from prose or poetry that seems to you to be good choral-reading material. Plan its interpretation by marking the phrasing, words that need emphasis, and any passages in which pronunciation and enunciation must aid. Indicate the rate necessary for interpreting mood and idea. Choose and arrange the types of voices necessary, and direct the reading of the selection.

RELATED ACTIVITIES

A. You can find interesting material for such special reports on choral reading as are suggested by the following topics: its history; its place in ancient drama; choral reading today; methods of choral reading; records of choral reading. Use your Speech Score Card, page 31.

B. You may have access to phonograph records of other choral readings. Those of the London Verse-Speaking Choir will be of much help. Note the attention to pronunciation, enunciation, mood, and ideas.

USING ENGLISH IN ALL CLASSES

If your school has a music department and a speech department, unite to produce a program of choral reading for an assembly.

7. MEETING AND INTRODUCING OTHERS

Poise in making and in recognizing introductions is a valuable asset. If you feel self-conscious either when you meet or when you introduce people, study the guides in this lesson; then go on to the learning activities based upon them.

PRELIMINARY ACTIVITY

Study the following drawings. Decide on names for the characters in them; then tell how you would introduce them. Make this an oral activity.

GUIDES FOR MAKING AND RECOGNIZING INTRODUCTIONS

1. In making an introduction, present people as follows:
   a) A man to a woman
   b) A young woman to an older one
   c) A young man to an older one
   d) Other guests to a guest of honor
   Never gesture toward those whom you are introducing.

2. Use these or similar expressions:
   a) Mother, I'd like you to meet April Meade.
   b) Major Lee, may I present Ensign Baker? (*formal*)
   c) Alice, this is my cousin, David Everett; Dave, Alice Evans.
   d) Mrs. Gray, Miss Hansen.

3. When seated, rise under these circumstances:
   a) If you are a young woman meeting an older one
   b) If you are a man

4. If you are a man meeting another man, to extend your hand is a friendly gesture. A woman need not offer to shake hands.

5. To acknowledge an introduction, say, "How do you do, Miss Stuart." (It is courteous to repeat the other person's name, as in the example.) Be sure to wait until the introducer has finished his introduction.

6. In leaving a group or a new acquaintance, say, "I'm glad to have met you," or "I've enjoyed meeting you," or some similar courteous phrase. (An exception to the rule is that a woman usually does not say that she is glad to have met a man.)

LEARNING ACTIVITIES IN MAKING AND RECOGNIZING INTRODUCTIONS

A. Discuss the following questions in class or in your small groups.

1. What are some correct forms for making and recognizing introductions? What forms can you suggest that should be avoided?
2. What determines which name should be spoken first?
3. What information should a good introduction supply?
4. Why are careful enunciation and pronunciation of names important? What should you say if you fail to catch a name?
5. Why is it discourteous to mumble or mispronounce names?
6. How can you train yourself to hear and retain names?
7. What governs rising? shaking hands?
8. How can you bridge the awkward pause that is likely to come just after two people have been introduced?

B. Consult an up-to-date book of etiquette to see whether you can find other acceptable forms for making and recognizing introductions. Report to the class what you find. Use your Speech Score Card.

C. Why are these poor introductions? In class, reword them properly.

1. Grace, this is my mother.
2. Mr. Stone, meet my grandmother.
3. Come here, Junior. This is my teacher.
4. Jim, shake hands with my cousin Peggy.
5. Uncle Bill, meet up with my history prof.

D. In class or in your small groups, practice the following introductions, impersonating the various individuals indicated.

1. Introduce a new classmate of your own sex to (*a*) your mother, (*b*) your father, (*c*) your best friend.
2. Repeat the preceding activity with a member of the opposite sex.
3. Introduce your mother and (*a*) a man teacher, (*b*) a woman teacher from your school.
4. Introduce your father as in the preceding activity.
5. Introduce a stranger to a group of your friends. You need not repeat the stranger's name after the first introduction.

8. Making Speeches for Special Occasions

Perhaps you have at some time been called upon to talk at a banquet or a pep rally, to introduce a speaker, to present or accept an award or a gift. Because you get so little actual practice in giving these "occasional" speeches, as they are called, you need to make careful preparation. The subject matter of the various types of occasional speeches will be different, but the basic techniques are the same.

GUIDES FOR MAKING OCCASIONAL SPEECHES

1. Be brief, especially when introducing a speaker or accepting an award.
2. Talk without notes, if possible; at least, do not read your speech.
3. If you use a joke, be sure (*a*) that it will be new to most of your hearers, (*b*) that it really fits and is not just dragged in, (*c*) that you do not laugh as you tell it, and (*d*) that it will amuse and not offend.
4. Avoid false modesty in accepting a gift or an honor. To say, "I don't really deserve this," is to criticize the judgment of those honoring you.
5. Avoid boasting or talking much of yourself.
6. Use simple language.
7. Apply the standards on the Speech Score Card, page 31.

LEARNING ACTIVITIES IN OCCASIONAL SPEECHES

Directions: The following activities will provide entertaining class periods at the same time that they give you useful experience.

It is suggested that these activities be worked out in the order given. Rate each other by the Speech Score Card, page 31. Listen actively.

A. *The speech of presentation*

Use as your topic the presenting of a contest prize, a medal for bravery, a good conduct award, a gift of farewell or appreciation, an athletic award, a scholarship prize, or any other special honor.

The following procedure is suggested. On the day before you are to give the speeches, draw names. You are to honor in your speech the person whose name you draw. It will add to the enjoyment if you keep the name a secret, announcing it only at the end of your speech, with some such words as, "Will Jack Barry please come forward." Then make the award. Pinning on an actual badge or medal or handing the honored individual an envelope or a package will add a realistic touch.

B. *The speech of acceptance*

As your name is called in *A,* come forward and wait quietly until the speaker has finished. If the speaker has not warned you in advance, your remarks will have to be made on the spur of the moment. Ordinarily this is the briefest of all occasional speeches. Begin, of course, by expressing your thanks. You may mention your surprise, your gratitude, the help given you by others, or the inspiration that the award will be. Close with another expression of thanks.

C. *The speech of introduction*

Draw names as in *A.* Have a chair placed at the front of the room. The person being introduced should sit here during the introduction.

You may introduce your speaker under his own name, if you like. However, you may give him an impressive fictional name or that of a famous living person. In any case, do not mention the name until your closing line: "It is a pleasure to present to you that great inventor, Waldemar Whifflewitz, who will speak to you on the unusual but intriguing subject 'Building the Better Mousetrap.' Mr. Whifflewitz."

Since this is primarily an exercise in introducing a speaker, the person introduced does not need to make the speech indicated by the announced topic. He should acknowledge the introduction, however. He may comment upon it or upon the person making it; he may express his pleasure at being present; he may make any fitting impromptu remarks that occur to him.

D. *The pep talk*

Draw names as in *A*. However, the one who calls upon a speaker need not make a real speech. He may simply say, "Next, let's hear from that hard-hitting tackle, Jake Brown."

The girls in your class may not carry on interschool athletics; in that case, introduce them as pep club officers or cheerleaders.

As a rule, this is probably the most poorly done of all occasional speeches. You are familiar with the husky football player who shambles to the front of the room, gets a death grip on the nearest piece of furniture, and mumbles in the general direction of the floor, "Well, Central's got a tough team, but if you all get out there 'n' yell, I think we c'n take 'em."

It is true that a pep talk should be brief, but it should contain something worth hearing. Give the rooters a few pointers on plays and players to watch among the opposition; compare the records of the two teams; report on the condition of your team; tell an amusing incident that happened at practice or in a recent game; pay a brief tribute to your coaches or to the student supporters. Above all, speak as though you have confidence in your team's worth and sportsmanship.

E. *The toast*

Before this school year is over, some of you undoubtedly will have had the experience of talking at a dinner or a banquet. Perhaps you will serve as a toastmaster. Carrying out the following project will make the real-life experience more enjoyable. Proceed as follows:

1. Divide the class into groups of four or five people each. The members of each group should decide on a banquet theme. They should likewise choose one of their group to act as toastmaster. Each remaining group member should be assigned a topic related to the banquet theme. Frame your speech by the guides on page 50.
2. On the day or days set aside for the banquets, if possible, arrange the chairs around a table, either real or imaginary. If this arrangement cannot be made, perhaps you will be able to use the teacher's desk as a speaker's table for those giving toasts.
3. The toastmaster, whose duty it is to keep the speeches moving pleasantly around the central theme, opens the program. He may begin with an appropriate incident or a humorous anecdote in order to make all feel at ease.

His duty is not to talk at great length. Rather, he should try to co-ordinate all the speeches with the idea of the occasion, to introduce each speaker cleverly and appropriately, and finally to close the entire program with a fitting conclusion, serious or humorous, as the occasion demands.

4. After all the banquets have been given, you may enjoy taking a written vote to see which banquet the class thought was most successfully carried out. To vote intelligently calls for attentive listening as the toasts are given. Omitting your own banquet, rank the other banquets in the order of their excellence. Appoint a committee to tabulate the results.

9. Using the Telephone

READ AND DISCUSS

Have you ever heard a one-sided telephone conversation like this one?

> Hello-o-o . . .
> Yah! . . .
> Oh, sure . . .
> Whadjussay? . . .
> Uh-uh . . .
> Naw . . . Well, goo-by . . . Beseeinya . . .

If you had nothing else by which to judge that speaker, would you form a high opinion of him as an individual? What do others hear as they listen to your telephone voice?

In modern daily life, the telephone is of inestimable value. It saves time and trouble for everyone who has learned to use it well, but it can be an instrument of confusion and irritation if used poorly. The following activities will help you improve your telephone technique and manners.

LEARNING ACTIVITIES IN USING THE TELEPHONE

A. Discuss the following questions or topics in class.

1. Make a list of the uses to which you put the telephone, both in social and in business activities. What local telephone numbers should you know?
2. Is voice important to a local operator? to the long-distance operator?
3. Though "hello" is a common expression in America, there are better forms for answering the telephone, especially in business calls. What alternatives can you suggest?
4. Make a list of the chief errors in expression that you have found common to your own and others' telephone language.

5. Explain the necessity of courtesy in using the telephone. What do anger, impatience, or shouting show of one's character?
6. Why is it necessary to use names more carefully over the telephone than in ordinary conversation? Why should a speaker give his name at once?
7. Make a list of vocations connected with the telephone. Discuss those in which training in good speech is essential. The *Readers' Guide* (see page 133) will help you to find magazine articles dealing with the subject.
8. What should a boy say when he calls a girl to ask for a date? What should she reply? Should a girl ever call a boy?

B. In your small groups, dramatize the following telephone conversations. Listen critically to the calls.

1. Call a local store; ask for a certain department; give an order for a number of items. When do you give your name and address to the clerk? How do you indicate the manner of payment?
2. You are in a business office and an important telephone message comes for your employer, who is out. Take the message so accurately that no detail of it is lost.
3. Make a social call over the telephone, using all the habits of good expression that you would use in a face-to-face conversation. Why should even social calls be limited as to time?
4. Dramatize a long-distance call. Note in your own telephone directory all instructions for making such a call.

C. Explain to the class how to telephone a telegram to Western Union. (Page 240 gives help in writing telegrams.) Write the message before telephoning it. Why? Why does the clerk read the message back to you? Why is clear enunciation important to the Western Union clerk?

10. TAKING PART IN INTERVIEWS

Many times in your schoolwork you will encounter situations in which you can profit by the experience or knowledge of someone else. To get such information, you should know how to arrange for and carry out an interview in a businesslike manner.

You need also to know how to conduct yourself while you are being interviewed. Too often a capable worker fails to get a good position because of the poor impression made during a job interview.

This section will give you practice—both in conducting interviews and in being interviewed.

GUIDES FOR TAKING PART IN INTERVIEWS

HOW TO CARRY OUT AN INTERVIEW

1. Arrange in advance for the interview; suit the time and the place to the convenience of the person whom you wish to interview. Explain why you wish to talk with him.
2. Plan your opening remarks carefully. Begin by introducing yourself and reminding him why you have come.
3. Prepare most of your questions in advance. Remember that *you* must guide the interview and keep it moving.
4. Listen with full attention to the answers to your questions. Take careful notes of any that you wish to use. Read those answers back to the interviewee, and ask, "May I quote you?"
5. At the close of the interview, express your appreciation for the time and information granted you.

HOW TO BE YOUR BEST SELF IN A JOB INTERVIEW

1. Dress neatly and conservatively; be well groomed.
2. Arrive punctually. Introduce yourself and remind the interviewer of your reason for being there.
3. Be prepared with all necessary information. Provide a written statement of your qualifications. Beforehand, decide what questions the interviewer might ask and how you would answer them.
4. Listen carefully so that you can decide both your fitness for the job and your willingness to work under the conditions named.
5. Be courteous and interested throughout. Answer questions fully and definitely, but do not boast or talk too much. Ask questions, if necessary, to learn what will be expected of you should you be hired.
6. If asked to fill out an application blank, do so thoughtfully and neatly.
7. Let the interviewer close the meeting. Thank him; then leave at once.

LEARNING ACTIVITIES IN TAKING PART IN INTERVIEWS

A. Discuss the following questions in class or in your small groups.

1. Why do employers stress neatness in prospective employees?
2. Why should you be careful not to volunteer many remarks while being interviewed for a job?
3. Why should you ask permission to quote remarks? Why should you take careful notes of such remarks?

B. In pairs, dramatize the following imaginary interviews.

1. A well-known musician, athlete, writer, or actor is making an appearance in your city. As a reporter for the school paper, interview him.
2. Your club has decided to purchase a certain plot of ground for use as a tennis court. You have the duty of conducting the purchase. Interview the owner or agent.
3. After the club has bought the land, you decide to erect fences in order not to disturb adjoining property owners. Their consent should be secured. Interview one of these owners.

C. Carry out at least one actual interview. Here are suggestions.

1. Interview a businessman about the qualifications and requirements for success in his field.
2. Interview a long-time custodian of your school building, with the aim of finding out whether students today differ from those of ten or more years ago, and if so, how.
3. Interview the head of some community organization to learn specific things that young people can do to improve the community.
4. Interview some elderly person about his youth: what schools were like; what recreation young people had; how he thinks boys and girls of today compare with those of his generation.

D. Take part in one of these imaginary job interviews. They will give you practice for actual job interviews later on.

1. The most exacting businessman in town has advertised a position that you think you can fill satisfactorily.
2. Your teacher has asked for a typist and clerk who can help in filing papers and preparing reports. Make a personal application for the position.
3. What position would you like to hold? Make an oral application that should secure the position for you.

FOLLOW-UP ACTIVITY

If you would like after-school or Saturday employment, scan the advertisements in your local newspaper. Try to get an appointment for an interview. If successful, review carefully the guides for being your best self in an interview, page 54.

CHAPTER 5

Improving Conversational and Discussion Habits

1. Practicing Courtesy in Speech

READ AND THINK ABOUT

Every day you are tested on your ability to say something and say it well. From the time that you get up in the morning until you go to sleep at night, you are called upon to express ideas. These include questions, directions, explanations, greetings, conversations, good-bys, introductions, and discussions. Can you be proud of your performance in those situations?

Unfortunately, there are many more ways of being a poor talker than of being a good one. Since much of your waking time is spent in talking with others, you form stronger and stronger conversational habits every day. Why not make them good ones!

GUIDES TO COURTEOUS SPEECH HABITS

1. Be courteous as you speak with others. Help to keep a conversation going, but do not try to dominate it.
2. Lead the conversation into fields of interest to your companions.
3. Avoid making remarks that may hurt or embarrass other people.
4. Avoid much talk of yourself.
5. Make every effort to draw shy individuals into the conversation.
6. If you disagree with someone, do so pleasantly and impersonally.
7. Let your voice show interest, enthusiasm, friendliness.
8. Listen attentively and sympathetically.
9. Do not interrupt another person's remarks.

The activities that follow should start you to thinking seriously about your possible shortcomings. Recognizing your conversational failings is the first step toward becoming a more likable person.

LEARNING ACTIVITIES IN COURTESY IN SPEECH

Directions: Take time to discuss each of the following activities thoroughly.

A. Explain what is discourteous about the following actions:

1. Talking constantly of self
2. Talking about others, especially of small personal matters
3. Talking loudly and boisterously, especially in public places
4. Repeating as one's own the statements made by others
5. Excluding certain members of a group from a conversation
6. Making sarcastic remarks in the effort to "show off" or be "funny"
7. Waiting impatiently for a chance to seize the conversation
8. Lapsing into a bored silence while others talk
9. Repeating unfounded rumors
10. Speaking from prejudices rather than from facts
11. Laughing at others' mistakes

B. Some of the following terms are slang expressions, but they characterize certain individuals accurately. Define each term. Why should you resent being called any of them? How would you label the persons in the drawing?

1. Know-it-all	6. Sarcastic person	11. Clam	16. Gossip
2. Windbag	7. Monopolist	12. Bore	17. Yes man
3. Blowhard	8. Bluffer	13. Whiner	18. Grouch
4. Smart aleck	9. Clown	14. Mule	19. Knocker
5. Sensitive plant	10. Boor	15. Croaker	20. Parrot

A. Rate yourself by the Guides to Courteous Speech Habits, page 56. In the following lessons, practice to overcome your weaknesses.

B. Almost everyone is puzzled over what is the proper thing to say and do in certain social situations. As a class project, build up a manual of social behavior that will cover in a practical way what you want to know. Use the following plan.

1. Let each one in the class jot down points on which he would like information. Put each item upon a separate slip of paper. Leave the slips unsigned so that no one need feel embarrassed. Make each inquiry definite; for example: "What should I say when a boy thanks me for a dance?" Drop the slips into a box designated for that purpose.
.2. Choose a committee to sort and classify the slips.
3. When the committee has completed its work, have each set of related questions brought up and discussed in class. Consult authorities, both books and people.
4. Appoint a committee to write down the conclusions reached.
5. Choose another committee to mimeograph and staple the material.
6. Give a copy to each student.

2. Becoming a Good Conversationalist

The section on courtesy in speech emphasizes that the way you speak may make you a conversational misfit. *What* you talk about also can make your conversation ineffective.

INTRODUCTORY ACTIVITY

Just what *do* you talk about? What do you talk about most? Try analyzing the content of your daily conversation.

1. Think back over yesterday. Jot down each conversational situation in which you can remember having talked.
2. Go over the following list of topics. Under each conversational situation that you named above, write the topics that you discussed. You may classify a topic under more than one head.

a) Lessons	*h*) Current events	*o*) Sports
b) Classmates	*i*) Personal problems	*p*) Food
c) Teachers	*j*) The opposite sex	*q*) Music
d) Parents	*k*) Your possessions	*r*) Clothes
e) Other adults	*l*) School activities	*s*) Weather
f) Social events	*m*) Your likes, dislikes	*t*) Books
g) Radio and TV programs	*n*) Your successes, failures	*u*) Films

3. Go over your paper carefully. What conclusions can you draw from it? Did most of your conversation deal with (*i*), (*k*), (*m*), and (*n*)? Concentrating on yourself as a topic is a short cut to unpopularity. Did you spend much time discussing (*b*), (*c*), (*d*), (*e*), and (*j*)? Unless you can speak favorably of other people, talking of them is dangerous business. If the analysis leaves you dissatisfied with yourself, study the following standards thoughtfully.

STANDARDS FOR THE INTERESTING CONVERSATIONALIST

1. The interesting conversationalist can talk on a wide range of topics.
2. He talks more about ideas than about persons or things.
3. He introduces topics that will interest those with whom he talks.
4. He listens attentively and appreciatively. He asks intelligent questions which show that he is listening.
5. He avoids embarrassing or painful topics.
6. He suits his language to the age and interests of his company.
7. He can defend his own ideas but is tolerant of others' ideas.
8. He does not go off on "sidetracks."

You cannot expect to become a good conversationalist overnight. You will need practice. The activities that follow will get you off to a good start. Then apply to daily life what you learn.

LEARNING ACTIVITIES IN CONVERSATIONAL SPEECH

A. In your small groups, prepare to dramatize for the class one of the following activities. Apply what you have learned about courtesy in speech. Remember that half of being a good conversationalist consists of being a sympathetic listener. To criticize helpfully, the audience will need to listen thoughtfully.

1. On your way to school, you pass the house of a classmate just as he or she comes out. Because you do not know this person very well, you are tempted to slow down in order to avoid a meeting. Instead, join this classmate and start a conversation. Remember, the other person may be just as self-conscious as you are.
2. Dramatize the same situation as in *1,* but stage this one in the school lunchroom. The classmate is alone at a table.
3. You are on a streetcar when a friend of your parents sits down beside you. Probably he will ask you some friendly questions. If he does, try to respond interestingly. Do not confine yourself to such remarks as "Yes," "No," "I don't think so."

4. At a school party you notice someone who seems left out of things. Begin a conversation with him or bring him over to join your group. Draw him into the conversation in a friendly but casual way. Avoid giving the impression that you feel sorry for him.
5. You arrive early at a school play and find yourself seated by one of your teachers. What can you talk about? See whether you can omit talk of your classwork.
6. You meet your principal in the corridor, and he stops for a brief chat. He may comment on your entry in a school contest or refer to your part in an assembly program. What can you contribute to the conversation?
7. You and a teacher are sitting in the classroom, conversing after school. Another teacher enters. Under what circumstances do you rise? When may you be seated?
8. Call on a friend who is in the hospital, recovering from an operation or an accident. What topics should you avoid?

B. Organize your class into rotating groups so that each of you progresses from one conversational topic with one classmate to a different subject with the next. As you advance from group to group, talk on the topic indicated on the slip of paper that each new partner wears. Use the following suggestions and any other topics on which you would like practice.

1. Greet a friend whom you chance to meet on the street, after not having seen him for weeks.
2. Apologize for a misunderstanding or a breach of etiquette.
3. Narrate a personal incident that will entertain or amuse.
4. Narrate an amusing anecdote just heard or read.
5. Extend an oral invitation to a picnic or a party.
6. Express your thanks for a favor or a gift.
7. Express sympathy for a disappointment, a grief, a loss.
8. Extend congratulations on an honor.
9. Recommend a book, an entertainment, a hobby, a game.
10. Ask for helpful suggestions to improve your own work.

C. Pleasant humor is a good "icebreaker" in conversation. Some people make a hobby of collecting jokes and anecdotes, which they bring into conversations. Discuss these problems that may arise:

1. What is a humorous bore?
2. Why is it rude to tell a humorous incident that may embarrass another person?
3. Why does it kill the humor to laugh at one's own jokes?

FOLLOW-UP ACTIVITY

The preceding exercises deal with dramatized conversational situations. Now apply to real life what you have learned. Take advantage of all conversational opportunities to improve your skill. Better yet, go out and make such opportunities.

3. Practicing Parliamentary Procedure

READ AND THINK ABOUT

Probably you have had the experience of being in a class or club meeting in which people argued violently without getting anywhere. If you have a knowledge of parliamentary procedure, you can put an end to such time-wasting arguments. Everyone will agree that good citizens, especially in a democracy, must be able to take an intelligent part in the meetings of organized groups such as clubs. The first step toward intelligent participation is to learn the basic parliamentary principles.

The sections that follow give in a practical fashion what you should know to organize a society and carry it on effectively. If you wish to go into the finer points of parliamentary practice, study the manual that your group selects as its authority.

To give you the necessary practice in applying the information contained here, organize your class into a society, real or imaginary. If you feel no definite need for a real club, you will find that an imaginary organization offers wide opportunities for interesting, enjoyable practice. For example, in a real club you might hesitate to attempt building a clubhouse, but in an imaginary club such a project will provide you with discussion material for many meetings. *The important thing is for you to get concentrated practice in parliamentary procedure that will carry over into any organizations to which you belong now or may belong in the future.*

Be word-wise!

Skim page 61 and the above paragraph for these words: *argued, intelligent, selects, hesitate.* Use the dictionary to find their synonyms. Which synonyms would not be good substitutes for the words as used in this lesson? Which synonym of *hesitate* would you say is illustrated by the drawing?

ACTIVITIES IN LEARNING PARLIAMENTARY FORMS

Before you begin the actual organization of your club, you should be familiar with the fundamentals of parliamentary law, at least to the extent of knowing where to find quickly the help that you need.

Directions: Take as many periods as you need to study and discuss the sections on pages 63–70. The four types of activities listed here suggest methods to guide you in this practice. Use any or all of these methods in connection with your study of each section.

A. Have each section read aloud. Take time to discover whether any points need explaining.

B. Assign each member of the class to talk on a certain section or part of a section. The class should listen attentively and be ready to offer corrections at the close.

C. Let each member of the class prepare twenty good fact questions based upon these sections. When a student has read one of his questions in class, the other members find the rule that answers the question. The questioner then asks someone to read the rule.

D. After considerable practice on *C,* vary the exercise by asking students to answer the questions without reading the rules. You may conduct this activity as you would a spelling match.

Primer of Parliamentary Practice

1. MOTIONS

The motion is the basis of all business in an organized group. All motions go through four stages: (1) *making and seconding* the motion, (2) *stating it*, (3) *putting the question,* and (4) *announcing the result of the vote.*

1. (*Making and seconding the motion*)
   Mr. A. (*Rising*): Mr. Chairman.
   The Chair (*Seated*): Mr. A.
   Mr. A. (*Makes the motion*): I move that our club employ a janitor.
   Mr. B. (*Seated*): I second the motion.

2. (*Stating the motion*)
   The Chair (*Seated*): It is moved and seconded that the club employ a janitor. Is there any discussion? (*Discussion follows.*)

3. (*Putting the question*)
   The Chair (*Rises*): Are you ready for the question? (*Pauses*) It is moved and seconded that the club employ a janitor. All those in favor signify by saying *aye*. Opposed, *no.*

4. (*Announcing the result*)
   The Chair (*Standing*): The *ayes* have it. The motion is carried. [*or,* The *noes* have it. The motion is lost.]

CLASSES OF MOTIONS

To take part intelligently in the work of a society, you should be familiar with certain motions. There are exceptions to the rules governing some of them, but for ordinary purposes the information given here is sufficient.

The first thirteen motions are listed here in the order of their rank, with the motion of lowest rank (the *main motion*) given last. When any one of them is before the house, all motions below it on this list are out of order, whereas those above it take precedence over it; that is, those above it may be made while the original motion is still being discussed.

*Undebatable * and Privileged*
1. Fix the time to which to adjourn. (*This one can be amended.*)
2. Adjourn
3. Take a recess. (*This one can be amended.*)
4. Raise a question of privilege
5. Call for orders of the day

*Undebatable * and Subsidiary*
6. Lay on the table
7. Previous question
8. Limit or extend limits of debate. (*This one can be amended.*)

* Undebatable motions must be voted upon without discussion.

Debatable and Subsidiary
9. Postpone to a certain time. (*This one can be amended.*)
10. Commit or refer. (*This one can be amended.*)
11. Amend (*This one can be amended.*)
12. Postpone indefinitely
13. Main motion. (*This one can be amended.*)

The following motions, as the name "incidental" indicates, arise out of some question already before the house and therefore must be settled first. They rank below the privileged motions.

Undebatable and Incidental
14. Question of order
15. Question of appeal
16. Suspension of rules
17. Objection to consideration
18. Division of the assembly
19. Leave to withdraw a motion

The following motions take precedence of no pending question. They may be made while any other question is pending, but their consideration has only the rank of the motion to be considered.

Unclassified
20. Take from the table
21. Reconsider

EXPLANATION OF THE MOTIONS

1. *Fix the time to which to adjourn.* Use this motion only if there is no definite time set for the next meeting. Say, "I move that when we adjourn, we adjourn to 3:00 P.M. on Friday, March 9."
2. *Adjourn.* Say, "I move that we adjourn." Use *1* instead if you do not have a definite time set for your next meeting.
3. *Take a recess.* Use this motion when you need an intermission for some purpose. Say, "I move that we take a recess until . . . "
4. *Raise a question of privilege.* Use this motion in any situation affecting your welfare or that of the group. For example, use it if you cannot hear what a speaker is saying or if you would like to have a window opened. Say, "Mr. Chairman, I rise to a question of privilege."
5. *Call for orders of the day.* Use this motion if you are sure that the regular order of business set for the meeting is not being followed. Say, "I call for the orders of the day."
6. *Lay on the table.* Use this motion if you wish to postpone a question temporarily in order to take up more important business. Say, "I move that the question be laid on the table."
7. *Previous question.* Use this motion to end discussion. If it carries, a vote on the main question before the group must be taken at once. Say, "I move the previous question."

8. (*a*) *Limit* or (*b*) *extend limits of debate*. Use the first if you feel that too much time may be spent on a question. Use the second if you want more time given it. Say, "I move that debate be limited [*or* extended] to . . ."

9. *Postpone to a certain time*. Use this motion if for any good reason you prefer that no action be taken upon a question until a later time. Say, "I move that the question be postponed until the next meeting."

10. *Commit or refer*. Use this motion to provide for careful investigation by a committee so that the group may have fuller information on a proposal before coming to a decision. Say, "I move that the question be referred to a committee," or, "I move that the subject be referred to a committee to be appointed by the chair."

11. *Amend*. Use this motion to change the wording of a motion that has been offered. Say, "I move to amend the motion by . . . "

12. *Postpone indefinitely*. Use this motion if you are against a motion being considered, but dare not at the moment risk a direct vote for fear that it will carry. Say, "I move that the question be postponed indefinitely."

13. *Main motion*. This motion presents a piece of business to the group for its consideration. Say, "I move that the club hire a typist." Motions 6, 7, 8, 9, 10, 11, 12, 17, 19, 20, and 21 always are made in connection with a motion already under consideration, usually a main motion.

14. *Question of order*. Use this motion whenever you notice an infraction of parliamentary rules. Say, "Mr. Chairman, I rise to a point of order."

15. *Question of appeal*. Use this motion if you disagree with a decision by the chairman. Say, "Mr. Chairman, I appeal from the decision of the chair." The chairman must then ask, "Shall the decision of the chair be sustained?" If the vote is in the negative, he must reverse his original decision.

16. *Suspension of rules*. Use this motion only in connection with *standing rules;* that is, rules that are not a part of the constitution or bylaws. Say, "I move to suspend the rules that interfere with . . . "

17. *Objection to consideration*. Use this motion if you do not want a main motion discussed at all. It must be made before discussion has begun on that main motion. Say, "Mr. Chairman, I object to the consideration of this question." At once the chairman must say, "Shall the question be considered?" He then takes a rising vote. If the vote is in the negative, the main motion must be dropped.

18. *Division of the assembly*. Use this motion if you think that the chairman has announced incorrectly the result of a *viva voce* vote (*aye* and *no*) or of a show of hands. Simply say, "I call for a division." Then the chairman must call upon each side to stand and be counted.

19. *Leave to withdraw a motion*. Use this motion if you wish to withdraw a motion that you have made. Say, "Mr. Chairman, I wish to withdraw my motion." If the chair has not yet stated the question, you need no one's consent. If he has stated the question, he asks whether anyone objects to its withdrawal. If so, he puts to a vote the request for withdrawal.

20. *Take from the table.* Use this motion to bring under consideration again a motion that has been laid on the table. It is out of order unless some business has been transacted since the motion was laid on the table. Say, "I move that the motion to . . . be taken from the table." This motion is undebatable.

21. *Reconsider.* Use this motion if you change your mind after you have voted upon a question. You may offer it only if you voted with the winning side and you must do so on the day that the vote was taken or at the next meeting. Say, "I move to reconsider the vote on . . . " If the motion to reconsider carries, the question is again open to debate. Use this motion also if you see that a motion which you oppose is sure to pass. Vote for that motion, and then move to reconsider the vote. This motion is debatable only if the motion to be reconsidered is debatable.

SPECIAL NOTES ON MOTIONS

1. The following motions need not be seconded:

Call for a division   Question of privilege
Objection to consideration   Withdrawal of a motion
Question of order   Orders of the day

2. These motions require a two-thirds vote:

Motion to suspend the rules   Previous question
Motion to amend the rules without notice   Motion to amend bylaws *
Motion to limit or extend debate   Objection to consideration †

3. Makers of these motions need not wait to be recognized:

Question of privilege   Question of order
Orders of the day   Objection to consideration
Call for a division   Motion to reconsider

* Previous notice must be given for this motion.
† Here the two-thirds vote must be *against* what the maker wants. The chair will say, "Shall this motion be considered?"

2. CONSTITUTION AND BYLAWS

Your group may wish to frame both a constitution and bylaws. However, many societies adopt instead only a set of bylaws. These are the fundamental rules that cannot be changed without previous notice to the members that a change is desired.

The following articles usually appear in the bylaws of a society that has no constitution.

    I. Name of the society
    II. Object
    III. Membership
        1. Classes (*active, associate*)
        2. Qualifications for membership
        3. Election of members
    IV. Dues and fees (*if any*)
    V. Officers
        1. Names (*president, secretary, . . .*)
        2. Election
        3. Term of office
    VI. Meetings
    VII. Committees
    VIII. Parliamentary authority
    IX. Method of amending bylaws

3. OFFICERS AND THEIR DUTIES

THE CHAIRMAN OR PRESIDENT

1. The presiding officer is addressed as *Mr. Chairman* or *Mr. President.* He speaks of himself as *the chair.* A woman is addressed as *Madam Chairman* or *Madam President.*
2. The chairman remains seated except in these cases:
   a) When he calls the meeting to order
   b) When he puts a question to a vote
   c) When he gives his reasons for a decision
   d) When he speaks upon an appeal
3. If voting is by ballot, he is entitled to vote. If some other form of voting is used, he may vote whenever his vote will change the result, either to break or to make a tie.
4. He should not take part in debate, nor should he indicate with which side he sympathizes when a motion is being discussed. He should see that all have a chance to talk.
5. He should be familiar with parliamentary usage.
6. He should use tact and common sense.

7. He announces the various items of business.
8. He states all motions and puts them to a vote.
9. He appoints committees.
10. He rules upon points of order and of privilege, subject to appeal.
11. With the secretary he signs all orders drawn on the treasurer, unless otherwise specified in the bylaws.

HELPFUL HINTS FOR THE CHAIRMAN

1. Keep at hand (*a*) a copy of the rules, (*b*) a copy of the parliamentary manual used by the club, (*c*) a list of members of all committees.
2. If you make an error, correct your mistake promptly.
3. Be considerate of all, but let no member monopolize the meeting.
4. Apply rules less strictly in a small group than in a large one.

THE VICE-PRESIDENT

The vice-president takes the president's place in his absence; his qualifications are the same as those for the president.

THE SECRETARY

1. The secretary has charge of all records except those, such as the treasurer's books, that are definitely assigned to someone else.
2. He keeps the roll and calls it as required.
3. He notifies members of their appointment as officers, delegates, or committee members. He provides them with necessary papers or credentials.
4. With the president he signs all orders on the treasurer unless the bylaws specify otherwise.
5. Unless there is a corresponding secretary, he carries on the correspondence.
6. He prepares for the chairman an order of business for the day.
7. He should have with him at each meeting a list of all standing committees and of any special committees whose work has not been completed. In addition, he should have a copy of the bylaws and of the manual of parliamentary practice named in the bylaws.
8. In the absence of the president and the vice-president, the secretary takes charge of a meeting long enough for the election of a temporary chairman.
9. He keeps all minutes and reads them to the group.

THE TREASURER

The duties of the treasurer, as a rule, are simply these:
1. He pays bills on the written authority of the president and the secretary.
2. He submits annual (and sometimes quarterly) reports. The group does not accept the treasurer's report. Annual reports should be referred to auditors or an auditing committee; their report is the one to be adopted.

4. THE SECRETARY'S MINUTES

The secretary's minutes should contain the following information:

1. Name of the organization
2. Kind of meeting (*regular, special, adjourned*)
3. Date, time, and place of meeting
4. A statement indicating the presence of the president and the secretary, or, if they were absent, the names of their substitutes
5. A statement concerning the minutes of the last meeting; whether approved, reading dispensed with, etc.
6. Committee reports
7. Lists of new committees appointed
8. All main motions (except any that were withdrawn) with the name of the maker but not of the seconder; whether or not they carried
9. All points of order and all appeals; whether sustained or lost
10. All other motions not lost or withdrawn
11. A record of the voting under these circumstances: (*a*) if a count is ordered; (*b*) if the voting is by ballot; (*c*) if the voting is by a poll of the members. In the last-named case, the record should show how each member voted.
12. A short statement about the program, if there was one
13. Time of adjournment
14. The secretary's signature

It is a good idea for the beginning secretary to take pencil notes. Later he should revise these notes and then write them neatly in ink in the permanent record.

5. ORDER OF BUSINESS

The following is the customary order of business:

1. Call to order by chairman
2. Roll call (*if desired*)
3. Reading of minutes of last meeting, and their approval
4. Reports of standing committees
5. Reports of special committees
6. Special orders (*business set for this meeting*)
7. Unfinished business (*not completed at last meeting*)
8. New business
9. Program (*if any*)
10. Adjournment

6. NOMINATIONS

Candidates may be nominated for office in various ways: (1) by a nominating committee, (2) by means of a nominating ballot on which the members name candidates, or (3) from the floor. Sometimes the by-laws name the method that is to be used.

Any member may move to close the nominations, but the motion needs a two-thirds vote to carry.

Nominations require no second.

7. VOTING

There are five common methods of voting: (1) *viva voce* (*aye* or *no*), (2) show of hands, (3) rising, (4) ballot (customarily used in elections), and (5) *yeas* and *nays* (each member responds as his name is called). In ordinary business, the first method is the one most often used.

In an election, the chairman names tellers to distribute, collect, and count the ballots. They then turn the ballots over to the secretary, who keeps them until it is certain that a recount will not be ordered. The first-named teller reads the results without saying who is elected. He hands the report to the chairman, who reads it again and announces the winners. If no candidate has a majority, balloting continues. To have a majority, a candidate must receive over half of all votes cast, not just more votes than any other candidate. If John has 12 votes, Tom has 9, and Jean has 7, John has a *plurality,* not a *majority.* He has more votes than either of the others, but he does not have over half of the 28 votes cast. In other words, he does not have enough votes to be elected.

8. STEPS IN ORGANIZING A CLUB

FIRST MEETING

1. Someone voluntarily calls the meeting to order. He then moves that a certain person be temporary chairman. Anyone who wishes may second this motion. The one who made the motion puts it to a vote.

2. The chairman thus chosen takes charge.

3. He calls for the election of a temporary secretary.

4. The chairman asks someone to state the purpose of the meeting.

5. The group members discuss the subject.

6. Someone moves that the group organize. He states the kind of club desired.

7. After this motion has been seconded and passed, someone moves that the chair appoint a committee to draw up a constitution and bylaws, or bylaws alone.

8. When the motion for a committee has been seconded and passed, a motion to adjourn, or one to adjourn to a certain time, is in order.

SECOND MEETING

1. The chairman and the secretary chosen at the first meeting serve until permanent officers are elected.

2. The chair calls upon the secretary to read the minutes of the last meeting. They are then approved, or corrected and approved.

3. The chairman of the committee on constitution and bylaws (or bylaws alone) reads the rules drawn up by the committee.

4. He moves their adoption.

5. These rules are taken up and discussed, paragraph by paragraph, and desired amendments are made.

6. The chair calls for amendments to the whole.

7. The group votes on the whole document. A majority vote will carry.

8. Members sign the roll and pay fees (if fees are required). A recess may be taken for this purpose.

9. The secretary reads the roll of members.

10. The group proceeds to the election of officers.

11. The new officers take their places as soon as elected.

12. The president appoints any standing committees named in the rules.

13. The meeting adjourns.

NOTE: It may be impossible to complete both the adoption of rules and the election at one meeting. In that case, their completion should follow immediately after the reading of the minutes at the next meeting. This type of meeting, continued from the previous one, is known as an *adjourned meeting*.

LEARNING ACTIVITIES IN CARRYING ON CLUB WORK

Directions: Try to carry out all the activities that follow. They give you the chance to apply in a practical fashion what you have been studying.

A. Go over carefully the various steps in organizing a club (page 71). Ask questions about any terms or procedures not clear to you.

B. Organize your class into a club. Until your club, real or imaginary, is running smoothly, you probably will want to meet during each English period. Later, one meeting each week will keep you in practice.

The following list of club names may suggest the kind of club that you would like to organize.

Hobbies	Travelers	The Readers	Radio Amateurs
Bug Club	Stargazers	Sports Fans	Curio Collectors
Art Club	Scribblers	Photographers	Citizens' League
Swimmers	Drama Club	Nature Lovers	Aviation Amateurs
Musicians	Journalists	Kitchen Crafts	Better Speech Club
Cyclists	Storytellers	Mathematicians	Hero Worshipers

C. Here is a plan that you can use to get everyone to take part in meetings. Prepare enough small cards so that there is a card for each member of the class, aside from the president and the secretary. On each card write the name and the number of one of the motions described on pages 64–66. If the class has more than twenty-one members, make more than one card for motions that may come up often, such as *4, 6, 7, 9, 10, 11, 12, 13, 14, 15, 17, 18, 19, 21.*

At the beginning of each meeting, distribute the cards among the members. It is the duty of each member to find an opportunity to offer the motion listed upon his card. Devise some method of checking to see that each person carries out his part.

D. Hold elections frequently, both to give you practice in carrying them on efficiently and to give more people the experience of serving as officers. If your bylaws as first drawn up do not provide for holding frequent elections, amend the rules.

E. Serving efficiently on committees takes practice. See that numerous questions are turned over to committees so that everyone serves, and, if possible, makes committee reports. A report is given by the committee chairman, who ordinarily is the first person named to the committee. As a matter of courtesy, the presiding officer usually names as committee chairman the member who moved that a committee be appointed.

RELATED ACTIVITY

Try to bring into class a copy of an issue of the *Congressional Record*. It is a very interesting report of the sessions of the greatest parliamentary organization in the country. Your public library should have copies on file.

4. HOLDING SPECIAL TYPES OF DISCUSSIONS

To be a happy and useful member of any group, you must be able to take a co-operative part in the discussion of ideas. Three useful methods of discussion are the *forum,* the *panel discussion,* and the *debate.*

The purpose of all discussion should be to clarify thinking, with the aim of reaching a truthful conclusion. The first requirement of a good discussion is that certain mental attitudes be developed.

GUIDES TO GOOD DISCUSSION HABITS

1. Remember always that any discussion question must have more than one side. Open the mind to new ideas; listening to and absorbing ideas is as important to a good discussion as talking is. Expect to have your ideas modified or even reversed sometimes.
2. Learn to follow the ideas as they change or develop.
3. Ask questions; be able to answer questions pertaining to your ideas.
4. Introduce only topics of real interest to the group.
5. Insist that every member feel free to present an opposing view. Insist also, however, that he show a considerate, co-operative spirit.
6. Limit the time for each speaker. Two minutes is long enough except in a debate or a planned panel.

THE FORUM DISCUSSION

The purpose of a forum discussion is to examine a topic by questioning, so that an understanding of the whole subject may be obtained. The steps to follow in setting up a forum discussion are these:

1. Choose a controversial question of interest to the group.
2. State it in exact words.
3. Define any terms that may cause difficulty.

DUTIES OF THE CHAIRMAN

1. The chairman may be responsible for doing (1), (2), and (3) above.
2. He points out the differences of opinion.
3. He keeps the discussion to the subject.
4. He leads all members to participate.
5. He explains points that are not clear.
6. He closes the discussion by summarizing the views presented.

The chairman stands during his preliminary speech, but during the discussion everyone remains seated.

The members of the group have these responsibilities:

1. To listen to and follow all views presented
2. To take part by question, illustration, or presentation of new ideas
3. To aid the chairman in keeping the discussion on the topic

If the discussion is planned, pupils should use the library and other sources of reference; they should outline the problems and relate the ideas so that the important ones are in their proper ratios. It is never wise to write these speeches and then try to give them word for word. Such procedure brings formality and a tendency to memorize. If one keeps thinking clearly, clear expression is likely to follow.

THE PANEL

If the discussion is to take the form of a panel, there is more planned participation than in a forum. (1) A few speakers are chosen to present the opposing views on the question. (2) The speakers sit before an audience in a semicircle about a chairman, and each develops his contentions in a well-planned speech. (3) Usually panels are followed by questions from members of the audience who may address any speaker and ask for clarification or proof or expansion of any ideas presented. (4) The chairman guides this audience participation in parliamentary form. (5) He concludes by summarizing both views.

LEARNING ACTIVITIES IN FORUM AND PANEL DISCUSSIONS

A. Let each of your small groups plan and carry out a forum discussion, with the rest of the class acting as a critical, thoughtful audience. Use the helps on pages 73–74 and the Speech Score Card, page 31. Here are suggested topics. Choose your chairman carefully.

1. Are radio, television, and motion pictures threats to leisure reading?
2. Are good manners important to business and social success?
3. Should slang have a place in one's vocabulary?
4. Should schools eliminate grading systems?
5. Should a married woman have a vocation?

B. Plan and carry out a panel discussion. Use the *Readers' Guide* (page 133) to help you locate helpful material. Here are suggested questions:

1. Should our school have (*or* abolish) student government?
2. Should high schools be tuitional rather than tax supported?
3. Should free public education be extended to offer two years of college training to all who wish it?
4. Does our school need to be more democratic?

C. Listen to radio or television forums or panel discussions. Talk about them in class. Continue one of them, imitating the methods used by the speakers.

The debate is the most formal discussion method. Properly used, it stimulates thinking and trains one in the clear development of proof. If you wish to learn to conduct this form of oral discussion, the following guides will help you.

GUIDES TO DEBATE PROCEDURE

1. A debate question should be one of policy rather than one of fact or opinion; in other words, it should state that something ought to be *done* rather than that something is so. Notice these examples:
   Good: *Resolved,* That the voting age in our national elections should be lowered to eighteen. (*Here you argue for a policy.*)
   Poor: *Resolved,* That men are more intelligent than women. (*Here you simply try to prove that something is true.*)

2. Topics that are clearly one-sided should be avoided.

3. The question should be put in the affirmative: *Resolved,* That Lincoln High School should limit each student to two extracurricular activities.

4. Those in favor of the policy stated are the affirmative; those against it, the negative. Usually each team has two speakers.

5. The burden of proof is on the affirmative. They must show (*a*) that their policy is needed, (*b*) that it is practical, and (*c*) that it will not lead to greater evils than now exist.

6. The work of the negative is largely one of tearing down that proof.

7. Each side prepares a case, usually based upon the points in 5.

8. Usually each speaker speaks twice: (*a*) in a main speech and (*b*) in a "rebuttal," his reply to the opponents' arguments. All speeches should have time limits, with the rebuttal time much shorter than that of the main speech. There should be a signal when a speaker has one minute left, and another when his time is up. He may finish a sentence but must then take his seat. The order of speaking usually is as follows:

Main Speech	*Rebuttal*
1. First affirmative	1. First negative
2. First negative	2. First affirmative
3. Second affirmative	3. Second negative
4. Second negative	4. Second affirmative

9. The chairman should understand his duties. He announces the topic, introduces the speakers, gives the order of speaking, explains the time limits and signals, and announces the decision, if there are judges.

10. Opponents are not addressed by name, but by such terms as "the first speaker for the negative" or "the preceding speaker."

LEARNING ACTIVITIES IN DEBATE

Directions: Spend as much time on these activities as you feel will be helpful. Conduct all debates in a courteous, businesslike manner. Review "Thinking Your Way through Debatable Questions," pages 8–10.

A. Discuss the following questions: *Where in the situations of life are debates held today? Who have been some of the famous debaters of history? In what manner does the presentation of a case in a court of law by opposing lawyers take on the nature of a debate? How are debates conducted in legislative bodies of state, federal, and local governments?*

B. From the discussion questions on page 74, choose several that would make good debate topics. Be sure that each topic meets the test of the first two guides on page 75.

C. Divide the class into groups to debate upon the topics chosen in *B.* As far as possible, let students make their own choice of question and side. Each person should also serve as chairman, timekeeper, or judge of another debate.

D. If your school has an organized debate class or an extracurricular debate organization, perhaps one or both of these groups will help you in planning your case. They can help you, too, in locating material to support your side of the question, as well as by suggesting ways of meeting your opponents' arguments.

FOLLOW-UP ACTIVITY

Perhaps this work in debate will have aroused interest in starting an organized debate group. Most states have high school activities associations. Write to the association in your state for information on debate organizations and on sources of materials that will be helpful to you in carrying on debate activities.

Judging Radio, Television, and Film Entertainment

1. EVALUATING RADIO AND TELEVISION PROGRAMS

READ AND THINK ABOUT

Young as they are, radio and television reach more people today and have a greater influence than any other organized means of oral communication. All day long and far into the night, stations pour out their programs, good, bad, or indifferent. To what programs do you listen? What educational values have television and radio to offer? How can they aid you in your mastery of the English language? How can you get increased enjoyment and profit from your listening and viewing?

77

GUIDES FOR EVALUATING RADIO AND TELEVISION PROGRAMS

1. To what interests or emotions does the program appeal?
2. Is its effect on the listeners, especially young people, likely to be wholesome rather than harmful?
3. What is the aim of the program? Is it to *inform,* to *convince,* to *stimulate thinking,* or to *entertain?* How well does it succeed?
4. What seem to be the standards in these categories:
   a) Humor: Is it clean, kindly, original? Is it overdone?
   b) Dramatic material
   Are the characters convincing?
   Is the material wholesome? Has it literary value?
   c) News programs, interviews, speeches
   Is news accurately and fairly reported?
   Does it contain harmful propaganda?
   Are news *reports* clearly distinguished from *commentaries?*
   Are enunciation and pronunciation clear and exact?
   d) Advertising
   How much time does it take? Is it effective? Is it honest?
   Does it detract seriously from the audience's enjoyment?
5. How does the program compare with others of the same type?

LEARNING ACTIVITIES

A. Carry out any of the following discussions, either as a class or in your small groups. Be sure to apply the Guides to Courteous Speech Habits, page 56.

1. Hold a discussion on the subject of radio and television advertising. As a preliminary, time various programs to see what share of their time is given to advertising. Decide what you think is a fair per cent of the broadcast time to use for selling the sponsor's product.
   What types of advertising seem most effective to you? What can listeners do to improve the quality of advertising?
2. Let each small group discuss, before the rest of the class, one of the following questions. Prepare carefully in advance. (See pages 73–74 for a summary of the chairman's duties and of those of the discussion group.)
   a) Are radio and television good substitutes for reading?
   b) Would government ownership of stations be a good thing?
   c) Should children be allowed to hear or watch "horror" programs?
   d) Do radio and television have harmful effects on family life?

B. Carry out one or more of the following individual projects. Use the Speech Score Card, page 31, in preparing and evaluating them.

1. Explain specifically why a certain program is your favorite.
2. Give a talk on the early days of radio. Some older person in your home will be glad to tell you about his first listening experiences.

3. Explain clearly how a radio or a television set works. Follow the Guides to Clear Explanations, page 35.
4. Imitate a famous announcer, commentator, entertainer.
5. Give your opinion on what makes the difference between a good dance band and one that you label "corny." Be definite.
6. As an announcer, give directions for the use of some product or for participation in a contest. Apply the guides on page 37.
7. Write a courteous letter criticizing a program, telling why you believe its influence may be harmful. (For the form of a business letter, see page 224.)
8. Perhaps a radio or television career appeals to you. Consult the card catalogue in the library (see page 127) for books that will give you information about such careers. Consult also the *Readers' Guide* (see page 133) for lists of helpful magazine articles. Talk to the class on one kind of work.

C. If it can be arranged, make a visit to a radio or television station. Before your visit, list things that you want to observe. In a following class period, discuss what you saw and heard. Let someone volunteer to arrange by telephone for this visit. Practice good telephone technique. (Review pages 52–53.)

D. Dramatize a short story that you have enjoyed; produce it as if for a broadcast. Make your voices do the entire work of carrying the full effect of the tale to the listeners.

RELATED ACTIVITIES

A. If your school has a radio or television club or special classes either in radio or in television, arrange for members to speak to your group. Introduce these speakers. (For help, see the guides and *C* on page 50.) Listen carefully so that you can discuss each speaker's ideas accurately afterwards.

B. Invite a staff member of a local station to talk to your class on some phase of radio or television. This project offers practical experience in telephoning, introducing a speaker, listening, taking notes, and reporting.

FOLLOW-UP ACTIVITIES

A. Plan a series of programs to publicize your school and its activities. If your school has no broadcasting facilities, use your imagination and present an imitation broadcast. Here are suggestions:
1. Conduct interviews with the superintendent, the principal, coaches, athletes, honor students, teachers, heads of organizations.
2. Present samples of the work done in representative school activities, such as music and dramatics.
3. Have talks by alumni, by board members, by parents.

B. Many stations offer free educational materials. If possible, secure some of these materials and use them for class study.

2. Selecting and Judging Motion Pictures

Are you like Doretta?

"HOW DO YOU CHOOSE MOTION PICTURES?"

"OH, I DON'T——I JUST GO! IF I DON'T LIKE THE MOVIE, I CAN ALWAYS WALK OUT!"

THINK IT OVER...

What is wrong with Doretta's attitude?
How do *you* choose motion pictures?

Doretta's attitude is about as sensible as that of a person who would walk into a shoeshop and say, "I want a pair of shoes. Size? Oh, any old size. That goes for style and price, too. I'm not fussy. If they don't fit or I don't like them, I just won't wear them."

Perhaps the customer might be lucky enough to get just the right pair of shoes, and perhaps the hit-or-miss movie-goer sometimes gets his money's worth. However, the odds are against both of those results.

PRETEST ON MOTION-PICTURE APPRECIATION

What do you get out of the films that you see? Why do you like or dislike certain pictures? Take fifteen minutes now for a test of your ability to analyze your reactions. Write a brief review of the most recent film that you have seen. Try to state definitely what pleased or interested you, as well as anything that you disliked. Use the guides on page 6. Read your review to the class, applying the Guides to Effective Oral Reading, page 41. File this review in your notebook. You will need it again.

Be word-wise!

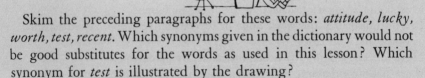

Skim the preceding paragraphs for these words: *attitude, lucky, worth, test, recent.* Which synonyms given in the dictionary would not be good substitutes for the words as used in this lesson? Which synonym for *test* is illustrated by the drawing?

GUIDES FOR SELECTING MOTION PICTURES

1. Learn the names of outstanding directors and producers. Their names on a picture are likely to assure good entertainment.
2. Study the reviews in newspapers and in quality magazines.
   a) Notice the names of the cast. Good supporting actors frequently contribute the best acting in a picture.
   b) Observe what the reviewer says about the acting, the photography, the use of sound and color, the sets, the costumes.
   c) Notice the theme. If it is outside your interests, the picture may disappoint you. However, it may offer something new and worth while.
   d) Analyze the writer's reactions. Does he seem to be giving an honest opinion, or simply to be making clever remarks?

GUIDES FOR EVALUATING MOTION PICTURES

1. How did the picture affect you? Did it leave you depressed? relaxed? unnaturally excited? uplifted? discontented?
2. If the story was intended to be realistic, how true to life were the situations, the language, and the characters?
3. Did the picture glorify crime? war?
4. In your opinion, was it a film that would tend to strengthen race, class, or national prejudice?
5. Were the actors well cast? Were they types, or real people?
6. How was any humor handled? Did you laugh *at,* or *with,* the characters? (There is a difference!)

The exercises that follow will help you to learn how to choose motion pictures wisely and how to judge them. They will help you to realize how the pictures that you see may exert a strong influence on your habits and your thinking.

LEARNING ACTIVITIES IN SELECTING AND JUDGING MOTION PICTURES

A. Do the following three exercises in the order given.

1. What types of plays seem to appeal most to the people of your community? For an answer, try to secure from the manager of your neighborhood theater a list of the pictures exhibited there during the past three months. Delegate one member of the class to make the request. Be sure to apply the guides for interviewing on page 54. If such a list is not available, appoint someone to consult the files of a local newspaper.

After the list has been secured, go over it in class. Have the following general classifications put upon the board. As the names of the films are read, decide into which group each picture fits best.

| Crime, horror | Fantastic | War | Musical | Adventure |
| Biographical | Family life | Love | Western | Historical |

Discuss these questions: *What possible reasons are there for the popularity of certain types? What do you think of the statement sometimes made by producers that they simply give the public what it wants?*

2. Why do people choose the particular plays that they do? The following reasons may sound familiar to you.
   a) My favorite star is in it. I never miss his (*or* her) pictures.
   b) A friend saw it and said he liked it.
   c) The title sounded interesting.
   d) I read the book it's taken from.
   e) The preview looked good to me.
   f) I just felt like a movie, and this was the closest one.
   g) A friend wanted to go. I went just to be agreeable.
   h) The ads in the paper sounded good.
   i) I read a good review of it.
   j) I always go on Tuesday.
   k) I see every Western (or some other type) that comes along.
   Discuss the preceding reasons. How many are likely to ensure one's seeing a worth-while play? Why are some of them poor reasons?

3. One of the safer guides in choosing pictures is the review. There are three types that you are likely to encounter:
   a) Previews in motion-picture magazines
   b) Reviews (advertisements) by the producer
   c) Independent reviews in newspapers or magazines
   Why should you not depend too much upon the first two? What probable difference is there in the motive behind them and that behind the third? Which makes more use of superlatives? Why should you not depend entirely even upon the independent reviewer? How may his opinions of a given picture be affected by his personal likes and dislikes, his health, his moods, the weather? Discuss these questions.
   If possible, bring to class at least three reviews of the same picture: one from a film magazine, one from an advertisement, and one by an independent reviewer in a newspaper or general magazine. Have the reviews read aloud without being identified. Listen thoughtfully. See whether you can tell which is which. Judge the reviews by the guides on page 81.

B. Here are two discussion exercises. Carry them out in class or in your small groups. Be guided by the Guides to Good Discussion Habits, page 73.

1. You may have heard someone complain that he disliked a certain picture because it was not true to life. However, a motion picture may be completely unrealistic, or different from real life, and yet be fine entertainment.

The inferior picture is one that pretends to be true to life and yet has impossible characters going through impossible situations. The average type is neither entirely realistic nor romantic (another name for *un-realistic*), although one element is usually stronger than the other. Honest realism makes you say to yourself, "Yes, that is just the way it would have to be." It should give you a greater appreciation of people and their problems. Honest romanticism, in contrast to realism, may be frankly of the escape type. If a romantic picture gives you wholesome pleasure, it achieves its aim.

Discuss films that you have seen recently. What romantic elements can you recall? How true to life were the attempts at realism?

2. Numerous charges have been made concerning the harmful influence of motion pictures. Discuss the accusations that follow. Give examples from plays that you have seen that tend to prove or to disprove any of the charges. Glancing through copies of motion-picture magazines will remind you of films to consider.

a) Many pictures build class and race prejudice.

b) They give people in other lands misleading and sometimes false ideas of American life.

c) They encourage crime and disrespect for law.

d) They make bad people seem more attractive than good people.

e) They lead to juvenile delinquency.

f) The many Hollywood divorces have a bad influence on the attitudes of young people toward marriage.

g) The films make attractive such harmful social activities as drunkenness, gambling, infidelity.

h) Hollywood stars have too much influence on what Americans do, think, and wear.

i) Many characters as portrayed are simply exaggerated types, not real individuals.

j) Many stars foster dishonesty by endorsing products that they themselves never use.

k) Motion-picture censorship is not strict enough.

l) The "glamour" of the films causes unhappiness by making people dissatisfied with their own lives.

C. Attend a motion picture in a group, using the film as a study case for class analysis. Be sure to apply the guides on page 81.

RELATED ACTIVITIES

A. Talk to the class about a book that you think would make a good film. Justify your choice by discussing plot, setting, and characters. If you like, tell how you would cast the play and whom you would choose as director. Use your Speech Score Card.

B. In addition to careers in the acting field, motion pictures offer a great variety of other vocational opportunities. Consult the card catalogue in the library (see page 127) for books about these vocations. Talk to the class about one or more of them. Use your Speech Score Card, page 31.

FOLLOW-UP ACTIVITIES

A. Make calendars of films that are coming to your community. Find out in advance as much as you can about them. On the school bulletin board, advertise with student annotations those that your group recommends.

B. Perhaps your school newspaper would like to conduct a column on local photoplays that students should attend. Use your group as a committee to write this column.

C. Begin a motion-picture record. List the name of each picture that you see. Include the name of the director and other information or comments that you wish. Use a rating system, such as *E* for *excellent; G* for *good; F* for *fair,* and *P* for *poor.* Check at the end of the year to see how many of the year's "best" pictures received your top rating.

CHECK TEST ON MOTION-PICTURE APPRECIATION

Applying what you have learned in this unit, write a review of the latest film that you have seen. After reading the reviews in your small groups, reread the ones that you wrote at the beginning of the unit. Listen to the reviews critically and judge how much growth there has been in the ability to analyze the qualities of a good motion picture. Use the guides on page 6 to help you compose good paragraphs.

READ AND

Grow

Improving Your Reading Comprehension

1. TESTING YOUR READING COMPREHENSION

Books can teach you much. They can give you pleasure; they can serve as inspirations to you; they can become old and trusty friends. In addition, books can help you in many daily-life situations. Just how well can you read? Suppose you test your ability.

Using your customary rate, read the following article through once. Other instructions will follow.*

HOW TO FIND TIME TO READ †

By Louis Shores

If you are an average reader, you can read an average book at the rate of three hundred words a minute. You cannot maintain that average, however, unless you read regularly every day. Nor can you attain that speed with hard books in science, mathematics, agriculture, business, or any subject that is new or unfamiliar to you. The chances are that you will never attempt that speed with poetry or want to race through some passages in fiction over which you wish to linger. But for most novels, biographies, and books about travel, hobbies or personal interests, if you are an average reader, you should have no trouble at all absorbing meaning and pleasure out of three hundred printed words every sixty seconds.

Statistics are not always practicable, but consider these: If the average reader can read 300 words a minute of average reading, then in 15 minutes he can read 4,500 words. Multiplied by 7 (the days in a week), the product is 31,500. Another multiplication by 4 (the weeks in a

---

* The test over this article is contained in the *Teacher's Manual* for this book.
† From *The Wonderful World of Books,* published by Houghton Mifflin Company and the New American Library. Copyright, 1952, by Alfred Stefferud, Editor.

month) makes 126,000. And final multiplication by 12 (the months in a year) results in a grand total of 1,512,000 words. That is the total number of words of average reading an average reader can do in just 15 minutes a day of one year.

Books vary in length from 60,000 to 100,000 words. The average is about 75,000 words. In one year of average reading by an average reader for 15 minutes a day, 20 books will be read. That is a lot of books. It is 4 times the number of books that are read by public-library borrowers in America. And yet it is easily possible.

One of the greatest of all modern physicians was Sir William Osler. He taught at The Johns Hopkins Medical School. He finished his teaching days at McGill University. Many of the outstanding physicians today were his students. Nearly all of the practicing doctors of today were brought up on his medical textbooks. Among his many remarkable contributions to medicine are his unpublished notes on how people die.

His greatness is attributed by his biographers and critics not alone to his profound medical knowledge and insight but to his broad general education, for he was a very cultured man. He was interested in what men have done and thought throughout the ages. And he knew that the only way to find out what the best experiences of the race had been was to read what people had written. But Osler's problem was the same as everyone else's, only more so. He was a busy physician, a teacher of physicians, and a medical-research specialist. There was no time in a twenty-four hour day that did not rightly belong to one of these three occupations, except the few hours for sleep, meals, and bodily functions.

Osler arrived at his solution early. He would read the last fifteen minutes before he went to sleep. If bedtime was set for 11:00 p.m., he read from 11:00 to 11:15. If research kept him up to 2:00 a.m., he read from 2:00 to 2:15. Over a very long lifetime, Osler never broke the rule once he had established it. We have evidence that after a while he simply could not fall asleep until he had done his fifteen minutes of reading.

In his lifetime, Osler read a significant library of books. Just do a mental calculation for half a century of fifteen-minute reading periods daily and see how many books you get. Consider what a range of interests and variety of subjects are possible in one lifetime. Osler read widely outside his medical specialty. Indeed, he developed from this fifteen-minute reading habit an avocational specialty to balance his vocational specialization. . . . But the important point for us here is that he answered supremely well for himself the question all of us who live a busy life must answer: How can I find time to read?

The answer may not be the last fifteen minutes before you go to sleep. It may be fifteen minutes a day at some other time. In the busiest of calendars, there is probably more than one fifteen-minute period tucked away somewhere still unassigned. I've seen some curious solutions to the problem of finding time for reading.

During army days in the last year of the war, I discovered a Pfc. in my squadron who seemed unusually well-read. I found in his 201 file a remarkable civilian and military biography. His four years of service included two overseas, all meritorious but without heroics. Had all his recommendations for promotion gone through he would have had not only his commission, but probably the rank of captain. But here he was, still a private first-class—because, despite the military emphasis on education, efficiency, loyalty, and all other criteria for determining promotion, accident plays a most important part. Every time this Pfc. had been recommended for promotion, except once, he had been transferred, or come up against table of organization limitations, or a new change in regulations, or a superior officer who had filled out the forms incorrectly or forgotten them in his third right-hand drawer. And so he had remained a Pfc., and had taken his reward in reading. The amount he did in the army was prodigious.

I was curious about his method. And one day, before I asked him, I found a partial answer. Every day the enlisted men put in an hour of drill and formations. During that time at least one fairly long period of rest was called. Imagine my surprise on my first visit to the drill field when, at the command "rest!" I saw one man in the whole long line pull out a paper pocket book and begin to read, standing up.

When I talked with him, I found that from boyhood he had developed the habit of carrying a little book in his pocket, from which he read every minute that he was not doing something else. He found a book especially useful and relaxing during the periods of waiting which all of us experience daily—waiting for meals, buses, doctors, haircuts, telephone calls, dates, . . . There were his fifteen minutes a day, or more. There were his twenty books a year—1,000 in a lifetime.

No universal formula can be prescribed. Each of us must find his own fifteen-minute period each day. It is better if it is regular; then all additional spare minutes are so many bonuses. . . .

The only requirement is the will to read. With it you can find the fifteen minutes, no matter how busy the day. And you must have the book at hand. Not even seconds of your fifteen minutes must be wasted starting to read. Set that book out in advance. Put it into your pocket when you dress. Put another book beside your bed. Place one in your bathroom. Keep one near your dining table.

You can't escape reading fifteen minutes a day, and that means you will read half a book a week, two books a month, twenty a year, and a thousand or more in a lifetime. It's an easy way to become well read.

If you failed to do well with the test, you will want to begin a course of improvement. Analyze your performance by these questions:

1. Did I fail to grasp the central idea of any paragraph? of the article?
2. Did I overlook important details?
3. Did I do poorly because I did not know the meaning of certain words?

2. Improving Reading Ability by Widening the Vocabulary

You may laugh at Arbee's remark, but there is a degree of truth in it. Everyone has two kinds of vocabulary: first, the *workable* vocabulary, or the number of words used in one's daily expression activities; and second, the *recognition* vocabulary, or the number of words that one should be able to recognize when they are heard or read, even though they are not a part of one's natural expression activities. This recognition vocabulary is always much larger than the workable vocabulary.

It has been found that there is a close relationship between the ability to use language well and success in any field. Think of successful people whom you know. What part do you think a wide vocabulary may have played in their success? Professional people are said to have the most extensive and usable vocabularies. How many vocations that you know depend much upon effective word usage?

To widen your knowledge of words, you must (1) really want to increase your vocabulary, (2) look for interesting facts about words, (3) pay attention to new expressions, and (4) study them for mastery.

GUIDES FOR IMPROVING THE VOCABULARY

1. Use the dictionary faithfully. Know what it contains and how to use it. Look up every puzzling or interesting word.
2. Pay attention to related words: *synonyms, homonyms, antonyms.* Know their meanings, spelling, and pronunciation.
3. Cultivate an interest in words so that *root words, prefixes,* and *suffixes* have association and exact meanings for you. A study of Latin helps.
4. Cultivate an interest in *word origins* and *growth* so that you learn to understand and enjoy the words that you use.
5. Widen your vocabulary. Do not limit it to trite expressions, slogans, colloquialisms, or slang. (If those terms are unfamiliar, use the Index of this book to find where they are explained.)
6. Learn that there is a vocabulary appropriate for informal expression (colloquial language), another for formal expression (standard English), and even one of loose slang usage.
7. Practice exact spelling, enunciation, and pronunciation of the words that you need in daily use.
8. Appraise yourself and watch your growth. Try to add at least one new *usable* word to your daily expression each week.

HOW TO ATTACK NEW WORDS

To understand what you read calls for the ability to grasp *central ideas.* Often a stumbling block in the way of getting an author's thought is the failure to understand the meaning of some *key word.* What you do about such a word is important to your mental growth.

There are three practical steps to take in attacking a new word:

1. Think through the sentence containing the word. Do any of the other words give you a clue? You may also find helpful clues in other sentences. This method is called "getting the meaning from the *context.*" Note this example from Parkman's *The Oregon Trail:*

   Bands of antelope would run lightly up the rocky *declivities* and stand gazing down upon us from the summit.

   Here the words *up, down,* and *summit* are clues that should tell you that *declivities* are *slopes.*

2. If the context does not help, or if you want to check your interpretation, consult the dictionary. For example:

Several times we quelled incipient fights.

Here are two strange words. Since the context does not help much, you should use your dictionary. You will find that *quelled* means "put down" or "subdued," and that *incipient* means "belonging to the first stages." From these definitions, it is easy to figure out that "the fights were stopped almost before they began." Notice that you do not need to use the exact dictionary wording. Often, as here, it is better to substitute your own.

3. Try out the various dictionary meanings. Choose the one that makes the best sense in your sentence. Note this example:

The Corn Belt needs new outlets that will *divert* some of the surplus crops into industrial use.

One meaning of divert is "to amuse" or "to entertain." That meaning does not make sense here. Therefore you try another meaning: "to turn aside." That one makes sense.

LEARNING ACTIVITIES IN ATTACKING NEW WORDS

A. Study the following quotations. Write each italicized word and beside it put your idea of its meaning. Check with the dictionary. If you were wrong, put a better meaning beside your first one. Go over the sentences orally, giving both your first interpretation and your final one.

1. Huck was sitting on the *gunwale* of a flatboat, *listlessly* dangling his feet in the water.—MARK TWAIN
2. Presently the boy began to steal *furtive* glances at the girl.—TWAIN
3. The moon through the *rifted* clouds looked down upon what had been the camp.—BRET HARTE
4. He was a tall, *shambling* youth, with a *cast* in his eye not at all calculated to *conciliate hostile* prejudices.—CHARLES LAMB
5. The figure was tall and *gaunt,* and was *shrouded* from head to foot in the *habiliments* of the grave.—EDGAR ALLAN POE
6. There were found none who put forth a hand to seize him; so that, *unimpeded,* he passed within a yard of the prince.—POE
7. When he got up into the drawing-room, and shut the door behind him, he was aware of a *respite* from alarms.—R. L. STEVENSON
8. In the *transports* of his *wrath,* he sent forth a roar, enough to shake the very hills.—WASHINGTON IRVING
9. Drawing his *falchion* and uttering a thousand *anathemas,* he strode down to the scene of combat.—IRVING
10. The *ponderous pericranium* of General Jan Risingh sank upon his breast; his knees *tottered* under him; a deathlike *torpor* seized upon his frame; and he tumbled to the earth . . .—IRVING
11. The inn was *capital;* we had a warm, carpeted room and beds of clean, *lavendered* linen.—BAYARD TAYLOR

12. He knew that denials would be *futile* with the terrible Stimson.

—STEPHEN CRANE

13. Never has George repeated his former *odious* habit of eating peas with a knife.—WILLIAM MAKEPEACE THACKERAY

14. I hate self-*laudation*.—THACKERAY

B. From your spare-time reading, copy sentences containing words that are new to you. Follow the steps on pages 91–92 to see whether you can clear up their meaning. Put interesting sentences upon the board and tell what you have learned about unusual words in them. If you prefer, exchange papers with a classmate. After working out the meanings, compare papers.

C. Decide what each italicized word means in the following paragraph. Then rewrite the paragraph, using your interpretation. Read the revisions in class to see how well your ideas agree. Be sure to apply the Guides to Effective Oral Reading, page 41.

> The Spaniards who came to Mexico heard tales of *opulent* cities to the north, called the "seven cities of Cibola." In these cities, it was said, the doors were *studded* with turquoises and whole streets had as *denizens* goldsmiths making jewelry and ornaments of gold. It was in *quest* of these cities that Coronado explored the *reaches* of the upper Rio Grande. Instead of gold and silver and precious stones, he found little but cactus and canyons and grazing buffaloes, with a few shabby *pueblos* in *lieu* of rich cities. *Propitiously,* perhaps, for those who came after, the Southwest was left in peace for a few centuries more. Coronado had no *prescience* of the treasures that lay within the canyons and beneath the trampling feet of the buffaloes.*

USING ENGLISH IN ALL CLASSES

From assignments in your other classes, bring sentences containing words that puzzle you. Use the class period to clear up their meaning. Be sure to bring *sentences,* not just isolated words. You must know in what connection a word is used before you can explain or define it intelligently. Work by yourselves, in groups, or as a class, whichever fits your situation best.

HOW TO USE THE DICTIONARY

An unabridged dictionary may contain and define as many as 600,000 distinct terms. Probably only a tiny fraction of those words are in your vocabulary. Naturally, you are not expected to master all 600,000. However, you can improve your vocabulary by getting better acquainted with the dictionary and the many kinds of information that it contains. This section of your text discusses certain helpful features contained in the dictionary.

---

* Katherine Glover, *America's Minerals,* page 7 (adapted). "Basic Social Education Series." Evanston, Illinois: Row, Peterson and Company, 1941.

ab·bre'vi·ate (ă·brē'vĭ·āt), *v.t.* [L. *abbreviatus*, past part. of *abbreviare*; see ABRIDGE.] To make briefer; specif., to shorten (words) by omitting terminal letters or sounds or by contraction (*Gen.* for *Genesis, bldg.* for *building*).

ab·bre'vi·a'tion (ă·brē'vĭ·ā'shŭn), *n.* The process of abbreviating; a form resulting from abbreviating.

A' B' C' (ā'bē'sē'). **1.** *pl.* The alphabet; as, to learn one's *A B C*'s. **2.** The first principles of any subject. **3.** The initial letters of the *A B C* powers.

Ab·di'as (ăb·dī'ăs), *n. Douay Bible.* Obadiah.

ab'di·cate (ăb'dĭ·kāt), *v.t. & i.* [L. *abdicatus*, past part. of *abdicare*, fr. *ab-* + *dicare* to proclaim.] **1.** To give up formally, as a throne; to renounce; as, a trust or duty. — **ab'di·ca'tion** (-kā'shŭn), *n.*

ab·do'men (ăb·dō'mĕn; ăb'dŏ·mĕn), *n.* [L.] **1.** The part of the body between the chest and the

———), *adv.* In bed; as, to lie abed.

A'bel (ā'bĕl; -bĭl), *n. Bible.* Son of Adam and Eve, slain by his elder brother Cain. See *Gen. iv.*

Ab'er·deen' An'gus (ăb'ẽr·dēn' ăng'gŭs). An animal of a breed of black hornless beef cattle originating in Scotland.

ab·er'rant (ăb·ĕr'ănt), *adj.* [L. *aberrans, -antis,* pres

a·bet' (á·bĕt'), *v.t.;* A·BET'TED; A·BET'TING. [OF. *abeter,* fr. *a* to + *beter* to bait (as a bear).] To urge on or encourage, usually in something wrong; as, to *abet* a criminal; to connive at; as, to *abet* a robbery.

a·bet'tor or **a·bet'ter** (á·bĕt'ẽr), *n.* One who abets.
Syn. Abettor, accessory, accomplice, confederate, conspir-

(-bĭd'ĕd; -ĭd); A·BID'ING. *Past part.* rarely A·BID'-DEN (-bĭd'''n). [AS. *ābīdan,* fr. *ā-* + *bīdan* to bide.] To continue in a place or in a condition; to remain; stay; dwell. — *v.t.* **1.** To wait for; await. **2.** To bear patiently; tolerate; as, I cannot *abide* him. — **Syn.** See RESIDE. — **abide by. 1.** To remain faithful to; as, to *abide by* a promise. **2.** To accept and be bound by; as, to *abide by* a treaty.

a·bid'ing (á·bīd'ĭng), *adj.* Continuing; lasting.

a·bil'i·ty (á·bĭl'ĭ·tĭ), *n.; pl.* -TIES (-tĭz) [through OF. fr. L. *habilitas* aptness, fr. *habilis* apt; see ABLE.] Condition of being able mentally, physically, or legally; power or capacity to accomplish things; skill, efficiency, or the like; in *pl.,* natural gifts or talents.

ab in·i'ti·o (ăb ĭn·ĭsh'ĭ·ō). [L.] From the beginning.

ab'ject (ăb'jĕkt; ăb·jĕkt'), *adj.* [L. *abjectus,* past part. of *abjicere* to throw away, fr

a'ble (ā'b'l), *adj.;* A'BLER (ā'blẽr); A'BLEST [OF., fr. L. *habilis* easily held or managed, apt, fr. *habere* to have, hold.] **1.** Having enough power, skill, or resources to do what one sets out to do; competent; capable. **2.** Talented; clever.
-a·ble (-á·b'l) Also **-i·ble** (-ĭ·b'l), **-ble** (-b'l). [F., fr. L. *-abilis, -ibilis, -bilis.*] A suffix meaning: 1.

a'ble-bod'ied (ā'b'l-bŏd'ĭd;2), *adj.* Having a sound, strong body.

ab·lu'tion (ăb·lū'shŭn), *n.* [OF. or L.; OF. fr. L. *ablutio,* fr. *abluere,* fr. *ab-* + *luere* to wash.] A washing or cleansing, as of vessels used in a religious service; also, the liquid used in washing.

a'bly (ā'blĭ), *adv.* In an able manner; with ability.
ab'ne·gate (ăb'nē·gāt), *v.t.* [L. *abnegatus,* past part.

āle, chāotic, câre (6), ădd, ăccount, ärm, ăsk (9), sofā, ēve, hēre (27), ĕvent, ĕnd, silĕnt, makĕr; īce, ĭll, chärĭty; ōld, ōbey, ôrb, ŏdd (73), sŏft (74), cŏnnect; fōōd, fŏŏt; oil; cūbe, ūnite, ûrn, ŭp, circŭs, F. menü;

Here are numbered items indicating various kinds of information that the dictionary gives about words. Examples in the excerpt on the opposite page are marked with corresponding numbers.

1. *Spelling.* (If the word has more than one spelling, the preferred form usually appears first.)
2. *Pronunciation.* (The note above applies here also. The pronunciation is shown by *respelling* and by *diacritical marks*, which are explained below.)
3. *Syllables*
4. *Primary (') and secondary (') accents*
5. *Hyphenated words*
6. *Parts of speech*
7. *Irregular plurals*
8. *Principal parts of irregular or difficult verbs*
9. *Comparison of irregular or difficult adjectives or adverbs*
10. *Derivation;* that is, the *source* or *history* of the word
11. *Numbered meanings*
12. *Proper nouns and proper adjectives*
13. *Synonyms and antonyms.* (Sometimes their shades of meaning are explained in detail.)
14. *Foreign words;* indicated by two parallel lines before a word. (Some dictionaries put foreign words into a special section.)
15. *Prefixes and suffixes*
16. *Cross references*

In addition, the dictionary often labels words to show (*a*) *specialized meaning,* (*b*) *levels of usage,* (*c*) *usage in a given geographical area.*

DIACRITICAL MARKS

These are the marks that show how certain letters, especially vowels, are to be pronounced. At the foot or the head of each page is a key giving sample words to use as guides. Here is a list of the commonest diacritical marks:

1. *Macron* (mā'krŏn). This mark (–) indicates the long sound of a vowel; its sound is the name of the letter over which it appears: *bāke, bē, fīne, ōld, fūse.*
2. *Modified macron.* This mark (⊥) shows a long vowel sound in an unaccented syllable: *dĕcide', ōmit'.*
3. *Breve* (brēv). This mark (˘) indicates the short sound of a vowel: *făt, lĕt, hĭt, nŏt, bŭt.*
4. *Circumflex.* This mark (^) indicates a broadened or lengthened vowel sound: *câre, côrn, bûrn.*
5. *Tilde* (tĭl'dĕ). This mark (˜) indicates an unaccented *e* before an *r: bakẽr, singẽr.*
6. *Two dots.* These indicate the broad sound of *a: bärn*

Dictionaries differ in the special sections of information that they include. The edition of Webster from which the excerpt on page 94 is taken includes the following special sections:

1. Guide to pronunciation
2. Correct English usage
3. Rules for spelling
4. Explanatory notes } (At front of book)
5. Abbreviations used in the vocabulary section
6. New words section

7. Abbreviations used in writing and printing
8. Signs and symbols } (At back of book)
9. Proper names (geographical and biographical)

LEARNING ACTIVITIES IN USING THE DICTIONARY

A. These exercises aim to help you to get acquainted with the many types of information contained in the dictionary. Make these oral or written activities, but be sure to compare notes in class or in your small groups.

1. Check your dictionaries to see (*a*) how many they contain of the sections named above and (*b*) where these sections are found. What other special sections, if any, are there? Compare your findings in class. Now check an unabridged dictionary (*Webster's New International Dictionary,* for example) to see what special sections it contains.
2. Find examples of the various kinds of information given about words. (Do not use the examples indicated on page 94.)
3. If possible, check a variety of dictionaries. Note any differences.

B. Explain to the class how to interpret accents and diacritical markings. Place on the board a list of words often mispronounced—for example, words from the list on page 29. Mark them and practice pronouncing them.

If any of you have difficulty in understanding the pronunciation of words, continue the drill on pronunciation. Note the keys given at the front of the dictionary and at the head or the foot of each page.

C. Efficient use of the dictionary requires a thorough knowledge of the alphabet, which you should be able to use readily, both forward and backward. Test the speed with which you can locate the following words: *business, prejudice, rascal, appeal, uniform, systematic, concise, fallacy, temperament, harass.* Jot down each word and beside it put the number of the page on which you found it. Write also its location on the page, such as *16,* signifying that it is the sixteenth word defined on the page. Stop at the end of ten minutes. Exchange papers and check them.

If most of your classmates outstripped you, plan a course of improvement. Make a daily habit of timing yourself in looking up a list of ten words.

D. Use *Webster's New International Dictionary* to find the answers to the following questions. Put the answers on the blackboard or on paper, as your teacher directs, and tell in what section of the book you found them.

1. What are *obsolete* words? *archaic* words? *rare* words? *colloquial* words? Give an example of each type.
2. What word is at the top of the column on the page on which you find the word *giggle?* Why may the guide word be called a "catch" word? What was the original meaning of *giggle?*
3. What kinds of words are included in the lower section of each page? (See the last page of the "Explanatory Notes" at the front of the dictionary.)
4. As how many different parts of speech may the word *down* be used? Illustrate each use by giving an example. From what different languages has it come? What scientific or specific meanings has it (in the *theater,* in *football,* in *botany,* in *navigation*)? What colloquial meaning has it? What slang uses? What obsolete meanings? How many compounds has it?
5. Find other words used as several parts of speech and with widely different meanings. Look up *die, flat, fly,* for example.
6. What is the population of Wichita Falls, Texas? of Richmond, Virginia? of Charleston, South Carolina? of Chapel Hill, North Carolina?
7. Who was Louis Hector Berlioz? What was his nationality? When did he live? How is his name pronounced?
8. Describe the flag of Mexico. Where did you find it pictured?
9. Is *grab-all* a good word for formal use? Explain.
10. How does a flying fish resemble a bird?
11. Is *foofaraw* an acceptable term? What is its origin? (Try the "Addenda" section, which contains words recently added to the language.)
12. With what are these "coined" words in the Addenda section associated?

a) boondoggle	*d*) recco	*g*) throwaway	*j*) brownout
b) goldbrick	*e*) schmaltz	*h*) typecast	*k*) minicam
c) maquis	*f*) snorkel	*i*) airmark	*l*) fratority

13. When and where was the Battle of Lepanto fought? Who were the participants? What was the outcome?
14. Who was Mark Hopkins? How old was he when he died?

E. Make a list of five questions similar to those in *D.* You may wish to choose sides and make this a speed contest in finding the answers.

RELATED ACTIVITY

Many companies that publish dictionaries offer pamphlets and illustrative material about their books. Interesting facts about the books themselves are included, as well as games, tests, and guides for study. Appoint a member of the class to write a letter, perhaps best sent under the signature of your teacher, requesting samples. If you are in doubt about correct letter form, turn to pages 222–25 for help.

READ AND DISCUSS

In Lewis Carroll's *Through the Looking-Glass,* there occurs this conversation between Alice and Humpty Dumpty:

"I don't know what you mean by 'glory,'" Alice said.

Humpty Dumpty smiled contemptuously. "Of course you don't—till I tell you. I meant, 'There's a nice knock-down argument for you!'"

"But 'glory' doesn't mean 'a nice knock-down argument,'" Alice objected.

"When I use a word," Humpty Dumpty said in rather a scornful tone, "it means just what I choose it to mean—neither more nor less."

What do you think of Humpty Dumpty's attitude? *Can* words mean just what you make them mean?

Whether or not you agree fully with Humpty Dumpty, you should realize that what a word means to you may be entirely different from what it means to someone else. Your experiences and your environment may cause certain associations to cluster around a word—associations that someone else may not have experienced. For example, "home" to you may mean a tiny, crowded apartment in a big city; to someone else, it may mean something far different.

In other words, there is more than one kind of meaning. If you are to understand what an author is trying to say, you must be aware of the *connotative* (emotional or associative) meanings that words have as well as of their *literal* (dictionary) meanings.

In addition to their connotative meaning, many words have "extended" meanings; that is, meanings that have been enlarged from their literal meanings so that they now have many additional uses, often ones that are figurative. In the process, the original meanings sometimes have dropped almost completely out of use. "Budget," for example, meant originally a *wallet* or a *leather bag*.

LEARNING ACTIVITIES IN EVALUATING WORD MEANINGS

A. Each of the following sentences contains at least two words having meanings that depend upon personal experience. Find those words and in your small groups talk over what they mean to you; that is, what you see in your mind when you read the words. How do these connotative meanings differ from their literal dictionary definitions?

1. The old man felt cold.
2. I come from a poor family living in a small town.
3. Many people in this neighborhood are wealthy.

4. He is too independent and selfish to suit me.
5. A large family moved into the little house next to ours.
6. He would do anything to be popular.
7. His grandfather is a man of education and culture.
8. She wears expensive clothes; yet she always looks untidy.

B. Here is a quotation from John Ruskin. Read and think about it; then talk over in class what you think he means. What are some of the words that he probably had in mind? In your discussion, apply the guides on page 56.

> There are masked words abroad, I say, which nobody understands, but which everybody uses and most people will also fight for, live for, or even die for, fancying they mean this, or that, or the other of things dear to them.

C. Bring into class a joke that depends for its humor upon different interpretations of a word. Here is an example.

> "Oh, boy, what a break!" said the office boy to the stenographer. "The boss just offered me an interest in this company."
> "He did?"
> "You bet! He said if I didn't take an interest in the business, I wouldn't be here long."

D. Here is a list of words having extended meanings. With the help of an unabridged dictionary, find the original meanings. Look both for the *source* and for any *obsolete* or *archaic* meanings. Note how different the current meanings are. Compare your findings in class. Here are the words: *worry, interval, interfere, eliminate, distract, defeat, default, result, fiction, lye, mingle.*

HOW TO DISTINGUISH RELATED WORDS

Another highly useful aid to vocabulary growth is an understanding of *related* words.

● **WHAT TO REMEMBER ABOUT RELATED WORDS**

1. (DEFINITION) *Synonyms* (dictionary abbreviation, *Syn.*) are words of the same or similar meanings. Knowledge of many synonyms and of the shades of meaning that they express is the best aid to the successful use of words.

2. (DEFINITION) *Antonyms* (abbreviation, *Ant.*) are words of opposite meaning. Antonyms are especially useful in showing a contrast; for example, in writing *balanced sentences.* (See page 411.)

3. (DEFINITION) *Homonyms* often cause trouble, because they are words having a similar sound but an entirely different meaning. Many confusing homonyms are treated in the chapter on spelling. (See the list on page 192.)

LEARNING ACTIVITIES IN DISTINGUISHING RELATED WORDS

A. How many of the following homonyms give you trouble in your writing? To show that you know the difference between them, write sentences using these homonyms correctly. As you go over the sentences in your small groups, read a sentence and then spell the word. If the members of your group reject your use of the word, you must try again.

1. cereal—serial	7. knew—new	13. heard—herd
2. vane—vein—vain	8. waist—waste	14. pain—pane
3. colonel—kernel	9. stake—steak	15. core—corps
4. holy—wholly	10. break—brake	16. forth—fourth
5. clause—claws	11. shear—sheer	17. aisle—isle
6. complement—compliment	12. soar—sore	18. beat—beet

B. In an oral activity, give and spell a homonym for each of the following words. Explain the difference in meaning between the two words.

1. peel	4. grown	7. maze	10. told	13. suède
2. fair	5. bridal	8. plum	11. mantle	14. sane
3. miner	6. lessen	9. rough	12. freeze	15. peak

C. In the dictionary find synonyms for the following words: (1) *decrease*, (2) *stout*, (3) *profuse*, (4) *ramble*. Decide which synonym of each is needed to give the right shade of meaning in the correspondingly numbered sentences.

1. Every week sees my money ·········· rapidly.
2. He was a ·········· man with powerful hands and shoulders.
3. As ·········· as he is with his money, he will soon be penniless.
4. It isn't safe to ·········· around this neighborhood at night.

D. Notice these words: *ludicrous, ridiculous, comical, droll, funny.* Each of them is related to the word *laughable.* Study the definition of each word, and then discuss in class the variations in meaning.

E. Discuss the significance of each of these related terms:

1. Do you *laugh? giggle? smile? grin? guffaw? chortle? chuckle? snicker? snort? roar? titter?*
2. Do you merely *walk,* or do you *amble, saunter, stroll, totter, toddle, shamble, glide, shuffle, creep, plod, tramp, waddle, skulk?*

F. Interesting word games may be made with related words.

1. Let the first speaker give a more vivid word for a common one such as *go.* Each contestant must add another substitute. Keep the game moving quickly.
2. In a given period of time, have each member of the class write a list of substitutes for common terms such as *see* or *hear.* Go over your papers in class and make a composite list. File this list in your notebook for use in your themes.
3. Conduct a contest to see who can give the greatest variety of meanings for each of these words: *still, take, bill, fast.*

HOW TO USE WORD ELEMENTS TO WIDEN THE VOCABULARY

The pupil who has studied a foreign language always has an advantage in mastering a vocabulary, for such study stresses the origins and relationships of words. The American language, like the American people, is a mixture of contributions from many nations. In fact, every known language has helped to make the American tongue the complicated mixture that it is; however, the basic vocabulary stems from the Anglo-Saxon.

Many words contain Greek roots, prefixes, or suffixes; still more have Latin roots, prefixes, or suffixes. The lists that follow indicate some of the contributions made by those two languages.

It is worth noting that of the words you use, most of the short, simple ones are likely to stem from the Anglo-Saxon; the longer, more high-sounding ones, from the Latin.

COMMON GREEK ROOTS

ROOT	MEANING	ROOT	MEANING
crat	rule	*graph*	write, describe
crit, cris	judge	*log*	idea, word, speech, science
cycl	circle	*phon*	sound
dem	people	*phos, phot*	light
ep	word	*phys*	nature
geo	earth	*trop*	turn

COMMON LATIN ROOTS

ROOT	MEANING	ROOT	MEANING
dic	say	*port*	carry
fac, fic, fact, fect	make, do, cause	*quer, quest, quir, quis*	seek, ask
flect, flex	bend	*rupt*	break
grad, gred, gress	step	*sci*	know
		sens, sent	feel
mitt, mit, miss, mise	let go, send	*sequ, secut*	follow
pell, pel, puls	drive	*sta, stat, stit, sist*	stand
pend, pens	hang, pay, weigh	*vid, vis*	see
		vit, viv	life

COMMON GREEK PREFIXES

PREFIX	MEANING	PREFIX	MEANING
a, an	without, not	*homo*	same
anti, ant	against	*hyper*	excessively
auto	self	*micro*	small
dia	through, across	*poly*	many
epi	upon, at	*pro*	before
eu	good, well	*syn, sym*	with, together

COMMON LATIN PREFIXES

PREFIX	MEANING	PREFIX	MEANING
a, ab	from, away, off	*non*	not
ad	to, near, toward	*ob*	toward, against, to, very
ante	before		
con	with, together	*per*	through
de	down, from, completely	*post*	after
dis	apart, not	*pre*	before
ex	out of, beyond	*pro*	before, for, forward
extra	beyond, outside	*re*	back, again
in, il, im, ir, en, em	in, into, not, on, within	*sub*	under
		super	above
inter	between, among	*trans*	across, beyond

SUFFIX	MEANING	SUFFIX	MEANING
ic	of the nature of, pertaining to	*mania*	madness for
		oid	like, resembling
ism	act *or* condition of being	*phobia*	dread *or* fear of
		phorous	bearing
ist	one who, one skilled in	*sis*	condition *or* state of
itis	inflammation of		
latry	worship of	*ty*	state, quality

COMMON LATIN SUFFIXES

SUFFIX	MEANING	SUFFIX	MEANING
able, ible	worthy of, able to be *or* do	*fy*	make, form into
an	pertaining to	*ine*	like, pertaining to
ance, ence, ancy, ency	action, state, quality	*itious*	of the nature of
		ity	condition of
ant, ent	habitually, one who	*ment*	act *or* state of
ery, ory	act of, place of	*or, er*	one who
		ous	full of, like
fic	making, causing	*sion, tion*	act *or* state of

LEARNING ACTIVITIES IN ANALYZING WORD ELEMENTS

A. In the following pairs of words, which would you guess are of Anglo-Saxon origin? Which come from the Latin? On your paper, mark off two columns. Above one of them, write *Anglo-Saxon;* above the other, *Latin.* Then classify the words in the pairs. Exchange papers and check with the dictionary.

1. emperor, king
2. freedom, liberty
3. fraternity, brotherhood
4. amicable, friendly
5. house, domicile
6. leave, depart
7. truthfulness, veracity
8. enough, sufficient
9. strength, power
10. reach, arrive
11. summon, call
12. begin, commence

B. Using the lists of common Greek elements on pages 102–3, figure out the meanings of the words that follow. Make this an oral or a written activity. If you write it, exchange papers; then check the answers by finding the words in the dictionary.

1. micromania
2. democrat
3. epigraph
4. geotropism
5. graphologist
6. homophonic
7. polygraph
8. cycloid
9. aphonic
10. phonologist
11. geologist
12. phosphorous
13. autocratic
14. euphonic
15. symphonist

C. With the aid of your dictionary, take the following words apart, telling what each prefix, root, and suffix means. Make this a written exercise; exchange papers for checking. Here are the words: *philanthropist, misanthrope, cacophony, heterogeneous, genealogy, heliograph, polyglot, pachyderm, petrology, plutocrat.*

D. Using the lists of common Latin elements on pages 102–3, figure out the meanings of the words that follow. Proceed as in *B*.

1. expulsion	6. infectious	11. intermittent
2. visibility	7. persistent	12. irresistible
3. inflexible	8. revivify	13. repellent
4. inquisitor	9. prescient	14. transgressor
5. fictitious	10. degradation	15. factory

E. As in *C*, use the dictionary to help you to analyze the make-up of the following words from the Latin: *colloquy, loquacious, dissimulation, magniloquent, vociferous, soporific, gustatory, insensate, recumbent, impeccable.*

F. What is the common root in each of the following lists of words from the Greek? What is the meaning of the root? What is the literal meaning of each word? Do some thinking before you use the dictionary. What other words can you add to each list?

1. synonym, patronym, anonymous, antonym, homonym, pseudonym
2. hexagonal, pentagon, diagonal, octagon
3. kleptomaniac, bibliomaniac, mania, maniac
4. practical, practice, malpractice, practitioner

G. Learn to look for familiar parts in words that seem new. Try to figure out their complete meaning from their relationship to words that you already know. Always consult the dictionary to be sure that your guess is correct. Many words look and sound much alike, and you might make a serious error. For instance, in Latin the root word *pes* means *foot;* and *expedite, pedestrian, quadruped,* and *expedition* all come from that root, as do many other words. But the Greek language has a root word *pais* (*paidos*), which means *child,* from which come words like *pedagogue, pediatrics, encyclopedia, pedantry.* Look in the dictionary to see how many others you can find with these two roots in them. Make this a class or a small-group exercise.

FOLLOW-UP ACTIVITIES

A. Begin the habit of analyzing strange words; look for the root word; then study any prefixes or suffixes to determine their effect on the root word.

Keep a special section of your notebook for new and unusual words. Underline the root words. Soon the number of new words that you can "unlock" will surprise you.

B. Each day bring into class a new and interesting word. Place it on the board so that all who wish to use it may have it. Tell its history and meaning. Pronounce it and use it in a sentence.

Perhaps words are also like people in this respect: few are really bad if given an opportunity to do their rightful work in their rightful places. Like people, however, words sometimes get out of their rightful places. Certain general classifications cover most of such words.

● WHAT TO REMEMBER ABOUT WORD CHOICE

1. (DEFINITION) *Trite* words and expressions are those that once were new and vivid but have been so constantly overused that now they are almost meaningless. Examples are *beat a hasty retreat, in the nick of time, wee small hours.* Other examples are overworked figures of speech (see pages 257–58). Avoid these phrases.

2. (DEFINITION) *Slang* is the popular expression of the moment. When it is really expressive, it may become established in the language. Much slang, however, soon dies, as you will see if you compare current slang expressions with any that your parents may recall from their youth— or even with those that were most popular a year ago! The important thing to remember is that you should not let slang take over your speech completely so that your expression has neither originality nor variety.

3. (DEFINITION) *Colloquialisms* are expressions that are suitable to informal and conversational situations but not to formal situations. Examples are *phone* (for *telephone*), *funny* (for *puzzling*), *fizzle, crook, brainy.* Many slang phrases eventually become colloquialisms. Every sport, every business, and every great author has contributed to the language certain phrases so expressive that they have become a lasting part of the daily vocabulary. Use them naturally in the right situations, but be able to replace them with more formal expressions when the need arises.

4. (DEFINITION) *Slogans* are catchwords used in advertising and elsewhere. Business, politics, crime, sports, and the entertainment world are full of these common expressions that creep into everyone's speech. Slogans such as these are particularly prominent in advertising: "Good to the last drop!" "The skin you love to touch," "Say it with flowers," "Like sleeping on a cloud!" When you can, coin a good slogan to fit some plan or project; it is the kind of thing that people remember— and are likely to believe if they hear it often enough!

5. "High-brow" language (if you do not know what it is, see the dictionary!), like trite expressions and overuse of slang, should be avoided. Train yourself to use simple words, except on a topic that demands scholarly and scientific terms. Keep the intelligence of your readers or your audience in mind; if they cannot understand you, your fine words will be largely wasted.

LEARNING ACTIVITIES IN CHOOSING THE SUITABLE WORD

A. Some of the trite expressions that follow are common in writing; others of them are frequently heard in conversation. In a class discussion, supply good substitutes.

1. Age before beauty
2. All work and no play
3. As if turned to stone
4. As luck would have it
5. Balmy breezes
6. Better late than never
7. Breathed a sigh of relief
8. Bright and shining faces
9. By the skin of my teeth
10. Delicious refreshments
11. Downy couch
12. Fair sex
13. Frozen North
14. In the twinkling of an eye
15. Led to the altar
16. Little did I think
17. Method in my madness
18. My better half
19. Perfect in every detail
20. Poor but honest
21. Pretty as a picture
22. Proud possessor
23. Psychological moment
24. Quick as a wink
25. Render a selection
26. Struck speechless
27. The worse for wear
28. Too funny for words
29. To make a long story short
30. View with alarm

B. What trite similes are associated with what is pictured on this page? What new comparisons can you suggest that will give the same idea as each of these trite expressions? Make this an oral activity.

C. Discuss the probable origin of each of the following colloquialisms. Some of them began as slang terms. Others are on their way to becoming standard English. Which of the expressions listed do you think are in that stage?

1. Can't stand her	8. Mighty glad	15. Have the blues
2. Feel below par	9. Newsy	16. Horse sense
3. Gave me the mitten	10. Fathead	17. Jaywalker
4. Get in some good licks	11. Put on your things	18. Sore (*angry*)
5. Get into hot water	12. Run a business	19. Spunk
6. Go back on someone	13. Send-off	20. Squelch
7. Draw a blank	14. Good and hot	21. Stick up for

MISCELLANEOUS ACTIVITIES IN WIDENING THE VOCABULARY

A. Now that you have seen how words are formed by the addition of prefixes and suffixes to roots, you can understand how new language (including slang, technical and scientific terms, and foreign words) is constantly developing. Words lose their original meanings, add new or different meanings, or are lost entirely.

1. What new words can you name that the inventions of Thomas Edison added to the American language?
2. Name words growing out of the invention of the airplane, the radio, the automobile, the motion picture.
3. Discover the nationality of each of the men who gave the following words to the language: *boycott, Braille, doily, fuchsia, galvanize, macadam, mackintosh, saxophone, shrapnel, silhouette, volt, watt.* Add other words to this list.
4. As a demonstration of the fact that many nations have contributed words to the American language, locate the original source of each of these words:

alfalfa	breeze	lilac	robot	taboo
amen	caviar	mammoth	shampoo	tattoo
bandit	cobra	pecan	sleet	tea
bantam	glamour	polo	spook	toboggan
boomerang	lemon	potato	squall	waltz

B. The following words have interesting origins. Choose one or more of the words and report to the class what you find.

absurd	buckle	explode	nice	salary
album	career	humor	orchestra	slogan
amateur	clinic	infant	pageant	sophomore
avoid	clock	insult	pavilion	splendid
blanket	corduroy	lynch	pill	test
bomb	curfew	mail	puppy	torpedo
bribe	derrick	nasturtium	rug	waist

C. Look in an unabridged dictionary to see whether you can find at least five other words of interesting origin. Tell the class about them.

D. There are many good words suitable for everyday use that are often mispronounced or poorly enunciated. Use at least five of those in the following list in oral sentences that show their meaning. Make your sentences about your own experiences. Your classmates will listen attentively to check your work. Repeat any of the words that you mispronounce or fail to enunciate well.

amateur	coupon	insidious	bouquet
performance	favorite	apropos	clique
partner	deficit	finance	suite
asked	attacked	status	Italian
defect	handkérchief	gratis	adult
quantity	exquisite	hundred	err
superfluous	apparatus	penalize	data
positively	research	theater	picture

E. Many college freshmen do poor work in English composition because they have only vague ideas of the meaning of common words that they see in print. The words below are typical of those that appear in average reading material. Test your recognition ability by them. Without any preparation, copy the words in a column. After each word write a synonym or as clear a meaning as you can give. When everyone has finished, assign the words proportionally among members of the class. Each student should look up his words, getting all meanings. Afterwards he may read his list orally as pupils check their papers, or those of others if they exchange. Score one point for each acceptable interpretation given.

1. admonition	13. dogma	25. laudable	37. proximity
2. analogous	14. effigy	26. manifest	38. sagacity
3. antithesis	15. fallacious	27. mobile	39. scathing
4. apparition	16. feasible	28. nocturnal	40. sequence
5. aspirations	17. felicitous	29. noxious	41. smug
6. candor	18. fidelity	30. palliate	42. somber
7. coherent	19. imminent	31. paradox	43. somnolent
8. condone	20. impact	32. partisan	44. succinct
9. controversial	21. impromptu	33. philanthropist	45. tangible
10. corroborate	22. incognito	34. plausible	46. traverse
11. cupidity	23. infamous	35. posthumous	47. verbose
12. dilemma	24. insidious	36. progeny	48. wistful

HOW TO EVALUATE YOUR VOCABULARY GROWTH

To make sure that your vocabulary grows in size and in effectiveness, make and keep in your notebook an appraisal chart. Two methods are given here; use one of them or plan one of your own.

1. Underline in your themes all new words that you are trying to use correctly and the substitutes that you have used for trite and extravagant words. Perhaps your teacher will give you added credit, just as he deducts credit for errors. Here is part of a student's theme to show you a way to do it.

(has)

(+3)   My pencil bears the aspect* of a battle—

(chewed)

(+1)   scarred* soldier. The tip is gnawed almost
all the way off so that it looks like an

(+1)   escapee* from no—man's land, with shell holes
marking its experiences.

Is it dangerous to chew a pencil? Only the
other day I read that modern people have much
more trouble with their teeth than did our

(−1. Trite)   primitive ancestors because we eat food that
is too soft. Now, a pencil is certainly

(+1)   tough food. It gives the same masticatory*
joy as does chewing gum. To a thinker it

(−1. Trite)   gives mental food and inspiration. If the
truth were known, I am sure it would be

(+1)   manifest* that many great authors have had a
(+1)   family of willow sticks on which to nibble
out their unusual thoughts.

(NOTE: The starred words are new ones that
I have not used before. The two words in
parentheses are ones for which I found more
vivid substitutes.)

The teacher has marked two expressions as *trite*. Do you agree? Notice the
indications of added and deducted credit in the margin.

2. Keep two lists of words in your notebook: (*a*) words that you add and
(*b*) words that you discard. Watch the first list outgrow the necessity of
keeping the second.

3. Learning to Find Key Words and Central Ideas

READ AND DISCUSS

Look at the following incomplete sentences.

Joe .... seen much .... four years .... hobo.
.... experienced .... cruelty .... suffering .... life
.... road as well as .... adventure .... freedom.

What words probably belong in the blanks? Why could you figure out
the meaning of those sentences even though almost half the words in them
are missing?

As that little experiment will tell you, some words in what you read are more important than other words. These important words are *key words*. (Why is "key words" a good name for them?)

● **WHAT TO REMEMBER ABOUT KEY WORDS AND CENTRAL IDEAS**

1. A *paragraph* should be built around one central idea.
2. A group of connected paragraphs should be built around one theme, or central idea.
3. Except in narration, the central idea of a paragraph often is stated definitely in a *topic sentence,* or *topic statement.*
   a) Usually the topic sentence opens the paragraph, though it may come at the end or within the paragraph.
   b) All other sentences should relate to the topic sentence.
4. To find the central idea in a paragraph having no topic sentence, one should find the *key words* and from them frame a topic sentence.

> My great-great-great-grandfather was 90 per cent self-sufficient; that is, he was able to produce 90 per cent of the goods that he needed. I am, you are, nearly every American is, at most 10 per cent self-sufficient. We cannot live unless millions of people, whom we have never seen, keep sending us goods. If we have no money, they will not send these goods, and then we must either starve or go on relief.*

Statement of central idea: *Unlike our great-great-great-grandfathers, we depend almost entirely upon others for the things that we need.* You can see that in your statement you do not actually need to use many of the key words. They simply give the information from which you draw your conclusion.

LEARNING ACTIVITIES IN SELECTING CENTRAL IDEAS

A. Think through the following paragraphs. Locate the topic sentence in each paragraph. Analyze each paragraph in class to determine whether all other sentences in it relate to the topic sentence.

> Young men filled the lobby of College Hall. Coming from various sections of the country, bewildered by their new surroundings, awed by passing faculty members, they walked around and around in a maze of confusion. Whether apparently calm and confident, or obviously high-strung and excitable, a question mark hung over each one. In a corner a few girls, although meeting for the first time, huddled together as though for mutual protection. Stranger looked at stranger with appraising glance, some solemn and grim-faced, others sociable and smiling. It was the opening day of school, . . .†

---

* Stuart Chase, *A Primer of Economics,* page 11. "Basic Social Education Series." Evanston, Illinois: Row, Peterson and Company, 1941.
† Victor Robinson, *Doctor Jad: The Way of Life of a Physician,* page 8 (adapted). "The Way of Life Series." Evanston, Illinois: Row, Peterson and Company, 1941.

Some soldiers are ambitious; some are lazy. Some soldiers seek responsibility; others shirk it. Corporal Hendricks, an artist with motors, is clawing his way through technical correspondence school courses to become a master mechanic when his present enlistment expires. Hendricks has had only three years of school. Although many, like Hendricks, are taking advantage of their leisure time, others have no ambition except to spend every last cent of each month's pay. The Army, like civil life, is made up of all kinds of people.*

Unfortunately the frontier did not attract only good citizens. It was also a sink into which drifted much of the riffraff of the country. Before those wanted by the law elsewhere could be caught, they slipped away into the West. Into every gold camp and trail-end town wandered gamblers, swindlers, criminals, and other parasites. Like leeches, they fastened on any place where there was business activity, favoring especially young boom towns which had not yet developed a civil sense of law and order.†

B. The following paragraphs have no topic sentence. Read each paragraph carefully. Jot down the key words. Then write a sentence that you feel sums up the central idea. Compare your sentences in class or in your small groups.

Although instructed to avoid shooting if possible, the Mounted Police are told also that if shooting is necessary, they should shoot to kill. Maybe this idea is behind that well-known phrase, "The Mountie always gets his man." Maybe that line came out of the movies, which have given a very queer slant on the work and purpose of our Force. Anyhow, despite the fact that "always gets his man" may be the ambition of the individual, it is not our motto. The true motto is *Maintiens le droit,* the English of which is "Maintain the right." The French words, appearing upon our badges, are engraved first upon our hearing, then upon our thoughts, and always upon our memories.‡

You cannot astonish an English gentleman. If a man goes into a fit at his side, or a servant drops a dish upon his shoulder, or he hears that the house is on fire, he sets down his glass with the same deliberation. He has made up his mind what to do in all cases, and he does it. At a first introduction, he is cold, and may bow stiffly, but it is only his manner. . . . Rather chilled by this, you are a little astonished when the ladies have left and he closes his chair up to you, to receive an invitation to pass a month at his country house. Then you discover that at the very moment he bowed so coldly he was thinking how he could contrive to facilitate your plans for getting to him or seeing the country to advantage on the way.§

* Lt.-Col. R. Ernest Dupuy, U.S.A., and Lt. Trevor N. Dupuy, U.S.A., *To the Colors!: The Way of Life of an Army Officer,* page 38 (adapted). "The Way of Life Series." Evanston, Illinois: Row, Peterson and Company, 1942.

† William M. Raine, *45-Caliber Law: The Way of Life of the Frontier Peace Officer,* page 23 (adapted). "The Way of Life Series." Evanston, Illinois: Row, Peterson and Company, 1941.

‡ Sydney R. Montague, *Riders in Scarlet: The Way of Life of the Mounties,* page 34 (adapted). "The Way of Life Series." Evanston, Illinois: Row, Peterson and Company, 1941.

§ From *Famous Persons and Places* by Nathaniel P. Willis.

C. Find a short magazine article on some subject that interests you. The *Readers' Guide* (see page 133) will help you to locate an article. Jot down the topic sentence of each paragraph, or frame the central thought, if no topic sentence is given. If the article has been carefully written, the sentences that you set down will form a brief, clear summary of the material. Give a short talk to the class, based upon the sentences that you wrote. Use your Speech Score Card.

USING ENGLISH IN ALL CLASSES

Bring to class a reading assignment from one of your other classes. Go over the paragraphs of that assignment carefully. Write the topic sentence of each paragraph. If no topic sentence is given, jot down the key words and then frame a sentence of your own that sums up the central idea. Go over your sentences in class. This is a profitable way to study any reading assignment.

4. Improving Your Reading Methods

Is there something that Arbee should know?

"WELL, MAYBE YOU DO READ FASTER —
BUT I READ EVERY WORD !"

THINK IT OVER . . .

Is Arbee's practice of always reading every word necessarily a good way to read? Why not?

Should the reader's purpose affect the way that he reads?

As is pointed out on pages 109–10, it often is possible to grasp the important ideas in a piece of reading matter by simply noting the key words. The more skilled you become in picking out such key words, the faster your reading rate will tend to become.

Rapid reading is not necessarily good reading any more than is the "I-read-every-word" kind. If you simply look at words quickly and as a result miss most of what they say, your rapid reading is a liability to you.

It is important to realize that you need to vary reading rate according to your *intention* in reading. Here are some points to keep in mind.

1. *Skimming* is the kind of reading in which the reader glances quickly through the material. It is suited to these purposes:
   a) Ascertaining whether certain topics, dates, or names are mentioned
   b) Getting a bird's-eye view to see whether the material sounds interesting enough for a more careful reading
   c) Keeping up with current news in the daily paper

2. *Careful reading* is reading for details. It is the kind of reading needed whenever one must remember what is being read or when one must find and understand the ideas presented. Textbooks usually require this type of reading.

3. *Critical reading* is the kind in which the reader stops to examine the ideas of the writer, weighs those ideas, and then forms an opinion about them. By its very nature, critical reading should be done slowly.

GUIDES TO EFFICIENT READING

1. *Learn to skim*
   a) Note each paragraph indention in an article or chapter. Read only the first sentence; if that does not indicate what the paragraph is about, read the last sentence of the paragraph. Proceed thus to the end of the material. In most instances, you will have grasped the main ideas in an orderly fashion.
   b) If you are looking only for information about a certain *person, date,* or *thing,* move your glance quickly over an entire page. Let your eyes stop only when they see the word for which you are looking; then read the sentence containing it to see whether the information that you want is given.

2. *Practice turning into your own words* the main thought of a paragraph.

3. *Pick out the key words;* if necessary, write them down and then see whether you can make sense of them.

4. *Practice to widen your eye span;* that is, to cut down the number of eye movements that you make in reading a line. The fewer eye movements, the rapider the reading rate will be and the better you will grasp ideas.

5. *Pay attention to mechanical aids;* for example, numbered headings, the use of italics, or the use of boldface (**heavy black**) type.

Skim the preceding paragraphs for these words: *rapid, intention, current, glance.* Which of their synonyms, as explained in the dictionary, would not be good substitutes for the words as used in this lesson? Which synonym of *glance* does the drawing illustrate?

LEARNING ACTIVITIES IN INCREASING READING EFFICIENCY

A. In class or in your small groups, decide which kind of reading is best adapted to the following:

1. Preparing a math assignment
2. Looking for a book to read for pleasure
3. Keeping abreast of the day's news
4. Using a telephone directory
5. Trying out a new recipe
6. Deciding whether an author is biased in his views
7. Using the dictionary
8. Comparing what two authors have to say on the same topic

B. In one minute, skim the Preface on page iii of this book to find what are indicated as being outstanding features of *The New Building Better English.* At the end of the minute, close your books and jot down on a sheet of paper what you found. Compare results in your small groups; then go over the Preface carefully to see how accurate your skimming was.

C. Use the *Readers' Guide* to help you find an article on some controversial subject. Read the article critically; then, in a talk to the class, present the writer's arguments and tell why you agree or disagree with them. Talk from an outline (see page 118), and use the Speech Score Card, page 31, both in preparing your talk and in rating your performance.

5. IMPROVING READING ABILITY
BY PARAPHRASING

One of the best ways to determine how well you understand what a writer says is by *paraphrasing.* The term may be new to you, but probably you have had some experience in paraphrasing even though you have not realized that fact. For example, a teacher who says to you, "Tell me *in your own words* what the author is saying," is asking you to paraphrase.

A good paraphrase is not easy to write, for it requires that you *think*—and think hard—about what you read. It is probably the best way of all, however, to prove that you really understand a difficult piece of writing.

● WHAT TO REMEMBER ABOUT PARAPHRASING

1. The purpose of a paraphrase is to express clearly, in definite, easy-to-understand language, exactly what an author is saying.
2. A paraphrase is not a shortened form; it *parallels* the selection that it interprets. For that reason, a paraphrase may be even longer than the selection itself.
3. A good paraphrase must fit these requirements:
   a) It must be definite.
   b) It must be worded in clear, simple language.
   c) It must not repeat the author's wording.
   d) It must contain all the main ideas of the original.
   e) It must not add any new ideas.

Here is a paragraph from *The Autobiography of Benjamin Franklin*. Following the paragraph is a paraphrase of it.

After ten years' absence from Boston, and having become easy in my circumstances, I made a journey thither to visit my relations, which I could not sooner well afford. In returning, I called at Newport to see my brother, then settled there with his printing-house. Our former differences were forgotten, and our meeting was very friendly and affectionate. He was fast declining in his health, and requested me that, in case of his death, which he apprehended not far distant, I would take home his son, then but ten years of age, and bring him up to the printing business. This I accordingly performed, sending him a few years to school before I took him into the office.

(*A Paraphrase*)

After having been away from Boston for ten years, and being now in comfortable circumstances, I went back there to visit my relatives, something that I could not before very well have afforded. On the way back, I stopped at Newport to see my brother, who had a printing-house there. Our past disagreements were forgotten, and our meeting was very friendly and affectionate. His health was rapidly growing worse; and he asked whether, in case of his death, which he was afraid was not far away, I would take his son, then only ten years old, into my home, and bring him up to be a printer. I did so, first sending him to school for a few years before bringing him in to work with me.

A. Here are paragraphs to give you practice in paraphrasing. Before doing them, study carefully the points on page 115 and the example of paraphrasing. Compare work in your small groups; then decide on a composite paraphrase to be read to the entire class.

Remember this saying, *The good paymaster is lord of another man's purse.* He that is known to pay punctually and exactly to the time he promises, may at any time, and on any occasion, raise all the money his friends can spare. This is sometimes of great use. After industry and frugality, nothing contributes more to the raising of a young man in the world than punctuality and justice in all his dealings; therefore never keep borrowed money an hour beyond the time you promised, lest a disappointment shut up your friend's purse for ever.

—BENJAMIN FRANKLIN

In coming to this country, our fathers most certainly contemplated, not merely a safe retreat beyond the sea, where they could worship God according to the dictates of their own consciences, but a local government founded on popular choice. That their foresight stretched onward through the successive stages of colonial and provincial government which resulted in the establishment of a great republican confederacy, it would be extravagant to pretend. But from the primitive and venerable compact signed on the eleventh of November, 1620, on board the *Mayflower,* while she yet nestled in the embrace of Princetown harbor, after her desolate voyage, like a weary child at even-song in its mother's arms, through every document and manifesto which bears on the question, there is a distinct indication of a purpose to establish civil government on the basis of republican equality.

—EDWARD EVERETT

B. Paraphrase the following selections from poetry. Proceed as in *A.*

My wealth is health and perfect ease;
　　My conscience clear, my chief defense;
I neither seek by bribes to please,
　　Nor by deceit to breed offense:
Thus do I live; thus will I die;
Would all did so as well as I.

—SIR EDWARD DYER

My mind lets go a thousand things,
Like dates of wars and deaths of kings,
And yet recalls the very hour—
'Twas noon by yonder village tower,
And on the last blue noon in May—
The wind came briskly up this way,
Crisping the brook beside the road;
Then, pausing here, set down its load
Of pine-scents, and shook listlessly
Two petals from that wild-rose tree.

—THOMAS BAILEY ALDRICH

C. Paraphrase (1) the first paragraph of the Declaration of Independence and (2) the Preamble to the Constitution. In class, discuss your paraphrases; then work out a good composite wording. Be careful to apply the Guides to Good Listening, page 17, and the Guides to Courteous Speech Habits, page 56.

USING ENGLISH IN ALL CLASSES

Bring into English class a reading assignment in one of your other classes. Use difficult paragraphs for small-group practice in paraphrasing.

FOLLOW-UP ACTIVITY

Whenever you encounter difficult reading matter, learn to do at least mental paraphrasing. If the material is something that you must understand in order to proceed with your work, make a written paraphrase. Not only will you understand what you are reading, but you will remember it better than you otherwise would.

6. Improving Reading Ability by the Use of an Outline

Perhaps you grasp central ideas fairly well but have trouble in keeping supporting ideas or details straight. A real help in learning to read for details, particularly in studying reading assignments, is the outline.

A good outline shows clearly the most important ideas in a piece of writing. However, it also shows plainly the less important ideas covered and their connection with the main points.

Outlines are of two types: *sentence* and *topic*. Here is an example of each type. As a rule, the sentence outline is more satisfactory than the topic outline if you want to refer to your outline at some future date.

Sentence Outline	*Topic Outline*
I. This is a main point.	I. Main point
A. This is a subpoint of *I*.	A. Subpoint of *I*
B. This is a subpoint of *I*.	B. Subpoint of *I*
1. This is a detail of *B*.	1. Detail of *B*
2. This is a detail of *B*.	2. Detail of *B*
II. This is a main point.	II. Main point
A. This is a subpoint of *II*.	A. Subpoint of *II*
1. This is a detail of *A*.	1. Detail of *A*
a. This is a detail of *1*.	a. Detail of *1*
b. This is a detail of *1*.	b. Detail of *1*
2. This is a detail of *A*.	2. Detail of *A*
B. This is a subpoint of *II*.	B. Subpoint of *II*
III. This is a main point.	III. Main point

GUIDES FOR OUTLINING

1. Use only one method in an outline. Do not mix *topics* and *sentences*.
2. Begin each point with a capital letter and place a period after each division number or letter.
3. If a topic is divided, have at least two subheadings; it is impossible to divide anything into fewer than two parts.
4. Indent correctly. See above how each type of division numeral or letter is placed in its own margin. Begin the figure or letter before a subheading directly below the first letter of the point to which it is subordinated.
5. Do not place periods after the points in a topic outline.
6. If a sentence is too long for one line, begin the second line under the first letter of the line above, as shown in this sentence.
7. Use the sequence of numbers and letters shown in the sample outlines: *Roman numerals* for main ideas, *capital letters* for chief subpoints, *Arabic numerals* for important details, and *small letters* for less important details.

Here is an article, followed by a sentence outline based upon it. (For an example of a topic outline, see pages 7–8.)

THE MEN OF THE COAST GUARD *

To be admitted to the Coast Guard Academy, a young man must be over seventeen years of age and under twenty-three, of good character, and with a fine athletic body. His previous education must be sufficient to admit him to a good college of engineering. Each June, in various parts of the country, competitive examinations are given.

Those selected by competition are given a four-year course in mathematics, navigation, engineering, and other subjects. The students are under military discipline, which fits them for command. Every summer the cadets make a three-month foreign cruise, and those voyages are so planned that by graduation day each man has visited the principal European and South American ports. These cruises provide practical training in the fields of seamanship, navigation, and engineering.

Upon graduation the cadet is appointed an Ensign in the Coast Guard, and all commissioned officers in this Service have the rank and pay of United States naval officers. Their commandant is a Rear Admiral.

The enlisted men of the Service also are chosen carefully. Enlistment is for three years, but 85 per cent of them re-enlist for term after term. To enlist for the first time, a man must be between the ages of eighteen and twenty-five. His health must be excellent and his record of conduct good. If not American-born, he must have applied for citizenship and must be able to read, write, and speak the English language.

There are opportunities for enlisted men to qualify for the pay and rating of petty officers and warrant officers. Furthermore, the Coast Guard Institute offers free instruction to men in the Service who are capable and ambitious. They may fit themselves to become accountants, experts on marine engines, navigators, or radiomen.

THE MEN OF THE COAST GUARD

I. Entrance to the Coast Guard Academy is restricted.
   A. There are certain requirements for admission.
      1. An applicant must be over seventeen years of age and not more than twenty-three.
      2. He must be of good character.
      3. He must have a fine athletic body.
      4. His previous education must be enough to admit him to a good college of engineering.
   B. He must be one of the winners in the competitive examinations given each June.

* Mary Kidder Rak, *They Guard the Gates: The Way of Life on the American Borders,* pages 47–49 (adapted). "The Way of Life Series." Evanston, Illinois: Row, Peterson and Company, 1941.

II. The training of a Coast Guard officer is broad and thorough.
   A. He takes a four-year course in mathematics, navigation, engineering, and other subjects.
   B. He is under military discipline.
   C. Each summer he goes on a three-month foreign cruise.
      1. By graduation he has visited the principal European and South American ports.
      2. During these cruises he receives practical training in seamanship, navigation, and engineering.

III. Commissioned officers have the rank and pay of United States naval officers.
   A. Upon graduation, the cadet becomes an Ensign.
   B. The commandant is a Rear Admiral.

IV. The Coast Guard also contains enlisted men.
   A. Original enlistment is for three years.
   B. Eighty-five per cent re-enlist for term after term.
   C. A man wishing to enlist must meet certain requirements.
      1. He must be between the ages of eighteen and twenty-five.
      2. He must have excellent health.
      3. He must have a record of good conduct.
      4. If foreign-born, he must meet special requirements.
         a. He must have applied for citizenship.
         b. He must be able to read, write, and speak English.
   D. The enlisted man has opportunities to advance.
      1. He may become a petty officer or a warrant officer.
      2. He may receive free instruction at the Coast Guard Institute if he proves capable and ambitious.
      3. He may become an accountant, an expert on marine engines, a navigator, or a radioman.

LEARNING ACTIVITIES IN MAKING OUTLINES OF READING

A. In a class discussion, check the outline of "The Men of the Coast Guard" by the guides for outlining, page 118. Go over the guides point by point.

B. In groups of four or more people, make a sentence outline of this article.

AUTOMOBILE ACCIDENTS*

No one really wants to have an accident. The trouble is that people do not want hard enough not to have an accident. They drive too fast! They pass other cars on hills and on curves. They do not look each way before they cross railroad tracks. They expect everyone else to get out of their way—both other drivers and those who are walking.

* Curtis Fuller, *The Motor Car in American Life,* pages 34–35 (adapted). "Basic Social Education Series." Evanston, Illinois: Row, Peterson and Company, 1941.

What are the most dangerous actions of drivers that cause fatal accidents? About two out of every five drivers are going too fast. About one out of every four is either on the wrong side of the road or has no right to drive where he is driving. About one out of six drives recklessly. These causes account for four out of every five automobile deaths.

Since 1922 the number of adults killed by automobiles has increased more than 100 per cent. During the same time, fewer children have been killed. This fact is especially true for boys and girls under fourteen years of age, most of whom are not permitted to drive cars. Their record is much better than that of young people between sixteen and twenty-five years old. Men and women over sixty-five have the highest traffic death rate. This counts persons walking, getting on or off streetcars, riding bicycles, or riding in automobiles.

Although accident deaths have continued as a serious problem in cities, they have become even more serious in the country. Most traffic deaths are in the country. The greatest increase in accidents has been on the country roads. Some persons believe that one reason for this is that cities are able to direct and control their traffic better.

Drivers under twenty years of age have the poorest accident record of any age group. Although he knows how to steer a car, the young driver is reckless and lacks judgment. He has forgotten that the automobile in the hands of some persons is a dangerous and even criminal weapon. Safety experts say that the young driver will continue to be a traffic menace until he changes his attitude. A new generation of drivers must take pride in driving safely rather than in driving recklessly. Until this happens, the reckless young driver of today will grow into the impatient older driver of tomorrow. Both are much more likely to be killed in automobile accidents than are the careful drivers.

C. With a classmate prepare a sentence outline of "How to Find Time to Read," pages 87–89. Choose a different title. Compare outlines in class.

D. By yourself, carry out one of the following activities in writing a sentence outline. Bring to class both your outline and the material upon which you based it. Exchange with a classmate and judge each other's work. *Proofread carefully.*

1. Find and bring to class a printed copy of a speech. Make an outline that will show clearly what the speaker had to say.
2. Make an outline of some article found in your daily reading in books, newspapers, or magazines.
3. Find an essay in a literature book. Make an outline of the main points.

RELATED ACTIVITY

Prepare a talk upon a magazine article that you have read. Make a topic outline from which to give your talk. Use the Speech Score Card, page 31.

USING ENGLISH IN ALL CLASSES

Bring to class a reading assignment from another class. Working either in groups, in pairs, or by yourself, outline the material in it. Attack puzzling words by the steps on pages 91–92.

"WHAT ARE YOU DOING?"

"I'M MAKING A PRÉCIS OF THIS SALT WATER."

7. LEARNING TO COMBINE MAIN IDEAS: PRÉCIS WRITING

Notice that word *précis* (pronounced *pray-see'*) in the above title. It is a French word applied to a form of writing that is much like, but briefer and more exact than, a *summary*. A good summary of any material is built from an outline of (1) the chief ideas and (2) their important details. A précis omits all details, illustrations, and repetitions. It "boils down," so to speak.

DIRECTIONS FOR PRÉCIS WRITING

1. Read through the entire selection to get the main idea.
2. Jot down that main idea in your own words.
3. Study the selection to see whether each paragraph makes a definite contribution to the main idea. If necessary, make a list of *key words, topic sentences,* or any *summarizing statements* in a paragraph. Jot down in your own words the important information that you find. Sometimes the main facts of two or more paragraphs can be combined. *Omit all details, illustrations, and repetitions.*
4. Using the ideas jotted down, write a paragraph that covers them concisely and accurately. Remember to use your own words. Be sure that the main idea stands out clearly.
5. If what you have written is more than one third the length of the original article, work the précis over until you have cut it down. The more concise it is, the better.
6. Work on your style so that it is not choppy. Make it fit the ideas that it carries. Keep the tone of the original article.

Directions: Except in *A* of the following activities, exchange papers and check them by the Writing Score Card, page 197. Afterwards, confer with the person whose paper you checked. If possible, read your work to the group, being careful to apply the Guides to Effective Oral Reading, page 41.

A. Divide the class into groups of three or four people each. Read the following article, a copy of a talk that Knute Rockne, famous football coach, once made to employees of the Studebaker Corporation. Discuss it in your group and then work out a précis of it. Be sure that everyone in the group contributes. Have someone in each group act as secretary to do the necessary writing. When all groups have finished, read and compare the précis.

Qualities That Make or Mar Success *
By Knute Rockne

I don't know anything about selling automobiles; I never sold one in my life; but perhaps a few remarks that apply to a football organization might not be out of place, because it seems to me that the same psychology that makes for success in a football organization will make for success in any organization, particularly in a selling organization.

Now, in the fall when we make our first call for the team, for the lads to come out, about three hundred fifty of them assemble in a large room somewhat like this one; and it is my idea to talk to them on the correct psychology before I take them out on the field. I talk to them on ambition, and I tell them that most of that which I read about ambition is bunk. There is not plenty of room at the top. There is room at the top only for the few who have the ability, the imagination, the daring, the personality, and the energy that make them stand out from their fellow men. But there is success for any man in his own job if he does it as well as it can be done. As far as I am able to observe, the greatest satisfaction I can get on this earth is to do the particular job I am doing as well as it can be done; and I think that holds good for anyone. There may be other things that are easy, but they generally leave a headache or a heartache the day after.

I tell the lads there are six types that I do not want. The first type that I have in mind is the swelled head, the man who was a success a year ago, who is content to rest on his laurels, who wants to play on his reputation. Dry rot sets in, and he ceases to make an effort. To that kind of boy, there will come quite a shock, because the chances are someone will be playing in his place.

The second type of lad is the chronic complainer. He crabs at everyone but himself. I say no organization can afford to have that kind of man, because he is infectious. He is in for a shock, too, because as soon as I find out who he is, someday when he comes out for practice, there will be no suit in his locker.

The third type is the quitter. He is the fellow who wishes he could play but is not willing to pay the price. And I tell the boys if any one of them is that type, he might just as well quit then and not wear out the equipment.

Fourth, I don't want boys to dissipate, physically or emotionally. I tell them that I hold no brief against playing pool long hours in the afternoon, dancing

* Used by permission of Mrs. Knute Rockne and the Studebaker Corporation.

half the night, or learning to drive a car with one hand; but I tell them that they have no time for it. If they are going to compete with organizations which do not do that sort of thing and which are saving all their energy for the contest, I say, they should not dissipate any energy emotionally. And by that I mean that they should not give way to emotions such as jealousy, hatred, or anything of that sort. That sort of thing destroys an organization.

And then I tell them that they should look upon one another in a friendly way—look for the good in one another and be inspired by the fine qualities in those around them and forget about their faults. I tell them that the chances are that I will notice the faults—and won't stutter when I mention them. The man who lacks friendliness, then, is the fifth type.

There is a sixth type of undesirable; he suffers from an inferiority complex. He generally comes from a small community; he says to himself, "What chance have I to get on the first string of thirty-three men here, when there are three hundred fifty boys trying out for it? I don't believe I have a chance; I don't believe I can make it." If there are any among you who feel that way, I say, forget about it and get a superiority complex. You are as good as any man out here. By getting a superiority complex, you can show the coach that you belong at the top of the thirty-three men where you would like to be.

. . . .

In two weeks I call them together again, and I tell them that there are certain ones among them who have great potentialities, but who have not shown any improvement. There are certain ones among them that I do not want unless they change. The first is the chap who alibis, who justifies his own failure. I tell them that a boy who does this had better watch out or he will get into another class, that of feeling sorry for himself, in which case the bony part of his spine turns into a soft colloidal substance known as "soap," and he is absolutely worthless.

The second class of lad—I generally have very few of them—is the slicker, the mucker, who tries to get by by playing unfair football. And I tell that type of boy that we cannot afford to have him on the team, for he will bring discredit on the school and on our organization. I also impress on him that slugging and unfairness do not pay, either in a game or in life after school.

Then, third, there is the boy who lacks courage, who is afraid. What is courage? Courage means to be afraid to do something but still to go ahead and do it. If a man has character, the right kind of energy and mental ability, he will learn that fear is something to overcome and not to run away from.

B. Write a précis of an essay found in one of your literature books.

C. Write a précis of a speech that you find printed in a newspaper, a magazine, or a book of collected speeches.

USING ENGLISH IN ALL CLASSES

A. Choose an assignment in some subject in which discussion material is given for mastery, such as in social studies or science. Write a précis of the information contained.

B. Go over a report or an article that you have written for one of your classes. Boil the material down into a good précis.

Making Use of the Library

1. TESTING YOUR LIBRARY KNOWLEDGE

Use the following test to check your knowledge of the library. Take the test to the library and look up any answers about which you are doubtful. Record your answers.

1. Give a call number for (*a*) a book of fiction and (*b*) a book of nonfiction.
2. Name the three types of cards used in classifying nonfiction books in the card catalogue.
3. Give the method by which fiction is arranged on the library shelves. How many cards does each book of fiction have?
4. Tell how nonfiction books are arranged on the shelves.
5. Give the classification numbers for each of the following:
   a) Fine Arts   *c*) Photography   *e*) Religion
   b) Music   *d*) Biography   *f*) European History
6. Find a book containing information on the following topics. Record the *title* of the book, the name of the *author,* and the *call number.*
   a) The Crusades   *b*) Helium   *c*) Amelia Earhart   *d*) Lake Tahoe
7. Give the author and the title of any book numbered as follows:
   a) 820.4   *b*) 284.6   *c*) 973.7   *d*) 728   *e*) 528.6   *f*) 645
8. Give the title and the author of a book that you would find useful in preparing a report on one of the following topics. Record its call number.
   a) Aviation Pioneers   *c*) Radium in Industry
   b) International Trade Methods   *d*) Habits of Hornets
9. Give the title and the call number of a book in which the following short stories or poems may be found. Give the authors' names.
   a) "The Outcasts of Poker Flat"   *c*) "King Robert of Sicily"
   b) "The Night the Ghost Got In"   *d*) "Birches"
10. Tell where the encyclopedias are located in your library.
11. Locate the biographical yearbooks. Give their titles.
12. Locate the informational yearbooks. Give their titles.
13. List all information given on a card in the card catalogue.

If you had trouble with the test, how many of these errors did you make?

1. Did you misread a card and write the *subject*, which is usually in red ink, instead of the *title?*
2. Did you fail to find a book because you did not take both the name of the *author* and the *call number?*
3. Did you fail to write the *complete* call number?
4. Did you fail to look under the *last name* of a person?
5. Did your errors come from the fact that you do not understand the system of numbers used on books and cards in the library?

2. THE DEWEY DECIMAL SYSTEM

Some years ago a man named Melvil Dewey worked out a scheme for classifying and shelving books in a library. This scheme is called the *Dewey Decimal System*, after its originator. He devised ten main *classes* of books, subdivided by the addition of decimal numbers in such a way as to make possible the quick locating of all books even in the largest libraries.

000–099 General Works: *encyclopedias, yearbooks, periodicals, . . .*
100–199 Philosophy: *psychology, character, behavior, . . .*
200–299 Religion: *religious beliefs, mythology, the Bible, . . .*
300–399 Social Sciences: *government, education, law, politics, . . .*
400–499 Philology: *languages, speech, grammars, dictionaries, . . .*
500–599 Pure Science: *mathematics, chemistry, astronomy, . . .*
600–699 Applied Science: *agriculture, medicine, mechanics, inventions, . . .*
700–799 Arts; Recreation: *music, sculpture, architecture, photography, painting, sports, . . .*
800–899 Literature: *poetry, essays, fiction, drama, . . .*
900–999 History: *biography, geography, travel, . . .*

The ten classes are broken down into ten *divisions*, and these divisions are further broken down into ten *sections*. Each section has *subdivisions*, which are further subdivided, as shown in the example.

700–799 Arts; Recreation (*Class*)
    790 Recreation (*Division*)
        796 Athletics and Sports (*Section*)
           796.3 Ball Games (*Subdivision*)
              796.35 Golf (*Subdivision*)

NOTE: Biographies of individuals (that is, books on the life of one man) usually are classed under the heading 92 (*not* 092) or B and are found on the shelves just before the 920 books, each of which contains *collections* of biographies rather than the life story of one person.

3. THE CARD CATALOGUE

The *card catalogue* is a system of cards, 3 x 5 inches in size, that are held in a drawer or tray on a metal rod that runs through a hole at the bottom of the card. Each card gives all the information that will classify a book and help one to locate it on the shelves.

The standards for the form of the cards are set up by the Library of Congress, which is the largest library in the United States.* (It contains two copies of every book that has been granted a copyright in this country.) Most libraries follow the forms on the Library of Congress cards.

● **WHAT TO REMEMBER ABOUT THE CARD CATALOGUE**

1. Certain information is listed on every card.
    a) The complete *call number* is shown in the upper left-hand corner. This call number tells you where the book can be found on the library shelves. (See the cards on pages 128–29.)
    b) The *author's name* is given, with the last name first, followed by a comma and the first and any middle names.
    c) The *title* is listed with only the first word capitalized, except that proper nouns are always capitalized.
    d) The *name of the publisher* and the *place and date of publication* are included.
    e) Other information may be given, covering such things as *illustrations,* the *number of pages,* the *height* of the book (in centimeters), *headings under which to classify* the book, . . .
2. Each nonfiction book has a *title* card, a *subject* card, and an *author* card.†
3. Books of fiction have only a *title* card and an *author* card.
4. Books of fiction are arranged alphabetically according to the last name of the author and according to their titles. "Sinclair Lewis," for example, would come after "Ring Lardner," and Lewis's *Main Street* would come after his own *Babbitt.* Fiction always is shelved separately from nonfiction.
5. The biography of an individual is alphabetized by the name of the person whose life is told rather than by title or by author.
6. The card catalogue contains many *cross reference* cards. These cards contain (usually in the first line) the word "see," to indicate that there is another heading or classification for this topic, field, or author. "See also" cards tell where to look for additional material.

* The Library of Congress has its own system of classifying books, but on the cards it likewise indicates the Dewey Decimal classification.

† There may be several subject cards for one book, depending upon the fields of interest that it covers.

Here are author card, title card, and subject card for the same book, *Lost Trails, Lost Cities,* by Percy Harrison Fawcett. As you will see by the bottom line on each card, these sample cards have been made by the Library of Congress. Such cards may be purchased from that library. Many libraries buy them; others prefer to make their own cards.

AUTHOR CARD

918.1 **Fawcett, Percy Harrison,** 1867–1925?
F22 1   Lost trails, lost cities, by P. H. Fawcett; from his manu-
        scripts, letters, and other records, selected and arr. by Brian
        Fawcett. New York, Funk & Wagnalls, 1953.

           xvi, 332 p. illus., ports., maps. 24 cm.

           "Published in England under the title, Exploration Fawcett."

         1. Bolivia—Descr. & trav. 2. Brazil—Descr. & trav.   i. Title.

         F3313.F3 1953   918.1   53—6980

         Library of Congress   ₍53q10₎

TITLE CARD

    Lost trails, lost cities
918.1 **Fawcett, Percy Harrison,** 1867–1925?
F22 1   Lost trails, lost cities, by P. H. Fawcett; from his manu-
        scripts, letters, and other records, selected and arr. by Brian
        Fawcett. New York, Funk & Wagnalls, 1953.

           xvi, 332 p. illus., ports., maps. 24 cm.

           "Published in England under the title, Exploration Fawcett."

         1. Bolivia—Descr. & trav. 2. Brazil—Descr. & trav.   i. Title.

         F3313.F3 1953   918.1   53—6980

         Library of Congress   ₍53q10₎

---

1. Bolivia--Descr. & trav.

918.1 **Fawcett, Percy Harrison,** 1867–1925?

F22 1   Lost trails, lost cities, by P. H. Fawcett; from his manu-scripts, letters, and other records, selected and arr. by Brian Fawcett. New York, Funk & Wagnalls, 1953.

     xvi, 332 p. illus., ports., maps. 24 cm.

     "Published in England under the title, Exploration Fawcett."

     1. Bolivia—Descr. & trav. 2. Brazil—Descr. & trav.   ɪ. Title.

     F3313.F3   1953   918.1   53—6980

     Library of Congress   [53q10]

LEARNING ACTIVITIES IN THE USE OF THE CARD CATALOGUE

A. Answer orally the following questions about the sample cards.

1. Who published the book? Where? When?
2. Who prepared the material for publication?
3. What kind of illustrative materials has the book?
4. How many pages has it? How tall is it?
5. Under what other title has it been published?
6. What does the question mark after "1925" signify?

B. Talk over the following questions: What is the value of putting the copy-right date on the card? If you wish information on the topic "Safety in Flying," which book will you be likely to choose, one with a copyright date of 1947 or one dated 1955? Why are the cards in the card catalogue kept on a rod? Who can remove them? When and why? (If you do not know, find out from a librarian.)

C. Find titles, authors, and call numbers of three books in one of the following fields: *baseball, radio, opera, fishing, skiing, photography, television, cooking, camping, wild flowers, stamp collecting.* Explain to your small group how you found the information. Use the Speech Score Card, page 31.

D. By using the card catalogue, find and list ten different subjects (*not* titles) that come under the numbers 700–799. Compare findings in class.

E. From the books available in your library, compile a list of books on some subject of interest to the student body. Use exact titles, authors' names, and call numbers. (For the form of a bibliography, see page 249.) Post the best work on the bulletin board. Make your bibliography on some phase of *sports, birds, hobbies, travel, wild animals, music, manners, vocations,* or any other field.

F. Here is a list of books. In which class of the Dewey Decimal System would they probably be classified? After deciding, check with the card catalogue to find whether any of the books are in your library. For any that are, note the call numbers to see how accurately you classified them.

1. Stern, Bill. *My Favorite Sports Stories*
2. Williams, Oscar (*editor*). *Immortal Poems of the English Language*
3. De Kruif, Paul. *Microbe Hunters*
4. Durant, Will. *The Story of Philosophy*
5. Clark, Arthur C. *The Exploration of Space*
6. Williams, T. Harry. *Lincoln and His Generals*

G. Each state has a call number in the 900–999 class. Look for the decimal number for your state; then find at least one book about it.

4. REFERENCE MATERIALS

In addition to knowing how to use the card catalogue, you should be familiar with certain special reference materials. These materials form the 000–099 section of a library classified by the Dewey Decimal System. Besides dictionaries, most libraries contain other reference books that you should know how and when to use.

ENCYCLOPEDIAS

Encyclopedias are books containing information on all important subjects. The material is prepared by eminent authorities and specialists. New editions are published from time to time to keep information up to date. The material is arranged alphabetically and is indexed under many helpful topics. Your library is likely to have one or more of the following sets of encyclopedias:

> *Compton's Pictured Encyclopedia*
> *Encyclopaedia Britannica*
> *World Book Encyclopedia*

You may also find encyclopedias dealing with special subjects, such as *medicine, sports, music, art,* ...

YEARBOOKS

Yearbooks are annual publications giving a great variety of information. The following are entirely biographical.

> *Who's Who* (a British publication)
> *Who's Who in America* (published once in two years)

Other types of yearbooks are general in content, giving information about people, places, industries, events, government, and so on. Some of those best known are the following:

> Information Please Almanac
> Rand McNally Commercial Atlas and Marketing Guide
> Statistical Abstract of the United States
> World Almanac

SPECIAL REFERENCES

Special reference books are of many kinds. The names of those given here indicate their nature.

> Bartlett, John. *Familiar Quotations*
> Crabb, George. *English Synonyms*
> Fowler, H. W. *A Dictionary of Modern English Usage*
> Rand McNally International Edition World Atlas
> Roget, P. M. *Thesaurus of English Words and Phrases*
> Stevenson, Burton. *The Home Book of Quotations*
> *Webster's Biographical Dictionary*
> *Webster's Geographical Dictionary*

In addition to the reference sources named, most libraries contain *magazines, newspapers, bulletin boards, maps, globes, exhibits, clipping files,* and other aids to readers. Usually these supplementary materials are prominently displayed in the library. Newspapers are as a rule placed on racks or in cabinet files, as are magazines. Old newspapers ordinarily are not kept, but important clippings may be filed. Many libraries have a year's issues of certain magazines bound into a volume that becomes a permanent part of the reference material in the library.

LEARNING ACTIVITIES IN USING REFERENCE MATERIALS

A. Investigate the reference resources of your library. Find out how many it has of those named on pages 130–31. Examine and discuss them. Will the publication dates of any of the references affect their usefulness?

B. Read the questions that follow. Decide what reference books you would consult to find the answers. In certain cases the answers can be found in more than one type of reference. Find the answers to as many of the questions as you can. Compare results in class.

1. What is the Taj Mahal? Where is it? When was it built?
2. What baseball player won the most valuable player award last year in the American League? in the National League? Name any players who have won the award more than once.
3. When and where were the senators from your state born? How long have they been in office?
4. What are two interesting inventions of the past year?
5. How did the Elberta peach get its name?
6. For how long was the Pony Express in operation?
7. Why was the Great Wall of China built? Where and when was it built? How high, wide, and long was it? Is it still standing?
8. What novel, if any, won the Pulitzer Prize last year? Who wrote it?
9. Who are the governors of the states bordering your state? Does their length of term vary? If so, how?
10. Who was Torquemada?
11. In what novel is Maggie Tulliver a character?
12. Under what name did Charlotte Brontë write *Jane Eyre?*
13. What motion picture won the top Academy Award two years ago?
14. How many college students were there in this country two years ago?

C. Read the quotations on page 133. Choose one that appeals to you; then answer these questions about it:

1. From what writing is the quotation taken?
2. Who is the author?
3. When was he born? Is he still living?
4. What is his nationality?
5. Where was he born? (Locate on a map.)
6. What important facts can you find about his life?

To locate a quotation, consult the index of a book of quotations. Bartlett's *Familiar Quotations,* for example, lists one or more of the most important words of every quotation in the book. Thus, the quotation "He jests at scars that never felt a wound" is indexed three times, under *jests, scars,* and *wound.*

What other references will you need to consult? Discuss this question in class before you begin to work.

In a talk to the class, tell what you have learned about the quotation and its author. Close with a sentence or two telling why the quotation appeals to you. Use your Speech Score Card.

1. We are here to add what we can *to,* not to get what we can *from,* Life.
2. That there should one man die ignorant who had capacity for knowledge, this I call a tragedy.
3. I have loved the principle of beauty in all things, and if I had had time, I would have made myself remembered.
4. Bravery never goes out of fashion.
5. It is almost a definition of a man to say that he is one who never inflicts pain.
6. What I like in a good author is not what he says, but what he whispers.
7. We pardon in the degree that we love.
8. Sin has many tools, but a lie is the handle that fits them all.
9. Tell that to the marines; the sailors won't believe it.
10. A man should never be ashamed to own that he has been in the wrong, which is but saying, in other words, that he is wiser today than he was yesterday.
11. The greatest pleasure I know is to do a good deed by stealth and have it found out by accident.
12. So long as we love, we serve; so long as we are loved by others, I would almost say that we are indispensable; and no man is useless while he has a friend.

D. Prepare a set of questions that to answer will require the use of various types of reference books. Exchange papers and locate the necessary information. In class, as the person who wrote the questions asks them, give the answers.

USING ENGLISH IN ALL CLASSES

Choose a person, an event, a place, a quotation, or a process mentioned in one of your study assignments for another class. Use the reference resources of your library to find fuller information about the person or the topic that you chose. Make a topic outline of your information (see page 118) and report to the class the results of your research. Use your Speech Score Card.

5. THE READERS' GUIDE

A highly useful reference source in the library is the *Readers' Guide to Periodical Literature,* which indexes the contents of more than one hundred magazines. Each article or other selection is listed under two heads: *author* and *subject.* An issue is published twice each month, except in July and August, which have only one issue each. From time to time, issues that have been published are combined into a larger pamphlet; and at the end of the year, all issues for that year are put into one volume. Every three years a volume is published combining the material of the past three years.

Here is an excerpt from the *Readers' Guide,* showing how the references are listed. All abbreviations are explained at the front of each issue.

(Excerpt from the *Readers' Guide*)*

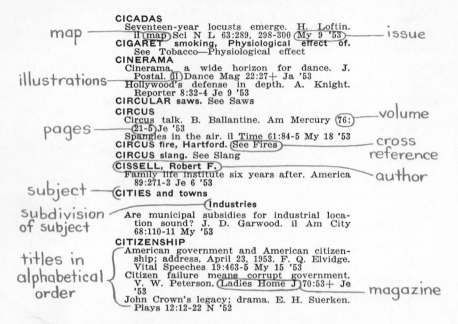

LEARNING ACTIVITIES IN USING THE *READERS' GUIDE*

A. Find answers to the following questions based on the above excerpt.

1. Which subject has a subtopic?
2. How many different magazines are referred to? What are they?
3. What three cross references are made?
4. Which magazine has published an article by A. Knight? How many pages does it cover?
5. Which article is accompanied by a map?
6. How many other articles contain illustrations?
7. Which article is a reprint of a speech?

B. With the help of the *Readers' Guide* in your library, find a recent article on some topic that interests you. Be sure to select one in a magazine that you can find either in the library, at home, or on the newsstand. Make a topic outline of the interesting information contained in the article; then, using the outline as a guide, tell your small group about the article. (For the form of a topic outline, see page 118.) Use the Speech Score Card, page 31.

* Used by permission of the H. W. Wilson Company, publishers of the *Readers' Guide to Periodical Literature.*

USING ENGLISH IN ALL CLASSES

If you have a report to prepare for one of your classes, use the *Readers' Guide* to locate helpful magazine articles. If the report is written, include a bibliography of all sources consulted. (See page 249 for bibliography form.)

RELATED ACTIVITIES IN THE USE OF LIBRARIES

A. In a panel discussion or a debate, decide whether books in school libraries should be divided among the classrooms and study halls or kept in a central library. Keep in mind the Guides to Courteous Speech Habits, page 56.

B. Carry out one of the following group projects.

1. If your school has no library or an inadequate one, use class discussion to find methods of improving your situation. If your state has a traveling library, find out how it is operated.
2. Plan and execute a display that will attract attention to good reading in your school library.

C. Carry out one of the following activities in making an explanation. Follow the Guides to Clear Explanations, page 35. Assign a committee to rate each speaker. Use the Speech Score Card, page 31.

1. Select one of the following as a topic:
   How Books Are Made
   Careers in Book Publishing
   The Training of a Librarian
2. Make an explanation of the parts of a textbook, telling the purpose of each part. Use a real book. If you lack information, look for help in the library.
3. Pretend that you have been asked to talk to a new student who has no knowledge of the use of a library. Explain to him what he needs to know in order to make good use of your school library.
4. Using an actual book for illustration, explain how a book should be treated. What are "dog ears"? If you know that you are guilty of making them, resolve now to break the habit. Interview the librarian to get information and suggestions. (Review the Guides for Taking Part in Interviews, page 54.)
5. Explain the rules governing the use of your school library.

FOLLOW-UP ACTIVITY

Begin a personal library scrapbook or clipping file on some subject that interests you. Arrange all material by *alphabetizing,* by *chronology,* by *subject matter,* or by any other method that suits the material. You may want to use one of these suggestions: (1) articles about prominent public figures; (2) pictures and articles about scientific advances; (3) articles and pictures about favorite sports; (4) literary selections; (5) information about authors, dramatists, statesmen, inventors, or scientists.

CHAPTER 9

Reading Books, Newspapers, and Magazines

1. READING TEXTBOOKS

Here, briefly summarized, are the reading principles covered on pages 90–124, with added helps for textbook study. Use any or all of them, depending upon the length and difficulty of an assignment.

GUIDES TO EFFICIENT STUDY OF TEXTBOOKS

1. Skim the assignment to get a bird's-eye view of the material presented.
2. If there is an introduction, read it carefully. Do the same for any summary paragraphs.
3. Read the assignment through, noting all unfamiliar words. If the context does not help, look up the words; then substitute usable synonyms.
4. Note chapter titles, section headings, marginal heads. They are clues to main ideas. Note also numbered or lettered items within a paragraph. Turn to the Table of Contents for an outline of the material covered.
5. Find the central thought in each paragraph. Look first for a topic sentence; if there is none, frame one of your own.
6. List the key words. Note words emphasized by italics or boldface (**heavy black type**). Use them in making a summary.
7. Study carefully any charts, maps, graphs, illustrations, or examples.
8. Do not neglect any explanatory footnotes that appear on a page. (In this text, red asterisks or other symbols indicate such footnotes.)
9. Write a précis of a reading assignment, such as one in social studies.
10. Make a sentence outline of the material in a reading assignment.
11. Paraphrase (see pages 114–15) difficult sentences or paragraphs.
12. Read difficult sentences or paragraphs aloud.

A. Here is part of a chapter from an economics text. Examine this selection in class or in your small groups. How many of the special aids to study (see guides 4, 6, 7, 8) are illustrated in this lesson? Point them out.

CHAPTER IV

How Much Do We Consume? *

We Shall Now Discover: *Which things are necessities, which are comforts, and which are luxuries, according to our mode, or standard, of living. Why it is sometimes so hard to decide between buying something now or saving the money for some future and perhaps greater need. What effect modern methods of advertising have on our efforts to spend our money wisely, and why it is foolish to try to "keep up with the Joneses."*

In Chapter III we examined some of the principles of human behavior that show why we act as we do in the process of satisfying our wants. We shall next consider the relative importance of these wants. This is the question of *standards of living*.

Standards of Living

We read in Chapter I that our wants are always expanding and that there is no limit to the range or variety of the things that we may desire. This statement is true. Yet the growth of wants is not a sudden expansion like the inflation of a rubber balloon when we blow into it. This growth is the result of an educational advance. We desire things as we learn about them. New wants are created by invention, which puts new goods on the market. New goods are put on the market by advertising and selling and by demonstrations of their uses.

Sixty years ago the want for automobiles did not exist, and forty years ago the want for the radio was unfelt. Strong potential wants for some such products did exist. Everyone wanted faster and more powerful transportation than the horse-drawn vehicle provided. Everyone likewise wished for a more efficient means of speedy communication than was afforded by the telegraph and the telephone. But no one had an idea of how to meet these wants. As soon as the automobile and the radio appeared, an immense demand quickly developed. It had simply been waiting for products that would satisfy it. There is always a great field for further expansion of wants, and this potential demand stimulates inventors to develop products that will awaken these desires.

---

* Harley L. Lutz, Edmund W. Foote, and Benjamin F. Stanton, *Getting a Living*, pages 59–63 (adapted). Evanston, Illinois: Row, Peterson and Company, 1941.

The pressure of our wants is an important factor in determining how much effort we shall exert in order to secure their satisfaction. The more things we want, the harder we are willing to work. If our wants, actual and potential, are limited, we have less incentive to work.

The list of our known and felt wants may be called our *standard of living*. We must distinguish between those vague desires that may be experienced while daydreaming or after reading an exciting novel dealing with the supposed luxuries of the rich, and those realizable wants that are a definite spur to action. All of us at some time or other may have dreamed of dwelling in marble halls, but this dream does not put a marble hall into our standard of living. As Dr. Hazel Kyrk expresses it, the standard is that "code or plan for material living which directs our expenditure into certain channels and satisfies our sense of propriety and decency as a mode of living." *

In general, we aim at securing a certain range of satisfactions, and this goal becomes our standard of living. Our success in reaching the goal is determined in part by our available income. This factor is discussed in the next chapter. We must first see what kinds of living standards there are and how they affect our consumption.

THE RISE OF REAL WAGES IN THE UNITED STATES

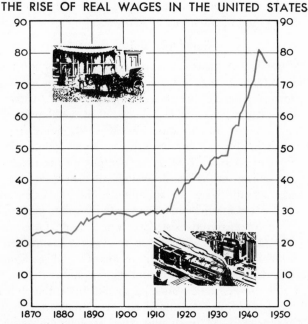

Real wages are wages measured by purchasing power rather than by money

Classes of wants. Since the most important thing in life is to keep on living, it is usual to classify our wants according to the way that they bear on this fundamental problem. Certain things are necessary to life.

* Hazel Kyrk, *A Theory of Consumption,* page 175. Boston: Houghton Mifflin Co., 1923.

The wants for these things are our most important wants. Other things make life more comfortable, more interesting, more enjoyable. We have, therefore, various classes of wants, or different possible standards of living. The usual grouping is as follows: (1) the necessary standard; (2) the comfort standard; and (3) the luxury standard.

The necessary standard. The things that are most essential to life are food, clothing, and shelter. Even in the tropics, where clothing and shelter would seem to be least essential, only the primitive tribes that have undergone a long process of adjustment can survive without clothes and dwellings.

The bare minimum that is required to keep a person alive is sometimes called the *subsistence standard,* or *subsistence minimum.* The truly necessary standard of living must be more liberal than this, for it must provide for health and for the maintenance of sufficient physical or mental vigor to enable the individual to keep at his work.

Since the average adult man must provide for a family as well as for himself, the necessary standard must include the essential family wants. Children must be properly fed, clothed, and educated. The requirements include also medical care and some provision for recreation.

In addition to the things that properly come within the necessary standard, there are other things that are so strongly desired, through the force of custom and habit, as to give them, for many people, a definite preference even over some of the essentials. These are called *conventional necessaries.* Illustrations are coffee and cosmetics.

The comfort standard. Beyond the things that are necessary, lie the comforts of life. We add to our comfort by securing even the necessary things in more pleasing variety. A limited amount of plain food and clothing will actually sustain life and preserve health. On the comfort standard, we can add to our enjoyment by having greater variety in our food, our clothing, and our houses. We can go further by getting other things that yield satisfaction, such as an automobile, a radio, and a piano. We aim also at better educational and recreational opportunities. We have more books, magazines, and pictures; we attend more plays and concerts. In general, the broadly cultural wants receive a recognition and satisfaction on the comfort standard that would be impossible for anyone living on the level of the necessary standard.

The luxury standard. One dictionary definition of a luxury is this: "Any article that ministers to comfort or pleasure and yet is not necessary to life or to what would be regarded as an ordinary degree of comfort." In other words, then, luxuries are those things that are neither necessaries nor ordinary comforts. But when does any article pass from one group to another? We find many shades of opinion, and the answer is often determined by the individual's personal attitude toward the thing in question. Men are likely to regard cosmetics as luxury goods; women may feel the same way about cigars and pipes.

B. List key words in the paragraph beginning "Sixty years ago." Next, close your book and with the help of the key words, write the paragraph as well as you can. Exchange papers for checking to see how well you have reproduced the thoughts in the paragraph.

C. Skim the selection to find answers to the following questions:
1. What, briefly, is meant by "standard of living"?
2. What three classes of standards of living are listed?
3. What are "conventional necessaries"?
4. In simple words, what are "luxuries"?

D. Write paraphrases of the following sentences from the selection. If necessary, find the paragraph in which a sentence appears and study it as an aid to understanding the sentence. Compare versions critically in class or in your small groups.

1. If our wants, actual and potential, are limited, we have less incentive to work.
2. We must distinguish between those vague desires that may be experienced while daydreaming or after reading an exciting novel dealing with the supposed luxuries of the rich, and those realizable wants that are a definite spur to action.
3. Even in the tropics, where clothing and shelter would seem to be less essential, only the primitive tribes that have undergone a long process of adjustment can survive without clothes and dwellings.
4. A limited amount of plain food and clothing will actually sustain life and preserve health.
5. In general, the broadly cultural wants receive a recognition and satisfaction on the comfort standard that would be impossible for anyone living on the level of the necessary standard.

E. Write a précis of the section labeled "Classes of wants." Be sure to follow the directions on page 122. Read work aloud in your small groups, being careful to apply the Guides to Effective Oral Reading, page 41. Choose the best précis to read to the entire class.

USING ENGLISH IN ALL CLASSES

Bring to English class the textbook in the subject that is hardest for you. Study reading assignments in it by applying the helps to study given in the guides on page 136.

FOLLOW-UP ACTIVITY

At home read aloud to yourself each difficult reading assignment in your school subjects. Apply also any of the other reading techniques given in the guides on page 136.

2. Widening Your Acquaintance with Books

What is the range of your reading? You know that a balanced diet is essential to your health and bodily growth. How about your mental diet? It is unbalanced if you are the kind of boy or girl who reads only dog stories, or love stories, or Western tales, or comic magazines, or crime stories, or science fiction.

According to reliable estimates, at least 225,000,000 books are bought in the United States every year. In addition, public libraries have an annual circulation of 500,000,000 volumes or more; 6,000 rental libraries scattered throughout the cities serve another large section of the reading public. Those are impressive figures. Americans do read books, but how many get full value from the time that they devote to reading? Do you?

Be word-wise!

Skim the preceding paragraphs for these words: *range, essential, scattered, devote.* Which synonyms for these words, as explained in the dictionary, would not be good substitutes for the words as used in this lesson? Which synonym for *scatter* does the drawing illustrate?

GUIDES FOR EVALUATING BOOKS

1. What is the author's purpose? How well does he achieve it?
2. What is the underlying idea?
3. Does the book reveal with truth any phases of human experience?
4. Does it have a universal human interest? What qualities will make the book live or not live?
5. Does the author have an original and powerful style of expression?
6. What is the effect of the book on me? Does it stimulate wholesome thoughts or pleasant memories? Does it leave me feeling depressed and discontented?
7. Does the book reflect the author's own life, his interests in life, the time in which he lives, the past . . . ?
8. For what qualities can I recommend the book?

LEARNING ACTIVITIES IN READING BOOKS

A. Analyze your reading food.

1. Make a list of various types of reading interests that you have or of other interests to which your reading contributes. Go over these lists in class. Which of the types illustrated on these pages make up most of your leisure-reading fare?

2. The chief difference between the reading attitudes and abilities of children and adults is that the child is concerned almost entirely with what "happens," whereas the adult mind analyzes *purposes, ideas, style.* How far have you progressed in your ability to discuss what you read?

   Divide the class, as far as possible, into small groups of students all of whom have read a certain book. Let anyone who does not fit into any such group be a listener. Use the guides on page 141 to analyze the book. Be sure to apply the Guides to Courteous Speech Habits, page 56.

B. Use any of the following methods to encourage more and wider reading within your class.

1. You have seen lists of so-called "best books." Compile a list of books that various students in your school name as their favorites. Make a similar list for faculty members and a third for outstanding citizens of your community. In interviewing these people, be sure to follow the Guides for Taking Part in Interviews, page 54. Compare the three lists; if possible, have them duplicated and distributed to the members of the class.

2. Consult some standard reading list for young people.* Make a list of ten titles that attract you. Compare lists in class.

3. Conduct question-and-answer forums about books. Apply the guides on page 73.

C. Choose one of the following ideas for a talk to the class. Use the Speech Score Card, page 31.

1. Get acquainted with at least one author. Use the card catalogue and the *Readers' Guide* to locate information about him.

2. Look up in the library the origin and purpose of one of these literary awards: the Nobel Prize, the Pulitzer Prize, the O. Henry Memorial Award, the Newbery Medal. Name some of the award-winning authors and the books chosen.

3. Select a book that is popular now but which you feel does not have the qualities to make it last. Prepare a critical analysis.

4. Using the questions in the guides on page 141, give a three-minute oral book report.

D. Write a carefully organized book report. You will find help on page 214. *Be sure to proofread.* Exchange reports for critical evaluation.

E. If you like to draw, make a series of illustrations for one of your favorite books. Below each drawing, copy the sentences that it illustrates. Good work should be displayed on the bulletin board.

* Two good lists are the following:
  Books for You by Mark Neville, Dwight Burton, *et al.*
  Good Reading by Atwood Townsend, *et al.*
  Both books can be ordered from The National Council of Teachers of English, 704 South Sixth Street, Champaign, Illinois.

Make a bibliography of books available in your library on some topic that you are studying in any class. (See page 249 for bibliography form.)

FOLLOW-UP ACTIVITIES

A. For the bulletin board or the school paper, make lists of recommended contemporary books. Think for yourselves in making the lists. Judge the value of your lists by the amount of reading that they stimulate.

B. Make a list of books that you want to read at some time. Indicate the reason for your interest. After you have read a book, check it from your list.

C. Keep a card file of your reading, using a form similar to the following example. Such a record will increase in value to you as the years go by.

Name—Jack Martin   Date—April 15, 19—
Author—John Buchan   Title—*The Thirty-nine Steps*
Type—Novel

Subject Matter   The story concerns Richard Hannay, a young mining engineer, who gets mixed up in a spy plot.

Central Idea   It shows how involved an innocent man can get when he is the victim of skulduggery.

Value   This book is of value principally for its exciting plot, which is concerned with an attempt to start a war, on British soil, between England and Germany.

BUILDING YOUR OWN LIBRARY

It is possible to collect a library at a small cost. Auctions of household furnishings sometimes offer excellent copies of books that are in good condition and will serve well as a beginning. Valuable and rare books have been obtained for almost nothing at such sales. The following publishing companies issue both classic and modern books in inexpensive editions.

E. P. Dutton & Co. (Everyman's Library)
Garden City Books
Grosset and Dunlap
Hamish Hamilton, London (The Novel Library)
Liveright Publishing Corp. (Black and Gold Library)
Modern Library, Inc.
Oxford University Press (World's Classics)
Tudor Publishing Company
World Publishing Co. (Rainbow Classics, Living Library)

As you can afford it, you will enjoy replacing inexpensive copies of your favorites with finer editions. They should become old and cherished friends.

3. READING NEWSPAPERS AND MAGAZINES

READ AND DISCUSS

The United States has more newspapers and magazines than any other country in the world. In a recent year there were 2,026 daily newspapers and 10,196 weeklies published in this country. In forty years, the volume of reading in the United States has increased 175 per cent. Every year Americans spend $727,880,000 on newspapers; $311,733,000 on magazines. Certainly those figures are impressive. However, it does not necessarily follow that this is the most cultured or the most literate nation in the world. How is the haste of modern life reflected in the reading of newspapers and magazines? How are a reader's interests and thinking revealed by the reading that he chooses? Think about and discuss those questions.

To study newspapers and magazines, you must have copies for class use. Try securing them by any of the following methods.

1. Make full use of newspapers and magazines available in your school.
2. Try to arrange to borrow back numbers of magazines from your public library. You may also be able to get old newspapers.
3. As a class project, collect old copies of magazines and newspapers from homes in the community.
4. Ask each pupil to contribute to a fund for buying material.
5. Go to your local newspaper office to see whether you may secure back copies of newspapers published in other cities.
6. If material and money are available in no other way, undertake a project for raising money to buy sufficient samples of magazines and newspapers for your class study.

Be word-wise!

Skim this page for the following words: *volume, haste, collect, sufficient.* Which synonyms for them would not be good substitutes for the words as they are used here? Which synonym of *volume* does the drawing illustrate?

GETTING ACQUAINTED WITH NEWSPAPERS

There are many different types of articles in a newspaper. The explanations on pages 146–51 will familiarize you with most of them.

The editorial page is the part of a newspaper that aims openly at influencing the thought of its readers.

● **WHAT YOU SHOULD KNOW ABOUT EDITORIALS**

1. The editorial is an article based upon some current question, situation, or news item.
2. An editorial may range from a eulogy of an individual, living or dead, to a discussion of local, domestic, or international problems.
3. Although it is an expression of one view of a question, the editorial should be the result of careful study of all sides of that question.
4. The reader should question the knowledge, the view, and the purpose behind an editorial. The best newspapers have the fairest, most thoughtful editorials.

EXAMPLE

A BRIGHT AND SHINING NAME[*]

Today the dawning atomic age remembers the man who inaugurated the age of electricity.

Thomas Alva Edison was born on February 11, 1847, into a world that moved under steam power and gaslight to the buoyant realization of its faith in enterprise, invention, expansion, material progress. As its prophet and instrument, he was interested not in ultimate implications but in practical results. And he got things done.

He wrote a success story that touched off the lights in millions of homes all over the world. With genius that was nine parts perspiration to one part inspiration, he helped launch industry on its dizzying, dazzling path toward the Bigger and Better.

The age of Edison began with an incandescent glow in a New Jersey laboratory. The atomic age began with a blinding flash in the New Mexico desert. One spelled emancipation; one threatened destruction. One offered endless opportunities; one demanded immediate controls. One was the individual achievement of a daring experimentalist; one emerged from the planned collaboration of the world's greatest physicists and technicians.

Edison expected his inventions to prove their value in profits of dollars and cents. The cost of atomic energy is reckoned in terms of civilization itself. We must of necessity look farther ahead than Edison to the end at which "material progress" aims. But we do well to look back to him also for an example of incandescent energy outshining every argument of doubt and defeatism.

[*] From *The Christian Science Monitor* for February 11, 1947. Used by permission of the *Monitor*.

THE NEWS STORY

The news story, as its name implies, is an account of something that has happened. Its aim is to keep readers up to date on news.

● **WHAT YOU SHOULD KNOW ABOUT THE NEWS STORY**

1. The most important news story usually appears in the right-hand column of the first page.

2. Usually the main headline (known as the *banner*) of that story will extend across the entire page. It, like all headlines, gives the main idea of the news story above which it appears.

3. The news story is written with the climax coming first; that is, the first paragraph (known as the *lead*) gives the gist of the entire story. The purpose is to give the hasty reader a chance to grasp the news quickly. Usually the lead contains the five *w*'s: *who, what, when, where, why. What* is the news? *When* did it occur? *Where? Who* was concerned? *Why?* Further paragraphs give details.

4. A good news story should be entirely impersonal, giving no expression of the writer's opinion. However, the very wording of an article sometimes indicates a biased view on the part of the persons who control the policies of the newspaper.

   Sources of news articles usually are indicated. At the head of each item may be initials of a news agency, such as the Associated Press (AP), United Press (U.P.), or International News Service (INS). Usually there is no *by-line;* that is, the name of the writer is not given, though the reporter who does an outstanding story sometimes has that distinction.

EXAMPLE

*350,000 Welcome Orioles Into Majors**

BALTIMORE, April 15 (AP)—Baltimore threw a wild welcome-home party for big league baseball today as a police-estimated crowd of 350,000 cheering fans lined the streets to watch the Orioles parade over a colorful carpet of 5,000 orchids.

The mammoth parade was the biggest thing this old tradition-bound city has seen in years. The new American League Orioles brought with them the first major league baseball that Baltimore has had in more than half a century.

---

* Used by permission of the *Chicago American* and the Associated Press.

Field Manager Jimmy Dykes was almost speechless. He said from his perch on a convertible:

"I've never seen anything like it before; it's absolutely wonderful to be here."

Almost as Dykes spoke and before the last float had crossed the parade's finish line, a drizzle began to fall in downtown Baltimore.

The two-hour parade ended in front of city hall. In its lineup appeared such old-time baseball greats as Connie Mack of the Philadelphia Athletics and Clark Griffith of the Washington Senators.

Baseball Commissioner Ford Frick rode with American League President Will Harridge in one car, and the widow of John J. McGraw, former Oriole, rode along in another.

Busts of the old Orioles who have been elected to the hall of fame were featured in another of the 60 floats in the parade.

Traffic inspector Bernard Schmidt, who gave the 350,000 crowd estimate, said he didn't include the thousands who probably saw the parade from windows.

Milwaukee police chief John Polcyn last year put the parade crowd there at 60,000 when the Braves were brought home for the Wisconsin city's entry into the National League.

The Braves had a red carpet to tread as they entered the city; for the Orioles, it was orchids.

Among the standouts in the welcome-back procession was a 14-foot papier-mâché statue of Babe Ruth.

THE FEATURE STORY

The feature story develops a news story from the angle of human interest. Every issue of a newspaper contains many good feature stories. They include such things as interviews with famous people or people in the news at the moment, stories about children and their pets, eyewitness accounts of important events, descriptions of unusual people, places, or occurrences. Note the comparison below, showing ways in which a feature story is likely to differ from a news story.

News Story	*Feature Story*
1. Tells the latest news	1. May (though not necessarily) grow out of current news
2. Gives climax first	2. May give climax at end
3. Is impersonal in tone	3. Is personal in tone
4. Aims to inform	4. Aims to appeal to the emotions; all details must strengthen the appeal.

ESCAPED MONKEY
SHIVERS IN COLD*

By MEYER BERGER

NEW YORK, Feb. 15.—The Mugg detests mankind. Today he brooded in the enshadowed girders underneath the roof of Pier 5 on the Bush docks in Brooklyn. He shivered in the winter blast and his protruding eyes glittered with loathing for the longshore crews and other men who labored on the wind-swept concrete, 50 feet below.

Ever since The Mugg and his childhood jungle chum, The Migg, escaped from their monkey cages on the pier last April while in transit from India's warm Deccan plains, men have bedeviled and made mock of him. Worst of all, they were the death of The Migg and of Juliet, a sister rhesus from the Deccan.

The Mugg and The Migg frolicked at will along the docks from last April through last October. They stole bananas and succulent grapes from clumsy traps set by the A.S.P.C.A. They nipped longshoremen who made awkward lunges at them. They had the run of visiting freighters and they prospered.

In October one of the men, a longshore worker, brought Juliet to the pier from some man's pet shop. He put her in a cage on the pier. He hoped her chatter would attract The Migg and The Mugg, and decoy them to capture. Instead, The Mugg and The Migg, somehow, snatched her from the cage and all three honey-mooned in the girders, feasted on stolen fruits and reminisced about the good old hot days in India.

On Dec. 6 Juliet developed a hacking cough. The men seized her and three days later she died in the A.S.P.C.A. shelter. The Mugg and The Migg wept in the girders and spat their hate at the men on the concrete. On Jan. 21, the cough got The Migg. He died in the shelter five days later.

Now The Mugg is alone, and hate and his brooding are magnificent, and men stare up at him and wait for the winter's snow and wind and ice to wither his strength and betray him into their hands. But The Mugg is valiant, and huddled in the girder shadows, he defies them and dreams warm dreams of the Deccan's lush greenness, and of The Migg—and of poor little Juliet.

THE SPORTS STORY

The sports story has a style all its own. The sentences are crisp and informal in style, and the words used are, in many cases, peculiar to the world of sports. Undoubtedly you are familiar with the sports story.

* Used by permission of the *New York Times*.

The column is a regular feature of most newspapers. It carries the author's name and is his personal expression of ideas concerning some subject that interests him. A columnist may write exclusively on one subject: *sports, politics,* or *television,* for example. On the other hand, he may simply comment informally upon what he sees, hears, reads, or experiences.

Rolling Along*

By Guy S. Williams

The Name Will Live

For some time now I've been scouting around for something that will keep my name from perishing when I do. There was a time when I thought maybe my writing might do it, but now I'm not so sure.

Still, I'm sure enough that I don't care to trust it.

I have no offspring to carry on my name except this dog, and he's 14 years old—or will be if he lives till next May —but I'd sort of like to have my name last a little longer than next May if it can possibly be arranged.

Well, I've finally hit upon an idea. Whenever I hear that a baby boy is being expected at the home of one of my colleagues, I begin hinting about how nice it would be if his prospective parents could see fit to name him for me.

If hinting doesn't do the business I come right out and openly suggest it. If that fails I begin to beg. So far I have hit the jackpot twice.

Not with my first name. They want no part of that. But with my middle name, which is Sidney. Two mighty promising young chaps now bear that name in my honor.

Not as their first name. Their parents wouldn't go quite that far. Even my own parents wouldn't. Sidney is their middle name, just as it is *my* middle name.

First, there is Richard Sidney Coffey, 6-month-old son of Mr. and Mrs. Max Coffey. Mr. Coffey, as you know, is our farm editor, and he can't possibly be any prouder of this young sprout he is raising than I am—nor than I hope the lad is going to be of himself when he grows up and learns whom he has been named for.

And now comes along James Sidney Robinson, born January 28 to Mr. and Mrs. Lawrence Robinson. Mr. Robinson is head of our photo department, and Young Sidney James—I mean James Sidney—is indeed a perfect picture.

If I could just get enough of the other boys interested—you know, if and when—I might outlive Shakespeare himself, although, if he were alive today, he could probably write rings around me.

Still, why would as great a writer as Shakespeare would be if he were alive today want to waste his talent writing rings around the likes of me?

---

* Used by permission of Guy S. Williams and the *Omaha World-Herald.*

THE COMIC STRIP

Many comic strips are pictured serials of sensational adventure, crime, or the supernatural. If a newspaper holds high standards, however, the comic features are likely to be wholesome in theme and content.

THE CARTOON

Newspaper cartoons should not be confused with the comic strips. Cartoons are drawings that express the opinions of the newspaper, often more clearly than do the editorials.

Badly Needed Education
*Safe-driving instruction is the answer**

SPECIAL INTERESTS

All newspapers devote space, sometimes entire pages, to *special interests,* such as *business and finance, literature, art, entertainment, homemaking, agriculture, fashions,* and *children's subjects.* Such features make it possible for a paper to appeal to a great variety of readers.

These features include such things as *book reviews, reports of exhibits, recipes, puzzles, patterns and designs, radio and television programs, shopping notes,* and *market reports.* There are many others.

PICTORIAL MATTER

Pictorial matter appearing in a newspaper reveals what the paper thinks will appeal to the public. Most dailies have a special page of *photographs* of people and events in the news. *Graphs* and *charts* also may be used freely to make clear the material contained in an article.

* Used by permission of the *Minneapolis Star.*

LEARNING ACTIVITIES IN READING NEWSPAPERS

A. Using a specific newspaper, hold small-group discussions or panels in which you analyze such features as those listed below. Read on the subject that you are to discuss; think it over with an open mind; talk to authorities about it.

1. What type of news is emphasized: the *sensational,* the *unusual,* the *important?* Note the use of headlines, the space given to various articles, the location of important news.
2. What proportion of news is local? national? international? Does this proportion seem in accord with the actual importance of the news?
3. Does the paper have a "point of view"? That is, can you find a strong expression of attitude on politics, foreign relations, local problems? What does the point of view indicate about the kind of thinking that you must do as you read?
4. What kind of amusement material does the paper run? Is there any relationship between the subjects of the comics and the kind of news emphasized? That is, if the comic strips emphasize *crime, marital difficulties,* and *wild escapades,* does the front page also feature them?

B. In class or in your small groups, talk over the following questions. Be sure to keep in mind the Guides to Good Discussion Habits, page 73.

1. How may a newspaper be influenced by the advertisements that it accepts?
2. What products advertised—patent medicines, for example—might come under the heading of valueless or even harmful to the average consumer?

C. In your small groups, study the front pages of several newspapers. What clues do they give to the news policies of the papers? What types of news are emphasized? Classify the papers according to their attitude toward the publishing of crime news and scandal.

D. Choose one of the following assignments as the basis for a brief talk to the class. Use the Speech Score Card, page 31. Those who listen should remember to apply the Guides to Good Listening, page 17.

1. Find a news story that interests you. Study the lead paragraph. See whether you can find the answers to the questions *who, what, where, when,* and *why.* Point these out.
2. Find a human-interest story in the news that has for its theme human sorrow, adventure, joy, or hate. Creative minds often find in these little features of the newspaper the germ of a short story or a novel. Tell how you would develop the story. You may wish to file the clipping for use when you study the writing of short stories, pages 267–77.
3. Report to the class on a newspaper vocation that interests you. Find out what preparation is needed, what abilities are essential, what the difficulties and the pleasures of such work are, and what your own aptitude for it is. Use the library and personal interviews to get the information. For example, discuss the career of a *reporter,* a *proofreader,* a *typesetter,* an *editor,* an *advertising manager,* a *photographer,* a *staff cartoonist* or *artist.*

4. Find an editorial on a controversial question. Analyze it by the following questions; then use your analysis as the subject of a talk to the class.

   a) What is the aim of the editorial?

   b) How do the views expressed compare with those in other papers?

RELATED ACTIVITIES

A. If it can be arranged, visit your newspaper office for an inspection of its files. How has the paper changed its appearance over the years? What difference, if any, is there in the types of news featured?

B. Perhaps some member of the newspaper staff in your community may be willing to talk to your class about how one should read newspapers, how standards for judging them should be set up, how news is gathered, how it is written, how editorial policy is determined. This activity will give you experience in telephoning, making introductions, and expressing appreciation. (For help in writing the letter of appreciation, see page 234.)

GETTING ACQUAINTED WITH MAGAZINES

Is there something that Arbee should know?

READ AND DISCUSS

A famous early governor of Virginia once said that he prayed God that the day of free public education would never come to America. Certain modern citizens echo that idea when they complain, "Why should we teach everyone to read? Worth-while reading is done only under compulsion in the schools. After school days are over, the average person reads only cheap and sensational magazines." Do you agree?

On every newsstand one encounters a bewildering variety of magazines. Nobody can read more than a fraction of them. How can one decide which magazines are worth reading?

Unlike radio or television offerings, printed material can be gone over thoughtfully as many times as one wishes. For that reason, magazines are likely to have more influence on what people think than have radio and television, important as they are in the communication of ideas.

Do you think that magazines are important enough to merit study in English class? What reasons can you suggest?

LEARNING ACTIVITIES IN STUDYING MAGAZINES

Directions: Working individually or in groups, carry out as many of the following activities as possible. In all discussions, maintain the attitudes listed on page 56.

A. Make a composite list of the magazines with which the members of your class are familiar.

After the name of each magazine, write the terms that indicate the field or fields covered: *adventure, romance, travel, crime, the West, the supernatural, news, aviation, the home, vocations, education, boys' interests, girls' interests, fashions, hobbies, leisure interests, travel, sports, science, . . .*

Classify the list of magazines on the basis of their appeal to the following types of readers:
1. Those with adult intelligence
2. Those with adult recreational interests
3. Those with light or frivolous interests
4. Those with picture-minded rather than reading-minded tastes

B. Carry out one or more of the following individual projects. Be sure to use your Speech Score Card.

1. Read to the class or to your small group a passage from a magazine article in which you think your classmates might be interested. Apply the Guides to Effective Oral Reading, page 41.
2. Summarize an article on some controversial subject; then tell why you do or do not agree with the author. Be specific in your comments. In analyzing the article, use any or all of the techniques given in the Guides to Efficient Study of Textbooks, page 136. Most of them apply to any careful reading that you must do.
3. Review the contents of a magazine that is unfamiliar to most of your group. Be sure to apply the Guides to Clear Explanations, page 35.
4. Talk on the topic "Why .... Is My Favorite Magazine."

C. Many magazine stories can be classified as "formula" stories; that is, the plot, characters, events, and ending follow the same pattern. Here is an amusing discussion of one type of formula story. Read it and then talk it over in class. Is the author, Mr. Morton, right? Think of pet stories that you have read recently. Except for details, do most of them fit the formula? If some of the stories are better than others, is it because of the author's style? Justify your answers.

FORMULA FOR PET STORY *

The pet story is a highly stylized job of writing: its beginning is prescribed by long custom; its mid-section is drawn from enthusiastic anecdote; it ends like a Greek tragedy. No matter what kind of pet is the subject, the stories themselves are remarkably interchangeable. One simply leaves a blank for the given species of pet, be it platypus or puff adder, and ho, for a quire of foolscap and a three-cent stamp!

"My Pet Blank" naturally begins with the very first arrival of the blank. No one in the family had dreamed it was coming, and they were all thinking about something else—Father about the bills, Sis her dress for the Freshman Prom, and Junior his bubble gum—when suddenly they were all aware of a faint scratching that had been going on at the back door (never the front door). The pros and cons of whether it was really a noise or just something they imagine are good for about a page of manuscript, and Dad finally settles it by stamping out to the back door and flinging it open.

At first, he sees nothing—looking out into the dark from the brightly lighted room. Dad is usually the bumbler in "My Pet Blank." He has no idea, at this stage, of a manuscript in the making. Dad can build a certain amount of low-grade suspense by slamming the door and going back to his check-book, but you and I know that the faint scratching noise will recur. It has to. Twice is enough for this sort of filler, and Dad had better strike pay dirt without too much fooling around.

"Mama! Sis! Junior!" he calls, and they go tearing out to look. What they find is a tiny, bedraggled, half-starved blank that can't be a day over six weeks old. It looks up at them appealingly.

The next major hubbub has to do with the baby blank's physical condition; the little thing is in bad shape; something broken, perhaps, with implications of cruel neighborhood boys or heartless motorists. Family uproar follows when Dad proposes to put the blank out of its misery. But it looks up at them appealingly. Not a chance. Outvoted, Dad is soon carrying on the classic medicine-dropper and warm-milk routine while the others make a bed of cotton in a candy box where the blank will be snug behind the stove. (The family must always keep a spare candy box on hand because they're going to need another to bury the blank in at the final curtain.)

They worry about it all night, and when they come down the next morning the blank is not there. Hubbub, lamentations, tearful search. They discover the blank suddenly; it has climbed into a saucepan and can't get out. The blank is chipper, merry, hardly the pathetic foundling they rescued from the storm the night before. (I forgot to say that these visitations are always accompanied by snow or rain and winds of gale strength.) "It wants to play!" screams Sis. And right here let's pin it down: there is nothing quite so playful as a six-week-old blank. It looks up at them appealingly.

* From *How to Protect Yourself against Women and Other Vicissitudes* by Charles W. Morton, 1948, Lippincott.

Even Dad comes to love the blank. He sits up with it half the night when it eats whatever it is that blanks should not eat. At the end, when the spare candy box makes its inexorable appearance—those cruel neighborhood boys again—Dad tries to cheer everybody up. "Never mind," says he. "We'll all miss the blank, but I saw a mighty fine hyena pup in a pet shop yesterday."

And that, the pet story concludes—or is it the next one just beginning?—is how the family got Robby, the winsome young hyena. Soon after, he was lost for a whole month, but one night there was a faint scratching at the back door. . . .

—C. W. M.

RELATED ACTIVITY

Your locality may have in it magazine publishers or writers. If it is possible, interview them or get them to talk to your group. Here is another chance to practice good form in invitations, introductions, and expressions of appreciation. If you invite and thank a speaker by letter, be sure that you check the letters by the forms on pages 222–23. For a letter of request, see page 227; for one of appreciation, page 234.

FOLLOW-UP ACTIVITIES

A. Set up a classroom library of magazines that offer good reading matter for high school students. You may want to divide the class into committees with the members of each committee to be responsible for reading carefully several issues of specified magazines. Each committee should then make a report to the class, recommending that certain magazines be purchased for the classroom library. The worth-while features should be pointed out in the recommendation. Before a vote is taken to decide which magazines to adopt for the class, the recommended magazines should be allowed to circulate for several days.

B. Because the aim of education is to lead you to mental growth, plan your growth in reading. To the list of magazines that you now read, add another list that will advance you step by step in reading ability and in thinking as you go on into adult life.

C. In your school paper, conduct a regular column of recommended magazine reading, or use your school bulletin board for that purpose. Name specific articles or selections that you think are worth reading. Appoint committees to prepare these recommendations.

WRITE AND *Refine*

Building Good Capitalization and Punctuation Habits*

1. Using Capital Letters Accurately

"WHY SHOULDN'T I CAPITALIZE 'ME'? THE RULE SAYS TO CAPITALIZE PARTICULAR PERSONS —— AND I'M VERY PARTICULAR!"

Doretta's argument sounds almost logical! She misquoted the rule, however; it says the *names* of particular persons. Her name is *Doretta,* not *me.*

Did the pretest show that you, too, are shaky in your usage of capital letters? If so, studying this chapter will help you.

---

* Pretests 1 and 2 should be given at this point. All tests called for in the text are contained in a test booklet that may be purchased for each pupil. The tests also appear in the *Teacher's Manual.* Schools not wishing to buy the booklets may mimeograph the tests.

RULES FOR CAPITALIZING: I

RULE 1. **Begin every new sentence with a capital letter.**

RULE 2. **Capitalize the names of** *clubs, associations, businesses,* **and** *other organizations.*

Salvation Army   National Geographic Society
Boy Scouts of America *   American League

RULE 3. **Capitalize the names of particular** *persons* **and any** *titles, nicknames,* **or other** *epithets* **referring to them. Capitalize** *personifications* **for special effect. (See page 258.) Do not capitalize words derived from proper nouns but having a specialized meaning, such as** *galvanize, saxophone.*

Wesley Oswald   the Red Sox (*The* is not part of the name.)
Old Hickory   William the Conqueror
pasteurize   the icy breath of Winter

RULE 4. **Capitalize common nouns or other words** (except those listed in the footnote) **that are used as part of a proper name.**

Duke University   a university   Baltimore Orioles
Professor Larrabee   Uncle George   Oak Street
Wrigley Field   Star Theater   the theater

RULE 5. **Capitalize the names of all** *countries, nationalities,* **and** *races,* **and of any** *proper adjectives* **derived from them. Exceptions are words no longer having a definite association with the proper noun from which they come, such as** *china* (dishes), *morocco* leather, *india* rubber, *champagne.*

England   Negro   Chinese boy   Indian customs

RULE 6. **Capitalize names of** *school subjects* **that come from the name of a** *country* **or a** *language.* **Capitalize names of other subjects only to indicate a** *specific course* **in some general subject.**

Latin   civics   Geometry II   United States history

LEARNING ACTIVITIES IN CAPITALIZATION: I

A. Rewrite the following sentences, supplying each needed capital letter. Check your papers in class; then analyze your own errors.

1. according to superintendent james ray, burke high school offers new courses in economics, english literature, and shop.
2. several american league baseball teams have cuban players.
3. "the big train" is the name often applied to walter johnson, for many years a great pitcher for the washington senators.
4. one of the famous figures of ancient history is alexander the great, son of king philip of macedon.

---

* Note that *of* is not capitalized. *Prepositions, conjunctions,* and the articles *a, an,* and *the* are not capitalized unless they come first or last in a name, a title, or other special word group containing capital letters.

5. the travelers' club heard an interesting report dealing with the civilization of the aztec indians before the coming of the spaniards.
6. the maiden spring has opened the buds in our garden.
7. a macadamized road led into musser air base.
8. oliver wendell holmes wrote a poem about *old ironsides,* a famous ship.
9. the high school that I attend is across from a park.

B. Write sentences applying correctly each rule that you failed to follow in *A*. Use the sentences for additional class practice. Read a sentence at a time and call upon someone to name the words that should be capitalized.

RULES FOR CAPITALIZING: II

RULE 7. **Capitalize the names of the *days* of the week and of the *months*, but not of the seasons, except when they are personified.** (See Rule 3.)

    Tuesday   April   summer   the footsteps of Spring

RULE 8. **Capitalize *personal pronouns* (and other words) *referring to the Deity;* the *Bible and its parts;* and all *religions, creeds,* and *religious denominations:*** Genesis, the Scriptures, God and His love, Buddhist.

RULE 9. **Capitalize titles of *literary, musical,* or *art works,* and of *magazines* and *newspapers.*** (Notice that the footnote on page 160 applies.)

    Life with Father   "The Blue Danube"   *Saturday Review*

RULE 10. **Capitalize the first word of every line of a poem.**

    By the rude bridge that arched the flood,
      Their flag to April's breeze unfurled,
    Here once the embattled farmers stood,
      And fired the shot heard round the world.
                —EMERSON

LEARNING ACTIVITY IN CAPITALIZATION: II

Rewrite these sentences, supplying each needed capital letter. Exchange papers and check your work in class. *Proofread carefully.* After analyzing your difficulties, prepare drill sentences that will give further practice to all who need it.

1. ring in the valiant man and free,
    the larger heart, the kindlier hand;
    ring out the darkness of the land,
    ring in the christ that is to be.
             —TENNYSON
2. Late in the summer our firm published *politics and the common people* by congressman walter bliss.
3. Arthur asked, "Did you see the statue called 'the thinker'?"
4. On the last tuesday in march, the club held its spring dance.
5. "Joe," asked the minister, "has the baptist picnic been held?"

6. He quoted the bible: "if god be for us, who can be against us?"
7. The *daily clarion* reviewed the play *the importance of being earnest.*
8. I transferred my membership to pearl methodist church in july.
9. In st. luke, in the new testament, we can read about the birth of christ.

RULES FOR CAPITALIZING: III

RULE 11. Capitalize only the *first word* of a *direct quotation*.
>Jim replied, "By tonight we should know."
>"By tonight," Jim replied, "we should know."

RULE 12. Capitalize the names of *official departments of government.* Capitalize the titles of *officials* when used *with or in place of a proper name*.
>Is it true, Senator, that you saw the Secretary of Defense?
>As a boy, I dreamed of becoming a senator.

RULE 13. Capitalize all important words in the names of *treaties, legislative acts* or *bills,* and *other documents*. (See the footnote on page 160.)
>Treaty of Ghent   Wagner Act   Declaration of Independence

RULE 14. Capitalize the pronoun *I* and the vocative *O*.
>As I've said, I was there.   It is my lady; O my love.

RULE 15. Capitalize the names of *holidays* and of *notable events* or *periods in history*. (Rule 4 applies.)
>Easter   French Revolution   New Year's Day   Dark Ages

RULE 16. Capitalize *specific geographical names*. (Rule 4 applies.) **Capitalize *north, south, east, west,* and their *derivatives* only if they refer to a *specific region*.**
>Rocky Mountains   the Indians of the Southwest   Lake George
>Gulf of Mexico   the farm southwest of ours   Yazoo River

RULE 17. Capitalize nouns that show *family relationship,* unless the noun is preceded by a possessive or other modifier and has no proper noun after it.
>Ask Mother to tell you about her father's boyhood.
>This is Aunt Minnie, my favorite aunt.

RULE 18. Capitalize the abbreviations for *ante meridian* and *post meridian* (or *meridiem*). [Some authorities permit small letters.] **Capitalize *initials* and *other abbreviations* if they stand for words that would be capitalized.**
>A.M.   P.M.   F.F.A. (Future Farmers of America)   B.C.   A.D.

RULE 19. Capitalize the names of specific man-made products, such as *buildings* and *other structures, ships, planes,* and *trains*. In *brand* or *trade names,* capitalize only the *specific part*.
>the Jefferson Memorial   the *Pinta*   Clearvu lenses

RULE 20. Capitalize the *first word* and *all nouns* in the salutation of a letter, and the *first word* of the complimentary close.
>My dear Sir: Yours very sincerely,   Dear Grandmother,

LEARNING ACTIVITY IN CAPITALIZATION: III

Rewrite these sentences, supplying needed capitalization. Exchange papers for checking. Analyze your errors; then proceed as in the activity on page 161.

1. The stamp act helped to bring about the american revolution.
2. During easter vacation father and i got up at 4:00 a.m. one day and hiked to heron lake, six miles north of rock city.
3. Yes, uncle john has lived in the south for many years. Often i've spent thanksgiving at his home in mobile, alabama, on mobile bay.
4. Supt. e. s. farley will attend the n.e.a. meeting in portland, oregon. He will leave just after the flag day program.
5. The new secretary of commerce served in the senate for twelve years.
6. Our new polaraire deep freeze arrived on mother's birthday.
7. The letter began "dear aunt eva," and ended "your loving grandniece."
8. My grandfather's law office is in the ludlow building.
9. Take, o take those lips away.—Shakespeare
10. "If i'm not mistaken," said ann, "the *santa fe chief* leaves at 2:00 p.m."

REVIEW PRACTICE IN CAPITALIZATION

A. The following sentences cover all the rules on pages 160–62. Use these sentences in any type of drill that will help you. One good method is to put the sentences on the board, insert capital letters, and then justify their use.

1. on monday dad sprinkled the vines with a paris green solution.
2. When i attended coe college, i studied shakespeare's *antony and cleopatra* in an english literature course.
3.   Take note, take note, o world,
   to be direct and honest is not safe.—Shakespeare
4. "if you go to the store," said harry's mother, "get a box of surelight matches."
5. living nature, not dull art,
   shall plan my ways and rule my heart.—Cardinal Newman
6. your devoted son,   dear uncle titus,   sincerely yours,
7. 'tis god gives skill,
   but not without men's hands: he could not make
   antonio stradivari's violins
   without antonio.—George Eliot
8. Early last spring, attorney will ellis was made a judge.
9. On august 15, 1914, the first ship passed through the panama canal. In that same summer, world war I began. It ended officially with the signing of the treaty of versailles.
10. The "gettysburg address" was delivered by president lincoln on thursday, november 19, 1863.
11. in the last election a. l. carter won a seat in the united states senate.
12. At bradley high school the pep club, with the help of the speech classes, stages some fine rallies.

13. "no, tom," said his uncle, "i've never visited the swiss alps or any other european spots. I have, however, traveled through the canadian rockies and the southwest."

14. Dennis said thoughtfully, "well, i think my favorite book is *a tale of two cities*. My favorite painting is 'the horse fair.' My favorite piece of music is a march, 'under the double eagle.'"

15. Last christmas my brother billy woke us all at 4:00 a.m. He put on the indian suit that he found under the tree and ran through the house, even into grandmother's room, giving a war whoop.

16. tonight i'd planned to see *the man from texas* at the palace theater over on third avenue, but i studied chemistry and american history instead.

17. at the methodist church last night dr. r. v. hill, who was born in canton, china, talked about oahu, in the hawaiian islands.

B. Write original examples of each rule that you violated in the preceding activity. Use these original sentences for group drill.

USING ENGLISH IN ALL CLASSES

Study each written exercise in any class for the teacher's marking of errors in capitalization. Restudy each rule that you have broken; then compose oral and written sentences that will fix it in your memory.

2. USING END PUNCTUATION AND INTERNAL PERIODS ACCURATELY

"YOU KNOW MY COUSIN HANK?
HE JUST LOST HIS JOB AT ACME FURS—
HE SOLD SIX FUR SCARFS
FOR $2.98 EACH.
HE ALWAYS DID PUT PERIODS
IN THE WRONG PLACES!"

Though you may not, like Arbee's cousin Hank, have trouble with decimal points, probably you can profit by a careful review of end punctuation and other uses of the period. To express the meaning that you intend, you must be sure of the significance of the punctuation that you use.

RULES FOR END PUNCTUATION AND INTERNAL PERIODS

RULE 1. **Use a** *period* **to end a** *declarative* **sentence; that is, one that makes a statement:** The sun shone brightly every day last week.

RULE 2. **As a rule, use a** *period* **to end an** *imperative* **sentence; that is, one that gives a command:** Pay attention to these directions.

RULE 3. **Use a** *question mark* **to end an** *interrogative* **sentence; that is, one that asks a question:** Where did you find your hat?
Use a *period* **after an** *indirect question:* He asked where I had been.
Use a *period* **after a** *simple request,* **one that the speaker assumes will be granted:** Will you come in now, please.

RULE 4. **Use an** *exclamation point* **to end an** *exclamatory* **sentence; that is, one that shows strong emotion or excitement:** We'll never give up!
Use an *exclamation point* **also after** *interjections;* **that is, words or expressions that show** *emotion.* (EXCEPTION: Mild interjections are followed by a comma.)
　　"Hurray! We won!" shouted the excited boy.　　Oh, I don't mind.
NOTE: It is *meaning* that determines the kind of end punctuation. See how a mere change of end punctuation affects meaning:

　　　　He was there.　　He was there?　　He was there!

Sometimes a command or a question becomes an exclamation. Here again, meaning determines the punctuation.

　　　　Drop that gun!　　Was I embarrassed!

RULE 5. **Use a** *period* **to show an** *abbreviation.* **However, in formal writing, as a rule, avoid abbreviations, except for such as these:**

　　a) *Mr., Mrs., Dr.,* and *St.* (Saint) before a name; and such academic degrees as *A.B., Ph.D.*
　　b) *Jr., Sr.,* and *Esq.* after a name
　　c) Abbreviations of other titles only before a full name, such as *Prof.* C. R. Steele. (Write *Professor Steele,* not *Prof. Steele.*)
　　d) A.M. and P.M. used with figures: 4:15 A.M.
　　e) Special abbreviations, such as *C.O.D.,* B.C., A.D., *G.O.P., U.S., P.S.*

RULE 6. **If an abbreviation comes just before any mark except a period, use both the period for the abbreviation and the other mark.**

　　　　"Do you weigh more than 250 lbs.?" queried the sign.

RULE 7. **Use a period after** *initials:* Call J. B. Allison.

RULE 8. **Use a period to show** *decimals* **or** *dollars and cents:* .25, $1.98.

A. Rewrite the following sentences, supplying periods, question marks, and exclamation points. *Proofread carefully*. Go over the sentences in class.

1. Capt O N Burt, of the USCG, is an accomplished speaker
2. "Is that a COD package" asked Dr Bowen "I hope not"
3. "Block that kick Block that kick" begged the crowd
4. Will you stand here, please, Mr Cunningham
5. "Am I addressing C Albert Payne, Sr" he inquired
6. (*Express the prices in decimals.*)
   Note our prices:
   > Butter, 3 lbs, $135
   > Eggs, 2 doz, $110
   > Potatoes, per bu, $165
7. "Stop Don't open that door" screamed Mrs Doane
8. The GOP candidate, Prof T L Royce, is due here on the 3:15 PM train.
9. St Benedict, born AD 480, died at the age of sixty-three
10. He belongs to the BPOE and the IOOF, I believe
11. Will you call back at 10:30 AM, please We should know then
12. On the name plate was a familiar name: E N Freeland, DDS

B. Write sentences similar to those in *A*. Use your sentences for class drill, or work with a partner.

USING ENGLISH IN ALL CLASSES

Bring into English class papers written for any class. Have you used abbreviations for words that should not be abbreviated? Correct any errors.

3. USING COMMAS ACCURATELY

SUE ELLEN, MARY ANN, AND GRACE CAME.   SUE, ELLEN, MARY, ANN, AND GRACE CAME.

One point about comma usage that needs to be emphasized over and over is that commas have only one real function: *to make meaning clear* or *more quickly understandable.* Inserting commas—or taking them out—may make a real difference in the meaning of a sentence. Note this example:

Do not be taken in by false or misleading advertising.

That sentence names two kinds of advertising (*false* and *misleading*). Now look at this sentence:

Do not be taken in by false, or misleading, advertising.

Putting in the commas makes *misleading* a synonym for *false;* the writer implies, perhaps incorrectly, that there is no difference.

One general rule should be your guide to using commas correctly: *Use a comma wherever it will make clear the meaning of a sentence.*

RULES FOR USING COMMAS ACCURATELY *

RULE 1. Use a comma or commas to set off a term in *direct address,* **also known as the** *noun,* **or** *nominative, of address.*

Tom, I need you.   Now, Tom, I need you.   I need you, Tom.

RULE 2. Use a comma to set off *yes, no, well; other introductory words or phrases;* **or** *mild interjections.*

Yes, he is here.   *By the way,* who is he?   *Oh,* you know him.

RULE 3. Use commas to separate the *parts of a date.* **Within a sentence, place a comma after the last part if it does not end the sentence. Use no comma between the month and the day.**

On Monday, May 7, 1956, he resigned.   In May, 1956, he resigned.
Wait until May 6 for my answer.

RULE 4. Use commas between *parts of an address.* **(City and zone number, if there is one, form one part.) Within a sentence, use a comma after the last part of the address if it does not end the sentence. Use a comma before an** *of* **preceding an address.**

She lives at 1812 Park Place, Austin 12, Texas, now.
James Brown, of Emporia, Kansas, called recently.

RULE 5. Use commas after *digits indicating thousands* **except in such items as dates or street numbers.**

15,265   A.D. 1607   1940 Sherman Avenue

RULE 6. In *alphabetical listings* **of names, as in directories or bibliographies, use a comma after the surname.**

Collins, Sheila Mary   Ingraham, Dr. Charles E.

RULE 7. Use commas to set off a *title,* **or the** *abbreviation of a title, following a name:* E. C. Baker, M.D., is his title now.   Lee Otis, Jr., is here.

---

* Other rules for comma usage follow on pages 168 and 170.

LEARNING ACTIVITIES IN USING COMMAS

A. Rewrite these sentences, supplying all necessary commas. Exchange papers for checking; then write original sentences for each usage that you missed.

1. By the way Dick the June 9 1954 edition is missing.
2. A 1650-pound steel beam crashed to the ground today in a building being constructed at 3715 Randolph Street Atlanta Georgia; but no one was hurt.
3. On June 20 1954 Fred became officially Fred H. Curtis M.D.
4. Well all I know is that she is listed as Roberts Arlene R.
5. No Henry in August 1952 I was in the hospital.
6. Mr. Davis paid $25500 for that farm in Knox County Nebraska.
7. As expected Grace Burns M.A. heads the list.
8. At least 49999 people agree with you David.

B. Write (1) a sentence containing a date and an address, (2) a sentence containing direct address and an introductory *yes*, (3) a sentence illustrating rules 6 and 7. *Proofread carefully*. Exchange papers for critical reading.

RULES FOR USING COMMAS—Continued

RULE 8. **Use commas to separate *consecutive* adjective modifiers.**

We stepped into a *clean, neat* room. (*clean* room, *neat* room)

If an adjective modifies an *adjective-noun combination*, omit the comma. (HINT: Omit the comma if *and* sounds queer between the adjectives.)

We saw a *red brick* wall. (*What kind of brick wall?* red)
(*We saw a red* **and** *brick wall* does not sound right.)

RULE 9. **Use commas to separate the *items of a series* of words, phrases, or short clauses.**

Pears, apples, peaches, and plums grow here. (*words*)
She ran up the stairs, down the hall, and into her room. (*phrases*)
Joe cut the grass, Ed raked it, and I hauled it away. (*short clauses*)

RULE 10. **Use commas to set off words or word groups that are *appositives* (pages 329, 354), unless the appositive is short and closely connected.**

Phil Gray, *our mailman*, is friendly.   My sister *Ila* was there.
A uniformed guard, *tall and forbidding*, barred our path.

RULE 11. **Use a comma to show the *omission* of words.**

Mary wore a white dress; Janet, a blue one. [*Wore* is omitted.]

RULE 12. **Use a comma or commas to set off a *direct quotation*.**

Mother said, "The plumber was here today."
"Today," said Mother, "the plumber was here."

RULE 13. **Use commas to set off *adjectives out of their natural order*.**

The puppy, *wet and muddy*, crept under the porch.

RULE 14. **Use commas to set off *contrasted elements*.**

Joe, *unlike Merton*, is musically gifted.   Use a pen, not a pencil.

A. Copy these sentences, supplying needed commas. Check papers in class. Write original sentences to illustrate each rule that you missed.

1. The boys tired but happy loaded bats balls and gloves into the truck.
2. "As a matter of fact" said Mr. Wilcox our grocer "oranges unlike grapefruit always sell well."
3. A tall thin man guarded one corner; a short fat man the other.
4. "I've looked upstairs downstairs and even outdoors" announced my brother Lowell.
5. The speaker said "A foolish little mistake not an intentional error cost me my job my home and my best friend."
6. Forrest eager and excited stood on the top step; his sister Kathlyn on the walk below.
7. The Sox my favorite team collected fifteen hits made four double plays stole three bases and committed no errors.

B. Write these sentences: (1) one containing *consecutive adjective modifiers*, (2) one containing *a series of phrases*, (3) one containing *an appositive*, (4) one containing *contrasted elements*. Compare work in your small groups. The drawing may suggest sentences.

RULE 15. Use a comma or commas to set off *parenthetical expressions;* **that is,** *words not necessary to the meaning of the sentence.*

I believe, however, that he is honest.

The woman, much to my surprise, knew my name.

He is, as I have said before, a good citizen.

RULE 16. Use a comma to separate the clauses of a *compound sentence* (see page 404) **unless they are very short clauses joined by** *and.*

Something must be done now, or the results will be serious.

The door opened and John came out.

RULE 17. Use commas to set off *adverb clauses* (see page 376) **that are** *introductory* **or that are** *noticeably out of their normal place* **in the sentence.**

As the words were spoken, a hush fell over the room.

Dick, *when he saw Mary,* quickly turned his head.

RULE 18. Use commas to set off *introductory* (*a*) *participial,* (*b*) *infinitive,* **or** (*c*) *absolute phrases;* **and** (*d*) *long or consecutive prepositional phrases* **or** (*e*) *those containing gerunds.*

a) *Whistling gaily,* Bert climbed the hill.

b) *To concentrate,* I closed my eyes.

c) *The ring being too costly,* Dan did not buy it.

d) *During the intermission between the acts,* I walked downstairs.

e) *After writing a letter,* I finished my knitting.

RULE 19. Use a comma or commas to set off *nonrestrictive clauses* **or** *participial phrases.* Such clauses and phrases merely give incidental or supplementary information. **Omit the commas if the clause or the phrase is** *restrictive;* **that is, if it is** *necessary to the sentence idea.*

Hal, *who thinks fast,* was off like a shot. (*nonrestrictive*)

The man *who helped me* is not here. (*restrictive*)

Russell, *feeling empty,* visited the refrigerator. (*nonrestrictive*)

The boy *standing beside me* is Leon Hall. (*restrictive*)

He was surprised, *although he did not say so.* (*nonrestrictive*)

Turn left *when you reach the next corner.* (*restrictive*)

RULE 20. Use a comma wherever needed for clear meaning.

In 1910, 579 new houses were built.

Where it is, is a mystery.

With Alice, Jane is a different person.

I smiled when he came in, and waited quietly for him to speak.

A week before, Larry had taken a new job.

RULE 21. Use a comma after *complimentary closings* in all letters. Use a comma after the *salutation of a friendly letter.*

Yours lovingly,   Sincerely yours,   Dear Katherine,

RULE 22. Use a comma before a *short clause that changes a statement into a question:* You have the keys, *haven't you?*

LEARNING ACTIVITIES

A. Copy these sentences, supplying commas wherever they are needed. After checking your papers in class, follow up as in the preceding two lessons.

1. In the calm cool stillness of the evening I swung in the hammock.
2. After marking the papers the teacher recorded the grades.
3. To illustrate his point the professor drew a diagram.
4. The entertainer after the applause had died down continued his act.
5. Since the place where he is is I believe unknown I am in favor of choosing someone else aren't you?
6. My father who is a lawyer has an office on Front Street; but my uncle interested only in his farm seldom calls there.
7. The same thing having happened before Ted watched as the man wearing the derby hat came in again and noted his exact movements.
8. Speaking from past experience I said that for 1956 340 copies should be enough; and my partner who often disagrees with me for once thought that I was right.
9. Just the week before Paul had resigned; now however regret that he had done so filled his thoughts.
10. As we stood there we heard the drone of a plane. We waved frantically but the pilot gave no sign that he had seen us.

B. The use of commas with nonrestrictive clauses gives many high school students difficulty. (Review Rule 19.) All modifying clauses beginning with *that* are restrictive; others may or may not be. Here is a group of sentences to give you practice in distinguishing restrictive from nonrestrictive clauses. Punctuate the sentences correctly. Make this an oral or a written exercise.

1. His latest book which you may have read is about the sea.
2. Automobiles which now crowd our streets create many problems.
3. Drivers that willfully violate the law should have their licenses revoked.
4. Workmen that refused to accept the new terms were not hired.
5. The leader who had once been a laborer was popular with his workers.
6. The book that you have in your hand is a favorite of mine.
7. I find no fault with your work which seems to be done well.
8. Take me back to the place where I was born.

REVIEWING ALL COMMA USAGE

A. Commas are used correctly in the following sentences. Analyze each use in class, citing the rule that justifies it.

1. "Well, Patty," conceded my sister Carol, "I am convinced. Patricia Farley, of Table Rock, Nebraska, does sound better."
2. On the afternoon of March 16, 1954, a letter containing important news was delivered at 646 Waller Lane, Portland, Maine. (Why is *containing important news* not set off by commas?)

3. Brooks, a scientific farmer, harvested 17,345 bushels of wheat; his neighbor, 5,320.
4. Bob, tired and angry, slammed the door, locked it, and strode off.
5. Yes, football, not baseball, is my favorite sport; but Ernie, on the other hand, prefers baseball.
6. After the car had come to a halt, smoking and steaming, Willis, who had been driving, climbed out.
7. The new directories having been delivered at last, Danny searched eagerly until he found it: *Casey, Daniel B.*
8. Smiling happily, Ralph left; ten minutes before, he had been scowling.
9. From George, Alfred Bates, Sr., learned that where the house once was, was now only a vacant lot.
10. In 1936, 1,700 farmers lost their farms when the drouth came, and moved to the city.
11. A shiny new automobile drew up before the house, paused there a moment, and then rolled on down the street. (Why is there no comma between *shiny* and *new*?)
12. At any rate, this man, as rumor has it, disappeared in May, 1952.

B. The following sentences cover all the comma rules that you have been studying. Copy the sentences, supplying needed commas. Go over your paper carefully after it has been checked. Decide which usages you need most to practice. Write original sentences to fix these usages in your mind.

1. "No" said Dr. Gray "you are wrong Sam in thinking that I was in Akron Ohio in May 1951. After all I was in Korea until August 6 1952."
2. The kitchen unlike the parlor was a cheerful little room very neat and clean. Here I decided the family must spend most of its time.
3. While they waited the message that was to change all their plans was being written in a dark dirty room only a mile away.
4. Feeling worse by the minute Agnes who had dragged unwillingly up the stairs read the name on the door: *R. L. Settell D.D.S.*
5. Well who won? Leo I suppose won the high jump; Art the discus throw.
6. "Bill you should have seen us" laughed Ed my younger brother. "There we sat eating the fish; and the cat licking her chops stared at us hungrily."
7. Gentlemen on July 1 1945 $2854785 was the surplus in the state treasury; one year later $1462390.
8. In the directory much to my confusion I found three Andrew Porters: *Porter Andrew C.; Porter Andrew H.;* and *Porter Andrew N.*
9. How if you don't mind telling us Joyce do you keep track of all those first cousins second cousins and first-cousins-once-removed?
10. "It happened on a wet cold Friday in April 1916; the place the Regis Hotel Buffalo New York" recalled Uncle Bill my mother's brother.
11. Outside the rain beat angrily at the door; inside however as we sat around the fire everything was warm cozy and pleasant.
12. To Barbara Jane first told the exciting wonderful news: they not the Mears twins had been chosen to sing at the concert.

13. "My daughter Susan" said Father impressively "is I am proud to say the winner of an art scholarship having been chosen incidentally from a group of 2500 applicants."
14. One entry having been overlooked the judges weary but honest reconsidered all entries revised the list of winners and at last announced the results of the contest.
15. Mark V. Brown Ph.D. spoke at the first one of these meetings; and our own dean at the closing afternoon session.

C. Write original sentences illustrating the rules for comma usage. After each sentence, write the number of each rule that applies. If a rule names *words, phrases,* or *clauses,* be sure to label each element. Use these sentences for class drill or in any other way that you feel will be most helpful.

D. From your reading, bring to class illustrations of comma usage. Explain each use. If you find a sentence that seems to violate the rules, try to decide whether there is a good reason for the breaking of the rule.

1. Is the meaning perfectly clear without the comma?
2. Are the elements so short that no comma is necessary?
3. Is the author writing for readers who can interpret the ideas easily?

E. Explain the difference in meaning suggested by the use or the omission of commas in the following sentences. Make this an oral activity.

1. Will you call Helen or Laura?
   Will you call Helen, or Laura?
2. Would you use red, or blue, as the color scheme?
   Would you use red or blue as the color scheme?
3. Give me $650 or 40 per cent of the profits.
   Give me $650, or 40 per cent of the profits.

USING ENGLISH IN ALL CLASSES

Make a definite effort to apply in all your written work the comma uses that bother you most. Read aloud in class sentences in which you have used commas. Explain each use. Exchange papers from other subjects and check each use of commas. Indicate also places where commas should have been used.

4. Using Apostrophes Accurately

Like the comma, the apostrophe causes confusion if it is omitted or incorrectly used. Its work is to make ideas clear by showing *ownership, contraction of words,* and certain *plural forms.*

RULES FOR USING APOSTROPHES ACCURATELY

RULE 1. Use an apostrophe with nouns to show *ownership*.

a) **To form the possessive of any** *singular noun,* **first write the noun.** *Make no changes in its spelling.* **Then add an** *apostrophe* **and** *s* **('s).**

      a woman, a woman's hat   Frances, Frances's hat *

b) **To form the possessive of a** *plural noun that ends in* s, **first write the noun.** *Do not change its spelling.* **Then add an apostrophe.**

      girls, two girls' hats   the Joneses, the Joneses' dog

c) **To form the possessive of a** *plural noun that does not end in* s, **follow the rule for singular possessives; that is, add 's.**

      two men, two men's hats   children, children's hats

d) **Use an apostrophe with possessive forms of** *indefinite pronouns: someone's, anybody's.* **Do** *not* **use an apostrophe with** *personal, interrogative,* **or** *relative pronouns* **in their possessive forms:** *yours, hers, its, ours, theirs, whose.* (*It's* means "it is" or "it has"; it is not a possessive pronoun.)

e) **Show** *separate ownership* **by making** *each name* **a possessive.**

      John's and Joe's boxing gloves. (*Each has a pair.*)

  Show *joint ownership* **by making a possessive of the** *name just before the thing possessed.*

      John and Joe's boxing gloves. (*They own them together.*)

f) **Make the** *last word of a compound word* **the possessive.**

      my son-in-law's house   everyone else's answer

RULE 2. Use an apostrophe to show *letters omitted* from words.

a) **In contractions of verbs with other words**

      they've (*they have*)   we're (*we are*)   isn't (*is not*)

b) **In other contractions; in year designations; in quotations of direct, colloquial speech**

      o'clock (*of the clock*)   Spirit of '76 (*1776*)   talkin' (*talking*)

RULE 3. Use an apostrophe and *s* to form the plurals of (*a*) *letters,* (*b*) *figures,* (*c*) *signs,* and (*d*) *words used as words.*

a) Make your *e*'s more carefully.

b) I can't tell your *3*'s from your *8*'s.

c) Count the number of +'s on each paper.

d) I found ten *very*'s on this page alone.

LEARNING ACTIVITIES IN USING APOSTROPHES

A. Each apostrophe in the following sentences is used correctly. Give the rule that fits each use.

1. In '44 he won the club medal, scoring *3*'s on nine holes.

2. Haven't you mistaken those *m*'s for *n*'s?

---

* Some authorities add only an apostrophe to form the possessive of singular nouns that end in *s:* Frances, Frances' hat.

3. Someone else's story may differ from yours. (What rule applies to "yours"?)
4. At ten o'clock we reached Joe and Ed's house. (Why is there only one apostrophe in the compound possessive?)

B. Rewrite the following sentences, replacing each expression in parentheses by a *possessive,* a *contraction,* or a *plural.* Be ready to explain why each apostrophe is needed.

1. That is (*someone else*) book. Where is (*you*)?
2. (*Sam and Ike*) eyes are blue, (*are they not*)?
3. The two (*Max*) hats (*do not*) seem to be here.
4. (*Cannot*) the (*men*) entries be marked with (2)?
5. The (*editor in chief*) train leaves at five (*of the clock*).
6. There are four (*A*) on (*James*) card.
7. (*It is*) too bad that you use so many (*and*).

C. Copy the following sentences, inserting apostrophes where they are needed. Exchange papers for checking.

1. Its odd about our names. Both hers and mine contain three *l*s, three *t*s, and three *r*s.
2. Arent there five *3*s in that column?
3. Will everyones work be finished by four oclock?
4. In the scoring, +s indicate true statements; and *0*s, false statements.

D. Write sentences illustrating each use of the apostrophe. Use these for class drill, or exchange papers with a classmate for checking.

E. Explain the difference in meaning given by the different possessives used in the following sentences. Make this an oral activity.

1. The boy's plans were practical.
   The boys' plans were practical.
2. Mr. Meyer's daughter is away at school.
   Mr. Meyers's daughter is away at school.
3. Milly and Dinah's brothers are hockey fans.
   Milly's and Dinah's brothers are hockey fans.

RELATED ACTIVITY

Study advertising signs, newspapers, and magazines. How accurate are they in apostrophe usage? Talk in class about your findings.

USING ENGLISH IN ALL CLASSES

Go over papers that you have written for other classes. Note whether you have been careful to use apostrophes correctly. Habitually correct usage is the real test of your mastery of their use.

5. USING QUOTATION MARKS ACCURATELY

READ AND DISCUSS

In your reading, how much do quotation marks help you to understand what is told? Try reading the following conversation between two people. All quotation marks and paragraph indentions have been omitted.

> Have you told Elmer the news? I think that you should break it to him. I haven't had time. Why don't you do so tonight?

Who is saying *what*? What happens to the meaning, depending upon where you put quotation marks and paragraph indentions?

RULES FOR USING QUOTATION MARKS ACCURATELY

RULE 1. **Always enclose in quotation marks the *exact words* that anyone uses.** Study the following examples.

"How do you like our idea?" asked Milton.
Ruth objected, "I don't approve of it."
"Well," I put in, "we haven't much choice."
"You're right," agreed Tom. "Tomorrow is the deadline."

Do *not* use quotation marks around an *indirect quotation*.
Ed said that he would go. (*Ed's exact words:* "I will go.")

RULE 2. **In writing conversation, begin a new paragraph each time that the speaker changes.**

RULE 3. **In quoting more than one paragraph, use quotation marks at the *beginning of each paragraph*, but at the *close of the final paragraph only*.**

RULE 4. **Use quotation marks to show words or phrases used in a special sense; that is, for (*a*) *technical*, (*b*) *ironical*, or (*c*) *unusual* words.**

a) This process is known as "annealing."
b) These so-called "reforms" are a mockery.
c) The "ins" were trying desperately to defeat the "outs."

RULE 5. **Quote titles of *short stories, short poems,* or *short musical works;* of *chapters, articles, essays,* or *speeches;* of *names of art works*.**

This chapter, "The Inner Beauty," analyzes Arnold's "Dover Beach."

RULE 6. **Use single quotation marks for a quotation within a quotation.**

"I like the poem 'Morning Mist' especially," said he.

RULE 7. **Place *inside* the quotation marks a *period* or a *comma* used with them; place a *colon* or a *semicolon* outside. Place *inside*, a *question mark* or an *exclamation point that is part of the quotation*. Place *outside*, a *question mark* or an *exclamation point* that is *not* part of the quotation.**

"He claims," said Mark, "that you lost."   Did you play "Dark Eyes"?
I like "Birches"; so does Elaine.   He shouted, "Wait for me!"

LEARNING ACTIVITIES IN USING QUOTATION MARKS

A. The following sentences illustrate correct use of quotation marks. Explain orally (1) the purpose of each set and (2) the reason for their location in relation to other punctuation marks used with them.

1. Do you know Browning's "The Lost Leader"?
2. The "also-rans" were sitting gloomily in the library.
3. I enjoyed the chapter called "Wake Up!"
4. "I've changed my mind," said Phil. "I'll go with Bob."
5. Ted insisted, "I know that Father's exact words were, 'Be here at noon.'"
6. "At dismissal we always marched out to the strains of 'Under the Double Eagle,'" recalled Mother.
7. "No wonder you can't forget that march!" laughed Dad.

B. Rewrite the following exercise, paragraphing it correctly. Go over your work in class.

"Have you asked Paul about this?" queried Fred. "No," replied his brother, "I haven't." "Well, will you?" "Oh, I don't know. Do you think it's really necessary?"

C. Rewrite the following sentences. Insert quotation marks wherever they are needed. In class explain why you inserted these marks, and why you put them where you did.

1. Here we go! shouted Don. We'll see you later!
2. The book that I mean, said Aunt Lucy, has a reprint of Millet's Man with the Hoe.
3. George remarked that he had heard Nelson Eddy sing Indian Love Call.
4. While Tim sat outside whistling Danny Boy, the so-called experts held a consultation in the kitchen.
5. Keep in a cool, dry place, the label says, announced Elaine.
6. Miss Ellis asked, Have you read that article called Traveler by Night?

D. Change the following indirect quotations to direct quotations. Punctuate them correctly.

1. Sue asked me to come with her.
2. Bart exclaimed that the cabin had been ransacked.
3. Father asked where I had been.
4. Maria begged Harry to sing "I Love Life."
5. The superintendent inquired whether any student had applied for a scholarship.
6. The children reported that they had found some arrowheads.
7. Gene said that he had found an old bicycle in the attic.
8. Mother asked whether we wanted waffles for breakfast.
9. Leon told Earl to follow him.
10. Bert exclaimed suddenly that he could hear footsteps.

E. Write sentences to illustrate each of the rules on page 176. Use your sentences for class drill or exchange for individual practice.

6. Using Colons and Semicolons Accurately

READ AND DISCUSS

Examine the following sentences. What seems to be the purpose of each colon or semicolon used?

At 3:15 P.M. tomorrow, I shall see these boys: Phil, Terry, and Ray.

Here is the explanation: no one had expected us.

We met delegates from Washington, Louisiana; Cuba, Missouri; and Florida, New York.

Like other punctuation marks, colons and semicolons are (1) guideposts to meaning and (2) aids to quick understanding of reading matter. The rules governing the use of these marks are simple; if you have only vague ideas about when they are needed, now is a good time to acquire the ability to use colons and semicolons with confidence.

178

RULES FOR USING COLONS AND SEMICOLONS ACCURATELY

THE COLON

RULE 1. Use a colon after the salutation in a business letter.

> Gentlemen: Dear Mrs. Frostenson: My dear Sir:

RULE 2. Use a colon before *listed items* introduced by such words as *the following, as follows, thus,* or *these,* or by a *number.* Do *not* use a colon before *predicate nominatives* or *objects.*

> RIGHT: He visited these places: Peru, Chile, and Ecuador.
> WRONG: He visited: Peru, Chile, and Ecuador. (*direct objects*)
> WRONG: The countries visited are: Peru, Chile, and Ecuador. (*predicate nominatives*)

RULE 3. Use a colon to introduce a *long* or *formal* quotation.

> Marcus Aurelius offers sound advice: "Be not careless in deeds, nor confused in words, nor rambling in thought."

RULE 4. Use a colon between numbers showing *hours and minutes.*

> Please call me at 8:30 P.M.

RULE 5. Use a colon between *chapter and verse* in *Bible references.*

> Job 6:25 (*sixth chapter, twenty-fifth verse*)

RULE 6. Use a colon between the clauses of a compound sentence when the *second* clause *explains the first* or *amplifies* it.

> His intention is clear: he does not plan to return.

THE SEMICOLON

RULE 1. Use a semicolon between the clauses of a *compound sentence* if the co-ordinate conjunction is omitted.

> The polls close at five; we must hurry.

RULE 2. Use a semicolon before *conjunctive adverbs* like *however, moreover, nevertheless, therefore, consequently, hence,* or *thus* when they connect the clauses of a compound sentence. To mark a pause after the conjunctive adverb, insert a *comma.*

> I shall try to convince him; however, I am not hopeful.

RULE 3. As an aid to clear meaning, use a semicolon between the main clauses of a compound sentence if those clauses contain commas.

> Jack, dressed in his best, waited impatiently; and his little sister, also in her Sunday attire, stood beside him.

RULE 4. Use semicolons to separate the *items in a series* if there are *commas within the items.*

> Winners are Ted Dixon, Bedford, Virginia; Bert Wallace, Aiken, South Carolina; and Myron Brown, Roxboro, North Carolina.

LEARNING ACTIVITIES IN USING COLONS AND SEMICOLONS

A. Copy the following sentences. Insert colons and semicolons wherever needed. Exchange papers and go over them in class, justifying the marks inserted.

1. Elbert Hubbard once wrote "Conduct, culture, and character are graces that go through life hand in hand, never separate or alone."
2. There is just one drawback there are no funds available.
3. *My dear Madam* is the salutation evidently the writer of this letter believes in being formal.
4. At 8 30 P.M., exactly on the dot, the wedding march began and the bride, dressed in white, came down the aisle.
5. On the committee I have named these people Alfred Beggs, of Canton Louis Gray, of Tyler and Howard Dalton, of Archer City.
6. We heard a fine sermon the text, taken from Proverbs 20 11, was as follows "Even a child is known by his doings."
7. Yesterday we made an important change Mr. Burke is now in charge of sales the rest of the staff remains as before.
8. In this connection, I am reminded of Emerson's words "Shallow men believe in luck."

B. Write original sentences using a colon (1) to introduce a lengthy quotation, (2) before an enumeration of items, (3) between the clauses of a sentence in which the second clause explains or amplifies the first. The drawings on these pages suggest some good ideas for sentences.

C. Write original sentences using a semicolon (1) between parallel constructions within which there are commas used, (2) between the clauses of a compound sentence containing no co-ordinate conjunction, (3) to clarify the meaning in a compound sentence containing several commas.

D. Bring in from an outside source five examples of colon and semicolon uses. Name the rule that each example illustrates.

Bring to class a theme or report that you have written. See whether you can improve it by using semicolons to form good compound sentences.

FOLLOW-UP ACTIVITY

Practice the use of colons and semicolons in all your writing. Be careful, however, to use them only if they help to make meaning clear; use other marks of punctuation if they will be more helpful.

7. USING HYPHENS, ITALICS, PARENTHESES, AND DASHES ACCURATELY

READ AND DISCUSS

Examine these pairs or sets of sentences. Which sentences are easier to understand? What conclusion do you gather?

Bring me forty five pound boxes of candy.
Bring me forty-five pound boxes of candy.
Bring me forty five-pound boxes of candy.

You use too many *and*'s and *and so*'s.
You use too many and's and and so's.

These men, Lester, Frank, and Clyde, deserve praise.
These men—Lester, Frank, and Clyde—deserve praise.

Miss Lee, the winner (so I've heard), grew up in Texas.
Miss Lee, the winner, so I've heard, grew up in Texas.

Applying the rules for good use of hyphens, italics, parentheses, and dashes can help you to more effective written expression. Here they are, in two groups.

RULES FOR USING HYPHENS

The hyphen has two primary uses: (1) to form certain compound words and (2) to divide words at the end of a line.

RULE 1. **Use the hyphen to form certain compound nouns.** If in doubt whether to hyphenate, see your dictionary. Many such compounds are made of a *noun* and a *prepositional phrase.*

man-of-war   movie-goer   teen-ager   fly-by-night

RULE 2. **Use a hyphen to form most compound adjectives used** *before* **a noun. Do** *not* **use a hyphen in a** *compound predicate adjective* **unless the dictionary indicates that the word always needs a hyphen.**

A dark-blue sky arched above us.   Her eyes are dark blue.

RULE 3. **Use the hyphen to form** *compound numbers* **from** *twenty-one* **through** *ninety-nine,* **and to form** *fractions* **used as** *adjectives.*

thirty-seven   a three-fifths share   one hundred fifty-two

RULE 4. **Use a hyphen in forming most compounds that begin with** *self* **or** *half:* self-starter, half-moon. Consult your dictionary for usage with other prefixes.

RULE 5. **Use a hyphen after any** *prefix* **that is combined with a** *proper noun:* un-Christian.

RULE 6. **If two or more compound words have the same base, hyphenate as in this example:** ninth- and tenth-grade students.

RULE 7. **Use a hyphen in a compound title that contains** *vice, ex,* **or** *elect:* vice-consul, ex-manager, captain-elect.

RULE 8. **Use a hyphen to show the omission of a connecting word.**
Read pages 1-2. (1 *and* 2)
He travels the Omaha-Chicago route. (Omaha *to* Chicago)

RULE 9. **Use a hyphen between syllables if you must divide a word at the end of a line.** Certain specific rules apply.

a) Do *not* divide *proper names* or *words of one syllable.*
b) Do *not* divide after a *single letter. Wrong:* a-long
c) **Avoid carrying over a** *single syllable* **that has** *no vowel* **except a silent** *e:* wear-able, *not* weara-ble
d) Try to avoid carrying over a two-letter syllable: *ended,* not end-ed.
e) **Do not make a division that will cause pronunciation difficulties;** for example, write busi-ness, *not* bus-iness.

RULES FOR USING ITALICS, PARENTHESES, DASHES

In handwritten or typed material, *underscoring* takes the place of *italics*.

RULE 1. **Italicize the titles of** *books; of magazines* **and** *newspapers;* **of** *long plays, poems,* **and** *musical works;* **of** *ships, airplanes,* **and** *trains.*

       Cimarron   Look   Il Trovatore   the *Humming Bird*

RULE 2. **Italicize** *foreign words or expressions.* **Italicize** *figures, signs, letters,* **or** *words referred to simply as words.*

    très bien   *3*'s and *4*'s   *&*'s   *p*'s and *q*'s   .too many *then*'s

RULE 3. **Use italics, but sparingly, for** *emphasis* **or for** *terms with special meaning.* **As a rule, use** *quotation marks* **for the latter.** (Rule 4, page 176.)

    You are *not* to go.   What is the meaning of *blitzkrieg?*

RULE 4. **Use** *dashes* (*a*) **to emphasize** *appositives* **or to set off a** *series of them,* (*b*) **to indicate an** *abrupt change of thought,* (*c*) **to emphasize a** *parenthetical clause,* **or** (*d*) **to show** *hesitation.*

    a) My friends—Kay, Lou, and Wanda—will arrive tonight.
    b) She is—well, you know what I mean!
    c) May first—a day I well recall!—began uneventfully.
    d) I—I don't know what to tell you.

WARNING! Guard against overuse of the dash, especially in writing letters.

RULE 5. **Use** *parentheses* **to set off material only loosely connected with the rest of the sentence:** The talk (what I heard of it, at least) was excellent.

Dashes usually *emphasize* what comes between them; parentheses show that what comes between them is *unimportant* or *incidental.*

LEARNING ACTIVITIES

A. (1) Copy the following words. (2) Draw vertical lines to show places where the words may be divided at the end of a line. (3) Circle words that should not be divided. Exchange papers and check by the rules on page 182.

1. instant	3. above	5. elegant	7. capable	9. reveal
2. laughable	4. Robert	6. wasted	8. hopeless	10. elusive

B. Express these numbers and fractions correctly in words: 54, 87, 33, 61, $\frac{2}{5}$ (*share*), $\frac{1}{3}$ (*reduction*).

C. In your literature books or elsewhere, look for examples of the use of parentheses and dashes. Bring several examples to class.

D. Copy the following sentences. Underscore any titles that you think need underscoring. Combine by the use of hyphens any words that you believe should be compounded in that way. Go over your work in class.

1. One third of our class have read Life with Father.
2. Before I was twenty one, I had many get rich quick ideas.
3. I ate alone in a self service cafe, with a copy of the Saturday Evening Post propped up beside me.

4. Tonight I heard the opera Carmen; it was a never to be forgotten thrill.
5. In yesterday's Daily Times I read of a stranger than fiction happening.
6. In the play The Barretts of Wimpole Street, the father is self centered.

FOLLOW-UP ACTIVITY

Go over papers written for other classes. Check each word that you divided at the end of a line. Correct any errors. Use the words for class practice.

Just to make sure! *

Directions: As you do this activity, refer to the rules in this chapter. If you write the activity, go over the sentences orally.

Copy these sentences, supplying needed capitalization and punctuation.

1. read these novels let the hurricane roar the yearling and northwest passage
2. Suddenly Ken was startled to hear the announcer say Ellsworth K W
3. Three of our football players made the conference team joel smith center ron hunt quarterback and ed sibley fullback
4. I heard ohs and ahs from the happy excited girls in the next room
5. Pillows were on the floor papers were scattered about and a chair was upset
6. The missionarys closing words were from matthew 19 26 . . . with god all things are possible
7. The contestant who sent the best letter praising trill bird seed is employed at hale and harts new hardware store
8. In april 1954 I was a guest at longhorn ranch greeley colorado
9. My aunt harriet shes the one who has been to europe is here
10. You cant expect me to well why didnt you tell me sooner
11. Does the empire builder leave la crosse at 5 21 pm
12. Your sister in law can play st louis blues cant she
13. Yes I would choose Jon not Ted but the choice as you know is not mine
14. To Al Ed said what the reason is is not important
15. Ernie my roommate celebrated his twenty fifth birthday yesterday
16. I ordered lamb chops harry lobster
17. Did Marie say, my aunt and I ate in that chinese restaurant on locust street
18. last friday a major from the air base spoke to our aviation club
19. On memorial day we decorated graves in maple lawn cemetery
20. Tornadoes recently swept across the middle west
21. the quartering act required civil authorities to provide barracks and supplies for the british troops
22. at iowa state college im to study chemistry english literature foods and design. I may take french
23. Tonight dad has a meeting at the ioof hall
24. o shades of night—o gloomy awesome night!

* Check Tests 1 and 2 should be given at this point. If the results show need for further study, pupils should do this review practice. They should then take Mastery Tests 1 and 2.

Building Good Spelling Habits

"No, no, Rameses! How many times do I have to tell you—*horse* before *cow* except after *sow*!"*

READ AND DISCUSS

Just how important is the ability to spell correctly? What vocations can you name in which spelling plays little part? Even in such vocations, what advantages are there in being able to spell correctly?

* Reprinted from the *Saturday Review*.

Certainly, many activities call for a mastery of spelling. No one who must make frequent use of written language in his work can escape the responsibility of being a correct speller.

If you want to spell accurately, you should acquire certain spelling habits.

GUIDES TO GOOD SPELLING

1. Establish the habit of using the dictionary to check your spelling.
2. Observe the form of words with your eyes; hear them with your ears.
3. Let correct pronunciation and enunciation aid you in spelling words that give you difficulty.
4. Learn the rules that govern the spelling of many words. Be certain of the meaning of terms used in spelling rules (*vowel, consonant, syllable, prefix, suffix*), or the rules will mean little to you.
5. Correct every spelling error that is called to your attention.
6. Be determined to spell correctly.
7. Make up your own devices to fix in your mind the spelling of troublesome words.
   a) Find words within words: ve getable, business, ache.
   b) Pair a troublesome word with one that you know how to spell: dance, balance; gain, certain; rich, sandwich. Make up a sentence to help you remember: You are *certain* to *gain* much.

Be word-wise!

Skim the preceding guides for these words: *form, difficulty, devices.* Which of their synonyms, as given in the dictionary, would not be good substitutes for the words as used here? Which synonym of *form* does the drawing illustrate?

1. SPELLING BY RULES

Although English has many spelling peculiarities, most of the words in the language are spelled according to rules. Master those that follow (pages 187–90), and most of your spelling difficulties will disappear.

THE RULES

RULE 1. (Adding suffixes) As a rule, *drop* a final silent *e* before a suffix beginning with a *vowel; keep* the *e* before suffixes beginning with a *consonant:* love, loving, lovely.

EXCEPTIONS

a) *Keep* the *e* before a suffix beginning with a vowel if any confusion in pronunciation or in meaning would result from dropping it.

singe, singeing (Without the *e*, what word would you have?)
dye, dyeing (Without the *e*, what word would you have?)
acre, acreage   shoe, shoeing   mile, mileage

b) Drop *e* before the consonants in these words: *acknowledgment, abridgment, ninth* (but *ninety*), *truly.*

c) When final silent *e* is preceded by *c* or *g,* keep the *e* before a suffix beginning with *a* or *o* (*able, ous*): peaceable, courageous.

d) If a word ending in *e* is compounded with another word, keep the *e:* somewhere, therefore, hereby.

RULE 2. (Adding suffixes—*Continued*)

a) Double a final consonant preceded by one vowel in these two cases:

(1) If the word has one syllable and the suffix begins with a vowel: drop, dropping; hot, hottest

(2) If the accent in a word of more than one syllable is on the final syllable: forget', forgetting

b) Do *not* double a final consonant in these cases:

(1) If the suffix begins with a consonant, such as *ment* or *ness:* equip, equipment; bad, badness

(2) If the accent is not on the last syllable: o'pen, opened; mur'mur, murmuring

(3) If the consonant is preceded by more than one vowel: cool, cooler

(4) If the word ends in two consonants: start, starting

LEARNING ACTIVITIES IN ADDING SUFFIXES

A. (*Rule 1*) Form new words by adding suffixes to the following words. Write this exercise; then exchange papers for checking.

1. advance	8. decide	15. like	22. reduce
2. bake	9. encourage	16. love	23. sense
3. become	10. exchange	17. move	24. smile
4. compare	11. excite	18. nerve	25. sure
5. complete	12. give	19. please	26. use
6. continue	13. imagine	20. practice	27. value
7. contribute	14. introduce	21. race	28. write

B. (*Rule 2*) Form new words by adding suffixes. Proceed as in *A*.

1. alter	6. deliver	11. limit	16. permit	21. resign
2. appear	7. dig	12. linger	17. prefer	22. shop
3. assist	8. feel	13. mean	18. put	23. star
4. clean	9. formal	14. omit	19. refer	24. stop
5. commit	10. govern	15. perform	20. repeat	25. strong

THE RULES—Continued

RULE 3. (Forming plurals) **To form the plurals of most nouns, simply add** *s* **to the singular.**

EXCEPTIONS

a) **Add** *es* **to nouns ending in** *s, sh, ch, x,* **or** *z:* gas, gases, box, boxes.

b) **For nouns ending in** *y* **preceded by a** *consonant,* **change the** *y* **to** *i* **and add** *es:* story, stories; baby, babies.

c) **For nouns ending in** *y* **preceded by a** *vowel,* **simply add** *s:* key, keys.

d) **Add** *es* **to most common nouns ending in** *o,* **but add only** *s* **to** *musical terms* **and to most words having the** *o* **preceded by a** *vowel:* hero, heroes; alto, altos; cameo, cameos. **Certain words ending in** *o* **may be spelled correctly with either** *s* **or** *es:* motto, mottoes, mottos.

e) **For a few words ending in** *f* **or** *fe,* **change the** *f* **to** *v* **and add** *es:* self, selves; knife, knives. Check by the dictionary when in doubt.

f) **Learn the spelling of certain plurals that follow no rules:** *man, men; tooth, teeth; foot, feet; child, children; goose, geese; mouse, mice.*

g) Here are guides to the formation of plurals of *compound nouns:*

   (1) **As a rule, add** *s* **to the** *main word:* passer-by, passers-by; sister-in-law, sisters-in-law.

   (2) **With a few words, however, make both parts compound:** men-servants, knights templars.

   (3) **Add** *s* **to compounds ending in** *ful:* basketfuls, mouthfuls.

   (4) **As a rule, add** *s* **at the end of a** *compound word not containing a noun:* mix-ups; stand-ins.

h) **To** *proper names,* **add** *s* **or (if the name ends in** *s, sh, ch, x,* **or** *z* **) es.**
Tommy, two Tommys   Barnes, Barneses   Schwarz, Schwarzes
For *proper names preceded by titles,* **use either of two forms.**

Singular	Plural
Mr. Cates	Messrs. Cates *or* the Mr. Cateses
Miss Brady	the Miss Bradys *or* the Misses Brady

i) **For certain nouns borrowed from** *foreign languages,* **keep the foreign plurals:** alumnus, alumni; erratum, errata; thesis, theses.

j) **For some nouns, use the** *same* **form in both the** *singular* **and the** *plural.* Examples are *salmon, heathen, Sioux.*

k) **To** *signs, numbers, letters,* **and** *words used simply as words,* **add** *'s:* %'s, 2's, *k*'s, *or*'s.

LEARNING ACTIVITIES IN FORMING PLURALS

A. Write the plurals of the following words. Exchange papers for checking as the plurals are spelled orally.

1. Mr. Roe	8. business	15. echo	22. silo	29. alley	36. pony
2. bathhouse	9. Iroquois	16. life	23. cuff	30. hoof	37. minute
3. go-between	10. railway	17. 5	24. buzz	31. lunch	38. bush
4. stiletto	11. library	18. solo	25. studio	32. thief	39. nobody
5. drum major	12. fireman	19. wolf	26. child	33. Jones	40. match
6. son-in-law	13. duty	20. inch	27. berry	34. gypsy	41. essay
7. talisman	14. *	21. calf	28. Healy	35. proof	42. woman

B. Write the foreign plurals of these words. (Some of them also have an English spelling.) Proceed as in *A*. Use the dictionary to help you.

1. crisis	4. index	7. tableau	10. señor	13. cumulus
2. beau	5. datum	8. alumna	11. stratum	14. vertebra
3. larva	6. oasis	9. chapeau	12. tempo	15. analysis

THE RULES—Continued

RULE 4. (Using prefixes) **In using the prefixes** *mis* **or** *dis,* **do** *not drop* **any letters** *from,* **or** *add* **any letters** *to,* **the original word.**

mis + spell = misspell	dis + satisfy = dissatisfy
dis + appoint = disappoint	mis + lead = mislead

RULE 5. (Words containing *ie* or *ei*)

a) **Use** *ei* **after** *c* **or if it has the sound of long** *a:* receive, weigh, ceiling.

b) **Use** *ie* **in cases not covered by (***a***).**

field	thief	fierce	apiece	lieutenant
niece	friend	sieve	yield	shield
relieve	cashier	pierce	priest	fiend

c) **Learn these exceptions to (***a***) and (***b***):**

either	species	efficient	leisure	forfeit
financier	weird	counterfeit	height	foreign
seize	neither	conscience	ancient	sovereign

LEARNING ACTIVITIES IN SPELLING WITH PREFIXES

A. Combine either *mis* or *dis* with each of the following words to form new words. Write this exercise and check it in class.

1. ability	6. solve	11. approve	16. advantage	21. sent
2. qualify	7. oblige	12. similar	17. pronounce	22. arm
3. please	8. state	13. appear	18. connect	23. step
4. doing	9. apply	14. behave	19. understand	24. obey
5. infect	10. agree	15. inherit	20. orderly	25. lay

B. Study the lists of *ie* and *ei* words carefully; then make a list in which you mix them. Choose a partner and work on spelling the words for each other.

THE RULES—Continued

RULE 6. (Words ending in *y*)

a) **When you add the suffix** *ing* **to a verb, do not change the spelling of the original word:** hurry, hurrying; delay, delaying.*

b) **When you write the** *third person present* **or the** *past* **or the** *past participle,* **follow these guides:**

    (1) **Change the** *y* **to** *i* **if preceded by a** *consonant:* try, tries, tried.

    (2) **Do** *not* **change the spelling if the** *y* **is preceded by a** *vowel:* dismay, dismays, dismayed. Exceptions are *laid, paid, said,* and *slain.*

c) **For most** *adjectives* **or** *nouns* **ending in** *y* **preceded by a** *consonant,* **change the** *y* **to** *i* **when adding a suffix:** dizzy, dizzily; glory, glorious. **If the** *y* **is preceded by a** *vowel,* **simply add the suffix:** gray, grayer, grayest; † joy, joyous, joyful.

RULE 7. **Learn the only three words that end in** *ceed:* exceed, succeed, proceed; **and the only one that ends in** *sede:* supersede. **For all others with a similar syllable sound, write** *cede:* precede, secede, recede, concede, . . .

LEARNING ACTIVITIES

The following activities call for the application of Rule 6. Conduct both oral and written practice over these activities.

A. (1) Add *ing* to each of the following verbs. (2) Form the *third person present* and the *past participle* of each.

1. pray	3. cry	5. pay	7. stray	9. study	11. enjoy
2. stay	4. imply	6. deny	8. annoy	10. defy	12. carry

B. Add *ance, ous, ment, ly,* or *ness* to each of the following words.

1. annoy	3. holy	5. juicy	7. showy	9. rusty	11. ghostly
2. defy	4. vary	6. injury	8. weary	10. worthy	12. harmony

REVIEW PRACTICE ON WORDS SPELLED BY RULES

Spell orally the following words and give the rule that fits each. You may prefer to use this exercise as a check test on words spelled by rules. In that case, write the words from dictation; then exchange papers for checking. As the

---

* For the few verbs that end in *ie,* drop the *e* and change the *i* to *y.* Examples: *die, dying; lie, lying.*

† Only three common adjectives have *y* preceded by a vowel: *gray* (or *grey*), *gay,* and *coy.*

words are spelled orally, explain the spelling by quoting from the rules that apply. Score two points for each correct spelling. A perfect score is 90.

1. acknowledgment
2. advantageous
3. advisable
4. excitement
5. buys
6. calves
7. ceiling
8. chopping
9. deceit
10. denying
11. denies
12. disagree
13. exceed
14. expedient
15. finally
16. forfeit
17. freight
18. generally
19. hoeing
20. hygiene
21. inches
22. lovable
23. loveliness
24. management
25. mileage
26. misinform
27. missent
28. monkeys
29. mosquitoes
30. mysteries
31. nervous
32. noticeable
33. pianos
34. practically
35. preferred
36. roofs
37. seize
38. serviceable
39. singeing
40. sopranos
41. studying
42. usually
43. wives
44. women
45. worthiness

2. MASTERING OTHER SPELLING DIFFICULTIES

Sometimes failure to spell a word correctly is not due to the violation of any particular rule. Some words contain trouble spots that are traceable to (1) mispronunciation, (2) silent letters in the word, (3) faulty knowledge of syllabication, or (4) faulty knowledge of the sound of certain letters or combinations.

Other difficulties are not a matter of misspelling a word but of confusing it with some other word. That other word may be (1) a *homonym* (pronounced like the word but spelled differently), (2) a *near-homonym,* or (3) a word that is similar in its spelling. For example, *their* and *there* are homonyms; *weather* and *whether* are near-homonyms; *angel* and *angle* are words similar in spelling.

ANGLE OR ANGEL?   CLOTHS OR CLOTHES?   DAIRY OR DIARY?

LEARNING ACTIVITIES IN MISCELLANEOUS SPELLING PROBLEMS

A. Here is a list of words that are often misspelled. Go over them in class. Decide where the trouble spots are and what makes them difficult. Think of devices to help you master the correct spelling. (See the list of guides, especially 7, on page 186.) Then use the words in a spelldown or a written lesson.

1. accommodate	18. destroy	35. philosophy
2. accurate	19. diphtheria	36. physiology
3. application	20. drowned	37. picnicking
4. appreciation	21. duchess	38. practicable
5. architect	22. equally	39. practical
6. assistance	23. familiar	40. prejudice
7. attacked	24. fatigue	41. psychology
8. awkward	25. galoshes	42. respectfully
9. barbarous	26. harass	43. rheumatism
10. brilliant	27. heir	44. rhythm
11. burglar	28. inconvenience	45. sufficient
12. character	29. lightning	46. superintendent
13. chasm	30. mathematics	47. synonym
14. conscience	31. nuisance	48. village
15. conscious	32. occupy	49. villain
16. courteous	33. often	50. witch
17. crowd	34. permission	

B. Here are pairs or groups of words often confused. Many of them are homonyms. To show that you can tell them apart, give sentences using the words. Pronounce a word; then spell it; then give the sentence. Make this a small-group activity. Be careful to pronounce the words accurately. As the sentences are given, the other members of the group should listen attentively so that they can judge spelling, usage, and pronunciation.

1. accept—except	15. desert—dessert	29. presence—presents
2. affect—effect	16. dual—duel	30. principal—principle
3. angel—angle	17. dyeing—dying	31. quiet—quit—quite
4. allowed—aloud	18. formally—formerly	32. rain—reign—rein
5. all ready—already	19. hear—here	33. right—rite—write
6. bare—bear	20. hole—whole	34. shone—shown
7. berth—birth	21. later—latter	35. stationary—stationery
8. born—borne	22. lead—led	36. steal—steel
9. capital—capitol	23. loose—lose	37. straight—strait
10. cite—sight—site	24. miner—minor	38. their—there—they're
11. clothes—cloths	25. passed—past	39. then—than
12. coarse—course	26. peace—piece	40. thorough—through
13. council—counsel	27. plain—plane	41. weather—whether
14. dairy—diary	28. precede—proceed	42. your—you're

C. Practice writing from dictation any of the following sentences that you and your teacher feel will be helpful to you.

1. I suppose that everyone except me will accept the invitation.
2. Did the rain affect your plans? No, it had no effect on them.

3. Just inside my angle of vision was a cake, an angel food.
4. Of course, it is better to use coarse thread for this work.
5. Mr. Hall, formerly our mayor, was dressed formally.
6. Do you know whether the weather forecast has been given?
7. I am quite sure that he will quit his job. He says that he needs a quiet place to work.
8. Just then a louder voice than mine spoke up.
9. In the past, many great men have passed this place.
10. I'm sorry to desert you before the dessert is served.
11. I could not bear to touch it with my bare hand.
12. Our clothes are made of many different cloths.
13. Milk comes from a dairy; thoughts go into a diary.
14. Tell me the whole truth. Who dug that hole in the yard?
15. The boys left their bicycles there in the shade. They're coming back for them later.
16. I hear that a circus will be here in June.
17. To keep the peace, I gave each child an equal piece of cake.
18. At the meeting we were not allowed to speak aloud.
19. I have already said that we are all ready.
20. The crimson glow of the dying sun was dyeing the landscape.
21. Just after the guide had shown us over the grounds, the sun came out and shone brightly.
22. Who would steal anything as heavy as a steel safe?
23. I hope that we shall be stationary at Fort Dix for a year. If so, I shall order some engraved stationery.
24. The latter of those two men will return later.
25. That lead pipe must be led through the opening.

D. What words within words can you find to help you to remember how to spell the troublesome words in the following list? Analyze each word first to find the troublesome part or parts. Make this either a class or a small-group activity. Be sure that your suggestions will help with the troublesome part of the word.

1. before	11. instead	21. afraid	31. resource
2. meant	12. congratulate	22. soldier	32. grateful
3. among	13. captain	23. against	33. pleasant
4. ninety	14. romantic	24. villain	34. cemetery
5. spread	15. beginning	25. museum	35. vacation
6. ghost	16. studying	26. expense	36. excellent
7. tenor	17. permanent	27. tragedy	37. dreadful
8. client	18. peaceable	28. referee	38. familiar
9. prairie	19. candidate	29. definite	39. parallel
10. wholly	20. personally	30. grammar	40. existence

E. Here is a paragraph containing misspelled words, all taken from actual student themes. In class or in your small groups, go over this theme. (1) Analyze the misspellings to see what may be responsible for the errors—*mispronunciation,* *lack of knowledge of spelling rules, confusion with another word,* . . . (2) Suggest how the writer might master the spelling of each misspelled word. (3) Rewrite the paragraph, correcting all misspelled words. Underline your corrections. *Be sure to proofread.* Exchange papers for checking as the sentences are read aloud and the words spelled.

Time was out with less than a *minite* remaining to be *plaid* in the *finial* quarter. The score at this point *favered* our team, 21–20. It had been a *wounderful* game to watch. During *practiclly* the entire second half the ball had been in *posession* of our *oponnents,* led by that *magnificient vetern athelete,* Projiliak, *thier* All-*Americian captian* who was being highly *reccommended* to *proffesional* football scouts. He had *definately* been the outstanding *indivitual preformer* on the field today, *overwellming* our players with his *beatiful* kicks, *terrizing* them with his *sparkeling* runs, and *litterally stagering* them with *surprize* passes when they were least *exspected.* But when he had put his team in *stratigic* scoring position on *differnt ocassions,* the home team had made *galliant, stuborn* defensive stands. Just *previus* to this time-out, the *vistors,* who *allways opperated* from a T-formation, had *oppened hugh* holes in the line on three *consecitive* plays with scatbacks *scurring* through for *substancial* gains. On the second-to-last play, they had *choosen* to run *arround* right end and again were *sucesful* in making the *neccesary destence* for a first down. Then the attack had *collasped* when Projiliak's *stradegy* had backfired. A *desparation* pass was attempted to the *elongaited* left end, *distination* end zone. It was an *ancious* moment as the pass appeared *compleeted, similiar* to *farely routeen* passes *whitch* he had *handeled* all during the game. A touchdown seemed *inevidable.* But from *knowhere* our safety man appeared, *streched* high into the air, and *cluched* the pigskin from the grasp of the *throughly puzzeled* end. We had the ball on an *interseption!* With play *interupted, ownly fourty* seconds of the quarter remained. *Knowone* knew what the final *decission* would be, *all though* it *dident* seem that our team would have any *troble* holding the ball *untill* the *offical's finial wistle.* Some *woundered wheather* it was too soon for *congradulations,* but just then the gun sounded, and it was *appearent* to all that this *extrordinary thieft* had *deceided* the outcome. What an *expierence!*

USING ENGLISH IN ALL CLASSES

For each of your classes, make a special list of difficult words that have to do with that subject. Bring your lists to class and practice spelling them from dictation or in spelldowns or in any other helpful way.

FOLLOW-UP ACTIVITY

If you are not already keeping and drilling upon your own list of troublesome words, begin such a list now. Put into it the correct spelling of any words that you misspell in any written work that you do; then practice to make their correct forms habitual. Use the guides on page 186 to help you.

Setting Standards
for Writing

"YOU'VE WRITTEN A MYSTERY STORY, ALL RIGHT—
I CAN FIGURE OUT ONLY
ABOUT HALF THE WORDS IN IT."

READ AND THINK ABOUT

What do you think should be the writing ability of students who have
had ten or more years of training in the public schools of America? Have
they had practice enough during those years to express themselves on paper
clearly, logically, and legibly? Can *you* express yourself in those ways?

195

As a measure of your present abilities in the field of written communication, follow carefully the directions for this pretest theme.

Directions: To ensure that all themes are written under the same conditions, proceed as follows:

1. Write the theme in the classroom, without outside preparation. Bring no notes, outlines, or first drafts to class with you.
2. Write a first draft in class and copy it before handing it in.
3. Do not take your paper from the classroom. If one class period is not long enough for completing the theme, perhaps your teacher will allot another period for it.
4. Form your own title, based upon one of the subjects listed below.
5. Use the customary tools and write in your best style.
6. Make your theme at least one page in length.

SUBJECTS

Habits I Want to Form	The Type of Person I Most Admire
Habits I Want to Break	My Most Serious English Problems
Things I Fear	Silly Habits (Styles, Games, . . .)
People I Want to Know	The Best Thing in the World

Your teacher will score this theme by the score card on page 197. Afterwards, he will help you to record the types of errors that you made and will point out your particular needs. Put this record into your notebook to use as a guide in your own practice writing.

1. STUDYING THE SCORE CARD

The items on the score card may not be new to you, but it is a good idea to review them in class to be sure that you understand them.

You will note that your themes are to be graded separately on form and content. Your teacher may indicate this grading on your themes by a mark such as *B/A,* with the letter before the line showing the grade on *content* and the letter after the line showing the grade on *form.* Why is it a good idea to have form and content graded separately?

Modify the score card, if necessary, to fit your particular needs. Make a copy of it to use as a guide in writing and as a means of scoring all your written activities. Check first on the chart the results of your test theme. Use that record as a standard to measure your improvement as you advance. Unless your teacher suggests other markings, use these symbols: *F* for *fair; P* for *poor; I* for *improving; G* for *good.* Under *Corrections made,* use *Ck* if your errors were few enough in number for you to rewrite only the parts containing them; use *Rw* if you have rewritten a paper completely.

196

Writing Score Card

Name *Lila Loring* Date	9/8							
Theme number	1							
I. Content								
A. Choice of topic	G							
B. Sticking to topic	F							
C. Development of idea	F							
D. Beginning and ending	P							
E. Vocabulary								
1. Variety	F							
2. Effectiveness	F							
II. Form								
A. Mechanics								
1. Manuscript form	P							
2. Capitalization	F							
3. Punctuation	P							
4. Spelling	G							
B. Structure								
1. Sentences								
a. Unity	F							
b. Variety	P							
2. Paragraphs								
a. One central thought	F							
b. Development	F							
c. Relationship to others	F							
3. Grammatical usage	P							
III. Grade (if given)								
A. Content	C+							
B. Form	D							
IV. Corrections made	Rw							

SUGGESTIONS FOR IMPROVING WRITTEN WORK

1. Organize into committees of students with similar needs. They should work together to set standards, score work, and help those who have difficulties. As one achieves a satisfactory degree of mastery of a problem, he should advance to another group.
2. Occasionally choose names and work in pairs. Read each other's work and mark it by the score card. Confer on methods of revision.
3. Never give the person who is to score your paper anything but your best work. Correct every paper in the way that the teacher suggests.
4. Unless directed otherwise, keep all your themes in consecutive order in a folder or notebook. Use them as a record of your growth.
5. Use errors made in your themes as material for practice. Sometimes write on the blackboard sentences containing errors. Ask classmates to help find and correct them. From your themes, make lists of spelling words, punctuation uses, and sentence difficulties that you need to master.
6. Bring into English class written activities from other subjects and use them for themes in English.
7. Confer with your teacher on points that trouble you.

2. Marks of Correction

Marks	Meaning
1. cap	(1) capital letter needed or (2) capital unnecessarily used
2. sp	mistake in spelling
3. p	mistake in punctuation
4. ¶	new paragraph needed
5. no ¶	new paragraph not needed
6. mar	faulty margin
7. head	heading incorrectly placed or incomplete
8. ill	illegible handwriting
9. syl	syllabication (*word incorrectly or poorly divided*)
10. F	fragment (*not a complete sentence*)
11. RO	run-on sentence
12. voc	vocabulary (*poor word choice*)
13. abb	(1) incorrect abbreviation or (2) no abbreviation permissible
14. K	clumsy or awkward construction
15. ?	not clear
16. #	more space needed between words
17. ∧	something omitted
18. agr	agreement (*pronoun with antecedent, verb with subject*)
19. u	faulty usage (*illiterate expression, slang*)
20. gr	faulty grammar
21. t	wrong tense of verb

Studying How to Build Paragraphs and Themes

1. LEARNING TYPES OF PARAGRAPH DEVELOPMENT

READ AND THINK ABOUT

Prose writing is divided into paragraphs. Each paragraph is built around a *central idea,* which may be stated in a *topic sentence,* or *topic statement.*

Careful thinkers form good paragraphs naturally and logically. Beginning writers can gain much by studying certain definite types of paragraph development and then practicing them. Many paragraphs are a combination of types, but practice in specific types offers good training.

GUIDES TO THE DEVELOPMENT OF THE PARAGRAPH

1. Make the central idea clear. In paragraphs of explanation, state that central idea in a *topic sentence,* which as a rule should be the first sentence, but which may come at the end or within the paragraph.
2. Check each paragraph to see that it has *unity;* that is, that every sentence in it is related to the central idea.
3. Check each paragraph for *coherence;* that is, to see that the ideas expressed by the various sentences are arranged in a logical order. (See page 254 for different types of order.)
4. Be sure that *emphasis* (sometimes called *force*) on the central idea is evident. Now and then you can secure effective emphasis by use of a *clincher sentence* that sums up the idea in the paragraph or reinforces the topic sentence. (Do not tack a clincher sentence to every paragraph; use one only for effective emphasis.)
5. Develop a paragraph by using *definitions, details, comparison or contrast, cause and effect, illustrations or examples, repetition,* or any *combination* of methods that will be most helpful.

DEVELOPING A PARAGRAPH BY DEFINITIONS

The kind of paragraph that develops an idea by defining words or explaining thoughts is common in your textbooks.

The word "liberty" is often interpreted incorrectly. The dictionary gives many exact definitions of the word; briefly, it means "freedom from restraint or control." Such a brief definition leads to misinterpretation. Many people think liberty means that they may do whatever they like, regardless of the effects. Liberty is not uncontrolled freedom. Real liberty involves thinking of the other fellow and giving up your desires if they will harm him. If it is to be enjoyed by everyone, then everyone must give up the idea that liberty means freedom from all restraint or control. Everyone must live by the true meaning, "self-disciplined freedom."

LEARNING ACTIVITIES

A. Study the paragraph defining liberty; then discuss the following questions or answer them in writing.

1. In how many ways does the paragraph define liberty?
2. Why is the dictionary definition alone unsatisfactory?
3. Quote the sentence that tells what liberty is not.

B. From various textbooks, bring other paragraphs developed by definition. Read one of your paragraphs to the class. Show how each sentence helps to bring out the meaning of the term being defined. Apply the Guides to Effective Oral Reading, page 41.

C. Develop one of the following ideas by the use of definitions. Tell what the word or thing *is not* as well as what it *is*.

1. A real sports fan is one who . . .
2. If one is called a "hard-boiled" person, it means . . .
3. Patriotism is . . .
4. "Now, James, just what do you mean by saying that you want an 'old-fashioned' girl?"
   "I mean just this: *The old-fashioned girl is* . . ."

DEVELOPING A PARAGRAPH BY GIVING DETAILS

A common way to expand an idea into a paragraph is to give details; that is, to add descriptive matter that fills out the picture.

Speed is the word that marks our time. Everybody is in a hurry to go somewhere, to do something, to see somebody. Industry is constantly demanding new inventions that will "speed up" production, and the constant cry of the bosses to the workmen is "Speed it up!" The maker of automobiles has as his proudest boast that the newest type of car goes faster than the old models. Shoppers push and shove each other all about the counters in a hurry to get something for nothing. People going to school, shop, or office rush breathlessly to unimportant tasks. They gulp their food and swallow it in haste. Restless "hunters of fun" crowd into places of entertainment. Most of these people cannot sit still. At a movie, they tap their feet or wiggle their tongues or click their teeth on gum; at a dance, they swing and whirl madly. It's a hurry-up time we are in.

LEARNING ACTIVITIES IN DEVELOPING A PARAGRAPH BY DETAILS

A. Study the preceding example. Find the topic sentence; then list the details that support it.

B. Find and read to the class a descriptive paragraph that makes good use of details. State the central idea and name the details added.

C. Add details to develop one of the following topic sentences into a paragraph. Think out your details carefully. Remember that the topic sentence need not come first. Read your paragraph to the class, applying the Guides to Effective Oral Reading, page 41. Call upon members to discuss your use of details. If you developed your paragraph either deductively or inductively, explain.

1. The ideal teacher has certain definite qualities.
2. The country is the place for a real vacation.
3. Early morning sounds in the country are pleasant (*or* annoying).
4. The movie . . . is outstanding.

DEVELOPING A PARAGRAPH BY COMPARISON OR CONTRAST

Sometimes the central idea of a paragraph is made clearer by a series of contrasts or comparisons. Often both methods are used in a paragraph.

With the coming of the automobile, life changed greatly in the country. Before they had automobiles, farmers could not go to town often because their horse-drawn wagons took so long to get there. Once a week or once a month, perhaps, the farmer went to town to get his supplies. Because of those infrequent visits to town, the farmer made more of the things he used than he makes today. He read less because he was not so well-educated as today and because there was no rural free delivery service. He had to go into town for his mail; now he has the daily paper delivered to his door. The farmer knows more people in town than he used to. Today most farmers' sons and daughters attend high school; before the automobile, few did so, because they had no means of transportation to town.*

* Curtis Fuller, *The Motor Car in American Life,* pages 43–44 (adapted). "Basic Social Education Series." Evanston, Illinois: Row, Peterson and Company, 1941.

LEARNING ACTIVITIES IN DEVELOPING A PARAGRAPH BY COMPARISON OR CONTRAST

A. Name the ways mentioned in which country life is different today from what it was before the days of the automobile. What other points of contrast can you add? What comparisons can you give to show ways in which life on the farm has not changed? If you live on a farm, talk these things over at home and report what your parents say about them. Use your Speech Score Card.

B. Use one of these five statements to develop a paragraph by comparison, contrast, or both. Vary your sentence structure to avoid monotony. (Pages 410–17 will give you help.) Read and discuss your paragraphs in class, or exchange them for written criticism.

1. City life offers many contrasts to rural life.
2. She reminds me of a girl I used to know.
3. In handling Father, different tactics must be used from those used on Mother.
4. My brother (*or* sister) and I are exact opposites.
5. Dogs make better pets than cats.
6. On the outside, the two houses are much alike.

C. Write a paragraph comparing or contrasting two men whom you have met in your reading for social studies, two characters in a book that you are reading, two processes or methods of conducting a science experiment or of solving a problem in mathematics. If you prefer, write a paragraph suggested by the drawings. Go over your paragraphs as in *B*.

DEVELOPING A PARAGRAPH BY CAUSE AND EFFECT OR BY GIVING REASONS

Some ideas are developed by stating either the causes or the results of incidents or actions. The following paragraph is an illustration.

> Beating full in our teeth, the snow came fast and blinding. To see was impossible; the fine particles so stung our eyeballs that we could not look ahead. My eyelashes were loaded with snow, which immediately turned to ice and froze the lids together unless I kept them in constant motion. Although there was a crust of ice a quarter of an inch thick on our cheeks, and the ice in our beards prevented us from opening our mouths, we kept warm. At one o'clock we reached the second station, Gefre, unrecognizable by our nearest friends. Our eyelashes were weighed down with heavy fringes of frozen snow; there were icicles an inch long hanging to the eaves of our mustaches; and the handkerchiefs which wrapped our faces were frozen fast to the flesh.*

LEARNING ACTIVITIES

A. State in a clear sentence the central idea of the preceding paragraph. List the effects of the severe snowstorm.

B. Develop one of the following statements by the use of cause and effect. Read and discuss your paragraphs in class.

1. The automobile has provided man not only with one of his greatest luxuries but also with a great enemy.
2. Ill health changes a person in many ways.
3. The people who settled America came for many different reasons.
4. Failure in a school subject may have serious results.
5. The home is no longer a center of family life.

USING ENGLISH IN ALL CLASSES

A. If you write science experiments in paragraph form, bring a sample to class for examination and criticism.

B. In your social science textbook, find a paragraph that shows this type of development. Read it to the class and justify your choice.

DEVELOPING A PARAGRAPH BY ILLUSTRATIONS OR EXAMPLES

The central idea of a paragraph may be developed by the use of one or more illustrations or examples. Read the following example. Select the topic statement and notice the illustration.

* From *Northern Travel* by Bayard Taylor.

My parents, like other fond mamas and papas, still repeat the "bright" remarks that I made as a small child. For example, one day I heard my mother say that she certainly had her hands full. I immediately informed her that she was just fooling herself, for she hadn't a thing in her hands! Another time, when I saw a team of horses with their tails knotted up in ribbons, I ran to tell Mother about the pretty horses with marbles in their tails. My grandfather, who visited us often, always began his opening remarks in the same way; therefore one day when I saw him coming, I exclaimed, "Oh, here comes Wella! Wella! Wella!" Mother also tells of my comment when I heard her read a letter in which my uncle, a waiter, wrote about spending his "tips." I wanted to know who in the world would sell him anything for *tips!* You see, I thought that the tips customers left were the chicken-wing-tips that they couldn't eat!

LEARNING ACTIVITIES IN DEVELOPING PARAGRAPHS BY EXAMPLES OR ILLUSTRATIONS

A. In class or in your small groups, analyze the preceding example.

1. What is the topic sentence?
2. How many examples support the topic sentence?
3. What would be a good clincher sentence?

B. Develop one of the following topic statements into a paragraph by the use of illustrations or examples. Read your paragraphs in class. Discuss the examples given. Do they clinch the central idea?

1. It is possible to have too many friends.
2. I can laugh now at some of my childhood fears.
3. You can't always believe what you hear.
4. Everyone has embarrassing moments.

C. Listen carefully to a radio talk, a sermon, or any public address. Notice how a good speaker uses illustrations to liven up parts of his talk that might otherwise lose the attention of his audience. Report to the class on specific examples that you have observed. Use your Speech Score Card.

USING ENGLISH IN ALL CLASSES

In textbooks for any of your classes, find paragraphs developed by illustrations or examples. Read at least one paragraph to the class. Apply the Guides to Effective Oral Reading, page 41.

DEVELOPING A PARAGRAPH BY REPETITION

Often a paragraph can best be developed by numerous repetitions, in different forms, of the topic sentence. This method is particularly valuable in trying to persuade people to believe something or in trying to impress them with a vivid picture of a situation.

Danger! In the piney woods and on the prairie, it stalked everyone—men, women, and children. Danger walked with them by day and lay down with them at night. Because the clearings of the settlers were far apart, the price of life was constant vigilance. Nobody could tell when the raiders would come whooping out of the brush to kill the settlers and run off the stock. Long and appalling is the record of Indian atrocities along the Texas frontier. Danger to life and property was in the very air that the pioneers breathed.*

LEARNING ACTIVITIES IN DEVELOPING A PARAGRAPH BY REPETITION

A. What point does the author make in the preceding paragraph? In how many ways does he express that idea? Discuss these questions in class.

B. Write a paragraph in which you develop an idea by the use of repetition. Build your paragraph around a specific mood or impression, such as *speed, fear, gloom, comfort, jealousy*. Read your paragraphs for class evaluation.

DEVELOPING A PARAGRAPH BY A COMBINATION OF METHODS

You have been studying six different ways of developing paragraphs. Oftener than not, paragraphs combine one or more methods.

The story of the Northwest Mounted is an inspiring one. They stamped out the illicit whiskey traffic and saw that the greedy traders paid the natives a fair price for furs. In their dealings with the Blackfeet and with the other Plains Indians, they dealt fairly. So great was their prestige, so sure were the wild red men of fair play, that Canada escaped the depredations and massacres so common in the United States. This situation was true not only because the troopers were exceptionally fine men, but also because the whole intent of the Canadian government was to treat the tribes justly. In our country . . . treaties made by one administration were ignored by the next. The Apaches and the Cheyennes, as well as the other tribes, learned that they could not depend upon pacts solemnly signed and ratified. This knowledge put them into a state of mind ready for war.†

LEARNING ACTIVITIES

A. In class, study the preceding paragraph carefully. Find in it examples of *cause and effect, details, examples, contrast,* and *repetition.*

* William MacLeod Raine, *45-Caliber Law: The Way of Life of the Frontier Peace Officer*, page 10 (adapted). "The Way of Life Series." Evanston, Illinois: Row, Peterson and Company, 1941.

† *Ibid.*, page 58 (adapted).

B. Use a combination of methods to develop one of the following topic sentences. Read and discuss your paragraphs in class.

1. Some people are very changeable by nature.
2. The weather affects our dispositions.
3. Even people who won't admit it enjoy being flattered.
4. Camping out has its drawbacks as well as its pleasures.

USING ENGLISH IN ALL CLASSES

Bring to class papers written for other classes. Decide how you have developed the paragraphs. Can you see ways in which a different method or a combination of methods would improve them? Try rewriting them.

2. BUILDING PARAGRAPHS INTO THEMES

Prose writing is broken up into paragraphs to make the development of ideas easier to follow. A well-written theme has a definite pattern.

● **WHAT TO REMEMBER ABOUT THE PATTERN OF A THEME**

1. A well-written theme begins with a *short introductory paragraph* that states the topic to be discussed.
2. It closes with a short paragraph that is a *summary*, a *climax*, or a *conclusion* drawn from the preceding paragraphs.
3. Between the opening and closing paragraphs are the paragraphs that make up the *main body* of the theme. They must proceed in a smooth, connected fashion.
4. A skillful writer uses special connecting devices, called *transition words* and *transition paragraphs*, to tie the theme together.
   a) Sometimes a *linking word* or *phrase* is used; that is, such an expression as *then, too, in like manner, in contrast, . . .*
   b) Often a *key word, phrase,* or *clause* from the central idea of the preceding paragraph is repeated, usually in the first sentence.

Be word-wise!

Skim the preceding explanation for these words: *pattern, proceed, smooth, special.* Which dictionary synonyms would not be good substitutes for the words as used in this lesson? Which synonym of *smooth* does the drawing illustrate?

Study the following theme; then answer in class the questions that follow it.

WHAT IT MEANS TO BE PRESIDENT *

Introductory paragraph

We can learn the powers and duties of the Chief Executive by reading Article II of the Constitution. But that Article will not tell us why the Presidency is now the world's most important and difficult job.

Transition

In doing this job, the President must first of all carry out the laws passed by the Congress. Second, he must keep order in all parts of the nation. He must see that each state is protected from invasion and violence.

Transition

In addition to the preceding duties, the President has another important task—that of appointing thousands of officials. These range from ambassadors down to postmasters for small towns. Although the Senate has to approve these appointments, the President's choice is usually final.

Transition

Thus the President is busy many hours day and night. He must spend much time studying, vetoing, or signing bills; appointing officials; holding Cabinet meetings; seeing foreign officials; discussing needed bills with members of Congress. Often he must talk over the long-distance telephone with an ambassador abroad.

Transition paragraph

For, throughout his busy hours, the President must keep in touch with all parts of the world. He is responsible for our relations with other nations. His words and actions may help to keep peace, or they may bring us close to war.

Transition

When war actually breaks out, the powers of the President become very great. During the War between the North and the South, for example, President Lincoln increased the size of the Army and the Navy. Usually this is the work of Congress. Lincoln also spent public money without the approval of Congress. He declared the slaves free. He deprived many citizens of their constitutional rights for a short time.

Transition

During the World War of 1914–1918, Congress granted President Wilson *even broader powers than Lincoln had taken* for himself. Wilson had the right to fix prices and to take over for war purposes railroads, factories, and supplies of coal and food.

Conclusion

Whether in peace or war, the states are united in "a more perfect union" by the leadership of their Chief Executive.

1. To what ideas in the preceding paragraphs do the various italicized transitional expressions refer? Be specific.

2. What two main ideas does the transition paragraph join? Are they indicated in the opening paragraph? Explain your answer.

3. Is the final paragraph a *summary,* a *conclusion,* or a *climax?*

* Benjamin Brodinsky, *Our Federal Government,* pages 16–17 (adapted). "Basic Social Education Series." Evanston, Illinois: Row, Peterson and Company, 1941.

3. Setting Standards for Building Themes

Use the following questions as a check on the development of each theme that you write. Until you have established the habit of careful paragraph organization, it may be a good idea to write complete answers to the questions. Hand them in with your theme.

APPRAISAL QUESTIONS ON THEME DEVELOPMENT

1. Have I a definite idea to develop in the entire theme? (*State it.*)
2. Is each paragraph organized about one central idea? (*In your theme, underline this idea; or, if it is not expressed, write a statement of it.*)
3. Have I used words, phrases, or short paragraphs to link paragraphs? (*In your theme, underline these links, or label them in the margin.*)
4. Does my introductory paragraph give the main idea?
5. Is there a satisfactory last paragraph?
6. Have I used varied methods of paragraph development? (*In the margin of your theme, label the methods used.*)

LEARNING ACTIVITIES IN BUILDING PARAGRAPHS INTO THEMES

Directions: If possible, do all the following activities. Check each theme by the appraisal questions and by the Writing Score Card, page 197. Read and criticize the themes in your small groups. Be fair but honest in your appraisal.

A. Develop one of the following topics into a theme of several paragraphs.

1. A bus station
2. Buying a pair of shoes
3. Little brothers (*or* sisters)
4. Women's clothes (*or* hats)

B. Here are two introductory paragraphs. Develop one of them into a theme. Perhaps you can use inductive or deductive reasoning. (See pages 10–12.)

> One of the easiest subjects to talk about in the whole world is how other people ought to run their lives.

> We should have won our last game. Look at the facts.

C. Here are two concluding paragraphs. Write a theme to fit one of them.

> It remains for all of us—parents, teachers, church leaders, and young people themselves—to attack the problem. Let's get to work!

> As I stagger home with my load of packages, one happy thought is in my mind. No more Christmas shopping for another year!

USING ENGLISH IN ALL CLASSES

If you soon will need to make a report or write a theme for any class, use the appraisal questions on this page to guide you.

Writing in Daily Living

What practical writing skills should you possess by the time that you are graduated from high school? Here is a list of some of them. Many of the items included are ones that you have studied and practiced in previous years of schoolwork.

Examine the list of skills thoughtfully; then enter in your notebook all those which you honestly feel that you still need to practice. If necessary, add to the list given here.

1. Tests
2. Records: diaries, budgets, notebooks, card files, expense accounts
3. Note taking
4. Directions and explanations
5. Reports: of speeches, plays, books or articles, interviews
6. Parliamentary forms: secretary's minutes, treasurer's report, committee report, resolutions
7. Newspaper writing: news items, features, letters to the editor
8. Business forms: checks and drafts, receipts, promissory notes, blanks and questionnaires, money orders, bills of sale
9. Correspondence: business letters, social letters
10. Telegrams and classified advertisements

1. TAKING TESTS

Writing tests successfully requires much more than the mere knowledge of subject matter. It requires the ability to *analyze,* to *interpret,* and to *follow directions.* It is a school activity that carries over into life beyond high school.

Certain colleges test applicants before admitting them; all test students on their achievements. The government tests applicants for civil service positions. Many factories and offices now give rigid written application tests. The activities that follow will help you to improve your ability to pass tests.

LEARNING ACTIVITIES IN ANALYZING TESTS

A. Do you know what to do when you meet these words in tests: *discuss, list, name, tell why, define, explain, show how, enumerate, describe, identify, classify, state?* Discuss their meanings in class.

B. Here is part of a test. Study each section of it carefully; then analyze it by writing answers to the questions that follow it. *Do not answer the test questions themselves.*

SAMPLE TEST

1. Write a paragraph that gives three causes of the Revolutionary War in the United States.

Analyze the above test assignment by writing answers to these questions:
  a) Should this paragraph be developed by the *inductive,* or the *deductive,* method? (See pages 10–12.) Explain.
  b) Why is "United States" rather than "America" used? Have there been other revolutions on this continent?
  c) How many causes are wanted? If one knows more, should he tell them?
  d) Why would it be incorrect to give a list of *topics* telling the causes?

2. Discuss the effect of small political groups on the election chances of candidates of large groups.

Analyze the above test assignment by answering the following questions:
  a) What form must the answer have? Must one make a list? state reasons? write a paragraph?
  b) May one give illustrations of any influence of such groups on elections? How would such a paragraph be developed?
  c) What would be the central idea of the discussion called for? Should one state it first or last?

C. Exchange your answers to the questions in *B.* Hold discussions to help one another find errors and methods of correcting those errors.

D. Make a list of your own difficulties in interpreting test questions and directions. For each difficulty write a paragraph telling how to overcome it.

USING ENGLISH IN ALL CLASSES

Collect sample test questions from various courses. Point out in class the key direction words, the steps that are to be followed, and the best way to present the answers required.

"DAD, YOU WON'T FIND ANY MISTAKES IN MY ADDITION THIS WEEK!"

2. Keeping Records

What kinds of records do you keep? In school there may be a *notebook*, perhaps a *science manual, score cards, card files* of reading and notes. Outside school there may be *club records,* that secret *diary* or journal, and possibly a *budget* and an *expense account.* How neat and accurate are you in keeping such records?

LEARNING ACTIVITIES IN KEEPING RECORDS

A. Your father has sent you on a business trip and has given you ten dollars and the use of the car. You have had to buy ten gallons of gas, a quart of oil, and a lunch at noon. You have paid your business host $3.75. You have bought your mother a box of candy. Make a complete expense account for your father.

B. Here are suggestions for some records that you might enjoy keeping. Try one of the suggested records as practice in writing. You may decide to continue keeping this record.

1. A record of interesting or humorous things that you observe or do each day
2. A record of your growth in breaking a bad habit, in forming a new one, in acquiring an ability or skill
3. A scrapbook in which you mount clippings, dated and labeled, about your favorite sports personality. If you prefer, make your scrapbook about someone prominent in another field.

3. Taking Notes

Unless you have a perfect memory, you will often need to take notes on information that you wish to use. Detailed help in taking notes is given on pages 245–47 of the chapter "Writing the Term Paper." For ordinary purposes, the following guides will be adequate.

GUIDES FOR TAKING NOTES

1. *Select key words, phrases, or sentences that summarize ideas.* Omit little details and useless illustrations; get chief ideas and main subtopics.

2. *Put into your own words what the author says.* If for any reason you want to use his exact words, put quotation marks around them and say definitely that you are quoting. Only dishonest people take what belongs to others and display it as their own.

3. *Check your notes to be sure that they will be clear to you later.*

4. *Respect the books that you use.* Never write in a book that is not yours. Do not turn down pages, use heavy markers that will injure the book, or place on its pages the paper on which you are writing.

LEARNING ACTIVITIES IN TAKING NOTES

Directions: Take the notes called for in any of the following activities; then use them as the basis of an oral report to your small group. Make a topic outline (see page 118) to guide you in giving your talk. Use your Speech Score Card.

A. Take notes for a report on outside reading in any class.

B. Take notes on a radio or television speech.

C. Take notes of an interview and organize them for an orderly report. (Review the guides for interviewing, page 54.)

4. Writing Directions and Explanations

As you learned in your study of oral expression, giving and understanding directions or explanations are abilities essential to successful work in any field. If you have not mastered those abilities, study again pages 34–38. Use any of the assignments on those pages as practice material for writing directions and explanations. Check all work by the Writing Score Card, page 197.

5. MAKING WRITTEN REPORTS

Learning to take notes is the first step in preparing a report. Once you have selected and organized the material, your task is to express the ideas well in your own words.

To guide you in preparing reports, use the appraisal records that follow. It is not necessary to answer all questions given for each type of report. Never be content with merely answering a question; give illustrations.

APPRAISAL RECORDS FOR WRITING REPORTS

FOR AN INTERVIEW

1. With whom was the interview held? When?
2. What was the subject? State it in one clear sentence.
3. What was the interviewee's reaction to each of the important topics discussed? (*Make a paragraph for each topic.*)
4. What proofs or examples supported each assertion?

Report Analysis

1. *Does my report avoid any comment on the answers given to the questions?* (If such reactions are given, the paper becomes a discussion or an analysis, not a report.)
2. *Have I checked it by the items on the Writing Score Card?*

FOR A REPORT ON LISTENING

1. Who was the speaker, and where did he speak?
2. What was his theme? Give it in a clear statement.
3. What authority did the speaker present?
4. Were the author's ideas free from prejudice and bias?
5. What was his conclusion?

Report Analysis

1. *Is my report entirely free from my own opinions?*
2. *Is the report in my own language? If not, have I given proper credit?*
3. *How well does my report conform to the standards set in the Writing Score Card, page 197?*

FOR A REPORT ON READING PLAYS

1. What is the title of the play?
2. Who is the author?
3. What is the underlying idea? What is the mood?
4. Is the purpose of the play to furnish entertainment, or does it aim to reform, to attack, to inform? How is the purpose revealed?
5. Is the play a *comedy,* a *tragedy,* a *melodrama,* or a *farce?* (If any of those terms are new to you, consult the dictionary.)

6. Who are the chief characters? What particular traits have they?

7. Is the end of the play fitting and satisfactory?

Report Analysis

1. *How does my report rank on the items in the Writing Score Card?*
2. *Have I given reasons for any opinions that I have expressed?*
3. *Does the report show clear thinking?*

FOR A REPORT ON READING BOOKS AND ARTICLES

1. What is the title, and what is the complete name of the author?
2. If it is an article, what is the source?
3. What is the central idea?
4. What was the author's purpose in writing it?
5. What is its form? (*fiction, essay, verse, biography, . . .*)
6. Give and illustrate the point of emphasis: *plot, idea, mood, character, persuasion, . . .*
7. Is the selection worth recommending? Why or why not?

Report Analysis

1. *Have I made good use of reasoning?*
2. *Have I tried to express myself interestingly as well as clearly?*
3. *Does the report meet the standards on the Writing Score Card?*

LEARNING ACTIVITIES IN WRITING REPORTS

A. You are sent to interview a businessman about the standards set for letter writing in his office. Use the Guides to Taking Part in Interviews, page 54. Write your report, using the appraisal record on page 213.

B. Listen to a radio play or watch a play on television. Write a report based upon the appraisal record on page 213. If all can listen to the same performance, you may be better able to criticize the play. Exchange papers for criticism.

C. Report on a motion picture that you have seen. Write your report as if for publication in your school paper or in the local paper.

D. Write a report based upon a book that you have read recently. If you have read one in class, hold a contest for the best and most interesting report on it. If you wish, make a "specialized" appraisal, such as one of the following:

1. List every date (or approximate time) given. Tell what happened then.
2. Make a statement about one character; then prove it.

USING ENGLISH IN ALL CLASSES

Bring into class any report that you have been asked to prepare for some subject other than English. Perhaps several of you may have the same assignment. Working in pairs or in small groups, prepare and test your reports.

6. Writing Parliamentary Forms

If you do not now have a class organization functioning according to the rules of parliamentary practice, review the material on pages 61–72.

LEARNING ACTIVITIES IN WRITING PARLIAMENTARY FORMS

A. Write and read to the class the report presented by a committee chosen to suggest a name for a proposed club. Here is a model to guide you.

Mr. President:

The committee appointed to select a club name offers these suggestions with the recommendation that the class choose one by majority vote.

English Improvement Club
Find Out Club

The committee recommends the adoption of this report.

Leo Murphy
Eleanor Carlson

B. Write the report of a resolutions committee appointed to express club views on the matter of abolishing interschool athletic contests. This type of report is formal in tone and follows a definite pattern. The report should be signed by the committee. Read and discuss your reports in class. Here is an example.

Mr. President, I move the adoption of the following resolution.

Whereas, The use of parliamentary procedures is becoming more necessary in all democratic procedures in America; therefore be it

Resolved, That this club organize itself into a group which shall continue the discussions introduced on radio or television programs.

C. As secretary, write and read minutes to cover the meeting for which you wrote the report in *A.* If there are corrections, revise your minutes.

D. Write the treasurer's monthly report for a real or an imaginary organization. Present a neat and accurate statement. Exchange papers for criticism.

RELATED ACTIVITY

How accurately can you pronounce and spell these terms: *parliamentary, motion, resolution, minutes, secretary, treasurer, procedure, organization, quorum?* In a class activity, test yourselves.

7. Writing for School Publications

What particular kind of newspaper writing interests you? The many types of articles that appear in newspapers are discussed on pages 145–51. If necessary, refer to those pages.

As you carry out any of the assignments in this lesson, make use of these suggestions. (1) Check all work by your Writing Score Card. (2) *Proofread critically*. (3) Exchange papers and score each other's work. (4) Hold conferences and point out to each other good qualities achieved and methods of correcting faults. (5) Make exhibits on the bulletin board of examples of successful work. (6) Read and discuss your work in class.

LEARNING ACTIVITIES IN WRITING FOR SCHOOL PUBLICATIONS

A. Write one of the following news articles. Be sure to answer the five *w*'s in your opening paragraph. (See page 147.)

1. Write a news story of an actual occurrence in your school or town.
2. Has your school new pupils, changes in daily routine, or assembly programs that merit a news article? Find something worth writing up.
3. Write an account of an exciting athletic event that has occurred recently in your school. Make the tone of your article carry the spirit of the event.

B. Try your hand at writing headlines. From one of last week's newspapers, clip a news article and bring it to class for exchange with a classmate. Before you exchange clippings, remove the headlines. Write a headline for the article that you receive. When you have finished, read the article and your headline aloud for criticism. Before working out this activity, review page 147.

C. Make a list of problems that should be brought to the attention of pupils in your school. Write an editorial based upon one such problem. (Review page 146.) Use the editorials in class as an exercise in studying all sides of a question.

D. Review pages 148–49; then write a feature story on a human-interest theme that you have found in your observation.

E. Try writing a column that will give interesting side lights on the usual experiences and observations of your day. (Review page 150.) If you like, imitate the style of some famous columnist. Imitation is excellent practice if you frankly acknowledge your imitation.

RELATED ACTIVITY

Persuade your publications staff to run a contest in writing editorials, feature stories, news stories. Open the contest to the members of all composition classes in your school.

8. WRITING BUSINESS FORMS

READ AND DISCUSS

The term "business English" is often used as if one should use a differen kind of expression in vocations from that used in other activities of life

True, there is a vocabulary belonging to business, but aside from that special vocabulary, business English is simply clear, concise expression, no different from that used in other areas.

To be ignorant of correct forms and interpretations of common business papers is likely to lead to costly results. Probably you have had practice in writing checks, receipts, money orders, and sales slips; and in filling blanks of various kinds. How many of the forms named can you read intelligently? How many can you write correctly?

THE BANK CHECK

Here is the form that the United States Department of Commerce has set as the standard for safe use. Study it; then answer orally the questions below.

STANDARDIZED BANK CHECK

Questions: Who is to receive the money? What is the amount? Why is it important to indicate the number of the check? Why is a line used to fill up the space in which the amount of the check is spelled out? Why is the amount indicated in two ways? Why is the indication of the number of cents written as the numerator of a fraction? Why is the indication of the number of cents placed close to the word *Thirty-five?* Where should John Doe endorse this check? Why is it important that the stub be filled in clearly and accurately?

CERTIFIED CHECK

Sometimes an individual or a firm does not know a customer who wishes to pay a bill by check. Time would be lost in investigating him. To avoid this delay, the customer may use a *certified check*. He writes his personal check, and the cashier of the bank then stamps it with a formal statement across the body of the check and signs it. This endorsement is proof that the bank authorizes the check drawn on it and immediately charges the check to the account of the writer.

A person who has no checking account can purchase a *cashier's check,* which is really a check drawn on its own funds by the bank. The customer pays to the bank in cash the amount of the check, plus a small service fee.

BANK DRAFT

The *bank draft,* like the cashier's check, is an order on a bank to pay a definite sum deposited with it by the person buying the draft. The draft differs from the cashier's check in that it is drawn by one bank upon another. You may have a draft made out either to yourself or to the person whom you wish to receive the money.

LEARNING ACTIVITY

Try to get from your bank sample forms of the certified check, the cashier's check, and the bank draft. Compare them with the ordinary bank check. Write examples of each type of check on forms that you make yourself. Exchange papers for critical examination.

THE RECEIPT

The receipt is a necessary business form in all transactions in which money is paid for goods or services received. (An endorsed check is a form of receipt.) Many unhappy experiences arise from the failure to demand a receipt, to read one carefully, or to file one after it has been received.

A receipt should state (1) the exact amount received, (2) for what the money was paid, (3) who paid it, (4) who received it, and (5) whether payment was in full, or merely on account.

LEARNING ACTIVITIES

A. Discuss these questions:
1. What difficulties might arise if the receipt for a final payment does not show that the payment is in full?
2. What might happen if an installment payment is made and not receipted?

B. Bring to class examples of receipts. Write a complete form of a receipt for payment in full; for payment on account. Exchange papers for checking.

MONEY ORDERS

Review the use of the money order by mail, by express, and by telegraph. Get a sample money order form from the post office. Use it as a model for interpretation and writing. Check one another's work carefully.

PROMISSORY NOTES

Secure a sample form of the promissory note. Examine carefully the phrasing. Why should one read it with special care before signing it?

BILLS OF SALE

Bring to class a bill of sale from your grocery or department store. If you have made out such a sales slip, explain each item that must be considered. Why should the purchaser read bills of sale carefully?

APPLICATION BLANKS, INCOME TAX FORMS, OTHER BLANKS

READ AND DISCUSS

Filling blanks of various kinds is a common requirement in the lives of most adults. How many different kinds of blanks or questionnaires can you name in addition to those in the heading of this lesson? With how many different kinds have you had experience?

Each set of blanks carries special instructions for filling the form. In addition, certain general guides apply to all.

GUIDES FOR FILLING BLANK FORMS EFFICIENTLY

1. Read carefully through the entire form. Do *not* begin to write until you have done this preliminary reading.
2. Study any introductory information or instructions. Know exactly what you are being asked to do.
3. Answer every question. If one does not apply to you, draw a line in the blank. To leave the space entirely blank might give the impression that you had overlooked the question.
4. Be complete and accurate in your answers.
5. Write or print answers as clearly and neatly as you know how.
6. After filling the blanks, check your answers carefully.

LEARNING ACTIVITIES IN FILLING BLANKS

A. Collect and bring to class as many types of blanks as you can find: college-entrance applications, job applications, order blanks, questionnaires, license applications, credit applications, . . . Practice filling these, using a fictitious name, if you like. Exchange papers for criticism.

B. If possible, arrange for an authority to talk to your class about income tax blanks and how to fill them. This activity offers an opportunity for practice in good telephone technique, in introducing and thanking a speaker, in listening, and in asking questions.

9. WRITING LETTERS

All through your years of schoolwork, you have had practice in letter forms and content. How much do you remember of what you have learned? Find out by taking the following pretest.

PRETEST IN LETTER WRITING

Directions: Write the answers to the test assignments entirely in the class period. Use no outside preparation or help. Score each assignment on the basis of the percentage indicated on the chart for letters, page 221.

1. Write in block form a letter of inquiry to the Newark (New Jersey) School of Aviation. Ask about their training courses for aviators or air stewardesses.
2. Write in semiblock form a letter to a business firm. Order three different items of merchandise.
3. Write in indented form a letter to a younger brother or sister, real or imaginary. Tell how high school differs from school in the lower grades. Do not be too serious.

After your test has been scored, confer with your teacher about your chief errors and needs. Copy the appraisal chart; then, under the place for tests, record your score for each part of the chart. Check those points on which you need most practice. In the learning activities in letter writing that follow, work constantly to strengthen your weak points.

"I READ ONLY THE P.S. IN AUNT CLARA'S LETTERS. THAT'S WHERE THE REAL NEWS ALWAYS IS."

APPRAISAL CHART FOR SCORING LETTERS

NAME *Charles Mason* DATE *October 6, 19—*   *Do not write in this book.*

LETTER TYPE	BLOCK				SEMIBLOCK				INDENTED			
	Test	1	2	3	Test	1	2	3	Test	1	2	3
100% I. Form*	70											
5% A. Choice of paper	5											
5% B. Choice of ink (handwritten letter)	1											
25% C. Neatness (no blots, cross-outs, erasures)	15											
15% D. Margins and page balance	10											
30% E. Punctuation	20											
5% F. Double spacing between parts and between paragraphs (typed letter)	5											
20% G. Envelope address and return	15											
100% II. Content	75											
20% A. Suitability of tone	15											
20% B. Clarity of expression	15											
10% C. Logical correctness of paragraph division	5											
25% D. Word choice and phrasing	20											
15% E. Quality of opening and closing sentences	10											
10% F. Suitable salutation and closing	10											

* As is indicated in this sample, if a letter has been typed, there will naturally be no score in B under "Form"; if, on the other hand, a letter has been handwritten, there will be no score under F.

221

Stan Hunt

"Gentlemen: Thank you for your courteous letter thanking me for my courteous reply to your courteous letter. . . ." *

Using correct forms is very important in writing good business letters. You should practice the forms carefully so that the appearance of your letters will make a good impression upon those who read them.

Most business letters are written in one of these two styles: (1) block or (2) semiblock. The chart below shows the two styles. What is the only difference between them?

Handwritten business letters usually follow semiblock style. As a rule, they are not double spaced between paragraphs.

BUSINESS LETTERS

(*Block Style*)		(*Semiblock Style*)
	Heading	
	Inside Address	
	Salutation	
	Body	
	{ Complimentary Close }	
	Signature	

* Used by permission of Stan Hunt and the *Saturday Evening Post.*

The form of the envelope address is the same for both block and semi-block styles. Note the chart below.

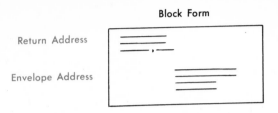

Letters should be inserted in the envelopes in such a way that when they are opened and unfolded, the name of the receiver is at once visible. The style of folding varies with the size of the stationery. Note the chart below.

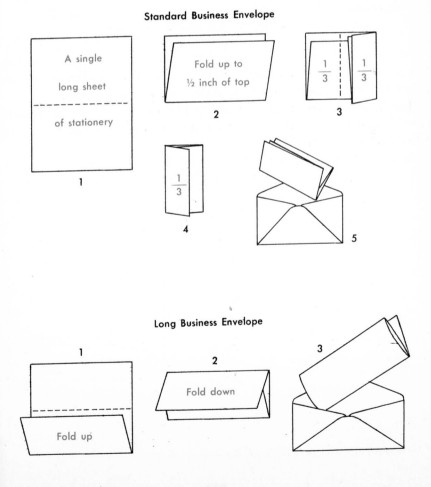

(Hotel Reservation)

1. Heading

4 1 6 Fulton Road
Lawrence, Kansas
March 15, 19—

2. Inside Address

Seaview Hotel
368 Shoreline Drive
Miami 10, Florida

3. Salutation

Gentlemen:

4. Body

I should like to reserve a double room for two weeks, beginning April 1. Mrs. Brooks and I plan to arrive about 6:00 P.M. of that day.

This will be the first time that we have visited Miami. We have chosen your hotel because of the fine recommendation given it by our neighbors, Mr. and Mrs. Craig Stevens, who have just returned after a month's stay at the Seaview.

5. Complimentary Close

Very truly yours,

6. Signature

Loren B. Brooks

Loren B. Brooks

THE PARTS OF A BUSINESS LETTER

1. The *heading* gives (*a*) the complete address of the writer and (*b*) the date.

2. The *inside address* is the same as the address used on the envelope, except that on the envelope the city and the state should be written on separate lines.

Miss Ruth Lee, R.N.   Mr. D. R. Cole, Secretary
City Hospital   Lakeland Country Club
El Paso, Texas   Oshkosh, Wisconsin

3. *Salutations* commonly used in business letters include these:

My dear Mr. Bailey: Dear Miss Phelps:
Dear Mrs. Rhoads: Dear Sir:

Gentlemen should be used in addressing a firm if one is writing to no specific person. *Dear Madam* is commonly used for either a single or a married woman; *Mesdames* or *Ladies* may be used when a plural form is needed.

Note that a colon follows the salutation.

4. The *body* of a business letter should be as brief as clearness and courtesy permit. In semiblock style, the paragraphs usually are indented five characters.
5. Typical *complimentary closes* include *Yours truly, Very truly yours, Yours very truly, Sincerely yours, Cordially yours, Sincerely. Respectfully yours* is usually reserved for letters to dignitaries of high rank, although it is good usage for young people who are writing to adults.
6. The *signature* is the writer's legal signature in his own handwriting. If the letter is typed, his name and his position, if necessary, are typed below the signature. A single woman should put *Miss* in parentheses to indicate the title to be used in addressing her. A married woman should sign her given name, but below it she should put her married name.

David C. Allen   *(Miss) Carol Scott*   *Ellen Lane*
                                                    (Mrs. R. V. Lane)

TYPES OF BUSINESS LETTERS

Before you do the activities beginning on page 229, study the following examples, which illustrate various types of business letters.

ORDER LETTER

450 Cliff Street
Battle Creek, Michigan
August 18, 19—

Evards Seed Company
Shenandoah, Iowa

Gentlemen:
     Please send by October 10, by American Express, the following bulbs selected from your fall catalogue.

No. ZX	2 doz.	Regal Lily	@ $ .35 each	$8.40
No. SX	5 doz.	Narcissus (royal)	@ .15 each	9.00
No. EX	6 doz.	Crocus (mixed)	@ .02 each	1.44
			Total	$18.84

My check for $18.84 is enclosed.

Yours truly,
Barbara Bannister
(Mrs. R. L. Bannister)

● POINTS TO REMEMBER IN WRITING ORDER LETTERS

1. Be specific in telling exactly what you are ordering. Tell sizes, models, colors, prices, and so on. State specifically the source (catalogue, advertisement, . . .) from which you are ordering.
2. Tell how you are paying. Is it a charge? a C.O.D.? If not, are you enclosing a check or a money order? Be sure to state the exact amount of your order.
3. If you must pay delivery costs, tell how to ship the goods.

LETTER OF COMPLAINT

Rural Route 3
Carbondale, Illinois
November 10, 19—

Bekins Sports Supplies
410 Tenth Street
Kansas City 3, Missouri

Gentlemen:

On October 15 we ordered from you six of the plastic football helmets advertised in your fall catalogue.

The helmets arrived yesterday. However, only five helmets were in the package, although on the invoice we have been charged for six.

We shall appreciate your attention to this matter. If possible, we should like you to ship us the missing helmet immediately.

Yours truly,

Kenneth Wills

Kenneth Wills
Athletic Director

● POINTS TO REMEMBER IN WRITING LETTERS OF COMPLAINT

1. Do not write when you are angry.
2. Explain the circumstances fully but as briefly as you can. Be careful to give exact details.
3. Be courteous in your attitude.
4. Tell what adjustment you would like to have made.

Scottsbluff High School
Scottsbluff, Nebraska
January 20, 19—

Mr. E. M. Willoughby
Gering, Nebraska

Dear Mr. Willoughby:

Our English class has been studying Francis Parkman's The Oregon Trail. We know that your great-grandparents were among the pioneers who made the covered-wagon journey to the West in 1848. We have learned that your great-grandfather kept a diary of their trip and that it is now in your possession.

We should like very much to have you talk to our class about that journey. We should especially appreciate your showing us the diary, if you would consent to do so.

Our class meets at 10:15 every morning. If you will agree to speak to us, we shall be glad to have you set any date convenient for you. In that event, we shall arrange to have someone meet you and bring you to our classroom.

Respectfully yours,

Paul Gregg

Paul Gregg
Class Secretary

POINTS TO REMEMBER IN WRITING REQUESTS

1. Be simple, brief, and definite. Avoid unnecessary details.
2. Include any information that the receiver needs if he is to answer your questions satisfactorily.
3. As a rule, tell why you need the information.
4. If only you are to benefit by the answer, enclose return postage or a stamped, self-addressed envelope. If the recipient also might profit (as by an order from you), you need not include return postage.
5. If you are requesting bulletins, catalogues, or samples, ask specifically for what you want.
6. Be courteous and appreciative.

4838 Lee Street
Columbus 12, Georgia
May 12, 19—

Mr. David Evans, Caretaker
Wilmont Golf Club
Columbus 15, Georgia

Dear Mr. Evans:

Mr. Samuel Carroll, a member of the Wilmont Golf Club, tells me that you are in need of a helper for this summer. I should like to apply for the position.

I am a junior at Central High School. I am 17 years of age, weigh 160 pounds, and am 6 feet in height. I am strong, healthy, and conscientious. The enclosed photograph was taken last spring.

For several summers past, I have done yard work for the following persons here in Columbus. They are allowing me to use their names as references.

Dr. Lee K. Maitland, 5420 Florence Drive
Tel. Elmwood 3-2456
Mrs. R. C. Lassiter, 5168 Franklin Avenue
Tel. Elmwood 3-4365

I shall be glad to come for an interview. My telephone number is Elmwood 3-2538.

Yours truly,

Jay E. Cardwell

Jay E. Cardwell

● POINTS TO REMEMBER IN APPLYING BY LETTER

1. Word the first sentence of an application carefully. (*a*) Be specific about the position. (*b*) Tell how you learned of the vacancy. (*c*) Do not go into the matter of your qualifications in this first sentence.

2. In stating your qualifications, avoid unessential information. Stress your fitness for the position, not your need of work. Neither emphasize nor belittle the matter of salary.

3. In writing your letter, be guided by the following questions:
   a) What are the abilities that you can contribute? What training have you had? What experience?
   b) Whom can you name as references?
   c) Do age and weight matter in this letter?
   d) In what order should you give the information?

GENERAL GUIDES FOR WRITING BUSINESS LETTERS

1. Write as correctly as you know how.
2. Get to the point quickly.
3. State definitely what you are writing about. Be sure to include all information that the recipient of your letter will need in replying.
4. Express yourself simply and clearly.
5. Always be courteous.

LEARNING ACTIVITIES IN WRITING BUSINESS LETTERS

A. Here are several preliminary activities for you to do before proceeding to actual letter-writing assignments.

1. Collect and bring to class sample business letters. Judge them carefully by the chart on page 221 and by the guides on this page. Use as models any that measure up to the standards on the chart. *Be careful to bring only letters that are impersonal in tone and that do not deal with private affairs.*
2. Find out for what words the following abbreviations stand: *acct., agt., art., asst., ave., bal., bbl., bu., Co., C.O.D., cwt., do., f.o.b., Inc., mfg., Mgr., Sec'y.* Go over these in class. Can you find others used frequently in business letters? Check the letters collected in the preceding activity. How many of the preceding terms are used? Do the letters include others? Make a composite list of all such abbreviations that you find.
3. Can you spell correctly words that often occur in business letters? Write the following list from dictation. In your notebook make a copy of words that you missed or were not sure of. Use them to check your letters.

1. acknowledgment	11. courteous	21. quantity
2. advertisement	12. depreciation	22. receipt
3. apologize	13. enclose	23. recommendation
4. application	14. forty	24. references
5. appreciation	15. fourth	25. remittance
6. arrangement	16. immediately	26. requirements
7. believe	17. maintain	27. sincerely
8. canceled	18. maintenance	28. specified
9. competition	19. possession	29. succeed
10. convenient	20. preference	30. truly

B. In class, point out the weaknesses in the following sentences from application letters. Improve each sentence.

1. I herewith present my application for the position advertised in the *Sunday Times.*
2. I don't know much about cooking, but I think I could manage it in the housekeeping work you advertise in the morning paper.
3. May I come in and see you about the position you advertised?
4. I have to have a job because my father doesn't have one.

5. I know I could do the typing work well. I am tall and slender.
6. I happened to hear that you need a boy, and I think I'd like the job.
7. The salary doesn't bother me. I just want to learn the work.
8. I left my last job because the boss was too cranky.

C. Write an application for a position advertised in a daily paper. Check your letter by the chart on page 221 and by the Writing Score Card, page 197.

When you are satisfied with your letter, show it, if possible, to some employer whom you know. Use his criticisms as guides for improvement. If you actually would like to have the position, mail your letter.

D. Write an order to a department store in a nearby city for several articles advertised in a newspaper. (Follow the model on page 225.) Exchange letters and score them by the chart on page 221.

E. You find that one of the articles that you ordered in *D* is defective. Write a letter in which you ask for an adjustment. State the matter fairly and courteously. See how clear you can be without being abrupt or critical. Let the points on page 226, the chart on page 221, and the Writing Score Card on page 197 help you to write an effective letter.

F. Write a letter of inquiry or a request for information. (Review the points on page 227.) If you cannot think of a topic, try one of these:
1. A letter to a travel company asking about summer tours
2. A letter to a college requesting a general catalogue
3. A letter to the game and forest commission in your state inquiring about the dates of this year's open season on wild fowl
4. A letter asking for someone's autograph
5. A letter to a vacation resort, asking about accommodations and rates
   Discuss your letters in class. If you wish, mail your letter.

G. Write a letter in which you request a room reservation. The example on page 224 will serve as a guide.

CHECK TEST ON WRITING BUSINESS LETTERS

Directions: Write these test assignments entirely within the class period.
1. Make lined forms of business letters in (*a*) block style and (*b*) semiblock style. Punctuate the forms properly. Label each style of letter. Label each part of each letter. (*Score:* 30 per cent)
2. Write a letter in answer to this advertisement. (*Score:* 60 per cent)
   Wanted: At the State Theater at ten o'clock Friday morning, May 1, high school boys and girls who can act in any of the following capacities: dancing, chorus or solo singing, simple acting, impersonations, ushering. Apply by letter. Cadet Lowes, Mgr., Amateur Community Theater.
3. Address an envelope for your letter. Write the return address. Fold your letter and place it in the envelope. (*Score:* 10 per cent)

Social letters usually are written by hand and in indented form. However, use of the typewriter in social letters is now acceptable. The chart shows you the customary forms for writing social letters and addressing the envelopes. Compare the forms carefully with those for business letters, page 222.

SOCIAL LETTERS (*Indented Style*)

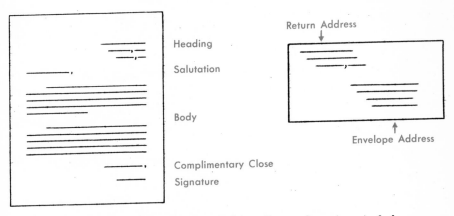

The chief principle to remember is this: *Always keep in mind the person to whom you are writing.* Write what you think he will enjoy hearing.

GENERAL GUIDES FOR WRITING SOCIAL LETTERS

1. Show good taste: avoid highly-colored stationery; use black, blue, or blue-black ink. Do not use a pencil.
2. Make the letter neat: avoid blots, cross outs, and untidy erasures; keep at least half an inch margin at the top and the sides and slightly more at the foot of the page.
3. Adapt your tone to the receiver's age, interests, and personality and to the nature of the relationship between you and him.
4. Do not waste the receiver's time and your own.
    a) Avoid unnecessary preliminaries like "How are you? I am fine and hope you are the same."
    b) Avoid writing anything about anyone that you would feel embarrassed to have that person read.
    c) Avoid long apologies for not having written sooner.
    d) Avoid the overuse of "I."
    e) Avoid the stereotyped closing, such as "Well, I haven't anything more to say, so will close."

Here are common types of social letters. Study the examples; then do the activities in which you need practice.

1. The friendly letter
2. The family letter
3. The letter of appreciation or thanks
4. The congratulatory letter
5. The letter of apology
6. The letter of sympathy or condolence
7. The invitation and the reply

THE FRIENDLY LETTER

> Sunny Rest Farm
> Halstead Road
> July 14, 19 —
>
> Dear Marvin,
> Now, isn't that a name for a farm where a fellow has to get up with the chickens and work all day in the hayfield! Don't make any mistake about it, though. I'm liking it fine. I came out here to get some soft muscles toughened up, and, boy, you wait until you see the results!
> There's nothing like this outdoor work for building up the body, believe me! Coach Thomas won't know his old halfback when I go out for guard. Have you heard anything from Tom Seaton since he went to work laying concrete with the construction gang? He and I should compare muscles when this "training season" is over.
> You city slickers might take a little time out to write a good letter with all the news. We do have rural mail delivery, you know.
>
> Yours for a husky football team,
> Don

● **POINTS TO REMEMBER**

1. Write informally but avoid trite expressions and overuse of slang.
2. Write fully about one or two items, not briefly about many.
3. Be sure to comment on the letter that you are answering.

At Home
Sunset Road
July 8, 19—

Dear Julia,

Now that you are all comfortably settled in Estes Park for a cool, woodsy vacation, I shall try to keep you informed of the joys that you are missing at home.

Lew Tully dropped in last night and sat out on the porch with the family for an hour. If he hadn't wiggled around so much and looked so forlornly at the moon, I'd have thought that he didn't know you were gone. He brought his little post card up for us to see. That was a good excuse for coming; just as if we didn't have some cards from you ourselves! Wonder if I'll ever get that way about some other fellow's sister!

Dad is going down to Turkey Run tomorrow to fish. I'm staying home to take Mother to her club. "Duty before pleasure" is my motto—or I should say that it is Dad's motto for me!

Speaking of duty reminds me that I'd better drag my trumpet out of its case and get in a little practicing or I'll be getting more than my share of black looks from Mr. Thompson during the band concert tonight.

Think of it — while you are relaxing under the stars, I'll be sweating it out (and I _do_ mean "sweating"!) on the old bandstand — and acquiring a new set of mosquito bites. Don't you wish you were here!

Love,
Kenneth

● **POINTS TO REMEMBER**

1. Write as interestingly as you would to a friend. Do not dash off a hasty note written purely from a sense of duty.
2. If you are writing to one of the family away from home, describe little "homey" events and activities.

1568 Park Avenue
Frankfort, Kentucky
October 10, 19—

Dear Anne,

Thank you for replying so promptly to my call for help. I was sorry to have to bother you, but I couldn't think of anyone else who might have Miss Franklin's new address. It was thoughtful of you to include her telephone number.

We expect to be in New York by Sunday, though Dad is the sort who likes to take little "side trips" whenever we travel by car. At any rate, I hope to be able to have at least a short visit with Miss Franklin after we _do_ arrive. I shall tell her that I owe it all to you! Thanks again, Anne.

Love,
Alice

● POINTS TO REMEMBER

1. If you are writing a "bread-and-butter" letter for the hospitality that you have enjoyed during a visit, you may send a small gift with your letter. Never suggest, however, that it is in payment of that hospitality. This letter should be sent to the hostess in the home.

2. Make the note short but sincere.

3. Mention specifically what pleases you about a gift or a thoughtful action; be just as specific in telling what made a visit enjoyable.

4. Write promptly.

Note that in the example the writer uses an inside address, since he is writing to a stranger.

3 Evergreen Avenue
Somerville, Massachusetts
April 29, 19—

Mr. Wayne Gard
3624 Normandy
Dallas 5, Texas

Dear Mr. Gard,

Congratulations on the publication of your latest book, The Chisholm Trail. As former Texans, my parents and I are looking forward to reading it. I hope to report on it for my history class.

Sincerely,

John Matthews

● **POINTS TO REMEMBER**

1. Keep the letter brief.
2. Avoid gushing, but show sincere pleasure at the success of the person to whom you write.
3. In writing to someone who has won over you in a competition, make a special effort to avoid showing disappointment.

THE LETTER OF APOLOGY

Ortonville, Minnesota
February 8, 1954

Dear Sally,

Can you find it in your heart to forgive me for my bad behavior yesterday? Just about the time that I think I have learned to control my tongue and my temper, I get angry about something — and away go all my good resolutions!

You were perfectly right in questioning my plans for the class party. I hadn't thought them through;

therefore it was inexcusable for me to fly out at you as I did. I can't call back the angry words that I said; I can only hope that you will try to forget them.

Sincerely,
Louise

● POINTS TO REMEMBER IN WRITING AN APOLOGY

1. Admit frankly that you were wrong. Do not make excuses.
2. Offer to make whatever restitution is possible.
3. Write promptly.
4. Keep your letter short.

THE LETTER OF CONDOLENCE

3825 O Street
Lincoln, Nebraska
May 12, 19—

Dear Tom,

The news about your father shocks me deeply. I know how devoted you were to each other and what a blow his sudden passing must be to all of you.

My own sense of loss is deep. I have been sitting here remembering his many kindnesses and the thoughtful interest he always took in the boyhood projects and enthusiasms that seemed so important to you and me. You have even richer memories, I know.

Just knowing your father has been an inspiration to me, as it has to so many others.

Sincerely,
Jack Harris

● POINTS TO REMEMBER IN WRITING CONDOLENCES

1. Write simply and sincerely.
2. Mention something specific about the one who has gone—his thoughtful acts, his cheery smile, his attitude toward life, . . .
3. Try to say something that will give comfort and hope.

Young people as a rule write only informal invitations. Their tone is like that of the friendly letter. Acceptance should be in the same tone as that of the invitation. Both should state specifically what the occasion is and when and where it is to take place. The invitation also should have in it any other information helpful to the prospective guest.

The formal invitation included here will guide you if you are on a committee to prepare invitations for a class banquet or other formal occasion. The replies on page 238 show the correct forms to use in replying.

Informal Invitation and Reply

Colburn, Indiana
July 10, 19—

Dear Carol,

Will you and Bob join us at dinner next Tuesday evening at the Cabin Lodge? Dinner (at eight) will be followed by a boat ride down the river in the moonlight.

Cordially yours,
Rhoda Roberts

Delphi, Indiana
July 10, 19—

Dear Rhoda,

What pleasant ideas you have! Nothing can keep river-loving Bob and me away.

Eagerly yours,
Carol Lancaster

The Formal Invitation

Mr. and Mrs. Kenneth Harvey
request the pleasure of your company
at dinner
on Wednesday, April sixth
at eight o'clock

R.S.V.P.
4624 Shady Lane

The Reply of Acceptance

Mr. and Mrs. Robert Davids
accept with pleasure the invitation
of Mr. and Mrs. Kenneth Harvey
to dinner
on Wednesday, April sixth
at eight o'clock

The Reply of Regret

Mr. and Mrs. Robert Davids
regret that serious illness in the home
prevents the acceptance of
Mr. and Mrs. Harvey's kind invitation
to dinner
on Wednesday, April sixth

● **POINTS TO REMEMBER IN WRITING FORMAL INVITATIONS**

1. Spell out the date and the time.
2. Write in the third person, not the first.
3. Follow the line arrangement and spacing shown in the example.
4. If you wish, write *R.S.V.P.* in the lower left-hand corner. Those letters stand for the French words "Répondez, s'il vous plaît." Translated, they mean "Reply, if you please."

LEARNING ACTIVITIES IN WRITING SOCIAL LETTERS

Directions: Do any of the following exercises in which you need practice. Check your writing by the chart on page 221 and by the model letters. Wherever possible, make these real letters that you will mail. *Be sure to proofread.* Read and discuss courteously at least the imaginary ones. (See the guides on page 56.)

A. Write one or more of these family or friendly letters.

1. Write a letter to a relative who lives at a distance.
2. Write a letter to a friend in another locality.
3. Suppose that you are a stranger visiting your home town. Write a letter to a distant friend, describing the place, the people, the activities.

B. Write at least one of the following letters of appreciation.

1. Write a note of appreciation for a birthday gift. Be sincere, not extravagant.
2. You have heard a fine radio program. Write a letter to the performers, the sponsor, or the broadcasting company.
3. You have been a house guest. Write a "bread-and-butter" letter.
4. You have received flowers, gifts, games, and cards during a recent illness.

C. You were in a competition and lost. Write a sincere note of congratulation to the classmate who won.

D. Write one or more of the apologies called for in these situations.

1. Your club held a picnic yesterday. Today you discover that it was held on private property and that rubbish and papers were left.
2. In an attempt to be humorous, you spoke rudely to a friend.
3. You have forgotten an important engagement or duty.

E. Carry out at least one of the following exercises.

1. Invite a friend in a nearby community to be your guest at a school play.
2. Write a formal invitation to a club banquet.
3. Write your acceptance or refusal of the formal invitation in 2 above.
4. Examine the society columns in the newspaper. Notice the various types of social functions recorded there. Write at least one invitation and a reply.

FOLLOW-UP ACTIVITY

Perhaps you would like to conduct a friendly correspondence with someone in a foreign land. There are agencies that arrange such correspondence. The names of several are listed in the *Teacher's Manual* for this book.

RELATED ACTIVITIES

A. Collect examples of good letters that are not too personal in tone to be used in the classroom as models. Read some of these aloud. Place model letters upon the bulletin board.

B. Illustrate for the class the use of the telephone for very informal invitations. (Review pages 52–53.)

CHECK TEST ON WRITING SOCIAL LETTERS

Directions: Write the test in class. Score each letter by the chart on page 221. Average the scores on form and content to get your final score on each letter. If you fell below 70 per cent on any letter, continue practice on that type.

1. You have received an invitation to spend a week with your uncle in the city. (*a*) Write the invitation. (*b*) Write your acceptance.
2. Write a friend at home about the things that you are seeing and doing.
3. Soon after your return, write a letter of appreciation to your uncle.

10. Writing Telegrams and Classified Advertisements

At present you may not need to write telegrams or classified advertisements, or "want ads," but being able to do so well is a useful skill.

1. Use as few words as possible in writing telegrams or classified advertisements, but do not omit any words needed for clear meaning. The basic rate for telegrams is for fifteen words, with an added charge for each additional word. Classified advertisements cost so much per word or line; often there is a requirement that the advertisement contain at least ten words. Note these examples, with unnecessary words crossed out.

Telegram

~~I AM~~ HAVING ~~A~~ WONDERFUL TIME UNCLE MIKE SAYS ~~YOU WILL NOT MIND IF I~~ STAY ANOTHER WEEK ~~IS THAT~~ OK WITH YOU ~~I SHALL BE~~ HOME NEXT SATURDAY ~~LOVE~~ GALEN

Classified Advertisement

~~I~~ lost ~~on~~ March 6 ~~a~~ brown morocco billfold. ~~It was~~ stamped ~~with the initials~~ JWK. ~~It~~ contains ~~a~~ driver's license ~~made out to~~ James W. King. ~~There is a~~ reward ~~for the finder. Please call~~ Davis 8–2345.

2. In a telegram punctuation marks must be spelled out and counted as words. Omit such marks if the message is clear without them.

LEARNING ACTIVITIES

Directions: In the following activities, exchange papers and score each other's work by these questions: (1) Is it clear? (2) Is every word necessary? (3) Is all necessary information given? Put models on the board.

A. Condense the telegram and the advertisement given here.

1. I am sorry that I shall be unable to meet your train at 6:30 P.M. on Friday, May 6. Upon your arrival call me at Graceland 4–2648.
2. I have for sale at a bargain price a like-new Speedster bicycle. It has attached a new lamp and a wire carrier basket. You may call at 673 Linwood Avenue or telephone Franklin 3–2065.

B. Write the telegram called for in one of these situations:

1. You have gone with the basketball team to an out-of-town game. A heavy snowstorm has blocked all roads. The host school has made arrangements for all of you to stay in local homes. Wire your parents in fifteen words that will free them from worry.
2. You are going to visit a cousin, and find that your train has changed time.

C. Write at least one of the classified advertisements called for in the following situations:

1. Your pet dog or cat has disappeared.
2. You would like to buy a secondhand typewriter.
3. You have homemade candy, cookies, or preserves for sale.
4. You wish to market some other product that you make.

Writing the Term Paper

Sometime during this school year, the teacher in one of your classes is likely to say, "The final requirement in this course is a term paper, which will be due on ..."

Whether it is called a "term paper" or a "long theme" or a "research paper" makes little difference. How you attack the preparation of that paper makes a tremendous difference. The purpose of this chapter is to teach you how to proceed in an orderly, time-saving, effective way.

Chapters 7–13 have laid the groundwork for this chapter. If you have already studied them, fine. If not, cross references in this chapter will guide you to the parts that will be most helpful in writing a term paper.

Be word-wise!

Skim the preceding paragraphs for these words: *final, course, tremendous, effective*. Which of their dictionary synonyms would not be good replacements for the words as used in this lesson? Which synonym of *course* does the drawing illustrate?

1. CHOOSING A SUBJECT

If you may write your term paper on a topic of your own choosing, you need to think carefully before you settle on a subject. The guides on page 242 will help you to select a good topic.

1. Choose a subject that really interests you but about which you still can learn much.
2. Choose a subject that is not too broad. For example, "The Automobile Industry" as a subject covers far more territory than you can treat in a term paper of some five thousand words. "Automobiles before 1900," on the other hand, is limited and specific.
3. Choose a subject not too difficult, one about which you can find material in popular magazines or in books aimed at the general reader.
4. Choose a subject that has some interest for the average reader.

LEARNING ACTIVITY

Decide in class which of these subjects do not fit the guides.

Guided Missiles	Farming in the United States
The Clipper Ship	Digging the Panama Canal
Teaching as a Career	Transcontinental Railroads
Irrigation	Washington as a Military Strategist
The Model–T	Descendants of Our Presidents
The Olympic Games	Ghost Towns of the West
The Oregon Trail	Careers for Women before 1890

2. GATHERING MATERIAL

Once you have settled upon a subject, you are ready to gather material. Begin by *defining the specific problem* with which you wish to deal. If, for example, your subject is "The One-Room School," you may define your problem thus: "Is the one-room school doomed?" Now, instead of collecting miscellaneous information about one-room schools, you will select only material related specifically to your problem.

WHERE TO FIND MATERIAL

1. *Observation or experience.* You will need to supplement this source with others, since your experiences or opportunities for observation are likely to be limited. Besides, you may gather hasty or false impressions.
2. *Interviews.* Persons in your community probably can give you helpful information. Apply the Guides for Taking Part in Interviews, page 54.
3. *The library.* Usually the library offers more help than any other source. Chapter 8 of this text tells how to make good use of the library. If you have not yet studied that chapter, do so before going further.
4. *Special bulletins and reports.* Government, industry, and various organizations are constantly publishing bulletins or reports. You can get from the

Government Printing Office, Washington, D.C., a list of the pamphlets that it has available. For a list of the leading associations in the United States, consult the *Information Please Almanac* or the *World Almanac*. In writing for material, state specifically what you are interested in finding out. (See page 227 for help in writing the letter of request.)

LEARNING ACTIVITIES

A. If possible, bring into class the almanacs named above. Examine them to get an idea of the many organizations listed.

B. Where might you write for information about some phase of the subjects listed in *A,* page 242? Discuss that question in class.

HOW TO MAKE A WORKING BIBLIOGRAPHY

You are ready now to make a *working bibliography*, which is a list of the *specific* sources that you plan to use.

GUIDES TO THE FORM OF A WORKING BIBLIOGRAPHY

1. Use ruled cards 3 x 5 inches in size.
2. Make a card for each book, bulletin, article, pamphlet, or interview.
3. Arrange the cards in alphabetical order.
4. Follow the same forms that you will use in the final bibliography (page 249). What to include depends upon the kind of source.
    a) A card for a book, a pamphlet, or a document should list these:
    (1) The author's name (*last name first*)
    (2) The title of the book (*underlined*)
    (3) The edition. (If none is given, the book is a first edition.)
    (4) The place of publication
    (5) The name of the publisher
    (6) The publication date
    (7) A brief statement about the contents, the call number of the book, and the place where the book is available.
    b) A card for a magazine article differs only slightly.
    (1) The title is put in quotation marks; it is not underlined.
    (2) The title of the magazine itself is underlined.
    (3) The volume number (in Roman numerals) and year are given.
    (4) The page or pages containing the article are named.
    c) A card for a part of a book is like that for a magazine article except that there will be no (3).
    d) A card for an encyclopedia article names the *article*, the *encyclopedia*, the *volume* and the *edition*, and the *page or pages* covered.
5. Follow *exactly* the forms shown on the cards on page 244.

Kaempffert, Waldemar
  Explorations in Science. New York: Viking Press,
1953.
    Has interesting material on supersonic speed.

500
K34E
Public Library

Sutton, Richard M.
  "A Family of Solar Eclipses." Scientific
American, CXC (February, 1954), 36-40.

  "Ancient Eclipses." Encyclopaedia
Britannica (1945 edition), VII, 912-14.

GUIDES FOR FINDING BIBLIOGRAPHY MATERIAL

1. Consult first of all general references, such as encyclopedias.
   a) If your topic is a narrow one, look under a related broad topic.
   b) Look in the *index* volume for additional references for a subject.
   c) Read carefully to get a general background for your subject.
   d) Make a bibliography card for each source that you read; also make cards for any references recommended in a source.
2. Look in special reference books (see pages 130–31) for additional sources that you may want to consult. Make cards for them. Make a card for a reference book itself only if it contains a discussion of your topic.
3. If *1* and *2* do not provide help, talk to your librarian. There are guidebooks and bibliographies to which she can refer you.
4. Make full use of the *Readers' Guide* (page 133).
5. Use the card catalogue. (*a*) If your topic is not listed, look under related topics. (*b*) For any titles for which you have already made cards, copy the call numbers to help you to get the books quickly.
6. As soon as you locate titles of pamphlets or bulletins not found in your library, order the material. Make out a card for each such item.
7. Write bibliography cards for any interviews. Give the date and the name of the person interviewed; tell why you think that he is reliable.
8. Hand in your complete set of cards for inspection by your teacher.

LEARNING ACTIVITY

Make bibliography cards for the following. Exchange papers for checking.
1. Man's Unconquerable Mind, a book written by Gilbert Highet. It was published by Columbia University Press, New York, in 1954.
2. An article in vol. 15 of the 1954 edition of the World Book encyclopedia. The title of the article is Sound, and it is found on pages 7559–7565.
3. Pacific Deeps Yield Strange Fishes, an article beginning on page 244 of Nature Magazine, vol. 47, the May, 1954, issue. The author is James Nevin Miller.

3. ORGANIZING THE MATERIAL

The next step in preparing your term paper is to consult and then classify the sources on your bibliography cards. To do so, make a *working outline* that covers the large subdivisions that you want in your paper.

TAKING NOTES OF YOUR READING

You are ready now to begin taking notes of material that has to do with the items in your working outline. Here you should make good use of the technique of *skimming* (page 113).

GUIDES FOR MAKING CARD NOTES

1. For each book named on a bibliography card, skim the *table of contents* and the *index* to find any parts of the books that concern your subject.

2. Skim those parts to see whether they contain usable material.

3. If a source has no usable material, toss out the bibliography card.

4. Continue checking until you have eliminated all but the cards that refer to really useful material.

5. Proceed to take detailed notes from the sources that remain.

   a) Use ruled index cards, preferably 4 x 6 inches in size.

   b) Cover only one point on each card; write only one note on it.

   c) Write the point in the upper left-hand corner so that you can file your notes according to the points covered.

   d) Name the exact source.

   (1) For a book or a pamphlet, give *author, title* (or enough of it to identify it), and *page*.

   (2) For a magazine article, give also the *volume number* and the *date*.

   (3) If it is an encyclopedia article, give the *name of the encyclopedia,* the *edition,* the *volume number,* and the *page*.

   e) Use *direct quotations* if you want to include in your paper an author's exact wording. Avoid too many quotations. (If necessary, review the rules on page 176.) To show that you are omitting certain words or phrases within a sentence, use three dots (...). If what you omit comes after a complete sentence, use four dots; that is, include the sentence period.

   f) Make most of your notes *brief statements in your own words*. For these, do not use quotation marks. You need not use complete sentences, but make sure that your notes are *exact* and *clear*.

A DIRECT QUOTATION

Temperature on Mars

"It has been found that in the south equatorial regions ... the surface temperature may be as high as 60 degrees Fahrenheit,..."

—Lewis, "As Mars Nears the Earth," *Nature,* XLVII (May, 1954), 274.

> *Surface of Mars*
> Believed less irregular than earth or moon. Probably real differences in level, however. Coblentz and Lampland suggest variations in temperature (noted by them) indicate such.
> —*Encyclopaedia Britannica* (1945 ed.), XIV, 961.

LEARNING ACTIVITY

For practice in making card notes, select a subject (or some phase of one) from *A,* page 242. Make at least three card notes, one note based on a book; another, on a magazine article; and the third, on an encyclopedia article. Quote directly in one of them. Exchange cards for criticism.

MAKING THE FINAL OUTLINE

This outline may well be made before you have finished your note cards, for it will help you to avoid taking notes that you cannot use. Page 118 explains how to make both the *sentence outline* and the *topic outline.* Decide for yourself which you wish to use. Keep your outline flexible; that is, feel free to shift sections or parts of sections. If your paper is to have an introduction and a conclusion, include those parts in your outline.

FITTING NOTE CARDS TO THE OUTLINE

After making your outline, go over your note cards carefully.

1. In the upper right-hand corner of each card, indicate the section and the subsection (of your outline) to which the note applies: IB3, for example.
2. Arrange the cards by the designations in the right-hand corner so that they are in the same order as the points of your outline. Then number the cards.
3. Compare the note cards with the outline. The Roman numerals will correspond to the main sections of your term paper. Do you have too much material for some sections and not enough for others? If so, discard some of your notes or find additional material for the weak sections.
4. If required, submit outline and note cards for your teacher's approval.

4. Writing the Paper Itself

THE FIRST DRAFT

1. Make a first draft of your paper, using your outline and the note cards. Concentrate on the *ideas* that you want to include; you can *polish* later.
2. If you include a long quotation (four lines or more), use no quotation marks. Instead, indent several spaces from right and left margins to show that you are quoting. If you are typing your paper, single space the quotation. Be sure to use quotation marks, however, for any short quotations.
3. Paraphrase the material contained on the note cards that do not have direct quotations. (Review pages 114–15.)
4. Use footnotes to give credit for the material, quoted or paraphrased, that you have borrowed from other writers. Use small figures ("superior numbers") to indicate these footnotes. There are different ways of numbering footnotes; for your purpose here, number them consecutively from the beginning of your paper to the end. Note these examples of the form for (1) a book, (2) a magazine article, (3) an encyclopedia article.

> [1] Durward Leon Allen, *Our Wildlife Legacy* (New York: Funk & Wagnalls Co., 1954), p. 87.
> [2] Isabel M. Lewis, "As Mars Nears the Earth," *Nature Magazine,* XLVII (May, 1954), 274.
> [3] "Atmosphere," *Encyclopaedia Britannica* (1945 ed.), XIV, 961.

LEARNING ACTIVITY

Write footnotes for the items on the sample bibliography cards, page 244. Supply your own page numbers for the book. Exchange papers for criticism.

REVISING THE FIRST DRAFT

After you have made the first draft, begin the process of revising and improving the content.

1. Analyze every sentence to see that it is clear and grammatically sound. Watch particularly for pronoun faults; be sure that you make clear to what noun (or equivalent word group) each pronoun refers. (See page 345.) Check also to see that modifiers are not located where they will cause confusion in meaning. (See pages 365, 380.)
2. This is a formal piece of writing; therefore you should avoid using colloquial English. (See page 105.)
3. Correct careless errors in spelling, capitalization, or punctuation.
4. Study consecutive paragraphs to see whether you have made smooth transitions. (See page 206.) Check all paragraphs for *unity, coherence, and emphasis.* (See page 199.)

MAKING A BIBLIOGRAPHY

The *bibliography,* which lists all books and other material that you read and made use of in the preparation of your paper, should be your last page or pages. Follow exactly the forms shown here, and group the sources as indicated, with the items in each group arranged alphabetically.

BOOKS

Calder, Ritchie. *Men against the Jungle.* New York: The Macmillan Company, 1954.

Rasmussen, A. H. *China Trader.* New York: Thomas Y. Crowell Company, 1954.

Vogel, Alfred A. *Papuans and Pygmies.* New York: Roy Publishers, 1954.

ARTICLES

Deevey, Edward S., Jr. "The End of the Moas." *Scientific American,* CXC (February, 1954), 84–90.

Hodge, Walter Henrick. "The Elusive Elephant's Foot." *Natural History,* LXII (September, 1953), 324–29.

Osborn, Fairfield. "People and Animals." *Atlantic Monthly,* CXIII (January, 1954), 37–39.

ENCYCLOPEDIA ARTICLE

"Papuans," *Encyclopaedia Britannica* (1945 ed.), XVII, 242–43.

PREPARING THE FINAL COPY

The final step in preparing your term paper is to copy it.

1. Type your paper or write it neatly in ink on good quality typing paper or theme paper. Write on only one side.
2. Center the title on the first line of the first page. Then skip a line before beginning the paper itself.
3. In a typed paper, put the title about an inch and a half from the top. Double space the material, except for long quotations, footnotes, and the bibliography, which should be single spaced.
4. Number pages consecutively in the center, about six lines from the top.
5. Begin each chapter or section on a new page.
6. Prepare a *title page.* Write the title just above the center of the page; below it put your name; below that, the name of the course. If required, add the date.
7. Make a *table of contents* to follow the title page. Show the title and page reference of each chapter or section and of the bibliography.
8. Proofread carefully for thoughtless errors in form.
9. Clip or staple the pages together or put them into a folder with your name on the outside.
0. Hand the paper in on the date specified.

CHAPTER 16

Writing Descriptions

The ability to describe vividly is an asset to anyone. No magic trick is involved in learning how to improve your descriptive powers. Just as there are basic principles to be mastered by the student of painting, music, or sculpture, so there are basic principles to be mastered by the writer. This chapter gives you ten practical helps to vivid description.

1. SEEING THINGS CLEARLY

The first requirement for good description is to see clearly what you plan to describe. Here are some helpful hints:

1. Be sure that the picture in your own mind is clear cut and vivid.
2. Try to describe from actual sight, not merely from memory or imagination.
3. Use the right words to help the reader see what you see. Notice, for example, the difference in the impression given by these two sentences:

> She was a thin, anemic-looking girl.
> She was a slender, ivory-skinned girl.

The girl may be the same person in both cases, but one image is attractive, and the other is not. What makes the difference? *Two different people are describing what they see.*

LEARNING ACTIVITIES

A. Practice sharpening your powers of observation. Professional writers use notes to record ideas, details, and expressions which they hope to use in some future writing. Try your hand at making such notes. For one week keep a record of *ideas* for descriptions, of *expressive words and phrases* that you read or hear, and of any *vivid original expressions* that occur to you. At the end of the week, hold a class or group conference in which you exchange and discuss your notes. File in your notebook any material that you think you may want to use.

B. Write two descriptive paragraphs. In one of them, give a pleasing impression of a place, a person, an object, or an activity. In the other, give the opposite impression. Read your work in class. The drawing offers a suggestion.

MOTHER BABY SITTER

2. KEEPING A CONSISTENT POINT OF VIEW

Point of view, or the way in which you look at what you are describing, is important in all description. You need to let your reader know what your point of view is so that he will not be confused. Keep these helps in mind:

1. When you describe the physical aspect of a scene, the position from which you are looking may be either stationary or moving.
2. If you view something from one spot, your viewpoint is of necessity limited. You must describe only what can be seen from that point of view.
3. If you choose to describe from a moving point of view, you must, when you change positions, make the change clear to the reader.
4. In keeping clear your point of view, you should use such expressions as *just beyond, to the left, opposite me, far below, across the road.*

Here is a description of what may be seen from a stationary point of view, that of a person standing before the inn described.

> At such a time one little roadside Inn, snugly sheltered behind a great elm-tree, with a rare seat for idlers encircling its capacious bole, addressed a cheerful front towards the traveler, . . . The ruddy signboard perched up in the tree, with its golden letters winking in the sun, ogled the passer-by from among the green leaves, like a jolly face, . . . The crimson curtains in the lower rooms, and the pure white hangings in the little bedchambers above, beckoned, "Come in!" with every breath of air. . . . Upon the window sills were flowering plants in bright red pots, which made a lively show against the white front of the house; and in the darkness of the doorway, there were streaks of light which glanced off from the surfaces of bottles and tankards.
>
> —CHARLES DICKENS

In contrast, note how the point of view changes in the description that follows.

> The man had hurried rapidly in the darkness along the main street of the Chelles; then he had turned . . . into the crossroad leading to Montfermeil, like one who . . . had been that way before.
>
> When he reached the wood, he slackened his pace, and began to look carefully at all the trees, pausing at every step, as if he were seeking and following a mysterious route known only to himself. There was a moment when he appeared to lose himself; when he stopped, undecided. Finally, by continual groping, he reached a glade where there was a heap of large whitish stones. He made his way quickly toward these stones, and examined them closely in the dusk of the night, as if he were passing them in review. A large tree, covered with those excrescences that are the warts of vegetation, was only a few steps from the heap of stones. He went to this tree, and passed his hand over the bark of the trunk, as if he were seeking to recognize and to count all the warts.
>
> —VICTOR HUGO

LEARNING ACTIVITIES IN KEEPING A CONSISTENT POINT OF VIEW

A. With your working partner, decide upon a scene that you may view from two different angles. One of you may describe what can be seen from the back of the school building; the other may describe what is visible from the front; or, if you like, you may stand together and describe what can be seen when you look in opposite directions. Read your descriptions in class. Be sure to apply the Guides to Effective Oral Reading, page 41.

B. Write a paragraph in which you describe something from a moving point of view. Follow the Guides to the Development of the Paragraph, page 199. *Proofread for careless errors.* In your small groups, exchange paragraphs for critical reading. Have good paragraphs read to the entire class. Here are possible topics:

1. The main street of your town
2. A hike through the woods
3. A trip through the zoo
4. A parade
5. The school cafeteria
6. The five-and-ten-cent store

3. CREATING A MOOD

The *mood,* or state of mind, in which you look at what you are describing will influence your description. If you feel gay and carefree, what you describe will undoubtedly reflect that spirit. If you are downcast and sad, your description will surely correspond to that mood. If your reader is to understand the mood that you are attempting to create, you must be very selective in choosing only details that will fit the mood.

Notice how simply yet effectively Stevenson creates a mood in this brief passage from *Treasure Island:*

I do not rightly know what it is to faint, but I do know that for the next little while the whole world swam away from before me in a whirling mist; [John] Silver and the birds and the tall Spyglass hilltop going round and round and topsy-turvy before my eyes; and all manner of bells ringing and distant voices shouting in my ear.

LEARNING ACTIVITIES

A. Bring to class a paragraph from literature that portrays a particular mood or feeling. Read your paragraph in class. Practice beforehand, applying the guides on page 41. Students will decide the mood or feeling that the paragraph conveys.

B. List five adjectives that describe a mood: one of *peacefulness, gloom, anger, lightheartedness,* . . . In your small groups, exchange lists. Write a descriptive paragraph using the adjectives on the list that you receive. *Do not use the word that names the mood.* Apply the guides on page 199. Give your paper to the person whose list of adjectives you used. As he reads the paragraph aloud, the other members of the group should listen critically to try to determine the mood.

4. Selecting the Right Details

READ AND DISCUSS

One common type of description uses the "catalogue" method; it gives a detailed, factual picture of what is being described. It is a method suitable for practical purposes; that is, for use in guidebooks, bulletins describing missing persons and those wanted by the police, "For Rent" and "Lost and Found" advertisements, accounts of scientific discoveries, . . .

Opposed to this type of description is the kind that appeals to the imagination. It uses only the details that will create a vivid impression; the catalogue method is likely to hamper it. All good literature abounds in description of this type.

In writing description, keep in mind that too many facts may bore or even confuse the reader. Whenever possible, *suggest* rather than enumerate. For example, instead of saying that someone is "generous," describe some generous action done by that person.

Read the following two descriptions of the same scene.

Twin rows of tall trees cast shifting shadows on the road lying straight and empty before us. Far ahead, it tapered to a point, like a drawing illustrating perspective.

On each side of the road there were trees. About half of them were elms; the rest were oaks and maples. They seemed to be about fifty feet high for the most part, and their branches had been trimmed to a height of fifteen feet. The road, which was paved with cement, was about twenty feet wide, but it looked narrower in the distance because it was so straight and the landscape was so flat. The sun was shining brightly and a breeze was blowing. It was not a very strong breeze, but it did move the leaves enough so that as the sun shone through them, it made moving spots of shade on the road. As far as we could see, nobody was traveling this stretch of road but us.

Which scene gives the clearer picture? How does it do so?

Be word-wise!

Skim the first two paragraphs under "Read and Discuss" for these words: *catalogue, suitable, vivid, hamper*. Which of their dictionary synonyms would not be good replacements for the words as used in this lesson? Which synonym of *catalogue* does the drawing illustrate?

LEARNING ACTIVITIES

A. Write a description of a valuable article that you have lost. This is a "catalogue-type" description. Use the exact words that will distinguish this article from others of its kind. Apply the paragraph guides on page 199.

B. Write a paragraph for a sales letter; describe an article so well that the reader will be eager to have it. Describe a *new car,* a *pet,* a *game,* a *book,* a *musical instrument,* . . . Read and discuss your paragraphs in class. Be sure to apply the Guides to Courteous Speech Habits, page 56.

5. ARRANGING DETAILS EFFECTIVELY

Once you have chosen the details that you want to include in a description, your next step is to put those details into some sort of logical order. Here are various methods:

1. Describing something *in relation to what surrounds it*
2. Describing a scene from *near* to *far,* or from *far* to *near*
3. Describing something from *top* to *bottom,* or from *bottom* to *top*
4. Describing from *left* to *right,* or from *right* to *left*
5. Going from *most important* to *least important,* or *vice versa*

No set rule for arrangement can be established. Just be orderly. This sketch from Sir Walter Scott's *Ivanhoe* shows logical arrangement of detail.

Accordingly he soon reached an open plot of turf, on the opposite side of which, a rock, rising abruptly from a gently sloping plain, offered its gray and weather-beaten front to the traveler. Ivy mantled its sides in some places, and in others, oaks and holly bushes . . . waved over the precipices below, . . . At the bottom of the rock, and leaning, as it were, against it, was constructed a rude hut, built chiefly of the trunks of trees felled in the neighboring forest, and secured against the weather by having its crevices stuffed with moss mingled with clay. . . .

LEARNING ACTIVITIES

A. List the items in the *Ivanhoe* description in the order that they appear. What arrangement does Scott use? Discuss that question.

B. Keeping in mind the order of details, write a short descriptive paragraph. *Be sure to proofread.* Compare work in class. Here are possible topics.

1. A church arranged for a wedding
2. A classroom
3. The stands at a ball game
4. A park
5. Any room in your home
6. A parade

6. APPEALING TO THE FIVE SENSES

READ AND DISCUSS

Inexperienced writers too often direct their descriptions to the eye and the ear alone. An appeal also to the sensations of smell, taste, and feeling can help to make your descriptions realistic. Analyze the following paragraph from Stevenson's *Treasure Island*.

The cold evening breeze of which I have spoken whistled through every chink of the rude building, and sprinkled the floor with a continual rain of fine sand. There was sand in our eyes, sand in our teeth, sand in our suppers, sand dancing in the spring at the bottom of the kettle, for all the world like porridge beginning to boil. Our chimney was a square hole in the roof: it was but a little part of the smoke that found its way out, and the rest eddied about the house and kept us coughing and piping the eye.

To how many senses does the author appeal? Name them.

Sometimes it is especially effective to concentrate on one of the senses, as Dickens does in this paragraph from *A Tale of Two Cities:*

The stillness consequent on the cessation of the rumbling and labouring of the coach, added to the stillness of the night, made it very quiet indeed. The panting of the horses communicated a tremulous motion to the coach, as if it were in a state of agitation. The hearts of the passengers beat loud enough perhaps to be heard; but at any rate, the quiet pause was audibly expressive of people out of breath, and holding the breath, and having the pulses quickened by expectation.

To which one of the senses does the author appeal primarily? What emotion is he trying to convey? How do you know?

LEARNING ACTIVITIES

A. Read and discuss the following quotations in class. To what senses do they appeal? How effective are the appeals? How much does the effectiveness of a sense appeal depend upon your familiarity with the sensations described?

1. . . . the warm, buttery smell from the popcorn machine.
2. The stiff collar sawed at his neck unmercifully.
3. He went down the dark streets, among the heavy shadows, with the moon and the clouds sailing high above him.—DICKENS
4. There drifted to him a mouth-watering hint of pickles in the making.
5. The world turned giddily before my eyes.—STEVENSON
6. The white fog creeps from bush to bush . . .—ARNOLD
7. The glow of the sun from above, its thousandfold reflection from the waves, the sea water that fell and dried upon me, caking my very lips with salt, combined to make my throat burn and my brain ache.—STEVENSON
8. Prickles of impending danger slithered down his spine.
9. The moan of doves in immemorial elms,
   And murmuring of innumerable bees.—TENNYSON
10. Of all flower scents, I remember most vividly the sharp, sweet fragrance from my mother's petunia bed in the cool of a summer evening.
11. The sudden cough of a rifle through the golden peace of the sunshine.
                                               —WALTER NOBLE BURNS
12. Again there came the shrill quaver of a hoot owl.

B. Find other descriptive sentences that have definite appeal to one or more of the senses. Try to find at least one sentence for each sense. Read these sentences in class; discuss their effectiveness. Save them for a later assignment.

C. Jot down specific sense details that you might use in writing a paragraph based upon each of the sentences that follow.

1. Dan was feeling thoroughly miserable.
2. I wish that I could really describe how it feels when you settle yourself in the line, waiting for the ball to be snapped.
3. The room was humming with activity.
4. It seemed hours that I crouched there in the dark.
5. An early breakfast in the open is something to remember.
6. During the final minutes of play, the gym was a madhouse.

7. Making Comparison with the Familiar

Comparing a thing to something else is one of the best ways to give a good picture—if the thing to which you make a comparison is familiar to the reader. Never use a comparison just for the sake of displaying how much you know. Notice the following comparisons:

Our tomatoes were the size of hens' eggs.
Our tomatoes were the size of one of the Cullinan diamonds.

Both comparisons may actually describe tomatoes of the same size, but only the first of them gives the average reader a clear picture. He knows how large hens' eggs are, but he has no idea whether the Cullinan diamonds are the size of peas or the size of golf balls. To use a comparison that carries no image to the reader only annoys and confuses him.

LEARNING ACTIVITIES

A. Using familiar comparisons, describe one of your favorite colors, tastes, or sounds. Compare these descriptions in class. File your work in your notebook.

B. Write a sentence in which you use a familiar comparison to describe each of the following. Read your comparisons aloud in class.

1. A thundercloud
2. The song of a cricket
3. A coolie hat
4. Hailstones
5. A dog's nose
6. Ginger ale

8. Using Figurative Language

A special type of comparison makes use of *figures of speech*. In a *literal* comparison, things are compared that belong to the same general class:

John is as tall as I am.

Both John and the speaker are human beings. In a *figurative* comparison, things are compared that are basically unlike each other but that have some quality in common:

John is as tall as a house.

You know very well that John is not so tall as a house, even a small one, but this comparison gives you a definite idea that he is unusually tall.

There are four types of figurative language that will be of special use to you. They are the *simile*, the *metaphor, personification*, and *hyperbole*.

1. A *simile* states a comparison definitely. It makes use of comparing words, particularly *like, as–as, so–as, than.*

Tom had leaped at the sound, *like a horse at the spur.*—STEVENSON

257

2. A *metaphor* implies a comparison between two things but does not actually state it. Notice this example:

> *The black flower of civilized society*—a prison.—HAWTHORNE

A prison is not actually a flower, of course; it is simply being compared to one.

3. *Personification* consists of giving human qualities or abilities to things or ideas. Notice this example:

> It was one of those dark *nights that hold their breath* by the hour together, and then *heave a long, low sigh,* and *hold their breath* again.—DICKENS

Often personification is combined with a simile or a metaphor:

> Terror of the people in the street sat down before his mind like a besieging army. (*personification and simile*)—STEVENSON

4. *Hyperbole* is deliberate and extravagant exaggeration. It is used oftenest for humorous effect: Before me stood a *mountain of a man.*

LEARNING ACTIVITIES IN USING FIGURES OF SPEECH

A. In class, discuss the following quotations. Classify the figures of speech used; then state as simply as possible the idea or impression that the writer wants to convey. Put your conclusions upon the board.

EXAMPLE: The days were like hot coals. (*Simile, showing extreme heat*)

1. Time has fallen asleep in the afternoon sunshine.—ALEXANDER SMITH
2. . . . a door with a weak rattle in its throat.—DICKENS
3. An hour and a half limped heavily away.—DICKENS
4. He would boil awhile to himself and then overflow and scald me again.
   —MARK TWAIN
5. My memory was never loaded with anything but blank cartridges.
   —MARK TWAIN
6. The sun, like a little man in a crowd at a puppet show, . . . endeavoring to get a peep between the unmannerly clouds.—IRVING
7. . . . hands that dangled a mile out of his sleeves.—IRVING
8. A whale ship was my Yale College and my Harvard.—MELVILLE
9. I love a broad margin to my life.—THOREAU
10. Who speaks the truth stabs Falsehood in the heart.—LOWELL
11. Come into the garden, Maud,
    For the black bat, night, has flown.—TENNYSON
12. From a proud tower in the town,
    Death looks gigantically down.—POE
13. The good Peter reeled with the blow and, turning up his eyes, beheld a thousand suns, besides moons and stars, dancing about the firmament.
    —IRVING
14. The whole wild night is in pursuit of us.—DICKENS
15. A buzz arose in the court as if a cloud of great blueflies were swarming around the prisoner.—DICKENS

16. Up the two terrace flights of steps, the rain ran wildly, and beat at the great door, like a swift messenger rousing those within.—DICKENS

17. He is a little chimney and heated hot in a moment.—LONGFELLOW

B. For each idea listed in *A*, write one or more different figurative comparisons. Read and discuss your work in class. Keep your paper for later use.

C. Try your hand at replacing with fresh, original figures the overworked similes and metaphors that follow. Compare your work in class.

1. Smooth as silk	5. A voice like thunder	9. Still as a mouse
2. Green as grass	6. Slippery as an eel	10. Brave as a lion
3. Thin as a lath	7. Cheeks like roses	11. Skin like velvet
4. Sly as a fox	8. Teeth like pearls	12. Sharp as a razor

D. Perhaps you can think of other worn-out similes. In class, make a list of them on the blackboard; then see how many effective replacements you can find. File the results in your notebook.

E. Besides similes, metaphors, personification, and hyperbole, writers often use certain other figures of speech. These include *allegory, metonymy, synecdoche,* and *apostrophe.* (The last-named is discussed on page 285.) Applying the Guides for Taking Notes, page 212, investigate one of the figures and report to the class what you find. Use your Speech Score Card. After you have listened to the reports and have copied the definitions for the four additional figures of speech, find at least five examples to illustrate each of them. Compare work in class; with your teacher, select the best ones from the entire class contribution. Place these in your notebook for future reference.

9. CHOOSING WORDS WISELY

Avoid the temptation of "dressing up" in a great many fancy words what you say. Search for interesting and effective new words, but use them only if they add to the picture. Compare these two examples:

> Slowly the sun sank.
> Dilatorily the refulgent orb gravitated below the horizon.

Does the second improve upon the first in any way? Note that here a few simple words give a far better picture than many elaborate ones.

GUIDES FOR CHOOSING EFFECTIVE LANGUAGE

1. As a rule, use simple words oftener than elaborate ones.
2. Use a vivid verb wherever possible instead of a colorless verb and accompanying modifiers. For example, say, "The stars *glittered,*" rather than, "The stars *shone brightly.*" (See page 311.)
3. Use exact or specific nouns. (See page 336.)
4. Use vivid adjectives and adverbs but avoid too many. (See pages 369 and 385.)

LEARNING ACTIVITIES IN CHOOSING WORDS WISELY

Directions: Do the following activities; then compare work in class.

A. Supply simpler words for the italicized words or word groups in these sentences. Rearrange the sentence order if you wish.

1. My *domicile* is one mile west of town.
2. A man should not drive a car when he is *under the influence of spirituous beverages.*
3. She *directed her gaze* at the letter on the table.
4. We *partook* hungrily of the *ambrosial viands.*

B. Supply one vivid verb to take the place of the italicized expressions in these sentences. You may take out or add a word if you wish.

1. The fisherman *waded noisily* across the mountain stream.
2. My friends *hinted slyly* that I knew more than I was telling.
3. You shall *pay dearly* for this.
4. The gossipy women *talked rapidly* about their new neighbor.

C. Substitute exact nouns for those italicized in these sentences.

1. The *storm* struck suddenly.
2. There was a slight *movement* in the grass.
3. The *passage* is blocked.
4. We drove mile after mile past fields of waving *grain.*

D. Make these sentences more graphic by the addition of adjectives and adverbs. You may add other words if you need them.

1. The bacon sizzled.
2. The water gurgled.
3. The sun blistered my back.
4. The moon peeked through the trees.

10. COMBINING THE AIDS TO DESCRIPTION

You have been practicing various aids to vivid description (pages 250–60). Now you are ready to combine them in your writing.

GUIDES TO GOOD DESCRIPTION

1. Be sure that your own impression is clear cut and vivid.
2. Make clear your point of view.
3. Create a dominant mood or impression.
4. Select only details that will strengthen the picture.
5. Be logical in the arrangement of details.
6. Appeal to as many of the five senses as you can.
7. Make use of familiar comparisons.
8. Use figures of speech, but use them sparingly.
9. Make use of interesting new words, but keep the general effect simple.
10. Choose vivid verbs, specific nouns, and vivid adjectives and adverbs.

LEARNING ACTIVITIES

Directions: Do as many of the following exercises as time permits. Follow the guides for developing paragraphs, page 199. *Proofread for careless errors.* Exchange papers for critical reading; then have good work read aloud in class or in your small groups. Apply the Guides to Effective Oral Reading, page 41.

A. On a vacation trip you have no doubt been attracted by the beauty of some scene. Try to make your reader see that scene.

B. Using any of these subjects, write a two-hundred-word description.

Snowfall	Grandmother's Garden	Night Sounds	A Canoe Ride
Full Moon	Along the Midway	Fall Landscape	Our Antiques

C. Describe an activity in such a way that you give the sense of movement. What length of sentence will best show speed? slow movement? What new comparisons can you make? Here are suggested activities.

Skiing	Fishing	Making a train	Packing for a trip
Skating	Rising late	Mowing the lawn	Riding a roller coaster
Diving	Boxing	Climbing a hill	Playing basketball

D. Shop windows are interesting subjects for description. Try to picture a local window so vividly that your listeners will recognize it. Follow the guides on this page.

RELATED ACTIVITY

If you have read any of the books of Charles Dickens, you will remember his way of using exaggeration of detail to secure a vivid impression. In any of his books, you can find excellent descriptions of odors, tastes, personal appearance, dress, manners, characters, places. Bring to class at least one example. Read it orally, being careful to apply the Guides to Effective Oral Reading, page 41.

Writing Essays

The word *essay* means "a trial" or "an attempt." Thus, whenever you try in a piece of writing to set forth your ideas or feelings on a subject, you produce an essay. You can be serious or humorous; you can offer information; you can persuade or argue; you can express your thoughts for no other reason than just that you feel like expressing them. Whenever you write *descriptions, explanations,* or *reports,* you really create different types of essays.

You need not classify by type each essay that you read or write, but it is wise to know the aim of each type. Elements of more than one type may appear in the same essay, but the writing should have one main purpose.

TYPES OF ESSAYS

1. Informative or instructive (*explanations, directions*)
2. Persuasive or argumentative (*editorials, discussions*)
3. Critical or analytical (*book reviews,* for example)
4. Historical
5. Personal (*moods and opinions*)
6. Descriptive
7. Entertaining or humorous
8. Biographical

It is always well to make some sort of outline to follow in writing your essay. For an informal essay, the outline need not be detailed. It need show only the main divisions of what you have to say. However, if an essay is to be formal, a careful outline is an excellent guide. If necessary, review page 118 for outline form. Appraise all writing by the Writing Score Card page 197.

LEARNING ACTIVITIES IN STUDYING ESSAYS

A. Here is a humorous essay written by a student. Read it and then discuss the questions at the end.

From Brother's Point of View

A mad rush of feet, a head-on collision, a slammed door—and she's there first, as usual. The kid sister, first to get up, last to breakfast, (and then in her pajamas), is the plague of every well-deserving, hard-working, self-sacrificing brother. Why is it, you wonder, that every great man is burdened by some such obstacle which he must overcome or ignore?

Muttering all sorts of wild wishes and hopes, you stalk back to your bedroom and savagely begin to dress. A malicious grin creeps across your face as you make mental plans for what you would do if she were your daughter! Fiendishly your fists clench and your teeth grit; you even debate the possibilities of an amendment to the Constitution, prohibiting these offensive creatures (your younger sisters) from even going into a bathroom until all the menfolk are properly bathed, shaven, clothed, and on their way to work.

Back down the hall you stalk, wondering "what in Sam Hill" she can be doing! You rap gently on the door and inquire sweetly whether she has died. Getting no response except a higher note of the song she is murdering for the thousandth time, you next pound on the door. That most savage of all threats, "I'll tell Mother!" brings only a cool retort, "Go ahead, and while you're at it, find out where she put the tooth paste." Next you dwell tearfully upon the calamities that will befall the entire family if you are late to work and lose your job. To back it up, you tell her the time—plus twenty minutes—only to have her give you the correct time from the watch she never takes off.

"Oh, well," you sigh, and lean against the wall. Eventually the door is thrown open, and she struts triumphantly forth, trailing her bathrobe and flopping her bedroom slippers in that irritating way that only she has. Calmly you survey the remains that she has left. As usual, she has borrowed your towel and completely exhausted the supply of hot water.

Presently you barge forth and down to breakfast. You are greeted by a few general reflections from Father on the subject of people who stay up all night and sleep all morning. During the course of breakfast, your artistic temperament causes you to wonder how Sister would look with your oatmeal decorating the end of her perky turned-up nose. It is difficult to restrain yourself from finding out.

In due time she arises with an air of superiority, trails out, and slip-slops back upstairs to complete the rituals and ceremonies she must perform before pronouncing herself ready for school.

Secretly resolving to remain a bachelor all your life, you proceed on your way to work. Of course you don't mind waiting in a pouring rain for Annette. She's different!

1. Prove that this is an essay.
2. What is the central idea?
3. Are *ideas* or *emotions* stronger in the essay?
4. What descriptive words or lines point up the humor?

B. Read the editorial on page 146. This is an impersonal essay. In one sentence, state the central idea.

C. In contrast to the impersonal essay is the *familiar* essay, which reveals the author's personality. Read and discuss this one by a man who was a great baseball player.

WHY I AM THANKFUL *

By Lou Gehrig

When I was seven or eight, I thought I would be the luckiest kid on earth if I could ever play football on the high school team. I did.

When I was in high school, I thought I would be the luckiest boy on earth if I could only go to college. I did.

When I was in college, I thought I would be the luckiest fellow on earth if I could just break into big-league baseball. I did.

When I fell in love with the Most Wonderful Girl in the World, I thought I would be the luckiest man on earth if she would really marry me. She did.

I could go on, but maybe that is enough to make my point.

In baseball we talk a lot about the breaks. But I figure the best break I ever got in baseball came when I was signed by the Yankees. When you're playing for the best team in the league, you get good breaks all the time, and you can take the bad ones and still come out on top at the end of the season.

This summer I got a bad break. The doctors said I couldn't play baseball any more. All right, I'm still the luckiest man on earth, when you add things up. I've still got a long season of life to play out, and my team—America—is absolutely the best in the league. That's what counts.

I was a poor kid. We lived in a poor neighborhood. But it was in America, where even poor kids in poor neighborhoods get good breaks—playgrounds, supervised athletics, good public schools. So I got to play on the high school football team—which made me the luckiest kid on earth.

My mother and father were hard-working people and they hadn't great educational advantages. But they were American parents, willing to work hard and skimp to give their son the advantages that they had missed. In America they could do it; so I went to college—which made me the luckiest boy on earth.

I was blessed with a good physique. In some countries that might have been just the thing to commend me to the attention of the authorities as a likely young man to carry a gun. But in America it commended me, instead, to the attention of the Yankee baseball scouts. So I became a big-league player—which made me the luckiest fellow on earth.

Just what my wife saw in me to make her consent to marry me, I've never fully understood. But I do know that if I hadn't been sure that I could support her, I wouldn't have had the gall to ask her to do it. In this America, the most prosperous country in the world, I had no qualms about making enough money. So we were married—which made me the luckiest man on earth.

There are plenty of other reasons why I claim that title. America has lavished opportunities upon me, wonderful friends and associates, great personal satisfactions—all good breaks. I can see no more reason to be overwhelmed by one bad break in the game of life than I could in the game of baseball. After all, I'm still playing on the top-notch team. And what better break could a man have than a chance to do his part for his country as an official of its greatest city? That break came to me recently when I was appointed a member of the Parole Commission of New York City.

In baseball you learn that it's team play that makes the good breaks pile up and makes up for the bad ones. I remember, several years ago, going up to Sing Sing with the Yankees to play an exhibition game. When we went out on the field, it sounded like old home week to me. A lot of the convicts in the stands were yelling: "Hey, Lou!" . . . "How're you, Lou?" . . . "Remember me, Lou?" I looked around, and there were several of the fellows who had been kids with me back in my old neighborhood. And I suppose they were thinking, "Lou got all the breaks."

Well, that's what I've just been saying. And I'm sorry for those poor fellows who got bad breaks and landed in Sing Sing. But they certainly got one good break, the most important break of all, the same break that I got. They were Americans. That made them members of the best team in the league, the team that spots a fellow more than his share of breaks before he starts.

Only they forgot—or never knew—that you don't get the breaks unless you play with the team, instead of against it. That's one thing that baseball has taught me. I've seen plenty of fellows come up to the big leagues and land on their ears, because they tried to chisel a little extra glory for themselves and let their teammates down. And they almost always blame the breaks—though they have had the best break of all in getting on the team in the first place.

I suspect it is just the same in any other field, or in life in general. My hunch is that if those fellows up in Sing Sing hadn't tried to chisel a little extra glory—or gravy—for themselves, at the expense of their fellow Americans, they would have had much better breaks all the way along. As a parole commissioner, I hope I can help youngsters who have got headed wrong to see that they make their own bad breaks—and good ones. I hope that I can help them to help themselves to breaks as good as I have had.

And I'm the luckiest man on earth.

1. What is the central idea?
2. How does repetition add to the effectiveness of this essay?

D. Read and discuss the column on page 150. What is the aim of the author?

265

E. Stephen Leacock, Clarence Day, Will Rogers, and Robert Benchley were masters of the humorous essay. Use the card catalogue (see page 127) to help you locate quickly any of their writings in your library. Read to the class one essay, or a part of it. Apply the Guides to Effective Oral Reading, page 41.

GUIDES FOR WRITING ESSAYS

1. Choose any subject that interests you.
2. Make an outline before you begin to write. (See pages 117–18.)
3. Treat your subject either seriously or humorously, as you wish. In writing a humorous essay, keep in mind these pointers:
   a) Never label your humor; let the reader discover for himself that this is a humorous piece of writing.
   b) Pretend to be serious even when you advance preposterous ideas.
   c) Be able to laugh at yourself.
   d) Keep your humor kindly.
4. Make no attempt to exhaust the subject. Write, as a rule, about only one phase or incident related to it.
5. Be natural and sincere.

LEARNING ACTIVITIES

Directions: Write any of the following themes. Read and discuss your essays in class. Check all work by the Writing Score Card, page 197.

A. Write a persuasive editorial for your school paper.

B. Write a book review that is a good sample of a literary essay.

C. Choose one of these titles and write the essay that it suggests.

On Being Tall (*or* Short)	I Teach My Girl to Drive a Car
People Are Funny	Advice to Entering Freshmen
Brotherly Love	Bargain Counter
Television Commercials	Spring Fever
Why Must Girls Wear Make-up?	Never Take a Girl to a Ball Game
Heart Trouble in the Classroom	In the Christmas Mood

USING ENGLISH IN ALL CLASSES

A. Many of your school subjects require essay development for assigned topics. Bring your work to English class for analysis and improvement.

B. From any of your classes, make a list of test topics that call for essay-type answers. Look for such words as *trace, describe, explain, tell why, compare discuss, summarize, justify, criticize, evaluate.*

Writing Narratives

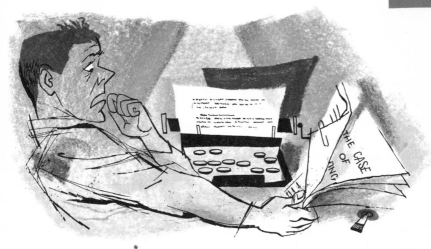

Telling a story may seem easier than writing one. However, writing a story has at least two advantages: (1) The author does not need an immediate audience. (2) He can polish and improve as much as he likes.

● WHAT YOU SHOULD KNOW ABOUT THE SHORT STORY

1. The story should create one sharp, central impression.
2. The heart of a good story is *conflict,* or struggle. This conflict may be between individuals, between people and ideas, between people and circumstances, or between a man and himself.
3. The progress of the struggle leads to what is called *suspense.* The author makes you eager to read on.
4. In a well-written short story, the action covers a comparatively short time. However, the author may bring in past events by means of a "flash back." For example, a character remembers something from the past, and that incident or scene is made a part of the story. The author introduces it by some such line as "John recalled the day that he and his father had first clashed," and then describes that scene.

1. CLASSIFYING STORY IDEAS

Long ago Solomon said, "There is no new thing under the sun." That remark is true of story ideas. The good storyteller simply gives a new twist to an old theme. He may treat it lightly or seriously, realistically or romantically. Underneath, it is still the same old idea.

Story ideas can be classified under certain main heads, which may, of course, overlap. Note these heads, with typical subdivisions.

1. *Courage:* in physical danger; in meeting defeat; in overcoming hate, prejudice, jealousy, or scandal; in physical or financial misfortunes

2. *Jealousy* or *hatred:* of a brother or a sister; of someone wealthier; of a business rival; of one who is more popular, successful, or beautiful

3. *Loyalty:* to home or family; to an ideal; to one's school, town, or nation; to a friend; to a belief; to one's religion; to a team or an organization

4. *Greed:* for money, power, popularity, possessions

5. *Rivalry:* in athletics, scholarship, politics, love, prize competitions, business

6. *Fear:* of physical danger; of discovery; of a parent; of making a mistake; of the mysterious or supernatural; of being laughed at

7. *Honesty:* in money transactions; in schoolwork; in competition (social, athletic, . . .); in family relationships

8. *Misunderstanding:* between parents and children; between brothers and sisters; between friends; between husband and wife; between employers and workers

9. *Love:* of a parent; of a son or a daughter; between sweethearts; between man and wife; of a friend; of justice, freedom, tolerance; of self

LEARNING ACTIVITIES IN STORY IDEAS

A. In class, go over the lists of story ideas. If you can, add to them.

B. Here are seven specific story ideas. Under which of the general themes might each of the ideas be classed? Could any of them fit under more than one theme? Think about these questions; then discuss the ideas in class.

1. A boy, injured in a football game, fears he may never walk again.
2. A girl is forbidden by her parents to see a boy whom she likes.
3. A teacher receives a note saying that someone is circulating damaging stories about him.
4. A plain, awkward girl has a pretty, popular younger sister.
5. A boy who has just scored the winning run in a baseball game knows that he failed to touch second base.
6. A boy boasts that he need not keep training rules, because he is so good that the coach will not dare take him off the team.
7. A boy is tempted to cheat in an important examination.

C. For each of the basic themes on page 268, write at least one specific story idea. Read and discuss each idea in class. File in your notebook any that your classmates approve.

D. Try to arrange for everyone in the class to read several selected short stories. See whether you can decide in a class discussion what is the basic theme and the specific idea of each story.

2. Developing the Plot

Once you have chosen a story idea, you are ready to work out a plot to fit it. This plot will be the series of incidents that form the skeleton, or framework, of the story.

GUIDES TO THE DEVELOPMENT OF A PLOT

1. *Set up a situation out of which the story will grow.* You may give it in the opening lines or develop it gradually.
2. *Introduce complications.* In this second stage, bring in elements or incidents that complicate or make more difficult the struggle of the main character. This is an important stage, for if nothing happens to interfere with the progress of the hero, there can be little story.
3. *Lead up to a crisis.* This is the stage in a plot at which matters come to a head. Here, you show the leading character faced with an all-important decision. Earlier in the story he probably has met more than one minor crisis and either has conquered it or has met defeat in it. Now he faces the greatest test of all. This crisis leads directly to the fourth stage of the plot.
4. *Bring the story to its climax.* Here you must resolve the crisis; that is, show the all-important action taking place or the all-important decision being made. This is the highest point of interest in the story. For that reason, place it as near the end of the story as possible.

The four stages of a plot are illustrated in this analysis of a familiar nursery tale, "Little Red Riding Hood":

Situation: Red Riding Hood sets out to visit her grandmother.
Complication: She meets the big bad wolf.
Crisis: At her destination she is faced with being eaten by the wolf, disguised as Grandma.
Climax: The woodcutter appears and cuts off the wolf's head.

LEARNING ACTIVITIES IN PLOT CONSTRUCTION

A. Choose several stories familiar to the class and analyze their plots. Since there may be disagreement, take special care to be courteous in the expression of your opinions. Stories that you have read for literature classes will provide good practice material.

B. In a class activity, outline a plot that might grow out of the following idea: *A boy borrows the family car without permission.* (See page 118 for outline form.)

C. Formulate a plot based upon one of the following ideas. Read your plots in class. After improvements have been suggested, file in your notebook any plots that appeal to you.

1. A girl finds her popularity threatened by a rival.
2. A boy is entrusted with class funds.
3. A girl has not been invited to a party that she longs to attend.
4. A man gets a letter meant for another man of the same name.
5. A mother is opposed to her son's desire to play football.

D. Work out and discuss a plot for one of the story ideas on page 268.

3. CREATING CHARACTER

A good plot is important, but if the persons involved in that plot seem unreal, the story is not likely to hold the reader's interest. In other words, the people must talk and act like real people.

There are at least six methods by which an author can indicate character. For example, suppose he wishes to portray a person who will never give up. Notice how he may give that impression.

1. *By what the person says:*
   "Give up? Don't be silly. I haven't even started yet!"
2. *By what someone else says about him:*
   "Jenkins? A bulldog is a quitter compared to him."
3. *By his actions:*
   Wearily Tom straightened his shoulders, took a deep breath, and tried again, as he had been trying for hours, to make the figures balance.
4. *By indicating his thoughts:*
   So they thought he would give up. What a laugh! He'd show them!
5. *By the way that other people treat him:*
   Here was a mission on which only a man who would never quit could succeed. The colonel's glance went swiftly down the eager line standing before him. Then, "Jenkins, you're my man," he barked.
6. *By the author's direct words:*
   Jenkins was a man who never gave up.

GUIDES TO THE CREATION OF CHARACTER

1. Use least often the sixth means of developing character.
2. Let the unfolding of character be gradual. Never try to tell everything at once about a person's character.
3. If you wish, let one person tell the whole story. Be careful that he reports only the actions and reactions of other people and not their thoughts.
4. Keep the persons in your story consistent. A man may reform, for example, but it is not human nature to do so overnight. Furthermore, you must have shown earlier that he has in himself the *possibilities* of reforming. In other words, play fair with your readers.

LEARNING ACTIVITIES IN CHARACTERIZATION

A. What is the author trying to tell you about the following characters? Discuss the method used in each case.

1. A rabbity little man stood on the doorstep, twisting a battered felt hat in his hands.
2. "Just wait! You'll find out. He's nothing but a big bluff."
3. Doctor Bob arrived, accompanied, as usual, by a swarm of youngsters.
4. "I tell you, Jake, nobody ever gives me a break."
5. Al was as big a boaster as he was a bully.
6. Let me see, *he thought*. Shall I wear my new green tie? No, Jane raised her eyebrows at it yesterday. This striped one? No, it clashes with this suit. I guess I'll wear this blue one. But it has a wrinkle in it! My, I wish I dared wear that red one!

B. Examine several short stories in books or magazines. Bring to class characterizations from them, one for each of the six types, if possible. Read these to the class. Be careful to apply the Guides to Effective Oral Reading, page 41. Classify the type used in each; then characterize the person in your own words.

C. Write one or more exercises in characterization. Exchange paragraphs for critical reading or have the paragraphs read aloud and discussed in your small groups. File good work in your notebooks. The drawings may suggest subjects.

4. Planning How to Use Setting

The third chief element in a story is *setting,* or the time, place, and circumstances under which a story takes place. It may be of vital importance to the story, or it may have a decided influence upon the development of character. Often, however, it is used to create mood or atmosphere. Notice this paragraph from Stevenson's "The Sire de Maletroit's Door":

> It was September, 1429; the weather had fallen sharp; a flighty, piping wind, laden with showers, beat about the township; and the dead leaves ran riot along the streets. Here and there a window was already lighted up; and the noise of men-at-arms making merry over supper within came forth in fits and was swallowed up and carried away by the wind. The night fell swiftly; . . . the wind rose and began to hoot under archways and roar amid the treetops in the valley below the town.

As you read that paragraph, can you doubt that it describes a night when exciting things are going to happen? (If you are not familiar with the story, use the card catalogue, page 127, to help you locate it. Then discover for yourself how well Stevenson has used setting to create mood.)

GUIDES TO THE USE OF SETTING IN THE SHORT STORY

1. If setting is relatively unimportant to your story, give little actual description of it. Let any use of setting be incidental: have a man take a milkpail from its hook, for example, and you give the idea that the story is laid on a farm. Go into details about the farm only if there is something unusual about it that will affect plot or character.

2. If you write of bygone days, be careful to use only details true of the period. For example, in a story of colonial days this sentence would show an out-of-place detail: "The children had many a game of hide-and-seek there, with the *corner telephone pole* serving as home base." Such a faulty element is known as an "anachronism."

3. If you write a "local color" story, make every detail of the setting help to locate the story in a certain region. Bret Harte's stories of Western mining camps, Kipling's tales of India, and Jack London's stories of the Far North—all are examples of the local color story.

LEARNING ACTIVITIES IN PROVIDING A SETTING ·

A. Using the guides, read and discuss these descriptions of story settings.

1. For days it had been raining, a slow drizzling rain that pattered against the panes and on the roof with a steady beat. Inside a little cabin, standing

alone not far from the banks of the big river, Tom and Mary sat huddled by the kitchen stove listening to Alice read . . .*

2. Snow lay five feet deep on the level and twenty feet at Dead Horse Pass. As night fell, a new storm headed down from the jagged peaks in a gray swirl. Driving white pellets almost blotted out the dim lights that marked the Lynx Creek Halfway Station, and obliterated the twisting string of road over which the stage passed four times a week.†

3. It was spring again. A soft south breeze said so; tender green leaves and swelling buds said so, too; and further proof lay in the timid wood thrush's liquid call. . . . Orioles and redbirds were in a fever of nest building . . . there was the rich smell of fresh-plowed, warm earth in the air . . . and fishing time had come again.‡

B. Find and bring to class at least one example of a story setting. Read the description to the class and explain briefly its importance to the plot or to the mood. Use your Speech Score Card.

C. Write a brief setting that suggests *cheerfulness, excitement, fear, mystery,* or *sadness*. Read your paragraph to the class. (Apply the Guides to Effective Oral Reading, page 41.) File the paper, if approved, in your notebook.

5. MAKING USE OF DIALOGUE

As you have learned, character can be indicated by what people in a story say. Dialogue, or *conversation,* also reveals and influences action.

GUIDES TO THE USE OF DIALOGUE

1. Suit the language to the speaker; speech is a key to character.
2. Avoid dialogue that neither advances the plot nor reveals character.
3. Keep speeches short, as a rule.
4. Use contractions. "Haven't I seen you before?" is more natural than "Have I not seen you before?" Reverse this rule if you wish to show someone who is stiff and formal by nature.
5. Omit "Jane said" or "replied Dick" except when necessary to identify the speaker. If you do use such labels, find good substitutes for *said*.
6. Occasionally let one speaker interrupt another.

* From "The Floating House" by Charlie May Simon. Used by permission of *Child Life* magazine.
† From "Lion Puss Rides the Stage" by L. C. Pritchett. Originally published in *The Open Road for Boys* magazine.
‡ From "Uncle George and the Doodle-Wimpus" by W. T. Person. Reprinted by permission of the author and of the Methodist Church School publications.

LEARNING ACTIVITIES IN WRITING DIALOGUE

A. Examine conversations in stories that you have been reading. Check them by the guides. How well do they measure up? Discuss your findings in class.

B. Write one or more of the following conversations. If you are not sure how to punctuate conversation, turn to page 176. Read the conversations in class. Criticize them by the guides on this page.

1. Between a mother and a daughter who "simply must have a new dress"
2. Between a salesclerk and a woman who is returning a purse
3. Between father and son over the latter's report card
4. Between two small boys boasting of their big brothers
5. Between two gossipy women
6. Between a boy and a girl on their first date together
7. Between a traffic cop and a woman driver

6. BEGINNING WELL

The opening lines should give some idea of the type of narrative that is to follow; that is, they should indicate whether it is a story chiefly of *mood,* of *action,* or of *character.* It may open with description, conversation, or action. The important thing is to catch the reader's interest.

LEARNING ACTIVITIES IN STORY OPENINGS

A. Read and discuss in class these opening lines; decide whether action, character, or mood would be likely to dominate in a story based upon each opening.

1. I think that I was jealous of Red Barker the first time I ever saw him.
2. Bill Scott stood outside the principal's office, his heart beating hard.
3. "For the last time, I'm warning you. Get rid of that dog!"
4. The night lay dark and heavy over the little prairie town. An uneasy quiet prevailed, a quiet only sharpened by the sound of footsteps, as a man, glancing fearfully behind him, hurried down the street.
5. Mary Lou sat in study hall, staring miserably and unseeingly at the open book before her. Tomorrow was the night of the football dance—and she didn't have a date!
6. "Well, we might as well face it. We're stuck. We should have known better than to try this short cut."
7. Dave Hill made his way blindly out of the gym, Coach Brown's words ringing in his ears. "I'm taking you off the team, Hill. I've no use for a player who folds in the clutch."
8. Elmer Eaves has always been the timidest little rabbit in the entire class. For that reason, I still can hardly believe what happened last Friday night.
9. Elizabeth sat up in bed, her heart thumping madly in the darkness. Surely that was a footstep outside on the porch roof!

B. Examine the opening paragraphs of stories that the class has read. Decide how well you think that the stories live up to the opening lines.

C. Write three story openings, one stressing *setting;* one, *character;* and one, *exciting action.* Read and discuss these in class; then file them in your notebook. As you write, apply the Guides to Good Description, page 261.

7. ENDING WELL

It is a good idea to end a story quickly once the climax has been reached. Tie up loose ends of the plot but avoid long explanations.

Sometimes, as in O. Henry's short stories and the "short shorts" with which you probably are familiar, the climax and the ending, or *denouement,* are the same, forming what is known as the "surprise ending." It can be effective, but only if it is reasonable enough to satisfy the reader.

LEARNING ACTIVITIES

A. If you have read short stories in your literature book, re-examine the endings. Discuss them in class. Are they brief but satisfying?

B. Find in a magazine a short story that you think has an effective ending. Sketch orally and as briefly as possible for the class the events that lead to the ending; then read the ending of the story. See whether your classmates agree. To comment intelligently, they will need to listen with thoughtful attention.

8. CHOOSING A TITLE

As a rule, you will want to write your story before giving it the final title. Note these points about titles:

1. A good title excites interest.
2. It should have a real bearing on the story.
3. It should not reveal the ending.
4. It should be simple but specific. (Why is "The Most Dangerous Game," for example, a better title than "An Adventure on an Island"?)
5. It should, as a rule, be short.

LEARNING ACTIVITIES

A. Examine a short-story collection in your library. List ten titles that arouse your interest. List ten titles that do the opposite. Compare lists in class.

B. Can you think of a good story that you have read which had a poor title? How would you have named it? Tell your small group why.

9. WRITING THE COMPLETE STORY

In the preceding lessons, you have had practice in writing the various parts of the short story. Now you are ready to write a complete story, applying what you have learned. Make free use of the materials that you have written earlier and filed in your notebook, those in description as well as those indicated in this chapter.

GUIDES FOR WRITING SHORT STORIES

1. Decide upon your story idea.
2. Plan the four stages of your plot; that is, *opening situation, complications, crisis,* and *climax.*
3. Name your characters. Jot down (*a*) the impression that you want each of them to make and (*b*) the part that he is to play in the story.
4. Write the first draft of your story. Do so as rapidly as you can; do not attempt a polished piece of work.
5. Rewrite your story.
   a) Read your story aloud to yourself to help you to decide where changes are needed.
   b) Eliminate everything that does not advance the plot or add to character or mood.
   c) Replace worn-out or hazy wording with vivid, exact language.
   d) Check all dialogue by the guides on page 273.
   e) Break up long, rambling sentences.
   f) Proofread carefully for errors in paragraphing, punctuation, capitalization, or spelling.

LEARNING ACTIVITIES

A. Write one or more of the stories suggested here. Hand your stories in unsigned. Let them be redistributed so that if possible no one knows whose story he has. Read carefully the story that you receive. If you believe that it is worth having read aloud, make a note to that effect on the first page. Have the stories thus selected read to the class. (Be sure to apply the Guides for Effective Oral Reading, page 41.) Discuss the merits of the stories; make suggestions for improving them. Try to arrange to have the best stories printed in a class magazine. Perhaps some of them will be considered worthy of being submitted in state or national contests.

1. Write a story based upon one of the ideas that you filed in your notebook (page 269).
2. Write a story in which the setting reflects or dominates the mood.

3. Write a story in which the development of character is your aim.

4. Write a story laid in some long-ago time.

5. Write a story in which action is more important than character or setting. Here you should keep description at a minimum. Avoid long sentences. Let the characters speak for themselves, but eliminate conversation that will slow up the story. You may choose to write an adventure thriller, a mystery, a supernatural tale, a science-fiction story, . . .

6. Write a story of the "tall tale" type. Perhaps you can create another adventure of the mighty Paul Bunyan.

7. Write a story told in the first person. Remember to give only the teller's thoughts, not those of other persons in the story.

8. Write a story giving another incident concerning the characters in a story that you have enjoyed, perhaps an incident mentioned in that story.

B. As a class, choose a theme for a story. Divide the class into groups, with one group assigned to write the tale for children under eight, one to write it for those from eight to twelve, a third to write it for the high school age group, and a fourth to write it for adults.

Writing Verse

1. Understanding What Poetry Is

READ IN CLASS AND STUDY

Everyone is a poet inside. Do you believe that? You are one yourself, even though you may never have written a line of poetry in your life. You *are* one—because poetry is primarily a matter of feeling. That glow inside you when you sink a clean shot in basketball; that warm response in your heart when your dog slips his nose into your palm; that shiver of excitement as you are dressing for a "special" date—all those are the stuff of which poetry is made. You may never have put those feelings into words, but they are poetic experiences.

Perhaps you are unlucky enough to be bored by the poetry that you "study" in literature. If so, try a change of attitude. Try thinking of a poem as someone's effort to put into words his impressions, his feelings, and his ideas. Every real poem is the result of an emotion so strong that the author felt that he simply had to tell about it. His poem has value if it makes even one reader say, "That is just the way I have felt!"

One good way to learn to appreciate poetry is to try writing it. To do so is easier than you think, once you are free of certain false notions.

1. *Get rid of the belief that poetry must rhyme.* Many poems do have rhyme, yet much great poetry has not a rhyme in it.
2. *Forget the notion that poetry is* "just a lot of fancy words strung together." A true poet uses short, simple words. Notice these lines by famous poets.

> Low on the sand and loud on the stone
>   The last wheel echoes away.—Tennyson

> Home is the sailor, home from sea,
>   And the hunter home from the hill.—Robert L. Stevenson

Do you find any "fancy" words in those lines?

2. Comparing Poetry with Prose

If poetry, then, needs neither rhyme nor an elaborate vocabulary, what distinguishes it from prose?

1. Prose and poetry differ in *form*. The *sentence* and the *paragraph* are patterns for prose. The *line*, the *thought phrase*, and the *stanza* are patterns for poetry.

2. The next most evident difference is *rhythm*. Both have it, but the rhythm of poetry tends to be stricter. The rhythm of most poetry follows a definite pattern, though in some poetry the rhythm is very irregular. However, if you read poetry aloud you will be conscious of the rhythm. Note these lines:

> One man with a dream, at pleasure,
> Shall go forth and conquer a crown.—W. E. O'Shaughnessy

Suppose, however, that the lines were changed to prose, like this:

> If he feels like it, one man who has a dream may go out and win a crown.

Do you feel the difference?

3. For the most part, poetry appeals to the *emotions;* prose, to the *intellect*.

4. Poetry is highly imaginative; prose often is matter-of-fact. The imaginative appeal of poetry is heightened by the use of vivid figures of speech.

> Deep in the sun-searched growths, the dragonfly
> Hangs like a blue thread loosened from the sky.—Dante Gabriel Rossetti

5. Poetry *suggests;* much prose *explains*. Therefore poetry is far more compact than prose. Because the poet uses connotative words (see page 98), a line or two of poetry may reveal as much as paragraphs of prose. Note how these short, simple lines suggest Tennyson's sorrow over the death of a friend:

> And the stately ships go on,
> To the haven under the hill;
> But O for the touch of a vanished hand,
> And the sound of a voice that is still!

6. Poetry is designed more for the ear than is most prose. The poet strives for words that are musical or that by their very sound create mood or feeling. Read aloud these lines, also from Tennyson; listen to the "mood-music."

> Here are cool mosses deep,
> And through the moss the ivies creep,
> And in the stream the long-leaved flowers weep,
> And from the craggy ledge the poppy hangs in sleep.

7. Both poetry and good descriptive prose appeal to the five senses.

LEARNING ACTIVITIES IN POETIC EXPRESSION

A. On page 280 are four pairs of lines. In each pair, one line is poetry (written here in prose form) and one is prose. Which is which? How do you know? Make this an oral discussion.

1. There is a garden in her face, where roses and white lilies grow.
   Her face is like a garden with roses and white lilies growing in it.

2. When we met, Jenny jumped up from her chair and kissed me.
   Jenny kissed me when we met, jumping from the chair she sat in.

3. My dearest, after I am dead, I do not want you to sing any sad songs for me.
   When I am dead, my dearest, sing no sad songs for me.

4. Happy, happy time, when the white star hovers low over dim fields fresh
   with bloomy dew.
   This is a very happy time; a white star hangs low over the faintly-seen
   fields with their fragrant dew-covered blossoms.

B. After writing any of the assignments that follow, read your work aloud
in class or not, as you choose. If you wish, your teacher will probably read it
for you without identifying you as the author.

The five senses provide the experiences out of which poetry comes. Here is
a student-written example that concentrates on one sense—that of *hearing*.

HOME SOUNDS

Home sounds are good sounds—
   A symphony of love;
The vacuum cleaner grumbling to
   The ticking clock above;

. . . .

The sizzling speech of frying pans
   That hints at what's inside;
The curt and crackling newspaper
   With worlds of news implied;

And, best of all, my mother's voice
   That makes my wrongs all right
By whispering these simple words:
   "God bless you, dear, good night."

Here are several exercises involving those senses. Do not try for length or for
elaborate effects. If your lines happen to rhyme, all right, but do not feel that you
must use rhyme. Try for rhythm and words that fit the way that you feel or that
suggest by their sound the effect that you want. Use figures of speech if they fit.

1. What sights bring you an inner glow or a feeling of happiness? Try to
   write a line or two of verse about several of them. Here are suggestions.

Shadows	Falling snow	Bare trees	Moonlight
Clouds	A child's smile	A horse race	Waving grain
Sunset	Trees in blossom	Lightning	Candlelight

2. The world is full of lovely sounds. What are some that appeal to you
   Write at least a line of verse about them. These suggestions may help yo

Laughter	"Hot licks" on a trumpet	A lark singing
Church bells	Train whistles at night	The drip of rain
An organ	The voice of a dear one	The hum of a motor
The sea	Cottonwood leaves rustling	Wind in the pines

3. What are your favorite smells? Can you describe them or their effect on you? Try it. The following may suggest others.

Lilacs in the rain	Fresh-turned earth	Fresh-cut grass	A cellar
New-mown hay	Baking bread	Clean hair	A bonfire
A perfume counter	Jelly making	Leather	Gasoline

4. What sensations are especially intense for you? See whether you can put those impressions into a bit of verse. The list below may suggest ideas.

Riding in an elevator	A cold shower	A roller coaster	Clean clothes
Downhill on a bicycle	Lying in the sun	A warm, wet wind	Velvet
Grass under bare feet	Iodine in a cut	A firm handshake	Fur

5. Describe the taste of some favorite food: *dill pickles, chili, a hamburger, watermelon, strawberry shortcake, . . .*

C. Have you ever fussed and worried about something, only to realize later that it was not very important, after all? Put your feelings into verse.

INSIGHT*

I had a new grief
   With a new grief's clamor;
Rattle, rattle in my mind,
   And on my heart, hammer.

But strangely and suddenly
   And just as I was weeping,
It seemed to be an old grief—
   And not worth the keeping.

D. Write a little poem in which the seriousness is turned to fun by its ending.

FOLK TUNE†

Other lads, their ways are daring;
   Other lads, they're not afraid;
Other lads, they show they're caring;
   Other lads, they know a maid.
Wiser Jack than ever you were,
   Will's with gayer spirit blest,
Robin's kindlier and truer—
   Why should I love you the best?
Other lads, their eyes are bolder.
   Young they are, and strong and slim.
Ned is straight and broad of shoulder,
   Donald has a way with him.
David stands a foot above you,
   Dick's as brave as Lancelot—
Why, ah why, then, should I love you?
   Naturally, I do not.

From *Any Spring.* Copyright, 1933, by Dorothy Aldis. Courtesy of G. P. Putnam's Sons.
From *Enough Rope* by Dorothy Parker. Copyright, 1926, by Dorothy Parker. By permission of the Viking Press, Inc., New York.

E. Falling in love is a rich experience. It is one of the favorite themes of poets. Here is a sample. Notice how simply this poem is written. Only one word has more than one syllable.

Song Is So Old*

Song is so old,
　Love is so new—
Let me be still
　And kneel to you.

Let me be still
　And breathe no word,
Save what my warm blood
　Sings unheard.

Let my warm blood
　Sing low of you—
Song is so fair,
　Love is so new.

Would you like to express your own feelings on this very personal matter of love? If you are shy, you need not show anyone what you write, but it is a worth-while experience to try putting your feelings into a poem.

F. Have you ever done something that seemed afterwards just like a bad dream? Have you thought, "I couldn't have done it! I'm not like that!" Read what a soldier says of such an experience; then write about one of your own.

Back†

They ask me where I've been,
And what I've done and seen.
And what can I reply
Who knows it wasn't I,
But someone just like me,
Who went across the sea
And with my head and hands
Killed men in foreign lands . . .
Though I must bear the blame
Because he bore my name.

---

* From *A Troop of the Guard* by Herman Hagedorn. Used by permission of Mr. Hagedorn.
† From *Battle, and Other Poems* by W. W. Gibson. Copyright, 1916. Used by permission of the Macmillan Company, Publishers.

3. Understanding the Technical Aspects of Verse

RHYTHM AND METER

Since rhythm is basic to all poetry, you should know certain terms pertaining to rhythm, particularly if you are to write poetry yourself.

● **WHAT YOU SHOULD KNOW ABOUT RHYTHM AND METER**

1. A *foot* is the unit of measurement in poetry. A foot consists of a set number of long, or *accented* (′), beats and short, or *unaccented* (˘), beats. Four kinds of feet are common to English verse.

Kind of Foot	Symbol	Example
iambic	˘ ′	Thĕ bést ĭs yét tŏ bé.—BROWNING
trochaic	′ ˘	Hére ă stár ănd thére ă stár.—DICKINSON
anapestic	˘ ˘ ′	Ĭn ă párk whĕre thĕ peách-blŏssŏms bléw.—LANG
dactylic	′ ˘ ˘	Hónŏr thĕ chárge thĕy mădĕ!—TENNYSON

2. *Meter* indicates the number of poetic feet in a line. (Most lines have more than one foot; few have more than five.)

   a) Monometer (mŏ·nŏm′ĕ·tēr) refers to a line having only *one* foot.

   b) Dimeter (dĭm′ĕ·tēr) refers to a line having *two* feet.

   c) Trimeter (trĭm′ĕ·tēr) refers to a line having *three* feet.

   d) Tetrameter (tĕ·trăm′ĕ·tēr) refers to a line having *four* feet.

   e) Pentameter (pĕn·tăm′ĕ·tēr) refers to a line having *five* feet.

   f) Hexameter (hĕks·ăm′ĕ·tēr) refers to a line having *six* feet.

   g) Heptameter (hĕp·tăm′ĕ·tēr) refers to a line having *seven* feet.

   h) Octameter (ŏk·tăm′ĕ·tēr) refers to a line having *eight* feet.

3. *Scansion* is the term applied to marking the feet in a line of poetry. A vertical line is used to show the feet. Each line below has four iambic feet.

   Whĕn Spríng | comĕs báck | wĭth rús|tlĭng sháde |
   Ănd áp|plĕ-blós|sŏms fíll | thĕ aír.|—ALAN SEEGER

Within one poem there may be many variations in rhythm; for example, the dropping of unaccented beats (especially at the ends of lines) or the substituting of one kind of foot for another. When there is variation, the kind of foot that predominates is the one that names the line. Therefore, the following line is classed as *anapestic tetrameter*.

   Tŏ thĕ lít|tlĕ grăy chúrch| ŏn thĕ wín|dy híll||—ARNOLD

Always choose a rhythm that fits the mood. Generally speaking, use *long* lines to express moods of *dignity, grandeur,* or *sorrow;* use *short* lines to express moods of *gaiety, lightness,* or *delicacy.*

From a technical standpoint, you should avoid these things:

1. Language not found in good modern speech
   a) Pronouns such as *thou, thee, thy, thine, ye*
   b) Verb forms like *dost, wert, shalt, mayst*
   c) *Do, does,* or *did* just to fill out a line; that is, such an expression as "When birds *do* sing" instead of "When birds sing"
   d) Contractions like *'tween* (for *between*), *e'en, ne'er*
2. *Unnatural inversions;* that is, lines like
   Sang merrily in the sun the maiden.
3. Hackneyed or trite expressions: *rosy cheeks, ruby lips, twinkling stars, whispering breeze,* . . . (See page 106 for other such expressions to avoid.)

LEARNING ACTIVITIES

A. Scan and label the following lines according to the example.

With lĭsp | ŏf leáves | aňd rĭp | plĕ ŏf raín | (*iambic tetrameter*)—SWINBURNE

1. Down to the depths of the sea.—ARNOLD
2. Past we glide, and past, and past!—BROWNING
3. This I whispered, and an echo murmured back the word "Lenore!"—POE
4. A sunny pleasure-dome with caves of ice.—COLERIDGE
5. A light of laughing flowers along the grass is spread.—SHELLEY
6. Bring me my bow of burning gold.—BLAKE
7. Our sweetest songs are those that tell of saddest thought.—SHELLEY
8. Every moment, lightly shaken, ran itself in golden sands.—TENNYSON
9. He rode all unarmed and he rode all alone.—SCOTT
10. Under the blossom that hangs on the bough.—SHAKESPEARE

B. Bring to class a poem written in a rhythm that especially fits the mood. Tell why you think so. Read the poem—or part of it—aloud, being careful to apply the Guides to Effective Oral Reading, page 41.

C. To learn more about the variations in poetic feet, see what you can find in a poetry handbook, the dictionary, or the encyclopedia about the *pyrrhic,* the *amphimacer,* and the *amphibrach.* Try to find examples.

4. USING FIGURES OF SPEECH AND SOUND DEVICES

One of the most effective devices used in poetry is the *figure of speech.* Besides the four figures of speech discussed in connection with description (pages 257–58), poetry often uses another, the *apostrophe.*

An apostrophe is a *turning away,* so to speak, to address (1) an absent person as though he were present, (2) a dead person as though he were living, or (3) an inanimate object as though it were alive.

Good-by, proud world! I'm going home.—Emerson

There are several ways of achieving sound effects in poetry. The chief means is through *rhyme.*

● **WHAT YOU SHOULD KNOW ABOUT SOUND EFFECTS IN POETRY**

1. *Rhyme* is the repeating of the same accented vowel sound, after differing consonant sounds, together with all the following consonantal and unaccented vowel sounds. All the sounds that follow must be identical. Here are rhyming words: *city–pity; cheerfully–fearfully; fright–bite.*

   The *rhyme scheme* for a poem or a stanza of a poem is the rhyming pattern that it follows. To figure out the rhyme scheme, letter the word at the end of the first line *a.* Mark also with *a* all corresponding rhyming words at the ends of lines. The first end-word that does not rhyme with *a* should be marked *b,* and so on, as follows:

   > Morning arises stormy and pale, (*a*)
   > No sun, but a wannish glare (*b*)
   > In fold upon fold of hueless cloud; (*c*)
   > And the budded peaks of the wood are bowed, (*c*)
   > Caught, and cuffed by the gale; (*a*)
   > I had fancied it would be fair. (*b*)
   >
   > —Tennyson

   Rhyme may occur elsewhere than at the ends of lines. *Internal rhyme* is the rhyming of words in the same line.

   > Back into the chamber *turning,* all my soul within me *burning.*—Poe

2. Another device if used sparingly that does much to add melody is *alliteration.* This device uses the same consonant sound to begin several not-far-apart accented syllables.

   > Blue *b*readth of sea without a *b*reak.—Browning

3. *Onomatopoeia* (on'oh·mat'oh·pea'ya) is the use of words that suggest their meaning by their sound. Examples are *hiss, crackle, sizzle.*

4. *Repetition* is another way of adding to the musical quality of poetry. Here is an example from Alfred Noyes's "The Highwayman."

   > And he rode with a jewelled twinkle,
   > His pistol butts a-twinkle,
   > His rapier hilt a-twinkle, under the jewelled sky.

LEARNING ACTIVITIES

A. Identify the figures of speech in the lines of poetry that follow on page 286. Make this an oral activity.

1. Love took up the glass of time and turned it in his glowing hands.
   —Tennyson
2. Blue were her eyes as the fairy-flax.—Longfellow
3. Here once the embattled farmers stood
   And fired the shot heard round the world.—Emerson
4. Sweet Thames! run softly till I end my song.—Spenser
5. O'er night's brim, day boils at last.—Browning
6. Our doubts are traitors.—Shakespeare
7. Exult, O shores and ring, O bells.—Whitman
8. All the perfumes of Arabia will not sweeten this little hand.—Shakespeare
9. Queen rose of the rosebud garden of girls.—Tennyson
10. Enjoy the honey-heavy dew of slumber.—Shakespeare
11. And a mouse is miracle enough to stagger sextillions of infidels.
    —Whitman
12. The sullen wind was soon awake.—Browning
13. And they whose hearts are dry as summer dust.—Wordsworth
14. Self is the only prison that can ever bind the soul.—Van Dyke
15. That old bald cheater, Time.—Jonson

B. Indicate the rhyme scheme of the following stanza:

> What is love? 'tis not hereafter;
> Present mirth hath present laughter;
> What's to come is still unsure:
> In delay there lies no plenty,—
> Then come kiss me, Sweet-and-twenty,
> Youth's a stuff will not endure.
>
> —Shakespeare

C. Point out examples of *internal rhyme, alliteration, repetition,* and *onomatopoeia* in the following lines.

1. Keeping time, time, time,
   In a sort of Runic rhyme.—Poe
2. The vow that binds too strictly snaps itself.—Tennyson
3. The viol, the violet, and the vine.—Poe
4. Over the cobbles he clatters and clangs in the dark inn-yard.—Noyes
5. O Mary, go and call the cattle home,
   And call the cattle home,
   And call the cattle home,
   Across the sands o' Dee!—Kingsley
6. "Thy life is his—thy fate it is to guard him with thy head."—Kipling
7. Oh, what a tangled web we weave.—Scott
8. Alone, alone, all, all alone;
   Alone on a wide, wide sea.—Coleridge
9. The cruel, crawling foam.—Kingsley
10. I bring fresh showers for the thirsting flowers.—Shelley

5. Writing Special Verse Forms

If you used *The New Building Better English* during your freshman and sophomore years, you had an opportunity to study and practice writing *limericks, couplets, quatrains, ballads, cinquains, triolets.* There, too, the difference between *lyric* and *narrative* poetry was explained. Here are other poetic forms that you will enjoy attempting.

BLANK VERSE

READ AND DO

Blank verse is *unrhymed* poetry that is written in *iambic pentameter.* (How many feet are in it, and what is the rhythm pattern?) Earlier poets had employed blank verse, but Shakespeare and Milton became its greatest masters. Blank verse is well suited to serious, dignified subjects. It is likewise well suited to drama, because of the lack of rhyme. In writing blank verse, avoid stopping the thought at the end of a line; allow the thought to continue into the following line when it seems natural for it to do so.

Note these lines spoken by Macbeth just after he has been told of Lady Macbeth's death. Practice reading them aloud to bring out their meaning as well as their beauty.

> Tomorrow, and tomorrow, and tomorrow,
> Creeps in this petty pace from day to day
> To the last syllable of recorded time,
> And all our yesterdays have lighted fools
> The way to dusty death. Out, out, brief candle!
> Life's but a walking shadow, a poor player
> That struts and frets his hour upon the stage
> And then is heard no more: it is a tale
> Told by an idiot, full of sound and fury,
> Signifying nothing.

LEARNING ACTIVITIES

A. Find and read in class ten or more lines of blank verse from one of Shakespeare's plays, Milton's "Lycidas," Tennyson's *Idylls of the King,* Arnold's *Sohrab and Rustum,* Robert Frost's "Mending Wall," or any other writing in blank verse. Read enough to get the feel of the rhythm. Be sure to apply the Guides to Effective Oral Reading, page 41. If you like, use a selection for choral reading. (See page 44.) Use the card catalogue (page 127) in looking for poems.

B. Write a short poem in blank verse. Use as your subject something about which you feel deeply.

Free verse has no definite accent and no set line length. However, it does have rhythm, with much of the rise and fall that one finds in speaking. Here is part of a student-written example of free verse.

This Is the House

This is where I live.

Here are the yard, the tulips, the bush where the bees swarm in the summer;

The trees we planted young in the hard black ground, the leaves we saw the wind take every fall, and every spring watched bud and blossom;

The sidewalk, which we walked up so many times that even the place where we carved our initials when the cement was soft is worn over;

The doorstep, where we sat in the hot sun shelling peas or braiding long chains of yellow dandelions from the lawn, and where, in a dark spring night, lighted cigarettes glowed as two people sat talking quietly.

This is the house.

Red brick, windows, and shingles, it is ours.

This frame has held our growing, our laughing, our loving.

Here we have been sick. We have run away from this place. We have fought and cried and slept and sung "I've Been Working on the Railroad" while we washed dishes in the kitchen sink.

This is where we peel potatoes and brush the dog and laugh at cartoons in the *Saturday Evening Post*.

This is the door we have opened for our neighbors and locked against prowlers, and to it a woman with a portfolio has come, marking us down as "American . . . with one bathtub . . . a washing machine . . . two children born in Chicago."

This is where one person on the 6:05 carries home his paper and brings the pay packet every other week and tells us the good joke he "heard at the office today."

And this is the place we come to after we've been away. . . .

This house has heard our music . . . the piano, the phonograph, a faulty cornet . . . Spike Jones and Tchaikovsky's *Symphony Number 5 in E Minor*. It has heard the radio blaring news of D day and announcing that men over thirty-five with a family would not be drafted.

And here a first corsage withered in the icebox; a boy ran crying into his room, with torn pants and a swollen cheek; a large black dog was hit by a truck in the street; a car dug deep grooves into the side lawn; and a girl walked slowly up the back steps with a kiss on her lips.

Here we earnestly repeated "Our Father who art in heaven . . ." at seven-thirty bedtime. Here report cards came, and as the seasons passed, mother talked to daughter and father to son.

. . . .

Our lives have been molded and torn and rebuilt in this house, but it stands apart, unchanged, only growing a little more worn each year.

The house will see us leave and watch those who stay, age and slow down. In it two will breathe in sobs and die.

Nothing of us will be left here. . . .

. . . .

Someday I'll come back.

I'll walk down the street through the spring rain and see buildings where the prairies used to be. Our house will look older than I remembered; the bricks will be faded.

The bee-bush will be chopped down and the trees that were once so scrawny will be thick spreading, and the rain drumming through the leaves will make a lonely sound.

I'll walk up the pavement and no dog will run to meet me. I'll stop and stare a while at the numbers that tell the address to which I came so many times.

On the pavement there will be a half-washed chalk picture and on the doorstep a forgotten dandelion chain woven by a strange girl.

I will lift my hand to ring the bell, but afraid of what will come, consider a moment, and then turn quickly down the street with the rain on my back.

For the echoes of our laughter, our heartaches, and our love will have died with our leaving;

And no one will know how important it all was to us then . . . the trees, the doorstep, the house, and one another.

And no one will care.

LEARNING ACTIVITIES

A. Read in class examples of free verse from the writings of Carl Sandburg, Walt Whitman, and Amy Lowell.

B. Try your hand at writing a piece of free verse. It need not be long.

THE SONNET

For your final study, here is a discussion of the *sonnet,* one of the loveliest of the fixed forms. The greatest English poets have written sonnets that rank with the finest literature in the language. Shakespeare wrote a sequence of one hundred fifty-four, most of which have never been surpassed.

● **WHAT YOU SHOULD KNOW ABOUT THE SONNET**

1. A sonnet has fourteen lines, written in iambic pentameter.
2. The lines rhyme according to a strict pattern.
   a) The *Italian* sonnet rhymes *abba abba cdcdcd* or *cde cde.*
   b) The *English* (also called *Shakespearean* or *Elizabethan*) sonnet rhymes *abab cdcd efef gg.* (In other words, it is made up of three quatrains and a couplet.)
   c) The *Spenserian* sonnet rhymes *abab bcbc cdcd ee.*
3. Usually the first eight lines, called the *octave,* set forth a problem (or question) or create a picture. The last six lines, called the *sestet,* resolve (or *answer*) the problem or comment upon it.

289

LEARNING ACTIVITIES

A. Find and place on the board Shakespeare's Sonnet XCI. Indicate the rhyme scheme. Scan the first four lines. Discuss the idea expressed in the first eight lines. What do the last six lines do with this idea? Note the epigrammatic quality of the couplet at the end.

B. Now write your own sonnet. Choose for your subject something that has stirred you emotionally. Make this writing your best effort.

RELATED ACTIVITY

One of the most beautiful series of sonnets is *The House of Life* by Dante Gabriel Rossetti. Do some research to find the fascinating story behind those sonnets. Then find and read some of them.

FOLLOW-UP ACTIVITIES

A. Begin a scrapbook of poems that you clip or copy from various sources; if you like, keep one section for your own work. Add something new every week. Such a scrapbook will record your growth in poetry appreciation.

B. Memorize poems or bits of poems that appeal to you. Like beautiful music, these lines will mean more to you every time that you say them. Try to learn a few new lines each day.

C. Make an anthology of poems written by the class. Let each person choose from his own writing one poem, or let poems be chosen by a committee, your teacher, or outside judges. If your class is small, perhaps copies can be handwritten; otherwise try to have them mimeographed and the individual poems autographed. You may want to include pictures of the authors.

FINAL TEST THEME IN WRITTEN COMMUNICATION

Bring to class all the tools for writing, including a clear mind. Without any outside preparation, write a theme of at least four well-developed and connected paragraphs.

Your teacher will score this theme by the Writing Score Card. Then he will hold a conference with you to compare your achievement with that in your first theme. This final theme will probably be filed with your permanent record in the office.

THEME SUBJECTS

My Most Serious Problem	Places I Remember
What I Like Best to Do	Am I Grown-up?

KNOW THE

Structure

Know How to Use Verbs*

"What do you mean, you 'don't need none'? Listen, lady, I'm selling grammar books!" †

1. RECOGNIZING VERBS

Because it is the part of speech around which the sentence idea is built, the verb is the chief sentence element. Try to express some idea in the briefest language possible. Unless you use an interjection such as *oh;* a pronoun that suggests a question, such as *what;* or a greeting like *hello,* you will use a verb. Even expressions without a verb imply one, for when you say, "What?" you really mean, "What did you say?"

---

* Pretest 3 should be given at this point. All tests called for in the text are contained in a test booklet that may be purchased for each pupil. The tests also appear in the *Teacher's Manual.* Schools not wishing to buy the booklets may mimeograph the tests.
† Used by permission of Bill Gray and *Redbook* magazine.

● WHAT TO REMEMBER ABOUT VERBS

1. (DEFINITION) **The** *verb*, **also known as the** *simple predicate*, **is the part of speech that expresses** (*a*) *action* **performed by or on the subject or** (*b*) **merely a** *state of being* **on the part of the subject. As the** *simple predicate*, **the verb** *makes a statement, asks a question*, **or** *gives a command:* Time *passes* slowly.   Who *is* the owner?   *Wait* for me.

2. (DEFINITION) **A** *verb phrase* **combines a verb of action or condition with one or more** *auxiliary*, **or** *helping*, **verbs. There are twenty-three auxiliary verbs:** *is, am, are, was, were, be, being, been, has, have, had, do, does, did, shall, will, should, would, may, might, must, can, could.*

    The wind *had been blowing.*   Today *has been* cold.

    NOTE: Use of auxiliaries as linking verbs is explained on page 323.

3. **The parts of a verb phrase may be separated by other words.**

    Have the boys *left?*   Jean *does* not always *wait* for me.

4. **Often a verb is part of a contraction:** *Is*n't John here?

5. **A sentence may have a** *compound predicate;* **that is, two or more separate verbs:** The days *came* and *went.*

6. (DEFINITION) **The verb and any words used to complete its meaning form the** *complete predicate:* Billy *went to the circus on Monday.*

LEARNING ACTIVITIES IN RECOGNIZING VERBS

A. Copy the following sentences. Draw two lines under each verb. Do not overlook any auxiliaries. Go over your papers orally.

1. The boys had played their final game on Saturday.
2. Have the results of the election been announced?
3. Surely Father closed and locked the door.
4. Lately business appears better than before.
5. His request may never even have been considered.
6. Can your brother identify this man?
7. Jean was ready at five o'clock.
8. Don't look at me.
9. Mrs. Anson closed the window and drew the shade.
10. The Carsons must have been walking the floor with the baby.

B. In an oral activity, fill each blank below with *should, may, must, can, might, could.* Explain the differences in meaning that the various auxiliaries give.

1. Mary .... wait for Fred.
2. We .... divide the money.
3. Jim .... be wrong.
4. He .... decide tonight.

C. Write sentences containing the following kinds of verbs: (1) *an action verb only,* (2) *two auxiliaries used with an action verb,* (3) *an action verb separated from an auxiliary,* (4) *a compound verb.* Compare sentences in class.

2. DISTINGUISHING VERBS FROM VERBALS

In the drawing, "practicing" looks like a verb; but, as you can see from Arbee's puzzlement, "practicing" here gives only part of an idea. If the auxiliary verbs passing through Arbee's mind are inserted, "practicing" becomes part of a verb phrase. Without the auxiliaries, the word is only a *verbal;* that is, a verb in *form* but some other part of speech in its *use.*

● **WHAT TO REMEMBER ABOUT VERBALS**

1. **(DEFINITION)** **A** *verbal* **is a verb form used as a** *noun,* **an** *adjective,* **or an** *adverb.* **There are three types:** *gerund, infinitive,* **and** *participle.*

2. **(DEFINITION)** **A** *gerund* **is a** *verbal noun;* **that is, a verb form used as a noun. It** (or its auxiliary) **always ends in** *ing.*
   Watching the clock is a bad habit. [*Is* is the verb.]

3. **(DEFINITION)** **An** *infinitive* **is a word group made up of the preposition** *to,* **expressed or understood, and a** *verb* **or a** *verb phrase.* **It is used as a** *noun,* **an** *adjective,* **or an** *adverb.* **After verbs like** *dare, feel, hear, help, let, make, see,* **the** *to* **is often omitted.**
   You need *to come* early. [*Need* is the verb.]
   Explain the plan *to be used.* [*Explain* is the verb.]
   This cleaner is easy *to use.* [*Is* is the verb.]
   Do we dare [*to*] *leave* now? [*Do dare* is the verb.]

4. **(DEFINITION)** **A** *participle* **is a verb form used as an** *adjective.* **It modifies a** *noun* **or a** *pronoun.* **The participle has several forms; for example, here are sentences using the participles formed from the verb "call":**
   Joe, *calling* for help, ran past. [*Ran* is the verb.]
   The name *being called* sounds familiar. [*Sounds* is the verb.]
   The boy *called* first must go. [*Must go* is the verb.]
   Having called early, Al was hired. [*Was hired* is the verb.]
   Having been called back, we began over. [*Began* is the verb.]

LEARNING ACTIVITIES IN RECOGNIZING VERBALS

A. Copy the following sentences. Underline *twice* each verb or verb phrase; underline *once* each gerund, infinitive, or participle. Exchange papers for checking.

1. Sue wants to be an actress.
2. The picture showed the church steeple slanting to the right.
3. Thank you for renewing your subscription.
4. In the eighth grade at our school, some girls learn to sew.
5. Don likes to go hunting.
6. Let's go to the store now.
7. Having sold her quota of tickets, Mary could relax.
8. We observed the reporters taking notes during the interview.
9. The letter, having been written, was mailed at once.
10. Clare studies singing and painting.

B. Some of the following groups of words are not sentences, since they contain no verb. Find the incomplete sentences and rewrite them so that each one is complete. Compare work in class.

> EXAMPLE: The game to be played Saturday. (*incomplete*)
> The game *is* to be played Saturday.

1. Feeling useless and unwanted.
2. To have a haircut at a barbershop.
3. Pumping gas is not an inspiring occupation.
4. My job, delivering magazines on my bicycle.
5. Painted a vivid blue-green.
6. Watching and waiting at the gate.
7. Do you dare to jump?
8. To have kept the light burning.
9. The wires being inspected.
10. Presenting the flowers without making a mistake.
11. To have gone on vacation.
12. The pencils, sharpened to a fine point.
13. Preparing sandwiches for sixty people takes time.
14. Dick, having been paid in cash.
15. The shells to be picked up.

3. CONJUGATING VERBS

Verbs, to provide for the many variations in time and meaning that they must express, take many forms. These numerous forms, when arranged in orderly fashion, constitute a verb *conjugation*.

1. (DEFINITION) A *conjugation* is an orderly arrangement of all the forms of a verb to show its five properties: *voice, mood, tense, person,* and *number.* (See pages 419–21 for a complete conjugation of the verbs *to give* and *to be.*)

2. (DEFINITION) A *synopsis* is a *shortened* conjugation that takes one person and number, usually the third person singular, through all tenses, moods, and voices.

3. (DEFINITION) The *voice* of a verb tells whether the *subject* is the *doer* (active voice) or the *receiver* (passive voice) of the action expressed. All *passive* verbs require some form of the verb *to be* as an auxiliary.

   a) (DEFINITION) A *transitive verb* requires a receiver of the action that it expresses; that is, a word answering the question, "To *whom* or *what* was something done?"

   b) Transitive verbs in the *active* voice act upon a *direct object;* in the *passive* voice, upon the *subject.*

   John *closed* the **door.** (*active*)   The **train** *was delayed.* (*passive*)

   Notice in the second example that the doer is not named.

   c) (DEFINITION) An action verb having no receiver of its action is an *intransitive* verb: The wind *blew.* Intransitive verbs are said to lack voice.

   d) (DEFINITION) An intransitive verb needing only a doer is an *intransitive complete* verb: The kitten *scampered.*

   e) (DEFINITION) An intransitive verb needing a word to complete it is a *linking,* or *copulative,* verb: The day *is* gloomy.

   f) Some verbs may be used either transitively or intransitively.

   The choir *sang* an **anthem.** (*trans.*)   The choir *sang* well. (*int.*)

LEARNING ACTIVITIES

A. Indicate whether the verbs in the following sentences are *transitive passive, transitive active,* or *intransitive.*

1. Who checked the roll?
2. The news was heard here.
3. Everything is ready.
4. Time waits for no one.
5. He was notified by letter.
6. Our plans have been laid.
7. Have you read that book?
8. You will not be needed.
9. We have tried your plan.
10. Is this your answer?

B. Here is a list of verbs that may always be used intransitively. Some of them may also be used transitively. Decide which ones may do double duty. Write sentences with those verbs, using them (1) as intransitive and (2) as transitive verbs. Compare your work in class. Here are the verbs: *run, lie, burn, listen, rise, wash, drive, happen, obey, sit.*

4. (DEFINITION) The *mood* of a verb indicates whether the action stated is a *fact* or merely a *wish,* a *possibility,* or a *supposition.*

    a) (DEFINITION) The *indicative* mood *states a fact* or *asks a question.* I saw you at the fruit stand. Did you see me?

    b) (DEFINITION) The *subjunctive* mood **expresses a** *wish,* a *possibility,* **or a** *condition contrary to fact:* **If he** *were* here, he would agree.

    c) (DEFINITION) The *imperative* mood **expresses a** *command* **or a re-** *quest: Go* at once.

5. (DEFINITION) The *tense* of a verb indicates the *time* expressed by it.

SIMPLE TENSES

    a) PRESENT TENSE: I give. (*present or habitual action*)
    b) PAST TENSE: I gave. (*action completed in the past*)
    c) FUTURE TENSE: I shall give. (*action to be performed in the future*)

PERFECT TENSES

    d) PRESENT PERFECT TENSE: I have given. (*action just completed or still in effect*)
    e) PAST PERFECT TENSE: I had given. (*action completed before some other past action*)
    f) FUTURE PERFECT TENSE: I shall have given. (*action spoken of as completed in some future time*)

6. (DEFINITION) *Progressive* verbs show action going on *at present* or *at some other indicated time. Active* voice adds the *present participle* of an *action verb* to the tense forms of *be. Passive* voice (which has only *past* and *present* tenses) inserts *being* between the *auxiliary* and the *main verb.*
    I *am washing* my hair. (*active*)   My hair *was being washed.* (*passive*)

7. (DEFINITION) *Emphatic* forms of a verb use *do* or *does* in the present and *did* in the past. Emphatic verbs have no passive forms.
    Jane *does* work hard. (*present*)   Miss Lang *did* live here. (*past*)

8. (DEFINITION) *Person* indicates whether the subject of the verb is the *speaker* (first person), **the** *one spoken to* (second person), **or the** *one spoken about* (third person).

9. (DEFINITION) *Number* indicates whether the verb is *singular* or *plural.*

LEARNING ACTIVITIES IN CONJUGATING VERBS

A. Using the above definitions and the table showing the conjugation of *to give,* pages 419–20, answer these questions. Make this an oral activity.

    1. In the active voice, what auxiliaries indicate *future tense? present perfect? past perfect? future perfect?*
    2. What do you notice about the *third person singular, present tense?*
    3. How is the passive voice formed in each tense?

4. What two tenses have no subjunctive? In what five other ways does the subjunctive mood differ from the indicative?
5. What kind of action do the perfect tenses indicate?
6. How are the progressive tenses formed? In the passive voice, what are the only tenses?
7. How are the emphatic tenses formed? In what voice and in what tenses may the emphatic forms be used?
8. How are infinitives, participles, and gerunds formed?

B. Other variations of meaning besides those given in the conjugation come from the use of the auxiliaries *should, would, may, might, must, can,* and *could.* Try substituting these for *shall* and *will* in the future and the future perfect tenses. Use *give* or some other verb. Make this oral or written work.

C. Notice this sentence: *Ruth lives nextdoor.* In an oral exercise, change the form of the verb to express each of these ideas:

1. She formerly lived there.
2. Possibly she lived there once upon a time.
3. She ought to live there.
4. She is going to live there in the future.
   Now restate the sentence in the *progressive present* and the *emphatic past.*

D. Classify the italicized verbs by indicating their *voice, mood, person, tense,* and *number.* Make this an oral or a written activity.

1. Peace *is desired* by everyone.
2. The fallen trees *have been removed* from the highway.
3. I *shall pay* my rent on the third day of each month.
4. "*Be* careful!" I shouted.
5. I insist that his request *be given* every consideration.

4. Forming the Principal Parts of Verbs

Foreigners who study the English language have a more baffling time with the principal parts of verbs than with almost anything else. The reason is that irregular verbs form their principal parts in many different ways. Learning English would be much simpler if verbs that are similar in sound or spelling formed their principal parts in the same way. The anonymous author of the poem beginning on this page demonstrates this "logical" method.

Sally Salter, a pretty young lady who taught,
Had a friend, Charley Church, a preacher who praught!
Though his enemies called him a screecher who scraught.

His heart, when he saw her, kept sinking—and sunk,
And his eye, meeting hers, began winking—and wunk;
While she, seeing him, fell to thinking—and thunk.

In secret he'd wanted to speak, and he spoke
(To seek with his lips what his heart long had soke);
So he managed to let the truth leak, and it loke.

He asked her to ride to the church, and they rode;
They so sweetly did glide, one might say that they glode;
And they came to the place to be tied, and were tode.

Then they to each other kept clinging, and clung;
While Time his swift circuit was winging, and wung;
And this was the thing Time was bringing, and brung:

The man Sally'd wanted to catch, and had caught—
That she'd wanted from others to snatch, and had snaught—
Was the one that she now liked to scratch—and she scraught.

"Wretch!" he cried, when she threatened to leave him, and left,
"How could you deceive me, as you have deceft?"
And she answered, "I promised to cleave, and I've cleft!"

● WHAT TO REMEMBER ABOUT THE PRINCIPAL PARTS OF VERBS

1. **The many forms of verbs are based on their** *principal parts:* **the** *present,* **the** *past,* **and the** *past participle.* Sometimes the *present participle* is listed as a fourth principal part.

2. (DEFINITION) *Regular* **verbs are verbs that form the past and the past participle by adding** *d* **or** *ed* **to the present.**

Present	Past	Past Participle
cover	covered	covered
close	closed	closed

3. (DEFINITION) *Irregular* **verbs are those that form the past and the past participle in other ways. Some irregular verbs have the same form in the past as in the past participle:** *teach, taught, taught;* **others make vowel changes:** *drink, drank, drunk.* Listed on page 422 are common irregular verbs as well as a few troublesome regular verbs.

4. **The spelling of principal parts sometimes causes trouble.**

   a) **Verbs ending in** *y* **preceded by a** *consonant* **change the** *y* **to** *i* **before adding** *ed:* fry, fried, fried.

   b) **Verbs ending in** *y* **preceded by a** *vowel* **add** *ed:* defray, defrayed, defrayed.

   c) **Verbs ending in a** *single consonant* **preceded by a** *single vowel* **usually** *double that final consonant* **before adding** *ed:* occur, occurred, occurred; rip, ripped, ripped.

   d) **Verbs ending in** *w* **preceded by a** *single vowel* **add only** *ed:* slow, slowed, slowed.

A. Write correctly the past and the past participle of each of these verbs.

1. compel	5. hinge	9. spar	13. build	17. hum
2. deny	6. age	10. meet	14. bat	18. hiss
3. free	7. plunder	11. fry	15. refer	19. tell
4. tiptoe	8. split	12. play	16. sleep	20. allow

B. As an oral activity, spell the present participle of each of the verbs in the list above. Refer to the rules on page 187.

5. USING PRINCIPAL PARTS CORRECTLY

Most errors in the use of principal parts come from substituting the past participle for the past form—or the other way round. Illiterate forms and the confusion of one verb with another make up most other verb errors.

THE RULES

RULE 1. **Do not confuse the** *past* **with the** *past participle.* **Use** *no auxiliary* **verbs with the** *past;* **use** *at least one auxiliary* **with the** *past participle.*

RULE 2. **Avoid such illiterate forms as these:** *attackted, brung* **or** *brang, busted, buyed, clumb, drug* (as a form of *drag*)*, drownded, blowed, drawed, et* **or** *aten, growed, stoled, throwed,* **and** *shined* (for *shone*).*

RULE 3. **Watch yourself constantly to see that you use correctly the principal parts of these common verbs:** *see, come, go, do, run,* **and** *give.*

LEARNING ACTIVITIES IN USING PRINCIPAL PARTS CORRECTLY

A. With a partner, practice the principal parts of the verbs on page 422.

B. Choose the correct verb from each pair of words in the parentheses. If you write the exercise, be sure to go over the sentences orally.

1. We (begun, began) to try harder. We were not yet (beat, beaten).
2. The line was (broke, broken) where the shark had (bit, bitten) it.
3. After we had (drank, drunk) the milk, we (become, became) sleepy.
4. Time has (flown, flew), but we've (done, did) much.
5. You who have (drove, driven) best will be (chose, chosen).
6. Night had (fell, fallen) before the news (came, come).
7. I've (forgotten, forgot) when those trees were (froze, frozen).
8. We were (showed, shown) how he had (got, gotten) the answer.

---

* When *shine* means *polish,* it is a transitive verb, its principal parts being *shine, shined, shined:* I *shined* my **shoes.** *Shine* in its other senses is intransitive: The moon *shone.*

9. I (seen, saw) that he was (shook, shaken) by the news.
10. By the time that we had (ridden, rode) ten miles, we had (drank, drunk) most of the water that we had (brung, brought) along.
11. I (run, ran) to see who had (gone, went) out the door.
12. The bell had (rang, rung) before Ike (give, gave) the signal.
13. After he had (spoke, spoken), he had (shrunk, shrank) back.
14. He has (sworn, swore) that no money was (took, taken).
15. Have you ever (wore, worn) a shirt that was (torn, tore)?
16. That song will be (sung, sang) just as it was (wrote, written).
17. We (swam, swum) out where the boat had (sunk, sank).
18. We (attacked, attackted) the weeds that had (sprung, sprang) up.

C. This activity deals with verbs for which illiterate forms are often substituted. Copy the sentences, putting in the right forms. Go over your work orally.

1. He (burst) into the room with the news that he had (buy) the house.
2. As the child (climb) the steps, he (drag) a toy behind him.
3. He (bring) the news that the enemy had (attack).
4. The sun had (shine) brightly all day.
5. No one has ever (drown) in this pool.

D. The verbs in this activity are two-way troublemakers. Not only are the past and the past participle often confused, but illiterate forms frequently are substituted. In your small groups, practice the sentences. Spell each form chosen.

1. The catcher (throw) quickly, but the runner (steal) safely.
2. Until now nobody has (know) who (draw) this sketch.
3. We had (eat) lunch before the whistle (blow).
4. I (know) then that he must have (grow) taller.
5. That picture was (draw) well. Who has (throw) it away?

E. Write sentences similar to those in *D*. Use the sentences for class drill.

6 USING OTHER VERB FORMS CORRECTLY

VERB PAIRS OFTEN CONFUSED: I

Because of spelling similarities and differences in meaning, the verbs in the three pairs in this lesson are often confused. Study them carefully. The present participles are included because they, too, are often confused.

Present	Present Participle	Past	Past Participle
lie	lying	lay	lain
lay	laying	laid	laid
sit	sitting	sat	sat
set	setting	set	set
rise	rising	rose	risen
raise	raising	raised	raised

THE RULES

RULE 1. (*Lie, lying, lay, lain; lay, laying, laid, laid*)
Use the forms of *lie* when the meaning is "recline" or "rest."

Please *lie* quietly.   Ted *lay* there for an hour.
The dog was *lying* nearby.   The mail had *lain* there unopened.

Use the forms of *lay* when the meaning is "place" or "put." The forms of *lay* require receivers for their action.

Lay careful plans.   Jim *laid* the book aside.
I've been *laying* out a pattern.   The grounds are *laid* out well.

RULE 2. (*Sit, sitting, sat, sat; set, setting, set, set*)
Use the forms of *sit* when the meaning is "rest in an upright position."

Tom *sits* there.   Marie *sat* near me.
You're *sitting* in my chair.   You have *sat* there before.

Use the forms of *set* when the meaning is "put" or "place." The forms of *set* require receivers for their action.

Set the lamp on the table.   He *set* a fast pace.
Don was *setting* the pace.   You have *set* a good example.

RULE 3. (*Rise, rising, rose, risen; raise, raising, raised, raised*)
Use the forms of *rise* when the meaning is "go up" or "get up."

Will prices *rise*?   Father *rose* early this morning.
The wind is *rising*.   Your land has *risen* in value.

Use the forms of *raise* when the meaning is "lift." The forms of *raise* require receivers for their action.

Can you *raise* the money?   I *raised* the window.
We are *raising* more corn.   This grain was *raised* in Ohio.

LEARNING ACTIVITIES

A. Copy these sentences, choosing the correct form of each verb in parentheses. Exchange papers for checking as the sentences are read aloud.

1. When I want him to (lie) down, my dog usually (sit) up instead.
2. I (lay) my glasses where you are now (sit).
3. When I (rise), I was stiff from having (lie) in one position too long.
4. Food costs are (rise); luckily, my salary has been (raise).
5. When I (set) them in a warm room, the rolls will soon (rise).
6. From where I was (sit), I saw that the fog was (rise) slowly.
7. When you grow tired of (sit), (lie) down.
8. I (rise) while everyone else was still (lie) in bed.
9. The dog (lie) on the porch did not (rise) as I drew near.
10. I was (sit) where I could not see what was (lie) on the desk.

B. Carry out a question-and-answer activity using the various forms of *lie, lay; sit, set; rise, raise*. In class or in your small groups, ask one another questions using the forms. The answers must contain another form of the same verb. If you like, conduct this practice in "spelldown" fashion.

EXAMPLE: Were you *sitting* here?   No, but I *sat* there yesterday.

VERB PAIRS OFTEN CONFUSED: II

Here are six other pairs of verbs often confused in meaning. Careful study of the rules for their use should clear up any confusion in your mind about these verbs.

THE RULES—Continued

RULE 4. (*Let, leave*)
Use *let* when you mean "allow" or "permit"; use *leave* when you mean "go away from" or "part with": Please *let* me drive.   We *left* in a hurry.

RULE 5. (*Learn, teach*)
Use *learn* when you mean "gather knowledge or skill"; use *teach* when you mean "give instruction": Jim *learned* how to play golf; I *taught* him.

RULE 6. (*Bring, take*)
Use *bring* for motion *toward* the speaker; use *take* for motion *away from* the speaker: Jane *brought* her tennis racket. You may *take* mine.

RULE 7. (*Borrow, lend*)
Use *borrow* when you mean "*obtain* temporary use of"; use *lend* when you mean "*grant* temporary use of": I *borrowed* a book. Sue *lent* it to me.

RULE 8. (*Imply, infer*)
Use *imply* when you mean "hint" or "intimate"; a *speaker* implies something. Use *infer* when you mean "assume" or "draw a conclusion"; a *hearer* infers something.

> The news commentator *implied* that the story was true.
> We *inferred* from the broadcast that the story was true.

RULE 9. (*Rear, raise*)
Use *rear* in reference to *children; raise,* in reference to *livestock* or *crops*.

> My parents *reared* nine children.   Father *raises* beef cattle.

LEARNING ACTIVITIES

A. Choose the correct or preferable word from each parentheses. Make this either an oral or a written exercise. Be ready to explain each choice.
1. Aunt Cora (raised, reared) Joe and Mary.
2. The speaker (implied, inferred) that he might compromise.
3. Will you (borrow, lend) me your pen? Please (leave, let) me use it.
4. I suggest that you (take, bring) this book home with you.
5. Who (learned, taught) your dog those tricks?

6. Ray (borrowed, lent) me his book.
7. Where were you (reared, raised)?
8. Who (left, let) that man into the room?
9. Are you (implying, inferring) that I'll not keep my word?

B. Write original sentences like those in *A*. Use them for class practice.

PROBLEMS IN THE USE OF TENSE

The purpose of tense is to make clear when events happen in relation to one another. Meaning becomes highly confused if tense uses are not logical; that is, if they violate proper *tense sequence*.

THE RULES

RULE 1. Observe the proper tense relationship between sentences.

Sidney *was* seriously *injured* yesterday. He *had seen* [not *saw*] a car approaching but *had thought* [not *thought*] that he could cross the street ahead of it.

RULE 2. Avoid shifting needlessly from one tense to another.

MIXED TENSES: He *heard* the telephone and *goes* to answer it.
RIGHT: He *heard* the telephone and *went* to answer it.

RULE 3. Suit the tense of a *dependent clause* or a *verbal phrase* to the time expressed in the *main clause*. Use *past perfect* tense to indicate a time earlier than that of a past-tense verb in another clause.

I *ironed* the dress that I *had washed* [not *washed*]. (The *washing* preceded the *ironing*; the past perfect, *had washed*, is needed.)
Having rung [not *Ringing*] the doorbell, George waited there impatiently. (The *ringing* preceded the *waiting*.)
I was hoping *to go* [not *to have gone*] to the party. (At the time of hoping, the party had not taken place.)

RULE 4. When an indirect quotation follows a *past* tense, use the auxiliaries *could, should, would,* **and** *might;* **use** *can, shall, will,* **and** *may* **after** *present* **or** *future* **tenses.** *

He **said** that I *could* [not *can*] win the championship easily.
He **says** that he *may* [not *might*] change his mind.

RULE 5. Express in the *present* tense the verb in a noun clause that states a *generally accepted truth* **or a** *fact that is true for all time.*†

Franklin proved that lightning *is* electricity.

RULE 6. Avoid using *says* **for** *said:* "Sit down," I *said* [not *says*].

---

* An exception is made if the idea is one of present action continued into the future: Mother said that she *is* still *waiting* for the package.
† Current usage often disregards this rule, though it is a logical one.

LEARNING ACTIVITIES

A. Correct any errors in tense or tense sequence. Go over your work orally.

1. Joe said that he can take a car.
2. I lived in Peoria only two months before I was drafted.
3. I should have liked to have seen the expression on his face.
4. He told me that money was not everything.
5. All that we could see is a cloud of dust.
6. He ran up to the fence and leaps it.
7. His headache came from a blow that he received the day before.

B. A wrong verb tense has been used in some of the sentences that follow. Correct those sentences orally. Justify each change.

1. That blood circulated was proved by Harvey, an English physician.
2. The man explained why pasteurized milk was safer than raw milk.
3. He agreed that rain, snow, and hail are forms of precipitation.
4. The botany class learned that the plum belonged to the rose family.
5. That Robert E. Lee was a great general is generally acknowledged.
6. Jane said that her brother now at home was her twin.
7. The speaker told how coral reefs were formed.
8. I says to Jim, "I can't stay," and walked out.
9. Jane disliked Sally because they quarreled long ago.
10. We were standing there for an hour when the bus came.
11. Completing the questionnaire, I sat down.

REVIEW ▸ *Follow through*

(*Based upon the sentences in* B)

1. Explain the uses of the commas in *1, 3, 8,* and *11.*
2. Why are there no quotation marks in *3* and *6?*
3. Which two sentences have passive verbs?

MISCELLANEOUS PROBLEMS IN VERB USAGE

INTRODUCTORY ACTIVITY

Study the sentences below. How many of them sound right to you?

1. Someone had better call Elizabeth. She had ought to be here.
2. If you would have ask me, I could of helped you.
3. It is better that everyone be told.
4. Tim is popular and often elected to office.
5. We ate our dinner, and the dishes were soon washed.

Now check your judgment by examining the rules that follow. Five of the sentences are wrong; in fact, one of them has three errors. Find the rules that apply; then correct the sentences.

THE RULES

RULE 1. **Be sure to sound the** *ed* **ending of the past tense and the past participle of a verb:** I *asked* [not *ask*] him yesterday.

RULE 2. **Do not misuse** *would have* **for** *had* **in "if" clauses, or use** *of* **as an auxiliary. Never say** *hadda, woulda, coulda,* . . .

RIGHT: If he *had* given, . . .   WRONG: If he *woulda* given, . . .
WRONG: If he *would have* given, . . . If he *would of* given, . . .

RULE 3. **Use** *had better,* **not** *better,* **as a synonym for** *ought to.*

RIGHT: I *had better* stay here.   WRONG: I *better* stay here.

RULE 4. **Use no auxiliary verbs with** *ought.* **Avoid using** *oughta.*

She *ought* [not *had ought*] to be here.

RULE 5. **Do not make a single form of the verb** *to be* **function as both the principal verb and an auxiliary.** *Repeat it.*

RIGHT: Jerry *is* a singer and often **is** *asked* to perform.
WRONG: Jerry *is* a singer and often *asked* to perform.

RULE 6. **Repeat a verb that is essential to clear meaning.**

CLEAR: Jim *likes* me better than he *likes* Ed or Tom.
CLEAR: Jim *likes* me better than Ed or Tom *likes* me.
CONFUSING: Jim *likes* me better than Ed or Tom.

RULE 7. **Use the** *subjunctive* **forms to express the following:**

Condition contrary to fact. This may be a *wish* or a *supposition.*

I wish that Jean *were* (not *was*) going. (*wish*)

Command.   I order that the boat *sail* (not *sails*) at midnight.
Demand.   I demand that Joe *give* (not *gives*) us an answer.
Desirability.   It is better that he *be* (not *is*) told.
Formal motion. I move that the meeting *be* (not *is*) adjourned.
Necessity.   It is essential that everyone *be* (not *is*) there.

NOTE: In colloquial usage, the indicative forms are common.

RULE 8. **Avoid unnecessary shifts of voice and subject.**

RIGHT: He *rushed* to the telephone and *called* the doctor.
WRONG: He *rushed* to the telephone, and the doctor *was called.*

RULE 9. **In standard expression, avoid using** *allow, calculate, expect, guess,* **or** *reckon* **as substitutes for** *think, suppose, believe, assume, gather.*

STANDARD: I *think* that I should go.   COLLOQUIAL: I *guess* I should go.

LEARNING ACTIVITIES

A. Copy the following sentences, making any changes called for by the rules. Exchange papers for checking as the sentences are read aloud.

1. If you would have helped me, I might of won.
2. He ask me what he had ought to do.

3. I calculate that I better see whether anyone else wants to go.
4. Ted found Ralph sooner than Bill or Bob.
5. The farmer went to the bank, and his savings were drawn out.
6. I expect that you are wrong this time.
7. When I ask him, he said that he had ought to wait for Tim.
8. Bert telephoned me before Don or Dave.
9. Jane is a good bookkeeper and employed at the bank.
10. If only he hadda ask, I could of helped him.
11. I reckon you don't remember me.
12. He knows me better than Lou.
13. She liked literature, but math was not enjoyed very much.
14. I guess you're surprised to see me.

B. Write sentences using correctly any forms that gave you trouble in *A*. *Be careful to proofread*. Use the sentences for class practice.

C. Rewrite the following sentences, changing the italicized verb to the corresponding tense of the subjunctive mood. Go over your work orally, telling in each case which subjunctive use (Rule 7) applies.

1. I insist that the charges *are* investigated.
2. It is necessary that everyone *is* there.
3. I wish that I *was* having a vacation now.
4. Suppose that John *was* our captain.
5. It is advisable that his reply *is* not quoted yet.
6. If this *was* yesterday, I'd change my answer.
7. The general ordered that his men *are* re-enforced.

DIALECTAL OR ILLITERATE VERB FORMS

This lesson and the next deal chiefly with expressions that the dictionary classifies as *dialectal* or *illiterate*. They are minor problems in the sense that for many people they are not problems. It will be worth while to go over the rules in class to see how many of them you really need to study.

308

THE RULES

RULE 1. **Do not use** *disremember* **for** *forget.*

> I *forget* [not *disremember*] the date.

RULE 2. **Avoid using** *didn't go to* **for** *didn't mean to* **or** *didn't intend to.*

> I *didn't mean to* [not *didn't go to*] hurt your feelings.

RULE 3. **Do not use** *invite* **or** *recommend* **as nouns.**

I received an *invitation* [not an *invite*] to the wedding.
The teacher wrote me a *recommendation* [not a *recommend*].

RULE 4. **Avoid using** *take* (or *took*) *sick* **for** *become* (or *became*) *ill.*

> The baby *became ill* [not *took sick*] during the night.

RULE 5. **Avoid the unnecessary use of** *take* (or *took*) *and.*

> She *doubled* [not *took and doubled*] the recipe.

RULE 6. **Avoid saying** *want in, want out, want off, want through.*

RIGHT: I *want to get off* here.   WRONG: I *want off* here.

RULE 7. **Avoid using** *used to could* **for** *used to be able to.*

> I *used to be able to* [not *used to could*] run fast.

RULE 8. **Avoid using the noun** *suspicion* **for the verb** *suspect.*

RIGHT: I *suspect* him.   WRONG: I *suspicion* him.
RIGHT: Our *suspicion* was correct.

RULE 9. **Avoid using** *ain't* **for** *is not* (*isn't*), *are not* (*aren't*), *am not, has not* (*hasn't*), *have not* (*haven't*). Do not say *aren't I.*

RIGHT: I am seated in the wrong row, *am I not?*

RULE 10. **Do not open a remark with an unneeded** *say, listen, look.*

POOR: *Say,* have you seen the new library?
BETTER: Have you seen the new library?

LEARNING ACTIVITY

A. Here is a conversation that violates many of the rules in this lesson. Study this conversation; then in pairs read it aloud, making the changes needed.

"Hi, Jean. Did you get an invite to Sue's party?"

"I don't know yet, but I suspicion that she won't send me one. Ever since I took and criticized her hairdo, she ain't had much use for me. I didn't go to make her angry; she used to could take a joke! Are you invited, Pat?"

"Yes, but maybe I'll not go. Joe says that he can't give Sue's parties much of a recommend. He's invited, but he ain't sure he'll go. Maybe he'll take sick, he says!"

"Listen, someone else told me the same thing. I disremember who . . . Oh, oh—here's our corner! . . . Look, conductor, we want off here!"

B. Write sentences to illustrate correct usage based upon the rules in this lesson. Read them in class or in your small groups.

COLLOQUIAL *versus* STANDARD VERB USAGE

THE RULES

RULE 1. **In standard usage, distinguish between the words in these pairs. Colloquially, little distinction is made.**

Shall, will

To express *simple future,* use *shall* with the *first* person and *will* with the *second* and *third* persons.

I *shall* bake a cake on Tuesday; she *will* bake one on Thursday.

To express *determination,* use *will* with the *first* person and *shall* with the *second* and *third* persons.

I *will* have my own way; he *shall* not have his.

Should, would

Use *should* like *shall* and *would* like *will* except as follows:

a) **Always use** *would* **to indicate** *habitual action.*

The children *would* play in the sandpile for hours.

b) **Always use** *should* **to express** *obligation* **or** *duty.*

You *should pay* your bills promptly.

May, can

Use *may* to ask *permission* or to indicate *possibility.* Use *can* to indicate *power* (or *ability*) *to do.*

May we go, Mother?   *Can* you lift this rock?

RULE 2. **Do not misuse or overuse the verb** *get.* **Never use** *gotta.*

Poor: I *get* irritated with him.   Better: I *become* irritated with him.
Poor: You're going to *get* it!   Better: You'll be punished!
Poor: I didn't get to go. [Was not *permitted,* or was not *able?*]
Better: I *was not permitted* to go.   I *was not able* to go.

RULE 3. **Avoid** *is* (or *are*) *done with, is* (or *are*) *finished with, is* (or *are*) *through with.* **Say** *has* (or *have*) *finished.*

Poor: *Are* you *done with* dinner?   Better: *Have* you *finished* dinner?

RULE 4. **Be sure to express a repeated verb if its form is different from that of the one already expressed.**

Right: He **works** as hard as he always has *worked.*
Wrong: He **works** as hard as he always *has.* (Has *what? works?*)

RULE 5. **Avoid using** *aggravate* **to mean** *irritate, provoke,* **or** *annoy.*

Please don't *annoy* [not *aggravate*] the kitten.

RULE 6. **In standard expression, avoid using** *proven, contact* **as a verb, or** *enthused* (except as a verb in the active voice).

Did you *get in touch with* [not *contact*] the owner?
I'm *enthusiastic* [not *enthused*] about the picnic.
That statement can't be *proved* [not *proven*].

Change to standard usage any faulty or colloquial usage in the following sentences. If you write this activity, go over your papers orally.

1. He can and has done much hard work.
2. Haven't you got any work to do? I'm through with mine.
3. His behavior aggravates me.
4. Are you done with the stapler? I shall need it soon.
5. The man has proven that he was not in California in August.
6. I would like to see the record of your purchases.
7. When I was a child, I would color by the hour.
8. Look, I've made up my mind. You can go, on one condition.
9. Phil went everywhere that Jack had.
10. Listen, I have important news for you. We have contacted Harry.
11. I got bored before the man was finished with his speech.
12. Madge is enthused about going to Colorado for the summer.

USING ENGLISH IN ALL CLASSES

Bring into English class papers that you have written or are writing for any class. Check them for (1) wrong tenses or shifts of tense, (2) the use of "of" as an auxiliary, (3) wrong uses of verbs in the pairs on pages 303–4.

FOLLOW-UP ACTIVITY

Ask someone to check your ordinary speech to see whether you use any of the illiterate forms named on page 309. Work to eliminate them one by one.

7. USING VERBS TO EXPRESS IDEAS VIVIDLY AND EXACTLY

Verbs, being the life of the sentence, are the words that determine the force of the entire expression. You should try always to use the verbs that will bring out your ideas most vividly.

GUIDES FOR CHOOSING VIVID VERBS

1. Choose verbs that will make the strongest appeal to one or more of the five senses. (See pages 255–56.)
2. Choose the specific verb that best fits the action involved or that gives a clue to character. *Laugh*, for example, has many vivid substitutes: *chuckle, giggle, snicker, titter, cackle, guffaw.*
3. Replace a weak or general verb and a modifier with a vivid verb.

LEARNING ACTIVITIES IN USING EXPRESSIVE VERBS

A. The verb *tell* has interesting variations, each of which expresses specific activities not suggested by the word itself. Some of those variations are *report, mention, relate, utter, assure, confess, disclose, inform, recount, narrate.*

Write a sentence using *tell* or *told.* Then substitute the preceding variations. Read your sentences in class.

B. Fill the following blanks with verbs that express different types of *walking.* Read your sentences aloud so that your voice adds to the meaning.

1. The fat man ·········· down the street.
2. Mary ·········· noiselessly from the room.
3. Dizzy from his fall, Ben ·········· across the field.
4. Keeping time to the music, the boys ·········· down the hall.

C. For each of the following general verbs, make a list of words that assert action more specifically. Present your list to the class for evaluation. Here are the verbs: *eat, sit, think, work, burn, sing, look, give.* Make a combined list to put into your notebook for use in original writing that you do.

D. Here are quotations from literature, with blanks used in place of the verbs. Decide what vivid verbs might fit the blanks; then check your choices with those of the authors. (All the quotations are found in Bartlett's *Familiar Quotations.* They are also given in the *Teacher's Manual* for your text.)

1. Death ·········· on every passing breeze,
   He ·········· in every flower.—HEBER
2. From peak to peak, the rattling crags among,
   ·········· the wild thunder.—BYRON
3. Out of the shadows of the night,
   The world ·········· into light.—LONGFELLOW
4. And the white magnolia blossoms ·········· the twilight of the pines.
   —WHITTIER
5. For somehow the poor old Earth ·········· along.—LOWELL
6. Joyous we too ·········· out on trackless seas.—WHITMAN
7. The ill-timed truth we might have kept—
   Who knows how sharp it ·········· and ··········?—SILL
8. Short swallow-flights of song, that ··········
   Their wings in tears, and ·········· away.—TENNYSON

E. Replace the italicized words with a one-word verb that expresses the idea more vividly. Make this an oral activity.

1. He *moved rapidly* through the line.
2. Tom *walked slowly* down the street.
3. Billy *went noisily* up the stairs.
4. He *gave an angry look* at his tormentors.
5. Tim, *using his elbows, made* his way through the dense crowd.
6. The candles *shone brightly* in the darkness.
7. The birds *sang merrily* in the treetops.

Just to make sure! *

Directions: As you do these activities, refer to the rules and definitions in this chapter. Go over orally any activities that you write.

A. Supply the correct form of each verb given in parentheses.

1. After Emma had (wear) the dress a few times, the seams (burst).
2. The well should be (sink) here where I have (drive) a stake.
3. He had (buy) the land before prices (rise). As a result, when he sold it, he (become) wealthy.
4. I could have (swear) that I had not (throw) the box away.
5. I should have (know) that you had (get) permission to leave.
6. He (begin) to ask about the missions on which I had (fly).
7. The Greeks (climb) out of the wooden horse and (attack) while many of the Trojans (lie) asleep.
8. The lion had (spring) upon its prey and (drag) it down.
9. The boy had not (eat) the sandwich; he had simply (bite) into it.
10. The bell must have (ring), for the noon whistle has (blow).
11. I (run) out early to see whether the plants had (freeze).
12. The parents were (show) the fine work that the boys had (do).
13. After he had (shake) the malted milk, he (drink) it.
14. Joe has (write) a story and has (draw) pictures to illustrate it.
15. You have (swim) a fine race; in fact, you have (break) the record.
16. If I had (see) you, I'd have (speak) about this matter.
17. He (give) me a smile and then (steal) softly away.
18. He had (sing) so loudly that he had (drown) out the rest of us.
19. I had (forget) that you had already (bring) your excuse.
20. I have (choose) this hat, but perhaps I should have (take) that one.
21. She had (sit) there until she had (fall) asleep.
22. Your plant has (grow) rapidly; it has (beat) mine.
23. Was this curtain (tear) in cleaning? It must have (shrink), too.
24. Suddenly the moon (come) out from a cloud and (shine) brightly.
25. I had often (go) to Chicago but had never (ride) there on a train.

B. Correct each wrong or poor form. Go over your work orally.

1. I disremember what Mother ask me to do.
2. Then I says to Jack, "You used to could take and lasso that pony."
3. I should of called Mother. I better do so at once.
4. If I would have kept my face straight, no one would of suspected me.
5. Jack mentioned the incident but decides to forget it.
6. I'd have liked to send you an invite.
7. If I was you, I'd tell her that I didn't go to slam that door.
8. Dyeing the dress, I hung it on the line.

* Check Test 3 should be given at this point. If the results show need for further study, pupils should do this review practice. They should then take Mastery Test 3.

9. I inferred from its meowing that the kitten wanted in.
10. Dad said that he may borrow me the car tonight.
11. Phil is a fine golfer and also known as a tennis player.
12. If he had not left us help, I expect that he might have took sick again.
13. People learned long ago that water was necessary for life.

C. Locate any colloquial expressions and change them to standard English.

1. Say, if I had known that you were done with the tin snips, I'd have contacted you.
2. Don't get aggravated until you are proven wrong.
3. I blew the same kind of sour note that Roger had; the conductor didn't seem enthused about mine, either.

D. Identify the verbs in these sentences as *intransitive complete, transitive active,* or *transitive passive.* Make this either an oral or a written exercise.

1. Maine High School has a new Student Council president.
2. Have the prices been raised?
3. Terry was standing at the bus stop.

E. Give the *mood, tense, person,* and *number* of the italicized verbs.

1. *Send* her a telegram.   3. The boys *will help* you.
2. I *have read* the lesson twice.   4. I move that Ted *be* chosen.

REVIEW

To keep you in practice

CAPITALIZATION AND PUNCTUATION

Supply needed capitalization and punctuation in these sentences.
1. weve no time to waste cried dr fisher our train the last one until tomorrow leaves from the union station at exactly 1005 pm
2. tell me lois do you have mothers keys or did aunt susie borrow them
3. my aunt and uncle live at 417 pearl street lewiston maine they moved there from the south on may 1 1927
4. by the way dan bring the following an ax a good knife and a compass
5. no terry said his father im not interested in such here today and gone tomorrow notions
6. arent you c t bryan from rye new york asked uncle joe yes the man replied on christmas day ill have lived there twenty seven years
7. our science class has been reading a book called men against death prof a d britt our teacher says that most people know very little about the heroes of science whose stories are told in this book
8. when i opened the suitcase i found much to my surprise the belongings of a stranger
9. im sorry john but your 2s and 3s and 8s look too much alike
10. as we sat around the fire we sang jeanie with the light brown hair when you and i were young maggie and let me call you sweetheart

Know How to Use Nouns*

"NO, ARBEE, I'M AFRAID YOU DON'T QUITE HAVE THE RIGHT IDEA."

Are you, like Arbee, slightly hazy in your knowledge of nouns? If so, here is a chance to brush up on these important words.

1. RECOGNIZING NOUNS AND REVIEWING THEIR PROPERTIES

The term "noun" is one that appears over and over in any study of grammar; before going on to a study of the ways that nouns are used, be sure that you understand what a noun is.

* Pretest 4 should be given at this point.

WHAT TO REMEMBER ABOUT CLASSES OF NOUNS

1. (DEFINITION) **Nouns** * **are** *name words* **applied to** *persons, places,* **or** *things.* ("Things" includes *ideas, actions,* and *qualities.*) **All nouns are either** *proper* **or** *common.*

2. (DEFINITION) **Proper nouns refer to** *particular* **people, places, or things. They are always capitalized:** Ted Williams, Sweden, Red Sea.

3. (DEFINITION) *Common* **nouns refer to any of a class:** *man, nation, sea.*

4. (DEFINITION) *Concrete* **nouns name things that can be perceived by one of the five senses:** *baseball, banana, sunset.*

5. (DEFINITION) *Collective* **nouns name groups:** *crowd, audience, herd.*

6. (DEFINITION) *Abstract* **nouns name qualities or ideas:** *truth, freedom.* NOTE: A noun may be classified in several different ways. For example, *Congress* is *proper, concrete,* and *collective.*

7. (DEFINITION) *Compound* **nouns put together** *two or more words.* Some are hyphenated; some are written solid; some have separate words: *self-will, baseball, roll call.* Use the dictionary to check.

WHAT TO REMEMBER ABOUT THE PROPERTIES OF NOUNS

Nouns have four properties: *person, gender, number,* **and** *case.*

1. (DEFINITION) *Person* **shows whether a noun denotes the** *speaker* (first person); **the** *person spoken to* (second person); **or the** *person spoken of* (third person).
   I, the *chairman,* called the meeting to order. (*first person singular*)
   We staff *members* are giving Joe a present. (*first person plural*)
   You, *Ed,* are to blame. (*second person singular*)
   You *people* in the front row must move back. (*second person plural*)
   He, that small *child,* saved my life. (*third person singular*)
   They, the *men* that you named, have joined the club. (*third person plural*)

2. (DEFINITION) *Number* **shows whether a noun refers to** *one* (singular number) **or** *more than one* (plural number): *boy* (singular); *boys* (plural).

3. (DEFINITION) *Gender* **is the distinction according to sex.**
   Masculine gender: The *man* did his work well.
   Feminine gender: Six *girls* volunteered to help.
   Neuter gender (without sex): Fill the *box* with *sand.*
   "Common gender" is a term sometimes applied to nouns that may be either masculine or feminine: *clerk, pianist, worker.*

4. (DEFINITION) *Case* **denotes the relationship of a noun to other words in the sentence. The English language uses** *three* **cases:** *nominative, possessive, objective* (sometimes called *accusative*).†

---

* Another name for "noun" is "substantive," a term applied not only to nouns themselves but to any word, phrase, or clause used as a noun.

† Nominative and objective case uses are treated later in this chapter. Possessive case is treated under apostrophes, page 174, and under adjective modifiers, page 354.

A. Select all nouns in the following sentences. Tell what kind of noun each is; classify it as to number and gender. Make this an oral or a written exercise.

1. Jim Lee is a member of the senior class of Lane High School.
2. Mother baked a cake and two pies for the picnic.
3. There has been a slight change in the plans.
4. Campers at Lake Breezy enjoy the sunshine.
5. At dawn airplanes brought help to the survivors.
6. Many explorers have described the loneliness of life in the Arctic.
7. In the nineteenth century, the United States rose to power.
8. Is that flock of sheep still grazing in the east meadow?
9. The treasure was found in the hold of the ship.
10. The bond of friendship held the students together.

B. See how many abstract nouns you can write in five minutes. Compare lists in class.

C. The italicized words in these sentences can be used either as nouns or as verbs. In an oral activity, decide what part of speech they are as here used.

1. The *sun* sank in a *blaze* of color. Soon the first *star* appeared.
2. I was watching your *face*. Why did you *smile*?
3. We can *sun* ourselves here on the *beach*.
4. We should *blaze* a trail. It can't do any *harm*.
5. You should *face* facts. Your actions may *harm* all of us.
6. His *smile* fading, Tom said, "*Beach* the canoe here."
7. In this particular *dream,* a man said, "I shall *star* you in my new *play*."
8. Did you *dream* that you could *play* the part?

D. Write a paragraph containing at least eight words that may be either nouns or verbs. (Refer to the Guides to the Development of the Paragraph, page 199.) *Proofread for careless errors.* Underscore the words; then exchange papers and label the words according to their use.

2. USING NOUNS AS SUBJECTS

Nouns have many uses in the sentence, including the following:
1. As subjects
2. As predicate nominatives
3. As direct objects (objects of verbs), objective complements, indirect objects, objects of prepositions, adverbial objectives
4. As appositives
5. As nominatives of address

The most important use of the noun is as the subject of a sentence, since subjects combine with verbs to form the basic sentence idea.

● WHAT TO REMEMBER ABOUT SUBJECTS

1. (DEFINITION) The *subject* of a sentence names the *person, place,* or *thing* talked about. It is in the *nominative* case. To locate the subject, ask *who* or *what* about the verb.

    Joe Day bought a tractor. (Who bought? *Joe Day.*)

2. The subject of a sentence may be compound.

    Wheat, oats, and *rye* are grown in this area.

3. The subject does not always directly precede the verb.

  a) Sometimes expressions come between the subject and the verb.

    A *box* of clothing was left here. (What was left? *Box.*)

  b) In questions the subject often separates the parts of the predicate.

    Has the *rain* stopped? (What has stopped? *Rain,* the subject.)

  c) If a sentence begins with the expletive *there,* the subject follows the verb: There was a sudden *cry* for help. (What was? *Cry.*)

  d) For variety or emphasis, the subject may follow the verb.

    Near the gate stood a *sentry.* (Who stood? *Sentry.*)

LEARNING ACTIVITIES IN USING NOUNS AS SUBJECTS

A. Name the subjects in the following sentences. Remember, locate the verb first; then ask, "Who or what . . .?" Make this an oral or a written exercise.

1. A clump of trees sheltered the house in the hollow.
2. Wind and weather had eroded the rocks.
3. Where did Arnold lose his watch?
4. Out of the darkness came a scream.
5. A box of books blocked the entrance to the room.
6. Men, women, and children filled the streets.
7. Has John announced the distribution of the prizes?
8. There must be some mistake in this matter.
9. Inside the cave were many stalactites.
10. There is no alternative.

B. For more practice, use the sentences in *A,* page 317.

C. Write the following sentences. Go over them in class.

1. A sentence containing a compound noun subject
2. A question containing a noun subject
3. A sentence beginning with *there* and containing a noun subject

Using Diagrams to Analyze Sentence Structure

Pictures often make clear what words themselves cannot. A *sentence diagram* is really a picture of the relationship between the various parts of the sentence. Diagrams can help you to understand sentence structure.

Except for the conjunctions joining compound parts, the diagrams given as examples omit sentence parts not yet studied.*

SENTENCE: A little child in the front row raised his hand.

The Steps in Diagramming

1. Draw a horizontal line. This is the line on which all basic sentence elements are placed.

2. Find the verb first. Place it on the right half of the line.

3. To the left of the verb, draw a vertical line that cuts through the horizontal line. This line separates the *predicate verb* and the *subject,* the two chief sentence elements.

4. To find the subject, ask yourself, "Who or what raised?" Place the subject left of the vertical line.

child | raised

Compound Verbs and Subjects

John eats and sleeps well.   The days and weeks went by.

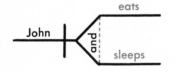
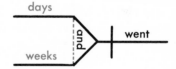

The boys and the girls laughed and sang.

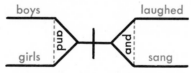

There † is some mistake.

---

* Diagramming in this book always follows complete instruction in the various sentence elements. If so desired, diagramming can be omitted without disturbing the sequence of instruction.

† An introductory *there* is called an *expletive;* it has no relation to the other parts of the sentence and therefore appears on a separate line of the diagram. Such a word is called an *independent element.*

A. Diagram verbs and subjects in the following sentences. Put diagrams on the board and go over them orally. Always name the verb first.

1. On the first day the boys hiked a distance of ten miles.
2. There is no substitute for hard work.
3. From the depths of the forest drifted the faint smell of smoke.
4. Here the sun does not penetrate at any time.
5. Have your friends ever visited Mexico?
6. Cattle and horses ran through the open gate and down the road.
7. There had been much mail and many callers in the past week.
8. At each exit stood a policeman.

B. For further practice, diagram verbs and subjects in *A,* page 317, and *A,* page 318. Put the diagrams on the board and explain them orally.

3. Making Verbs Agree with Noun Subjects

THE JURY INCLUDES TWO WOMEN.

THE JURY DISAGREE.

You have heard again and again the basic rule that *a verb agrees with its subject;* that is, a singular subject needs a singular verb; and a plural subject, a plural verb. That general rule, however, has specific subdivisions that you should know. One of them covers the situations pictured above.

THE RULES

RULE 1. Use *is, was, has, does,* and their *contractions* with a *singular* subject; use *are, were, have, do,* and their *contractions* with a *plural* subject. (*Don't* and *doesn't* cause most difficulty; watch them.)

> **Jane** *does*n't live here now.   The **boys** *are*n't working.

Do not be confused by (*a*) *words or phrases between verb and subject,* (*b*) *an introductory* here *or* there, (*c*) *questions with verb before subject.*

> *a*) A **list** of ten names *was* read.   **Ed,** as well as the girls, *is* here.*
> *b*) Here *are* the **papers**.   There *goes* **Jim**.
> *c*) *Has* that little **boy** been found yet?

RULE 2. **Do not be influenced by** a *predicate nominative* differing in number from the subject: Our **problem** *is* the crowds in the street.

RULE 3. Use a *plural* verb with *compound* subjects joined by *and* except when they form a unit.

> **Ham and eggs** *is* a good dish.   **Eggs** and **butter** *are* sold here.

RULE 4. Use a *singular* verb with *singular compound subjects* joined by *or, nor, either-or, neither-nor;* use a *plural* verb with *plural subjects.* If they *vary,* use a **verb agreeing** with the *nearer* subject.

> Either **Dean** or **Mark** *helps*.   **Rats** or **mice** *are* in the loft.
> Two boys or a **man** *is* enough.   A man or two **boys** *are* enough.

RULE 5. **If one subject is** *affirmative* **and another** *negative,* **make the verb agree with the** *affirmative* **subject: Tom,** not his brothers, *works* here.

RULE 6. Use a *singular* verb with *subjects,* **either** *simple* **or** *compound,* **that are limited by** *each* **or** *every:* Every **boy** and **girl** here *is* welcome.

RULE 7. Use a *singular* verb with a *collective* noun subject if the group acts as a *unit.* Use a *plural* verb if the members act *individually.*

> The **audience** *has* grown.   The **audience** *were* whispering.

RULE 8. **As a rule, use** a *singular* verb after *the number;* use a *plural* verb after *a number:* The **number** of cases *is* small.   A **number** *are* better.

RULE 9. **If** a *fraction* **or** a *per cent* **is the subject and is followed by an "of" phrase, use a verb that agrees with the** *object in that phrase.*

> **Two thirds** of the pie *remains*.   **Ten per cent** of the books *are* new.

RULE 10. Use a *singular* verb with words *plural in form* but *singular in meaning:* **Essays of Elia** *is* a book by Lamb.   **Ten dollars** *is* left.

RULE 11. **In most cases, use a** *singular* **verb with these subjects:** *civics, economics, mathematics, measles, molasses, mumps, physics, United States;* **use a** *plural* **verb with** *ashes, athletics, clothes, hysterics, pliers, politics, scissors, shears, slacks, statistics, suds, thanks, tongs, trousers, tweezers.*

---

* If in doubt, reword the sentence: *Ed is here, as are the girls.*

321

LEARNING ACTIVITIES IN MAKING VERBS AGREE WITH SUBJECTS

A. Choose the correct form from each pair in parentheses in the following sentences. If you write this exercise, go over your work orally.

1. Either Nona or her cousins (has, have) always helped us.
2. Three fourths of a cup of milk (is, are) enough.
3. *Tales of a Traveler* (was, were) written by Washington Irving.
4. The council (disagree, disagrees) on the matter.
5. Usually the girls, not their mother, (prepare, prepares) the dinner.
6. Every seat in the auditorium (has, have) been sold.
7. Politics (interest, interests) my older brother.
8. Neither the shrubs nor the grass (is, are) green.
9. This edition of *The Canterbury Tales* (is, are) beautiful.
10. Each boy and girl on the committee (has, have) worked hard.

B. Complete the following sentences, using one of these verbs in each of them: *is, are, was, were, don't, doesn't, has, have.* Compare sentences in class.

1. A basket of eggs . . .
2. The number of entries . . .
3. The dress, not the gloves, . . .
4. Either the cake or the pies . . .
5. Bread and milk . . .
6. Tom, as well as his friends, . . .
7. Ila and her dog . . .
8. Every boy and girl in the class . . .

C. Correct orally any errors in verb-subject agreement in these sentences.

1. The tree with its pink-and-white blossoms were a lovely sight.
2. My only regret is the hours wasted.
3. The boys was waiting for me.
4. A crate of peaches was delivered today.
5. Elms and maples grows on our lawn.
6. My answers on the test was right.
7. The sun don't shine often enough.
8. A new hat, as well as new shoes, was bought.
9. The owner and manager are my father.
10. Peaches and cream is a good dessert.
11. When was those letters mailed?
12. From this plant comes many useful products.
13. The sugar, together with the other staples, are on that shelf.
14. Liver and onions hit the right spot with Father.

USING ENGLISH IN ALL CLASSES

Go over papers that you have written or are writing for other classes. Correct any errors in verb-subject agreement.

FOLLOW-UP ACTIVITY

Form the habit of listening carefully to your own speech and that of other people. Work to correct one at a time your errors in agreement.

4. Using Nouns as Predicate Nominatives

● WHAT TO REMEMBER ABOUT PREDICATE NOMINATIVES

1. (DEFINITION) The *predicate nominative* (or *predicate noun*[*]) is a word that completes the predicate verb and renames the subject. The predicate nominative, like the subject, is in the *nominative* case.

   Rod Hayes is the *pitcher*. (Rod Hayes = pitcher)

2. (DEFINITION) A predicate nominative completes the kind of intransitive verb known as a *linking* verb. Linking verbs (also called *copulatives*) link the subject to the word that completes the meaning of the verb. Verbs that may be used as linking verbs (or as a part of them) include *is, am, are, was, were, be, being, been, seem, appear, become, continue, grow, look, stay, taste, feel, smell, sound.*

3. Predicate nominatives may be compound.

   The girls in the beauty contest are *Betty, Ann,* and *Margaret.*

LEARNING ACTIVITIES IN USING PREDICATE NOMINATIVES

A. Select *verbs, subjects,* and any *predicate nominatives* in the following sentences. Two sentences have no predicate nominative. Compare your work.

1. The smaller child is Betty's brother.
2. John seems a stranger to us now.
3. Did George once live in Elm City?
4. Those girls have been friends for years.
5. The little boy in the back seat is my nephew.
6. The younger women are Miss Strong and Miss Ellis.
7. Alice became chairman of the committee.
8. Is that woman your mother or your aunt?
9. Suddenly a man burst into the room.

B. Complete the sentences with predicate nouns. Compare work in class.

1. Jack Smith is . . .
2. Our doctor seems . . .
3. Elmer may become . . .
4. My father was once . . .

DIAGRAMMING PREDICATE NOMINATIVES

Predicate nouns, or *predicate nominatives,* are essential parts of any sentences in which they appear. Therefore, they belong on the main base line of a diagram. In other words, they are part of the *sentence skeleton.*

---

[*] This lesson covers only *nouns* used as predicate nominatives. Pronouns can also be used in that way. The term "predicate nominative" covers both predicate nouns and predicate pronouns.

The line separating the predicate nominative from the verb slants toward the subject to show that the predicate noun refers to it.

Predicate Nominative

The book is a novel.

Compound Predicate Nominative

The leaders are Bill, Tom, and Jim.

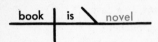

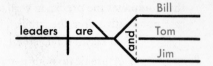

LEARNING ACTIVITIES IN DIAGRAMMING PREDICATE NOMINATIVES

A. Diagram *verbs, subjects,* and *predicate nominatives* in these sentences. Put your diagrams on the board and analyze them orally.

1. The winner of the contest was a Will Dawes, Jr.
2. Fruits in season now are peaches, pears, and plums.
3. The Oakland eleven appears the stronger team.
4. To my way of thinking, a change would be a good idea.
5. That man must once have been a farmer or a dairyman.
6. The new hired man seems a hard worker.
7. At that time the Smiths were our nearest neighbors.

B. Diagram verbs, subjects, and any predicate nominatives in the sentences in *A,* page 323. Go over your diagrams orally.

REVIEW

Follow through

(Based upon the sentences in A)

1. In sentences 1, 2, and 4, account for the commas.
2. In sentence 5, how would you write the plural of *dairyman?*
3. In sentence 7, why is there no apostrophe in *Smiths?*

5. USING NOUNS AS DIRECT OBJECTS AND AS OBJECTIVE COMPLEMENTS

READ AND DISCUSS

Like predicate nominatives, *direct objects* complete sentence ideas. They should not be confused, however. Look at these sentences:

Mr. Rand is our *mayor.*   Mr. Rand bought a *farm.*

Which italicized word renames the subject? Therefore which sentence has a predicate nominative? Which sentence has an action verb? On what does the subject act? Then what do you call that word?

The direct object usually is easy to locate. Slightly more difficult is the *objective complement,* which follows and renames a direct object.

● **WHAT TO REMEMBER**

  1. (DEFINITION) **A** *direct object* (object of the verb) **receives the action performed by the subject of a** *transitive active* **verb.***

  2. **To find the direct object, say the subject and the verb; then ask** *whom* **or** *what:* Mary bought a *hat.* (*Mary bought* what? *hat*)

  3. **A direct object may be compound:** Jane plays the *piano* and the *cello.*

  4. **Usually, except in some questions, the direct object follows the verb. Sometimes for special effect it comes first:** This **book** I really *enjoyed.*

  5. (DEFINITION) **A noun used as an** *objective complement* **follows and renames a** *direct object:* Christopher calls his **dog** *King.* (*Dog* is the direct object.)

  Verbs that often have objective complements include *make, name, call, choose, elect,* **and** *appoint.*

LEARNING ACTIVITIES

A. Complete these sentences with direct objects of your own choice. Compare your papers to see how direct objects affect sentence meaning.

  1. A messenger brought the .... 3. That color matches your ....
  2. Our school needs some .... 4. Uncle Carl bought a ....

B. (1) Copy the following sentences. (2) Draw two lines under verbs and one line under subjects. (3) Circle direct objects and enclose objective complements in parentheses. One sentence has no objects. Exchange papers for checking.

  1. Many Americans called Robert A. Taft "Mr. Republican."
  2. Always before, the plumber had brought his tools with him.
  3. Ted has won every match by a wide margin.
  4. Our neighbor named his farm Plentywood.
  5. Joe carried the cups and saucers to the kitchen.
  6. Miss Boyd appointed Ruth leader.
  7. Diligent practice made the boy a skilled pianist.
  8. Have the dinner dishes been washed yet?

C. Use the sentences in *A,* page 317, and those in *A,* page 318, for more practice.

D. Write sentences using the following verbs: *bought, have chosen, began, carried, appointed, should have been written.* Go over your work in class, naming each *verb* and *subject* and any *direct objects* or *objective complements.* Classify the verbs as *transitive active* or *transitive passive.*

---

* Occasionally a direct object follows a passive verb, being called then a *retained object:* You *will be given* a **choice.** Careful writers avoid overuse of retained objects.

Diagramming Direct Objects and Objective Complements

Direct objects and objective complements are diagrammed on the horizontal base line with the verb and the subject. All words that belong on this base line make up the *sentence skeleton*.

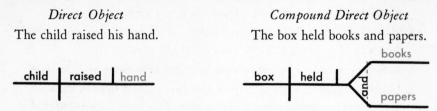

Direct Object	*Compound Direct Object*
The child raised his hand.	The box held books and papers.

Notice that the direct object is part of the complete predicate. The vertical line between the verb and the direct object meets the base line but does not go through it.

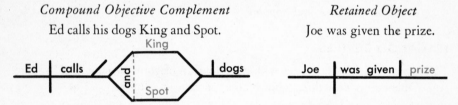

Compound Objective Complement	*Retained Object*
Ed calls his dogs King and Spot.	Joe was given the prize.

Note that the objective complement follows the verb. The separating line leans toward the direct object, since that is the word to which it belongs.

LEARNING ACTIVITIES

A. Diagram *verbs, subjects, predicate nominatives, direct objects,* and *objective complements* in these sentences. Put the diagrams on the board and go over them orally. Explain fully, thus: "The verb in this sentence is *calls;* the subject is a proper noun, *Ed;* there is a direct object, *dog;* there is a compound objective complement, *King* and *Spot.*"

1. In my algebra paper yesterday, Nona found several errors.
2. The children called their two poodles Nip and Tuck.
3. After long years of study, Jack became a doctor.
4. There have never been twins in our family.
5. The coach appointed Neil Thomas acting captain.
6. In this game Phil made two baskets and two free throws.
7. What fruits does Uncle Ed grow in his orchard?
8. The minister pronounced the couple man and wife.
9. Often new students lose their way in the building.
10. The candidate made the Plaza Hotel his headquarters.

B. For more practice, diagram and explain the sentences in *B,* page 325.

6. Using Nouns as Objects of Prepositions, Indirect Objects, and Adverbial Objectives

Other important uses of nouns are as *objects of prepositions, indirect objects,* and *adverbial objectives.**

● WHAT TO REMEMBER

1. (DEFINITION) **The *object of the preposition* is the word that a preposition joins to some other word in the sentence.** (If you need to review prepositions, see page 388.)

Judy *swam* **in** the *sea.* (The preposition *in* joins *sea* to *swam.*)

To find the object of a preposition, ask the question *whom* or *what* after it: *Judy swam in* what? *sea,* the object of *in.*

2. (DEFINITION) **An *indirect object* is a word that *receives* what the direct object *names.* To check a word that you think is an indirect object, place *to, for,* or *of* in front of it. If it is an indirect object, the sentence meaning will not change.**

Mother baked [for] *Betty* a cake.   He asked [of] *me* a question.
Fred gave [to] *Vern* a slap on the back.

3. (DEFINITION) **The *adverbial objective* is a *noun* used like an *adverb.* It generally tells *amount, direction, distance, time, value,* or *weight.***

Dick paid two *dollars* for the sweater. (*amount*)

4. Objects of prepositions, indirect objects, and adverbial objectives may be compound.

Mary traveled by *plane* and *bus.* (*objects of* by)
Mr. Smith gave *Bob* and *Joe* good advice. (*indirect objects*)
He works *mornings* and *evenings.* (*adverbial objectives*)

LEARNING ACTIVITIES

A. Copy these sentences. Place prepositional phrases in parentheses; underscore nouns used as objects in them. Exchange papers for checking.

1. The curtains at the window were flapping in the breeze.
2. On Monday I am invited to a friend's home for lunch.
3. At the end of each day, Al rushes for a seat in the subway.
4. A thick layer of cardboard covered the tables in the warehouse.

---

* The diagramming of these constructions is covered on pages 361 and 377–78, under adjective and adverb modifiers.

B. Copy these sentences. Circle direct objects; underline indirect objects. Read the sentences in class, turning the indirect objects into prepositional phrases.

1. Father gave Millie a scolding.
2. Mother sent Jane and Jim books for graduation.
3. On Sunday afternoons Grandmother reads the children Bible stories.
4. Reporters asked the President and his wife many questions.

C. Copy these sentences, underlining the adverbial objectives. Compare papers in class.

1. This package is ten pounds overweight.
2. Several times I have been paid five dollars for my help.
3. The speed of the car averaged fifty miles per hour.
4. Move the table a foot this way.

D. Write and read in class original sentences using as adverbial objectives *pounds, dollars, evening, minute, week.*

7. USING NOUNS AS APPOSITIVES AND AS NOUNS OF ADDRESS

"SUSIE, CAN YOU GIVE ME A NOUN OF ADDRESS?"

"THAT'S EASY. OURS IS RIGHT HERE — 912 SHADY LANE!"

THINK IT OVER...

As you probably know, Arbee's little sister has a wrong idea of the noun of address. What would *your* answer have been? And what would you say if you were asked to explain an *appositive?* How would you distinguish between an *appositive* and a *predicate nominative?* How would you distinguish between a *noun of address* and a *subject?*

1. (DEFINITION) **An** *appositive* **is an expression that** *explains* **or** *identifies* **a noun or a pronoun within a sentence. It is always in the same case as the word that it explains.**

   Tom Dale, my *uncle,* lives in Paris.   Jane has a new **ring,** a *diamond.*

2. **An appositive expression usually comes** *after* **the word that it explains, but occasionally it comes first.**

   A skilled *draftsman,* **Mr. Barnes** sketched a plan quickly.

3. **Appositives may be compound.**

   Jack Dunn, our *quarterback* and *captain,* spoke first.

4. **Appositives, or the word groups containing them, are set off by commas unless closely tied to the word explained.**

   My cousin *Jim* won the cup.   Bill, *my best friend,* lost to him.

5. **The appositive is useful in combining or shortening sentences.**

   Jim has a new car. It is a convertible. (*two sentences*)
   Jim has a new car, a *convertible.* (*one sentence*)

6. (DEFINITION) **The** *noun* **(or** *nominative) of address* **is a name or names used in** *speaking* **directly to a person or persons. It is always in the** *nominative* **case. It is set off by a comma or commas.**

   Dora, watch me.   This, *Mary,* is Sam.   Come here, *Doug.*

7. **A noun of address may be compound:** *Jon* and *Roy,* wait here.

8. **A noun of address is an** *independent element;* **that is, it is not an essential part of the sentence.**

LEARNING ACTIVITIES

A. Improve the following pairs of sentences by using an appositive to combine each pair into one sentence. Turn the less important sentence into the appositive. Make this an oral activity.

1. The new teacher is Mr. Belden. He is a graduate of Ohio State.
2. The county seat is Center. It is a small town in Nebraska.
3. *Present Indicative* is the autobiography of Noel Coward. It is delightful.
4. George Washington's native state was Virginia. Virginia was the home of the first permanent English settlement.
5. Mother is canning peaches. They are my favorite fruit.
6. Eli Whitney was the inventor of the cotton gin. He was not a Southerner.

B. (1) Write sentences using *captain, poem, neighbor, city* as appositives; let one appositive precede the word that it renames. (2) Write sentences using these words as nouns of address: *Mr. Average American, Ladies and Gentlemen, Senator, Mr. President, Sheriff.* Compare these sentences in class or in your small groups. *Be sure to proofread.*

C. (1) Copy these sentences. (2) Draw a straight line under each appositive and a wavy line under each noun of address. (3) Punctuate properly. Exchange papers for checking.

1. Boys and girls I am your new teacher Miss Gordon.
2. Your friend that Jones boy was looking for you Ernest.
3. Come over fellows if you want to see my new pet a chihuahua.
4. No class I have not visited Monticello Jefferson's famous home.
5. Henry what is the meaning of the word *gullible?*

D. Bring in from magazines several clippings that contain appositives. Tell orally what condensation has been made by their use.

Diagramming Appositives and Nouns of Address

As you will see by the following diagrams, appositives are placed in parentheses after the nouns that they rename. Nouns of address, like the expletive *there,* are diagrammed on a separate line.

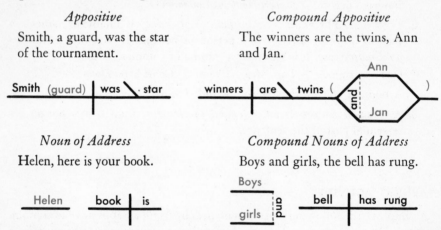

Appositive	*Compound Appositive*
Smith, a guard, was the star of the tournament.	The winners are the twins, Ann and Jan.

Noun of Address	*Compound Nouns of Address*
Helen, here is your book.	Boys and girls, the bell has rung.

LEARNING ACTIVITY

In the following sentences, diagram all the sentence parts that you have learned to diagram thus far. Put the diagrams on the board and explain them, naming each part specifically.

1. Mr. Malone, president and owner, dictated the letter of apology.
2. Roger Martin, a ranger, spotted the fire and sent for help.
3. Coach, is Elroy Dahl our best miler?
4. Mr. Leigh, your report omits two months, May and June.
5. Has Miss Case changed her mind, Rudy?
6. The new manager is Carl Gray, author and lecturer.
7. Sir, there has been a mistake.
8. Mr. Briggs, the court appoints your father guardian of this child.

8. Using Gerunds and Infinitives as Nouns

Two special word types that look much like verbs but that can do the work of nouns are gerunds and infinitives. Examine these sentences:

Swimming gives some people great pleasure.
To swim gives some people great pleasure.

How is each of the italicized expressions used?

● **WHAT TO REMEMBER**

1. **The** *gerund,* **a verbal noun, can be used in a sentence in most of the ways that nouns can.**

   Swimming requires muscular co-ordination. (*subject*)
   Her job is *filing.* (*predicate nominative*)
   Bob's summer job, *stripping* bluegrass, pays well. (*appositive*)
   Millie enjoys *wading* in the pool. (*direct object*)
   Does Tom object to *being nominated?* (*object of preposition*)
   Louise gives *typing* too little of her time. (*indirect object*)

2. **A gerund retains certain verb characteristics; that is, it may have** *complements* **and** *modifiers.*

   My hobby is *building* **boats.** (*Boats* is the object of *building.*)
   Clever *questioning* won the case. (*Clever* modifies *questioning*)

3. (DEFINITION) **A** *gerund phrase* **is made up of a** *gerund* **and any** *complements* **or** *modifiers.*

4. **The** *infinitive* **can be used in most of the ways that nouns can.**

   To ask questions is a sign of interest. (*subject*)
   Dave's job is *to plan* the stunts. (*predicate nominative*)
   Why don't the boys want *to go?* (*direct object*)
   Alice wants nothing but *to help.* (*object of preposition*)

5. **An infinitive may have** *complements* **and** *modifiers.*

   My job is *to set* the **table.**   Our plan was *to leave* **early.**

6. (DEFINITION) **An** *infinitive phrase* **is made up of an** *infinitive* **and its** *complements* **or** *modifiers.* In the examples above, *to set the table* and *to leave early* are infinitive phrases.

7. **After such verbs as** *wish, want, perceive, command,* **or** *advise,* **an infinitive may have a subject:** I want **Jane** *to sit* here.

8. **After such verbs as** *hear, help, feel, make, dare, see,* **and** *let,* **the to of an infinitive often is understood:** *Did Lou hear Dad* [to] *call him?*

9. **Infinitives and gerunds may be compound.**

   Collecting stamps and *reading* are good pastimes. (*gerunds*)
   His problem is whether *to go* or *to stay.* (*infinitives*)

LEARNING ACTIVITIES IN USING GERUNDS AND INFINITIVES

A. Locate the gerunds and the infinitives in the following sentences. If a gerund has an object or a predicate nominative, name it. If an infinitive has a subject, an object, or a predicate nominative, name it. Make this an oral exercise.

1. Taking an umbrella was a good idea.
2. His first task was to cut the grass.
3. Alfred helped his father trim the trees.
4. To be a guest at the party was Jane's secret hope.
5. My favorite pastime has always been reading.
6. Mother enjoys working in her flower garden.
7. To land safely seemed impossible.
8. Washing dishes does not appeal to many people.
9. The police let only one man leave the place.
10. The counselor's job, being a peacemaker, is not easy.
11. The mayor's chief interest now is in winning re-election.

B. Write sentences to fit the following requirements: (1) use *to umpire* and *to be admired* as subjects, direct objects, and predicate nominatives; (2) use *boating* and *entertaining* as subjects, appositives, and objects of prepositions. *Be sure to proofread.* Read and criticize the sentences in your small groups.

C. Improve the italicized parts of the following sentences by changing them to infinitive expressions. If you write this exercise, go over your sentences orally.
EXAMPLE: John hopes *that he may return* soon. John hopes *to return* soon.

1. The first requirement is *that one should keep cool.*
2. *That he may make the football team* is Fred's ambition.
3. The chief told his followers *that they should return to their homes.*
4. *That such changes can be made now* is impossible.
5. The miners' final decision was *that they would return to their jobs.*
6. *That he will be needed by someone* is every man's hope.
7. Martha believed *that the man was a stranger in the village.*
8. George would prefer *that Alfred should not leave until later.*

DIAGRAMMING GERUNDS AND NOUN INFINITIVES

Gerunds and noun infinitives are diagrammed in the same way, with the exception of infinitives that have subjects.

Subject
Buying new clothes is fun.

Direct Object
Jim hopes to play baseball.

Predicate Nominative

My idea is to leave early.

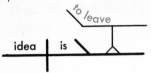

Appositive

His hobby, skiing, takes skill.

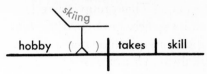

Infinitive with a Subject

Hal wants Bill to meet the train.

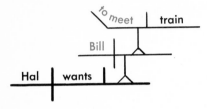

Tim let Alvin go with him.

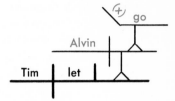

Compound Forms

Dan enjoys fishing and hunting.

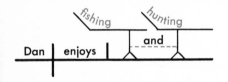

To go or to stay is a problem.

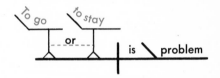

LEARNING ACTIVITIES

A. In the following sentences, diagram all the sentence parts that you have studied thus far. Put the diagrams on the board for orderly, specific analysis.

1. Collecting autographs is his hobby.
2. To meet the winner was a great pleasure.
3. Father asked Jim to buy a paper.
4. The fielder let two high flies slip through his fingers.
5. My job, filing the bills, takes time.
6. Debating and playing my clarinet occupy my leisure moments.
7. Most boys like to swim and to skate.

B. For more practice, diagram and explain the sentences in *A,* page 332.

9. USING DEPENDENT CLAUSES AS NOUNS

Just as the gerund or the infinitive may be used as a noun, so may a lause. (If you are not sure what a clause is, see page 404.) Notice this sentence: *What John said surprised his father.*

If you ask yourself, "What surprised?" the answer is the entire group of words *What John said*. In other words, *What John said* is the subject of the sentence. That group of words is a *clause,* because it has a predicate (*said*) and a subject (*John*). *What John said* is used merely as a part of speech; therefore it is known as a *dependent,* or *subordinate,* clause. Such a clause is always part of a *complex sentence.* (See page 404.)

● **WHAT TO REMEMBER ABOUT NOUN CLAUSES**

  1. (DEFINITION) **A dependent clause that does the work of a** *noun* **is a** *noun clause.* A good way to identify a noun clause is to substitute a third-person pronoun for what you think is the clause.
  What he said surprised me. *It* surprised me.

  2. **A noun clause is always a part of an independent clause.**
  Who he is does not interest me. (*subject*)
  The entire class saw *where he went.* (*direct object*)
  His excuse is *that the roads are muddy.* (*predicate nominative*)
  The fact *that no funds were available* worried me. (*appositive*)
  It is clear *that help is needed.* (*appositive:* It [that help is needed] is clear.)
  He gave *whoever had a perfect record* special praise. (*indirect object*)
  Joe paid no attention to *what I told him.* (*object of a preposition*)
  Hard work has made me *what I am.* (*objective complement*)

  3. **Words used to introduce noun clauses include** *that, whether, who, whom, what, how, why, when, where, whoever,* **and** *whomever.*

LEARNING ACTIVITIES IN USING NOUN CLAUSES

  A. Go over the following sentences orally. Locate each noun clause and tell its use. Decide whether certain sentences would be more effective if they were reworded to eliminate the noun clause. Reword any such sentences.

  1. That the door was locked is a fact.
  2. Jack wondered where his mother had gone.
  3. A change of scenery is what Mother needs.
  4. The teacher asked what was puzzling the class.
  5. His excuse is that the roads were blocked.
  6. It is certain that Alfred needs exercise.
  7. Why the bell was rung remains a mystery.
  8. Tom has given his answer, that his mind is made up.

  B. In each of the following sentences, substitute a noun clause for the italicized words. Use this as an oral class activity.

  1. The farmers hoped *for a change in the weather.*
  2. His excuse is *lack of time.*
  3. *Your actions* show a generous nature.
  4. Does Father know *your problem?*

5. *His whereabouts* did not concern us.

6. *The operation of the machine* is a puzzle.

7. Bob explained *his absence from the meeting*.

C. Bring into class an original sentence to illustrate each use of noun clauses explained in this lesson. Put sentences on the board for class practice.

Follow through

(*Based upon the sentences in* A, *page 334*)

1. Why are there no quotation marks in *2, 4, 5,* and *8?*

2. Why is *Mother* capitalized in *3?*

3. How would you spell the plural of the predicate nominative in *7?*

DIAGRAMMING NOUN CLAUSES

Here are diagrams of noun clauses. (Noun clauses as objects of prepositions are diagrammed on page 362; as indirect objects, on page 378.)

Subject

That the game ended in a tie was a surprise.

Direct Object

Mr. Gray doubts that prices will go up.

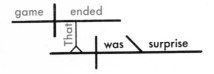

Predicate Nominative

My guess is that the owner will not return.

Objective Complement

Hard work has made Mr. Ayers what few men become.

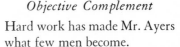

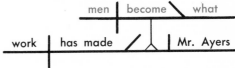

Appositives

It is a fact that a change is needed.

Chris brought the news that the loan had been granted.

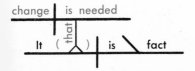

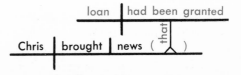

Compound Noun Clause

The article told where the men had been and why the trip had been a secret.

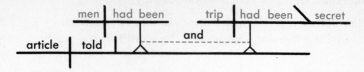

LEARNING ACTIVITIES IN DIAGRAMMING NOUN CLAUSES

A. In these sentences, diagram all sentence parts studied thus far. Put diagrams on the board and explain them in orderly, specific fashion.

1. Allen could not believe that he had been hypnotized.
2. The truth is that Kate would rather go by plane.
3. What you do with the money does not concern me.
4. It has been said that money talks.
5. Why Sue came, the committee cannot understand.

B. For more practice, use the sentences in *A,* page 334.

10. USING NOUNS TO EXPRESS IDEAS EXACTLY AND VIVIDLY

READ AND DISCUSS

Some students can write correctly according to the rules of grammar and usage, yet never write anything very interesting, because they have not learned to use words effectively. Instead of finding the vivid or unusual word, they use the commonplace, inexact word over and over. They pay little attention to the fact that words have strong powers of suggestion, or *connotation.* What is the difference, for example, between a *listener* and an *eavesdropper?* a *habit* and a *custom? fame* and *notoriety?*

GUIDES FOR USING NOUNS EFFECTIVELY

1. Learn to use effective *synonyms* for nouns. (Synonyms are words of similar meaning.)
2. Learn to distinguish between *general* and *specific* terms. Note how these nouns become increasingly more specific: *human being, man, Frenchman, Parisian, Pierre Cartier.*
3. Find the *exact* word that will best carry your meaning.
4. Use *simple* nouns oftener than flowery or big-sounding nouns.
5. Use words that have strong *connotations;* that is, words which suggest specific shades of meaning. (See page 98.)

LEARNING ACTIVITIES IN CHOOSING EXACT AND VIVID NOUNS

A. Arrange the following groups of words in order, beginning with the most general term and ending with the most specific. Go over these in class.

1. Potato, vegetable, Idaho, plant
2. Cake, angel food, dessert, food
3. Papoose, child, baby, human being
4. Plant, pine, tree, evergreen, piñon

Now take the most general terms that you found and have them written on the board. See how many different specific degrees you can name for each.

B. *House* is a general noun, but *cottage, mansion, hut, shack, bungalow, palace,* and *shanty* are specific nouns. Here are five general nouns: *story, road, hill, song, tree.* Write a paragraph using them; then rewrite it, substituting a specific noun for each. *Be sure to proofread.* Compare work in class.

C. From your listening or reading, bring to class illustrations of specific words that add to the effectiveness of the author's expression.

D. Replace each italicized noun with a simpler word of similar meaning. In class, decide which word is more effective. Use a dictionary or a book of synonyms.

1. His *pauciloquy* amazed us; before, he'd *fulminated* for hours on that topic.
2. John's *indefatigability* should win him a promotion.
3. We were looking for some unusual *divertissement.*
4. Don't let your head be turned by *blandishments.*
5. She has *orbs* of blue.
6. After *cogitation,* Father said, "I've seen this *chirography* before."

Just to make sure! *

Directions: As you do these activities, refer to the rules and definitions in this chapter. Go over orally any activities that you write.

A. Give the use of the italicized nouns or word groups used as nouns.

1. I was trying *to do* my *duty.* Honesty has been my *watchword.*
2. That mountain to the *left* is twenty *miles* away.
3. Did the *teacher* give *Earl* an *Incomplete* in biology?
4. Do you enjoy *being* field *representative, Elmer?*

B. Select noun clauses in these sentences. Give the use of each.

1. It is apparent that only a few will be chosen.
2. Her ambition is that she may become a dental assistant.
3. Have you heard who was elected?
4. Report the loss to whoever is at the desk.
5. Hand whoever is nearest you the baton.

C. Correct any errors in agreement in the following sentences.

1. *Coleridge's Poetical Works* gives a brief account of the poet's life.
2. Every man, woman, and child knows the danger of the hydrogen bomb.

---

* Check Test 4 should be given at this point. If the results show need for further study, pupils should do this review practice. They should then take Mastery Test 4.

3. Our home room have cast their ballots for class officers.
4. On the wall was several colorful posters.
5. A pile of old newspapers were stacked in the basement.
6. There have been several good plays at the Civic Opera House lately.
7. Another difficulty during our journey was the sandstorms.
8. Neither Bruce nor his parents know about the celebration.
9. George don't care much for cantaloupe.
10. Milo, not his sisters, are spending the summer at Skyline Lodge.

To keep you in practice

CAPITALIZATION AND PUNCTUATION

Copy these sentences, supplying needed capitalization and punctuation.

1. Confucius the chinese philosopher said when you see a good man think of emulating him when you see a bad man examine your own heart
2. One of my favorite pieces of art is whistlers London bridge
3. A story in this months womans day is no kiss for kate by timothy acres
4. Poise charm beauty these are qualities that each contestant has
5. The twenty five year old man was filled with self reproach
6. The minister read his text which was psalms 128 1
7. My sixteenth birthday how well I remember it was a thrilling one
8. We completed our plans for the easter program mona would direct the choir susan would take charge of the play

PLURALS

Write the plural form of each of these words or symbols.

1. thrush	3. pass	5. volley	7. sheaf	9. chef	11. &
2. onyx	4. glory	6. rodeo	8. corps	10. vortex	12. Mr. Gray

VERBS

Number your paper from 1 to 10. Decide on the correct form of each verb in parentheses. Write it after the corresponding number.

1. After the guests had (go), the chairs were (take) back.
2. Someone has (tear) a page from the book that you (give) me.
3. At once he had (spring) upon his horse and had (ride) away.
4. After we had (beat) the rugs, we (attack) the rest of the work.
5. Last time I (come) early and (bring) a friend with me.
6. Tom had (get) some new plants, but they had (freeze).
7. The bell will be (wear) out if it is (ring) much oftener.
8. The contract that we (draw) up last year has (run) out.
9. Our hearts (sink) at the task, but we (do) our best.
10. The late whistle had (blow) before we (drag) ourselves home.

Know How to Use Pronouns*

"MR. DIXON SAYS THAT THEY CALL THEIR DOG 'PRONOUN' BECAUSE, WITH THE TWINS AROUND, IT REALLY HAS TO STAND FOR A LOT OF THINGS!"

1. Understanding Pronouns and Their Uses

Mr. Dixon is making a play on words, of course; but it is true that pronouns "stand for a lot of things." Pronouns are used in most of the ways that nouns are. In any of their uses, they may be compound.

Subject: *I* called the fire department. (In a command or a request, the subject is *you* understood: [*You*] Come here.)

Predicate Nominative: The announcer is *he.*

Direct Object: Does Angela prefer *these* or *those?*

Indirect Object: The author wrote *me* a letter.

Appositive: Two boys, *he* and *I,* attended the jamboree.

Object of Preposition: Pay no attention to *him.*

Possessive: This raincoat is *mine.*†

---

* Pretest 5 should be given at this point.

† Possessive pronouns are sometimes used as adjectives. See *3a,* page 354.

1. (DEFINITION) **A** *pronoun* **is a word that takes the place of a** *noun.*

   a) (DEFINITION) *Personal* **pronouns refer to the** *speaker:* I, my, mine, me, we, our, ours, us; **the** *one spoken to:* you, your, yours; **or the** *one spoken of:* he, his, him, she, her, hers, it, its, they, their, theirs, them. (Note their declension on page 421.)

   b) (DEFINITION) *Compound personal* **pronouns combine** *personal* **pronouns with** *self* or *selves:* myself, yourself, himself, herself, itself, ourselves, yourselves, themselves.

   (1) (DEFINITION) **A** *reflexive* **pronoun when used as any kind of** *object* **renames the** *subject:* **John** did *himself* an injustice.

   (2) (DEFINITION) **An** *intensive* **pronoun** *emphasizes* **another** *pronoun* **or a** *noun;* **it is in** *apposition* **with the word to which it refers:** I made that rug *myself.* He *himself* came.

   c) (DEFINITION) *Relative* **pronouns are both** *pronouns* **and** *connectives.* **As connectives, they** *introduce a dependent clause* **and** *refer to an antecedent* **in an** *independent clause.* They include *who, whose, whom, which, that, whoever, whomever, whichever, whatever.*

   Show me the book *that* you wrote.   He is the one *who* called me.

   d) (DEFINITION) *Interrogative* **pronouns ask** *questions.* **They are** *who, whose, whom, which,* **and** *what:* With *whom* did you come?

   e) (DEFINITION) *Demonstrative* **pronouns** *point out.* **They are** *this, that, these, those: This* is one hat that I really like.

   f) (DEFINITION) *Indefinite* **pronouns do** *not* **point out specifically. They include** *another, any, anybody, anyone, anything, both, each, either, everybody, everyone, everything, many, neither, nobody, none, no one, one, other, some, somebody, someone, such.*

   Everyone has agreed.   I don't know *anyone* in Detroit.

2. (DEFINITION) **The** *antecedent* **of a pronoun is the word or words for which it stands:** Has **Phil** come? Usually *he* is here early.

LEARNING ACTIVITIES IN RECOGNIZING PRONOUNS

A. List each personal pronoun in the following sentences and tell how it is used. Name the antecedent if it is expressed. Exchange papers for checking.

   1. Mr. Wood, the sheriff has made you a deputy.
   2. My employer is he in the brown suit.
   3. Do you see them often? Do they ever ask you about me?
   4. The teacher appointed two girls, her and me.

B. In these sentences locate each pronoun and tell how it is used. Make this an oral or a written exercise.

   1. Who likes these better? Has everybody seen them?
   2. Those are some of the best samples. Nobody likes this or that, however.

3. Such are the plans. To which of them does anyone object?
4. What can anyone suggest? Many of you have much to offer.

C. These sentences contain compound personal pronouns. Classify them as *intensive* or *reflexive*. Tell how they are used.

1. Clyde painted the house himself.
2. Jones hurt himself on that play.
3. Give yourself a fair share.
4. She herself saw you.

DIAGRAMMING PRONOUNS

Pronouns are diagrammed just as nouns are.

Subject
He has been here often.

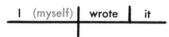

Compound Subject
You and I can help.

Predicate Nominative
The winner is he.

winner | is \ he

Direct Object
Who has done this?

Who | has done | this

Intensive as Appositive
I wrote it myself.

I (myself) | wrote | it

Subject Understood
Sell the house.

(You) | Sell | house

Subject of Infinitive
James wants us to be there.

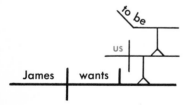

Object of Gerund
Seeing you is a pleasure.

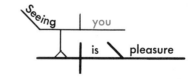

LEARNING ACTIVITY IN DIAGRAMMING PRONOUNS

Diagram and explain all sentence parts that you have learned thus far.

1. I shall go myself.
2. You yourself told the secret.
3. Do you need these?
4. That is she in the red dress.
5. Whom shall I select to help you?
6. Move the cars—these and those.
7. I shall ask to see no one.
8. We elected him president.

"Who shall I make it toom?" *

2. USING THE CORRECT CASE OF PRONOUNS

Most pronoun errors are due to the fact that certain pronouns change form. See the table of pronoun case forms, called "declensions," page 421.

RULES FOR USING PRONOUN CASE FORMS

RULE 1. **Use the** *nominative case* **for** *subjects* **and** *predicate nominatives.*
She watched the fight.   This is *he* speaking.

RULE 2. **Use the** *objective case* **for** *objects.*
I shall call *her* soon. (*direct object*)   Tell *us* a story. (*indirect object*)
Wait for Albert and *me.* (*objects of preposition*)

RULE 3. **Watch out for errors when using a pronoun as part of a** *compound.*
When in doubt, try eliminating the other member of the compound.
Mr. Jay gave ~~Tom and~~ *me* tickets to the game.

RULE 4. **Keep an** *appositive pronoun* **in the same case as the word with which it is in apposition:** Ed chose two **boys,** John and *me.* (*app. with d. o.*)

RULE 5. **Use** *who* **and** *whoever* **as** *subjects* **or** *predicate nominatives; whom* **and** *whomever* **as** *objects.*† **Do not be misled by the insertion of such an expression as** *do you think.*
Who is here? (subject of *is*)   *Who* do you think is here? (subject of *is*)

RULE 6. **Use the** *objective case* **for the** *subject* **or the** *object* **of an** *infinitive.*
Jean wants *me* **to call.**   Jack wanted Ted **to help** *him.*

RULE 7. **If a form of the infinitive** *to be* **links two pronouns, use the** *same case* **for both:** *I'*d like to be *he.* (*nom.*)   She took *me* to be *him.* (*obj.*)

---

* Used by permission of Bob Barnes and the *Saturday Review.*

† In informal use, *who* often replaces *whom*, especially at the first of a sentence: *Who* did you call?

342

LEARNING ACTIVITIES IN USING PRONOUN CASE FORMS

A. Choose the correct pronoun from each pair in parentheses. Make this an oral exercise, giving the rule that applies in each case.

1. Joan and (I, me) wanted her to see Phil and (him, he).
2. Why didn't you wait for Leon and (us, we)?
3. Harry and I need Jack and (him, he).
4. Mother wants Joyce and (me, I) to be musicians.
5. Coach Evans gave Hal and (I, me) a chance to play.
6. I should like to be (her, she) for just one day.
7. You and Bob should precede us, Gene and (I, me).
8. (Him and me, He and I) don't know (who, whom) to ask.

B. Write sentences using the objective pronoun forms that differ from the nominative forms. (See the declension on page 421.) Use your sentences for class drill. Include compound expressions like *you and me, him and me, her and me.*

C. In an oral activity, fill the blanks with *who, whoever, whom,* or *whomever.* Tell how each of them is used in its own clause.

1. I have extra drill material for ‒‒‒‒‒ needs it.
2. I learned nothing about ‒‒‒‒‒ the stranger was.
3. My cousin, ‒‒‒‒‒ you have not met, is visiting me.
4. Name the boys ‒‒‒‒‒ you think deserve the Good-Will Awards.
5. He is the man ‒‒‒‒‒ I thought called my name.
6. Tell ‒‒‒‒‒ is at the door to return in half an hour.

RULES FOR USING PRONOUN CASE FORMS—Continued

RULE 8. Use *we* with *nominative* nouns and *us* with *objective* nouns.

We boys are ready. (*subject*)   Father needs *us* boys. (*object*)

RULE 9. Use the *possessive case* before a *gerund* to show *ownership.*

Everyone was surprised by *his* [not *him*] coming.

RULE 10. *Never* use an *apostrophe* in *possessive personal pronouns* or in *whose.* **Write** *its, hers, ours, yours, theirs.* **Avoid confusing possessive pronouns with contractions that sound like them:** *it's* (it is *or* has); *you're* (you are); *they're* (they are); *who's* (who is *or* has).

Are these *our* seats? If *they're* ours, *whose* are those?

RULE 11. **Use an** *apostrophe* **and** *s* **to form the possessive of** *indefinite pronouns,* **except when followed by** *else;* **then add the** *s* **to that word.**

Here is *someone's* key. Is it *Jim's,* or is it *someone else's?*

RULE 12. **In choosing the case of a pronoun after** *than* **or** *as,* **be guided by the complete meaning of the sentence.**

I like her better *than* (he, him). [If you mean *I like her better than I like him,* use the objective form; if you mean *I like her better than he likes her,* use the nominative form.]

343

A. Practice the following sentences orally in your small groups, choosing the correct forms from the parentheses.

1. (Us, We) boys are glad not to be (them, they).
2. The earliest arrivals were (we, us) three girls.
3. Doesn't (him, his) going interest you?
4. I weigh more than (he, him).
5. You do your work as neatly as (she, her).
6. Yes, we visited Ellen as well as Nancy. However, we visited Nancy longer than (her, she).
7. (You, Your) making the team pleases (us, we) boys.
8. No one hopes for the best more than (I, me).

B. Rewrite the following paragraph, correcting all pronoun errors. *Be sure to proofread* before exchanging papers for checking.

Us boys need to make our plans for the picnic. The other groups have already made their's, but we should be able to come up with something better than them. Fred, you being here is lucky. Your ideas are twice as good as anybody elses.

C. Give oral sentences to illustrate the preceding rules. Listen closely to one another; make corrections if needed.

USING ENGLISH IN ALL CLASSES

Check papers written for any class to see whether you have violated Rule 10. If so, correct the errors; then make a note to yourself to check your next paper for similar errors before handing it in.

FOLLOW-UP ACTIVITY

Work constantly to improve your pronoun usage. Perhaps some of the correct pronoun forms do not sound right to you because you often hear incorrect uses. Some of those incorrect uses may eventually become acceptable English. In fact, "It is *me*," and "*Who* did you see?" are now allowed by some authorities as acceptable colloquial usage. However, it is a good idea to continue to practice the forms that authorities give as preferred expressions.

3. AVOIDING ERRORS WITH PRONOUNS AND THEIR ANTECEDENTS

The word "antecedent" comes from the Latin. *Ante* means "before"; *cedent* is from a root meaning "go." Therefore, *antecedent* means "going before," a good description of an antecedent, for it is the word to which a pronoun points back, or *refers*. For example, in the preceding sentence, *it* refers to *antecedent*, and *which* refers to *word*.

THE RULES

RULE 1. **Be sure that a pronoun agrees in** *person, number,* **and** *gender* **with its** *antecedent.* **(DEFINITION) An** *antecedent* **is the noun** (or other substantive) **to which the pronoun refers.**

> Tom laughed as *he* made the remark. (*third person, singular number, masculine gender; antecedent,* Tom)

RULE 2. **Unless you know that the antecedent is feminine, use** *his* **to refer to these singular indefinite pronouns:** *another, anybody, anyone, each, either, everybody, everyone, neither, nobody, no one, somebody, someone.*

> **Neither** of the girls did *her* share.   Did **anyone** give *his* name?

RULE 3. **Use either** *one's* **or** *his* **to refer to the antecedent** *one.* Some authorities consider *one's* the better usage.

> **One** needs to keep *one's* [or *his*] head in an emergency.

RULE 4. **Use** *their* **to refer to the antecedent** *both* **and** *his* **or** *her* **to refer to the antecedent** *each.* **Use** *his* **or** *her* **also to refer to an antecedent limited by** *each, every, either,* **or** *neither.*

> *Both* wore *their* [not *his*] medals.   *Each* one has *his* [not *their*] lunch.

RULE 5. **Avoid using a** *possessive noun* **as an antecedent.**

> WRONG: This is my **aunt's** car *who* lives in Cleveland.
> RIGHT: This car belongs to my **aunt** *who* lives in Cleveland.

RULE 6. **Use the neuter personal pronoun** *it* **whenever the sex of a person or animal referred to is unknown.**

> A dog loves *its* master.   My puppy Polo loves *his* master.

RULE 7. **Be sure that the reference to an antecedent is clear.**

> VAGUE: George told Phil that *he* [who?] was expected at the party.
> CLEAR: George told Phil, "*You* are expected at the party."
> CLEAR: George told Phil, "*I* am expected at the party."

RULE 8. **For clarity, avoid using** *which, it,* **or** *that* **to refer to the whole idea of a clause or a sentence.**

> POOR: I received an *A* in trigonometry, *which* pleased me.
> BETTER: The fact that I received an *A* in trigonometry pleased me.
>
> POOR: He was criticized by some of his friends. *That* worried him.
> BETTER: He was worried because some of his friends criticized him.

RULE 9. **Avoid reference to an** *implied* **antecedent.**

> We took a trip to England. *They* are hospitable people.
> We took a trip to England. *The English* are hospitable people.

A. Some of the following sentences contain errors in agreement of a pronoun with its antecedent. Others do not refer clearly to an antecedent. Rewrite the sentences correctly. Go over them in class, explaining each change that you made. Use the preferred form if there is a choice.

1. This purse came from Cuba. They do fine work with leather.
2. Each of you should check your own paper carefully.
3. I borrowed the Bakers' rake who live nextdoor.
4. Somebody left their notes on the desk.
5. A crow perched on a nearby fence post. I watched him curiously.
6. Nobody has called for these papers. That surprises me.
7. Everyone should enjoy their work.
8. Both of the women forgot to wear her earrings.
9. A baby soon develops its own personality.
10. Everyone in the girls' camp had their own work to do.
11. Elaine told Marilyn that she was expected to leave early.

B. Practice reading these sentences correctly in your small groups.

1. Hasn't either of them finished their translation?
2. Neither one is wearing their new shoes.
3. A black cat made his way across our path.
4. Charles wrote David that he could help him.
5. Neither Lavonne nor Frances has given their book report.
6. Each of the girls has their own choice to make.
7. Everybody in school has had their lungs X-rayed.
8. We had our cameras with us but didn't take many.
9. Tell me again your cousin's address who moved to Waco.
10. We won the game, which surprised me.
11. Every plate and cup was in their place.
12. Does either of you want their coffee now?

FOLLOW-UP ACTIVITY

Watch your daily speech for errors in pronoun agreement. Perhaps you and a classmate can check each other's usage.

4. MAKING VERBS AGREE WITH PRONOUN SUBJECTS

You have learned that a verb should agree in person and number with a noun subject. That fact is also true of the pronoun subject.

THE RULES

The first five rules for agreement of verb and subject on page 321 apply also to pronouns. Refer to those rules as you do the practice in this lesson.

RULE 6. **Always use a** *plural* **verb with the pronoun** *you.*

> **You** *are* my friend.   **You** *are* my friends.

RULE 7. **Always use a** *singular* **verb with these indefinite pronoun subjects:** *another, anybody, anyone, anything, each, either, everybody, everyone, everything, neither, nobody, no one, other, somebody, someone, one.* **Use a** *plural* **verb with** *both* **or** *many.* **Use either a** *singular or a plural* **verb with** *any, such,* **or** *none,* **depending upon their meaning in the sentence.**

> **None** of the cake *is* gone.   **None** of us *were* ready.
> **No one** *is* exempt.   **Both** *are* wrong.   **Either** *is* welcome.

RULE 8. **Use a** *singular* **verb with subjects, whether compound or simple, that are limited by** *each, every,* **or** *many a.*

> **Many** a man *is* honest.   **Each** boy and girl *has been notified.*

RULE 9. **If the subject is** *all, more, most, part,* **or** *some* **and is followed by an "of" phrase, use a verb that agrees with the** *object* **in that phrase.**

> *All* of **it** *is* mine.   *All* of **us** *want* to go.
> *Part* of the **ribbon** *has been used.*   *Part* of the **ribbons** *are* blue.

RULE 10. **Make a verb that has a** *relative pronoun* **as its subject agree with the** *antecedent* **of that pronoun.**

> John is one of the **boys** who *were* here. John is one **boy** who *is* helpful.

LEARNING ACTIVITIES IN MAKING VERBS AGREE WITH PRONOUN SUBJECTS

A. Choose the right word from each pair of words in parentheses. Go over your work orally, justifying each choice.

1. (Was, Were) you expecting company?
2. Each player and coach (is, are) invited.
3. Everyone in these classes (is, are) helping in the contest.
4. He (don't, doesn't) remember me.
5. Jim is one of those boys who (go, goes) out for all sports.
6. You, not he, (have, has) been selected.
7. Neither of you (look, looks) like your mother.
8. Both of us (was, were) there early.
9. She is one of those women who (belong, belongs) to many clubs.
10. Will everybody who (is, are) ready stand, please?
11. Neither of us (has, have) bought his ticket yet.
12. I bought one of the coats that (was, were) on sale yesterday.
13. She (don't, doesn't) sit near me this semester.
14. Many a long day and night (has, have) passed since that time.
15. Every man and woman (are, is) expected to help.

B. Write sentences to illustrate the first five rules on page 321 and the additional rules given in this lesson. Use the sentences for class drill.

USING ENGLISH IN ALL CLASSES

Go over papers that you have written or are writing for any class. Correct any errors in verb and pronoun-subject agreement. Bring your sentences to class and explain your corrections if you have the opportunity.

5 Avoiding Other Pronoun Errors

In addition to errors in case and agreement, there are other common faults made in the use of pronouns. Study the rules that follow.

THE RULES

RULE 1. **Avoid using** *hisself, theirself, theirselves, ourself.*

RULE 2. **Avoid the** *double subject.*
That *substitute* [not That *substitute he*] made five free throws.

RULE 3. **Avoid the use of** *this here, that there, these here, those there.*
These [not *These here*] are mine.   *That* [not *That there*] is yours.

RULE 4. **Generally, use** *who* **or** *whom* **to refer to** *persons* **and** *which* **to refer to** *animals* **or** *things.* **Use** *that* **to refer to** *persons, animals,* **or** *things.*
The man *whom* [not *which*] I met in El Paso is a rancher.
The squirrel *that* [not *who*] lives in our hickory tree is tame.

RULE 5. **Avoid using a** *redundant* (unnecessary) **pronoun.**
Let's [not *Let's us*] do the dishes for Mother.

RULE 6. **Avoid using** *what* **as a relative pronoun.**
He is the man *who* [not *what*] delivered the order.

RULE 7. **In compounds, put** *second* **person** *before first* **and** *third,* **and** *third before first: You, she,* and *I* have been named on the committee.

RULE 8. **Never use** *them* **as a demonstrative pronoun; that is,** *to point out.*
Those [not *Them*] are my books.   Mine are *those* [not *them*] on top.

LEARNING ACTIVITIES

A. Orally, explain why *a* is preferable to *b* in the following pairs of sentences. They cover rules on page 345 as well as those in this lesson.

1. *a*) He won the race. As a result, he was awarded a medal.
   b) He won the race, which meant a medal for him.

2. *a*) Don informed Mike, "Your uncle is in town."
   b) Don informed Mike that his uncle was in town.
3. *a*) Bob is a friend who never fails me.
   b) Bob is a friend which never fails me.
4. *a*) Joe always comes late.
   b) Joe he always comes late.
5. *a*) Those are my favorite flowers.
   b) Those there are my favorite flowers.
6. *a*) He can blame only himself.
   b) He can blame only hisself.
7. *a*) Let's go for a walk.
   b) Let's us go for a walk.
8. *a*) This car belongs to my brother who lives in Wyoming.
   b) This is my brother's car who lives in Wyoming.
9. *a*) You, they, and we should be neighbors.
   b) They, we, and you should be neighbors.
10. *a*) George is the one who broke the test tube.
    b) George is the one what broke the test tube.

B. The following sentences contain pronoun faults covered by the rules on pages 345–48. Rewrite the sentences correctly. Go over them in class, explaining how you corrected or improved each faulty construction.

1. Ruth reminded Laura that her mother would arrive soon.
2. My father he is a good golfer. He and you should play together.
3. She is a girl which I admire.
4. On the trip we lost our way, which delayed us.
5. This here is my magazine. Is it the one what you want?
6. We boys cannot put up the aerial by ourself.
7. The neighbor's house who lives next to us has a tile roof.
8. The horse ate his oats.

FOLLOW-UP ACTIVITY

Watch your own usage to see that you avoid the pronoun faults covered in the rules on page 348. Correct every error that you notice.

6. Distinguishing between Colloquial and Standard English

The following are less important or disputable items in pronoun usage. Most of the "errors" in the rules that follow, though not standard English, are acceptable in colloquial (informal) expression.

RULES FOR DISTINGUISHING BETWEEN COLLOQUIAL AND STANDARD USAGE OF PRONOUNS

RULE 1. **Avoid the careless use of** *you, it,* **and** *they* **as indefinite pronouns.**

FAULTY	BETTER
You **see** few icemen nowadays.	*One* **sees** few icemen nowadays.
They **mine** diamonds here.	*Diamonds* **are mined** here.
In this book *it* **tells** about Cuba.	This *book* **tells** about Cuba.

RULE 2. **Use** *either* **or** *neither* **to refer to** *one or the other of two;* **use** *any one* **to refer to** *one of more than two.*

Neither of the *two* suits me.   **Any one** of the first *ten* will do.

RULE 3. **Use** *each other* **to refer to** *two;* **use** *one another* **to refer to** *more than two:* **Mary and I** know *each other.*   We **three** boys know *one another.*

RULE 4. **Avoid using** *compound personal* **pronouns for** *personal* **pronouns.**

COLLOQUIAL: Everyone but John and *myself* has left.
STANDARD: Everyone but John and *me* has left.

RULE 5. **Do not use** *both* **for** *each. Both* **refers to** *two* **things together;** *each,* **to** *one* **thing. Be sure also that verb and subject agree.**

MISLEADING: *Both* of them **cost** a dollar.
BETTER: *Each* of them **costs** a dollar.

RULE 6. **Avoid shifting** *person* **needlessly.**

POOR: A *person* should choose his own work if *you* are to be happy.
BETTER: A *person* should choose his own work if *he* is to be happy.

RULE 7. **Do not use** *same* **as a substitute for** *personal pronouns.*

I wrote the letter and mailed *it* [not *same*] this afternoon.

RULE 8. **Avoid** *weak reference* **of pronouns.**

POOR: Father wants me to study music, but I do not care to be *one.*
BETTER: Father wants me to study music, but I do not care to be a *musician.*

LEARNING ACTIVITY

The following sentences contain expressions that do not conform to the rules in this lesson. Change the expressions to standard English. If you write this exercise, go over the sentences orally in class.

1. In this story it tells of a ballplayer who became famous.
2. The teacher was patient with us and didn't mind helping one.
3. Dad is a farmer. This is an occupation that I plan to follow.
4. They make many automobiles in Detroit.
5. Both sundaes cost a quarter.
6. Mary and myself write to one another often.
7. Neither of the four girls answered the telephone.
8. You don't need fur coats in the tropics.
9. I have found your key and I am sending same to you this afternoon.

350

Just to make sure!*

Directions: As you do these activities, refer to the rules and definitions in this chapter and to rules 1–5, page 321. Go over orally any activities that you write.

A. Correct any errors that you find.

1. Nobody feels like doing their homework. Let's us go for a walk first.
2. It don't look like rain, after all.
3. Is Ed one of those boys who are always late to study hall?
4. Wasn't you riding in that speeding car?
5. Neither he nor she have been absent this year.
6. I shall cast my vote for whomever pleases me.
7. Martha, not her brothers, are invited.
8. Do you approve of him taking over his father's business?
9. Who would care to be him? (You know the boy which I mean.)
10. Mother she never fails to call Joe and I early.
11. Henry told Dick that he might wait for him.
12. Is this the hassock what you ordered?
13. These here are my brother's boots who lives in Wyoming.
14. She, as well as two of her friends, works hard in the Pep Club.

B. Pick out the personal, relative, indefinite, and interrogative pronouns in the following sentences. Give the case of each pronoun.

1. We called on Alfred. Had you heard about his being ill?
2. No one enjoys reading more than she.
3. What does he want? Can anyone tell me that?

C. Change the colloquial expressions to standard English; make clear any misleading sentences.

1. I angrily threw the paper away—and then picked up same.
2. My brother is studying law, but I could never become one.
3. In this book it tells about Tibet. Joe and I read it to one another.
4. Nowadays you don't hear much about that country.
5. First I tie a knot in this corner; then you cut an opening here.
6. Both Dean and myself ate a hamburger.
7. The three boys, neither of whom you know, are juniors.

To keep you in practice

CAPITALIZATION AND PUNCTUATION

Copy these sentences, supplying needed capitalization and punctuation.

1. The great charter was signed on june 15 1215 by king john at runnymede
2. Did you hear the presidents address to congress

---

* Check Test 5 should be given at this point. If the results show need for further study, pupils should do this review practice. They should then take Mastery Test 5.

3. Have you ever read the book the wind in the willows
4. My uncle the one you have met was born on independence day
5. when I am a junior at crofton high school ill take american history latin typing II and physics
6. one of the chief crops of the middle west is corn
7. According to the springfield times the all state winners are les brown of spencer al cooper of storm lake and biff wilson of madrid
8. elmer made a frank unbiased statement im proud of him

PLURALS

Write the plural form of each of the following nouns.

1. muff	3. domino	5. flurry	7. bellows	9. ax	11. abbey
2. Amy	4. bronchus	6. tango	8. brooch	10. 9	12. Ellis

VERBS

Number your paper from 1 to 9. Decide on the correct forms of the verbs in parentheses. Write them after the corresponding numbers.

1. The flowers that I had (grow) so carefully were (steal) last night.
2. Two men had (fall) overboard, but neither had (drown).
3. I've not (forget) my promise. So far I have not (break) it.
4. Nobody (know) at that time that he had been (choose).
5. After she had (sing) that lovely air, we (sit) in silence.
6. Have you (show) anyone the poems that you have (write)?
7. I have (fly) for many years, but I (buy) an airplane only recently.
8. Mark had (drive) over to see what had (become) of us.
9. We had just (rise) from the table when Dick (burst) in.

NOUNS

Underline all nouns in the sentences; tell how they are used.

1. Mother, did you send your mystery friend a gift last week?
2. I call Bill Casey, the club president, a real trouper.
3. Miss Hinkle, my assistant, will issue a receipt.

AGREEMENT

Choose the correct verb form from the parentheses.

1. How (is, are) your sister and brother?
2. A box of cookies (is, are) on the table. (Don't, Doesn't) Ray want any?
3. The chief problem (is, are) too many visitors on the campus.
4. Neither Santa nor his helpers (look, looks) unhappy.
5. Our family (watch, watches) different programs.
6. Every man and woman (need, needs) to cast his vote.
7. Three fourths of the voters (has, have) registered.
8. Jean, not her sisters, (work, works) in the library.

Know How to Use
Adjective Modifiers*

1. RECOGNIZING VARIOUS TYPES
OF ADJECTIVES

"YOU NEEDN'T BE JEALOUS, DORETTA. SHE'S JUST A--A-SKINNY LITTLE BLONDE WITH A--A-RECEDING CHIN AND STRINGY HAIR."

What do *you* say when you try to describe a friend to someone who has never met him? If you succeed in creating a clear picture of your friend, you undoubtedly use *adjectives,* those useful words for limiting or making more vivid the meaning of nouns or pronouns.

* Pretest 6 should be given at this point.

● WHAT TO REMEMBER ABOUT ADJECTIVES

1. (DEFINITION) *Adjectives* are words that *modify* or *change* the meaning of *nouns* or *pronouns* by (1) *describing* or (2) *limiting* them.

2. (DEFINITION) *Descriptive* adjectives create a picture: *red, lonesome.*
   a) Descriptive adjectives are either (1) *proper: Paris* fashions, *French* cooking; or (2) *common: red* hair, *simple* language.
   b) (DEFINITION) *Participial* adjectives (or *participles*) **are present or past participles of verbs:** The dog, *growling,* crouched by the *broken* window.

3. (DEFINITION) *Limiting* adjectives *point out* or *specify.*
   a) (DEFINITION) *Pronominal* adjectives are *pronouns* **used to limit nouns or pronouns:** *this* car, *some* rain, *which* one, *our* house.
   b) (DEFINITION) *Numeral* adjectives may be either *cardinal* **numbers:** *five* men; or *ordinal* **numbers:** *fifth* man.
   c) **The articles** *a, an,* **and** *the* **are limiting adjectives. The** *definite* article *the* points out *specifically: The* food is good. **The** *indefinite* articles *a* and *an* **point to** *no particular* **object:** Bring me *a* cup.
   d) *Possessive nouns* **may be limiting adjectives:** *John's* hat.

4. **Sometimes adjectives are classified according to** *position.*
   a) (DEFINITION) **An** *attributive* or *direct* adjective *precedes* **the word modified:** We received generous donations.
   b) (DEFINITION) **An** *appositive* adjective *follows* **the noun that it modifies:** Trees, tall and leafy, shaded the path.
   c) (DEFINITION) **A** *predicate adjective* **completes a** *linking verb* **and** *describes the subject:* The windows are open.
   d) **An adjective used as an** *objective complement* **follows the** *direct object:* His good humor makes **him** *popular.*

LEARNING ACTIVITIES IN RECOGNIZING ADJECTIVES

A. Locate each adjective in the following sentences and tell what kind it is. Name also the noun modified. Make this an oral exercise.

1. Three crying children sat on the deserted porch.
2. My older brother gave these skates to me as a Christmas gift.
3. Whose pen has a wide gold band near the upper end?
4. The inspector, conscientious and honest, pronounced the building unsafe.
5. One dog in this neighborhood is old and blind.

B. Add adjective modifiers to the nouns in the following sentences. Put your sentences on the board. Point out the adjectives and name the nouns modified.

1. There stood a man.
2. Maizie bought a hat.
3. A sound startled us.
4. A package lay on the floor.

C. Copy the sentences that follow. The italicized words may be used as adjectives and also as other parts of speech. Label these words as used here.

1. This money will *square* accounts and put us on a *sound* financial basis.
2. *Open* your *paper* to page 16. What is the *price* of the *fall* coats advertised?
3. The *second blind* from the left has a large *square* patch.
4. Our *class* meetings fall into no *set* pattern.
5. Early in the *fall* our *blind* friend *set* out for Denver.
6. Will you *back* us in this *price* war?
7. Did you *second* the motion to post the list of *back* dues?
8. Would you *class* this *set* of books as a bargain? I don't like the *paper* covers.

2. FORMING ADJECTIVE COMPARISONS

To make it possible to tell differences between things or people, adjectives take different forms, or *degrees of comparison.*

● **WHAT TO REMEMBER ABOUT COMPARING ADJECTIVES**

1. (DEFINITION) *Positive* degree names a *quality:* good, bad, tall.

2. (DEFINITION) *Comparative* degree expresses a comparison between *two:* better, worse, taller than another.

3. (DEFINITION) *Superlative* degree expresses the *highest* degree of quality; it compares *more than two:* best, worst, tallest of a group.

4. Adjectives of *one syllable* and *some* adjectives of *two syllables* are compared by adding *er* or *est* to the *positive* degree.

POSITIVE:	sweet	noble	pretty	grim
COMPARATIVE:	sweeter	nobler	prettier	grimmer
SUPERLATIVE:	sweetest	noblest	prettiest	grimmest

5. Adjectives of *three or more syllables* and *some* adjectives of *two syllables* are compared by prefixing *more* or *most* to the *positive* degree.

POSITIVE:	improbable	unusual	helpful
COMPARATIVE:	more improbable	more unusual	more helpful
SUPERLATIVE:	most improbable	most unusual	most helpful

6. Some adjectives may be compared in *both* ways: *able, abler, ablest; able, more able, most able.*

7. Several adjectives have *irregular* comparisons.

POSITIVE:	bad, ill	good, well	little	much, many
COMPARATIVE:	worse	better	less	more
SUPERLATIVE:	worst	best	least	most

8. *Less* and *least* express a *diminishing* degree: *gay, less gay, least gay.*

9. Some adjectives cannot *logically* be compared: *perfect, round, final, square, dead, unique, correct, immortal, exact, equal, right.* For example, if something is really *square,* nothing else can be "squarer." In actual usage, however, many of these adjectives are compared.

Directions: Write any of the following activities. Check your spelling by Rule 1 and Rule 2, page 187, and Rule 6, page 190. Go over your work in class.

A. Compare the following adjectives: *fine, handsome, easy, tactful, small, excitable, good, large, helpless, foolish, red, industrious, tiny, noisy, gay, honorable, lovely, shrill.*

B. Make a list of ten adjectives not named in *A.* Exchange papers and write the comparison of the adjectives on the list that you receive.

C. Copy these sentences, filling each blank with the adjective form called for in parentheses.

1. We planted an .... variety of corn. (comparative of *early*)
2. This is a .... offer. (superlative of *unusual*)
3. He did his .... work on this machine. (superlative of *good*)
4. The lights seem .... here. (comparative of *dim*)
5. The .... problems are on the next page. (comparative of *simple*)

3. USING PHRASES AS ADJECTIVE MODIFIERS

READ AND DISCUSS

To give variety to your writing or speaking, you may sometimes use a phrase instead of a single-word adjective. Notice these sentences:

> The *corner* house is for sale.   The house *on the corner* is for sale.

What does the italicized word in the first sentence tell? How is it used? What do the italicized words in the second sentence tell? Then how are they, too, used? Such a word group is called a *prepositional phrase.* Since it modifies a noun, it is an *adjective phrase.*

Now look at these two sentences.

> *Wearing a happy smile,* Andrew walked toward the platform.
> The money *to cover our expenses* is here in my pocket.

What do the italicized word groups tell you? Then they, too, must be *adjective phrases;* specifically, *verbal phrases used as adjectives.*

Adjective phrases, like one-word adjectives, help to make ideas clear and definite. As the first example shows, phrases and one-word adjectives are sometimes interchangeable. Many times, however, single adjectives cannot take the place of adjective phrases.

> A basket *of rosy apples* stood on the porch.

Experiment to see whether you can find a one-word adjective that will take the place of the italicized phrase.

● WHAT TO REMEMBER ABOUT PHRASES USED AS ADJECTIVES

1. A *prepositional phrase* may be used as an *adjective.*

2. (DEFINITION) **A** *prepositional phrase* **consists of a** *preposition* **and a noun or pronoun** *object.* **The object may be** *compound,* **as in the first example. It may have** *adjective modifiers,* **as in the second.**

   Is the lunch for *you* and *me* ready yet?

   Jane broke the dish with *the gold* inscription.

3. **Frequently a prepositional phrase may have a** *verbal* **object.**

   Your plan for *selling* tickets seems practical. (*gerund*)

   I have no choice but *to stay.* (*infinitive*)

4. **Sometimes a** *noun clause* **is the** *object of a preposition.*

   My information about *how the process was developed* is incomplete.

5. (DEFINITION) **A participle and other words used to modify it or to complete its meaning form a** *participial phrase.*

   The stranger, catching my eye, beckoned to me.

   Showing my anger at his manner, I walked away.*

6. **An** *infinitive* **is often used as an** *adjective.*

   The man to ask is Mr. Gray.   Who gave the order to move?

7. (DEFINITION) **An infinitive and other words used to modify it or to complete its meaning form an** *infinitive phrase.*

   We have no reason to expect an answer today.

   A motion to adjourn until Friday was made.*

8. **Present participles that end in** *ing* **should not be confused with** *gerunds.* **Gerunds are used as** *nouns;* **participles, as** *adjectives.*
   Walking gives one an appetite. (*gerund*)
   The man, *walking* swiftly, turned the corner. (*participle*)

LEARNING ACTIVITIES IN USING ADJECTIVE PHRASES

A. Locate each prepositional phrase and each one-word adjective in the following sentences. Name the word that is modified by each. Make this an oral exercise.

1. The cellar under this house has walls of thick stone.
2. Letters from home are welcome.
3. Every player on the team is a member of the Science Club.
4. A tall man with a satchel in his right hand rang the bell of the small house.

---

* Note that a verbal phrase may have a prepositional phrase within it.

5. The driver paid no heed to what the sign said.
6. Several members of our class have written papers on the subject of developing atomic energy for peacetime uses.

B. Several of the following sentences would be more effective if certain adjective phrases in them were changed to one-word adjectives. Change any phrases that you think sound stiff or wordy. Go over your sentences in class.

1. Lincoln was born in a cabin of logs.
2. She has bought a new dress of a red color.
3. He bought some melons at a stand by the side of the road.
4. People with pleasant dispositions make great numbers of friends.
5. He was wearing a jacket with a tear in it.

C. In an oral exercise, locate each participle or participial phrase and each infinitive or infinitive phrase in these sentences. Name the words modified.

1. Having changed his mind, Father opposed the plan to raise fees.
2. The new road to be built will affect the value of our property.
3. Having been spanked, the small boy on the front steps howled noisily.
4. Dennis, plunging through the line, was the first to score.
5. Using her own money, Mary bought a purse to match her new shoes.
6. Blake, having made the trip often, knows the road to follow.
7. The clubs sponsoring the drive appreciate your desire to help.

D. Classify the italicized words in the following sentences as *gerunds* or *participles*. In class, give your reason for each classification.

1. I enjoy *riding* horseback.
2. The name *following* mine is that of my cousin.
3. *Riding* hard, the scout outdistanced his pursuers.
4. *Listening* courteously is a good habit to acquire.
5. George has finished *mowing* the grass.
6. Clouds, *racing* across the sky, blotted out the moon.
7. I have no intention of *going* alone.
8. I picked up the package *lying* on the table.
9. The flowers *blooming* near the fence are zinnias.

E. Use a *participle*, a *participial phrase*, an *infinitive*, or an *infinitive phrase* to modify each italicized noun or pronoun in the following sentences. Put sentences on the board. Note how the choice of modifiers changes the picture.

1. A *stranger* called at our house.
2. Sue struggled with the *bundles*.
3. We approve the *plan*.
4. Howard must be the *one*.

Follow through

(*Based upon the sentences in* C)

1. Account for the use or omission of commas in *1, 3, 4, 5, 6,* and *7*.
2. Which sentence has a linking verb? an intransitive complete verb?
3. How would you write the plural of the subject in *4?* in *5?*

4. Using Clauses as Adjective Modifiers

Pages 333–36 deal with the use of dependent clauses as nouns. Dependent clauses may also be used as adjectives.

● **WHAT TO REMEMBER ABOUT ADJECTIVE CLAUSES**

1. (DEFINITION) **A dependent clause that modifies a noun or a pronoun is an** *adjective* **clause:** Here are the measurements that you need.

2. **An adjective clause is joined to the rest of the sentence by** (*a*) **a** *relative pronoun:* who, whose, whom, which, that, **or** (*b*) **by the** *subordinate conjunctions* when **or** where.
   He is the one *whom* I mean.   I live in the house *where* I was born.

3. **The relative pronoun always is an** *essential part* **of the adjective clause; it may be a** *subject,* **a** *direct object,* **an** *object of a preposition,* **or a** *possessive modifier.*
   The girl *who* called is my sister. (*subject of* called)
   He is the man *whom* I mean. (*object of* mean)
   There is the dentist to *whom* I go. (*object of* to)
   Joe is a boy *whose* word I trust. (*modifies* word)

4. (DEFINITION) **An adjective clause that is** *necessary* **to the meaning of the sentence is a** *restrictive* **clause; it tells** *which particular one* **or** *ones.* **Commas should** *not* **be used to set it off from the rest of the sentence.** Adjective clauses introduced by *that* are always restrictive.
   George made the play *that brought us the victory.*

5. (DEFINITION) **A** *nonrestrictive* **adjective clause is one that merely gives** *additional information;* **it can be omitted without changing the basic meaning of the sentence. Commas should set it off from the rest of the sentence:** Tom Jenks, *who made that touchdown,* is a senior.

6. **Adjective clauses should** *never* **express the chief idea. That idea should be put into the** *independent* **clause.**
   The mayor, *who is sitting over there,* is seeking re-election.

7. **Adjective clauses are useful in** *combining* **sentences.**
   The all-state team was announced today. Two of us made it.
   Two of us made the all-state team *that was announced today.*

8. **Often an adjective clause can be condensed to a** *participial phrase* **or an** *infinitive phrase.*
   Alfred, *who was dressed in his best,* was ready. (*clause*)
   Alfred, *dressed in his best,* was ready. (*participial phrase*)
   This is the club *that you should use for that shot.* (*clause*)
   This is the club *to use for that shot.* (*infinitive phrase*)

359

LEARNING ACTIVITIES IN THE USE OF ADJECTIVE CLAUSES

A. In an oral activity, locate each *adjective clause, adjective phrase,* and *one-word adjective* in the following sentences. Name the word that each clause modifies and the connecting relative pronoun or subordinate conjunction. Name also the word modified by each of the other adjective modifiers.

1. The game, which was a close contest, marks our first defeat.
2. This is the place where I lost my fountain pen.
3. Jim told a story about a man whose hobby became his vocation.
4. I remember the time when our home had many pets.
5. This news, which is confidential, may cause a change in your plans.
6. A friend who can be trusted is a priceless possession.
7. A player whom the pitcher had walked scored the winning run.

B. The following exercise contains short simple sentences. Combine each set into a good complex sentence by the use of adjective clauses. Give the important information in the main, or independent, clause. Punctuate your sentences correctly. *Be sure to proofread.* Exchange papers for checking.

1. The class play will be given tonight. It has a cast of twelve characters.
2. He lives in a lonely spot. Visitors rarely come there.
3. We camped in a wooded valley. A shallow stream ran through it.
4. Philip Molloy is a three-letter man. He holds several county records.
5. Just then a bearded man tapped me on the shoulder. I did not know him.
6. Paul Farrell is the new 4-H leader. He lives four miles east of Waverly.
7. Fred is our dealer. He sold us our new car. We like it very much.

C. Add information to the following sentences by supplying adjective clauses. *Proofread carefully.* Put your sentences on the board. Name each adjective clause and the word modified. Explain each use or omission of commas.

1. The letter was missent.
2. The speaker was interesting.
3. My childhood was spent on a farm.
4. My last name is a common one.

D. Some nouns need clauses to define or limit them. Add to the following sentences any adjective clauses that will make the meaning clear. Why will you need no commas to set off these clauses? Read your sentences in class.

EXAMPLE: Children are afraid. (*What* children? Not all children are afraid.)
Children *who have been treated cruelly* are afraid.

1. Men cannot succeed.
2. Dogs become sullen.
3. Boys and girls should not drive cars.
4. Students do not deserve good grades.

E. Orally, change adjective clauses in the following sentences to verbal phrases.

1. I have just read a fine story that was written by Richard Connell.
2. The books that should be read first are on this list.
3. Here is the man who can help you.
4. Follow the directions that are printed on the label.
5. All of a sudden a woman who stood near me screamed.

DIAGRAMMING ADJECTIVE MODIFIERS

Study the following diagrams carefully. They show you how to diagram the various types of adjective modifiers. Notice how the diagrams make clear the relations between various parts of a sentence.

Direct Adjectives

That car needs a new motor.

They own a small but busy hotel.

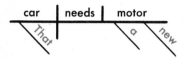
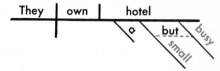

Predicate Adjectives

Do you feel happy?

She looks tired and lonely.

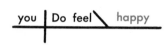
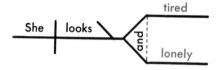

Prepositional Phrases

We have bought the house at the end of the lane.

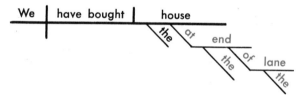

Note that the phrase *of the lane* modifies the object in the phrase *at the end.*

Possessive Noun

My father's watch is a family heirloom.

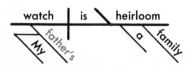

Note that the possessive noun also has a modifier.

Objective Complement

The blazing heat made the baby cross.

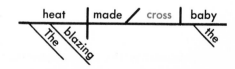

Note that the adjective as an objective complement is diagrammed like a noun so used.

Participles* and Infinitives

Crane Lake, having been improved, is a fine place to camp.

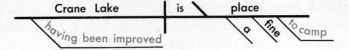

Note that these constructions are put on a broken line.

Infinitive Phrase as Object of a Preposition

I want nothing but to finish this project.

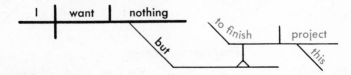

Adjective Clauses

The book that I lost was new.

This is the spot where we met.

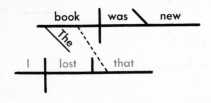
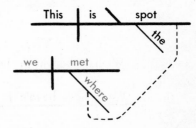

Note that a relative pronoun is joined to its antecedent.

Note the diagramming of the joining word *where*.

Noun Clause as the Object in an Adjective Phrase

He has no ideas about what you should do.

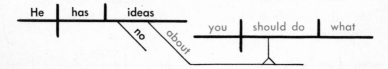

LEARNING ACTIVITIES IN DIAGRAMMING ADJECTIVE MODIFIERS

Directions: Do the following activities as listed. Put your diagrams on the board; then explain them, using a definite order.

---

* A simple participle may be diagrammed on a straight line. See *blazing* in the last right-hand diagram on page 361.

EXAMPLE: Bill Jones, who made the first touchdown, is a senior in Alton High School.

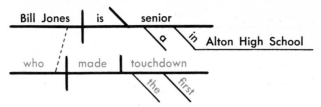

EXPLANATION: This is a complex sentence. The independent clause is *Bill Jones is a senior in Alton High School.* The verb is *is;* the subject is a proper noun, *Bill Jones;* and *senior* is a noun used as the predicate nominative. *A* is an adjective modifying *senior.* *In Alton High School* is an adjective phrase modifying *senior.* *In* is the connecting preposition and *Alton High School* is a proper noun used as its object.

Who made the first touchdown is an adjective clause modifying *Bill Jones,* the subject of the independent clause. *Made* is the verb. The relative pronoun *who* is the subject. *Touchdown* is a noun used as the direct object. *The* and *first* are adjectives modifying *touchdown.*

A. Diagram these sentences containing one-word adjectives.

1. Tall, dark buildings lined the narrow streets.
2. The smallest child seemed tired.
3. That young lady is her father's secretary.
4. A weary voice announced the final score.
5. Four or five books will be enough.
6. The other golfers called him lucky.
7. My brother's score was low.
8. Send me some pink and green ribbon.
9. The Indians, straight and lithe, were dancing a tribal dance.

B. For practice with the other types of adjective modifiers, diagram the sentences in *A,* page 357; *C,* page 358; and *A,* page 360.

Follow through

(*Based upon the sentences in* A)

1. Account for the commas in *1* and *9.*
2. Spell the plurals of the subject and the predicate nominative in *3.*
3. Which sentences have linking verbs?

5. USING ADJECTIVE MODIFIERS CORRECTLY

The next four lessons deal with correct use of adjective modifiers. Study any or all of them, depending upon your needs.

THE RULES

RULE 1. **Use the** *comparative* **degree of adjectives in comparing** *two;* **the** *superlative,* **in comparing** *more than two.* (See point 5, page 355.)

Jerry is the *older* [not *oldest*] of the two boys.

Of the eight designs, yours is the *most original* [not *more original*].

RULE 2. **Avoid** *double comparison.*

John's paper is *neater* [not *more neater*] than mine.

RULE 3. **In making comparisons within a group, say** *any other,* **not** *any; any-one else,* **not** *anyone.*

Tom is younger than *any other* [not *any*] boy in our class.

RULE 4. **Use** *less* **for** *quantity; fewer* **for** *number.*

I have *less* money now.   I have *fewer* dimes than pennies.

RULE 5. **Use the articles** *a, an,* **and** *the* **correctly.** (Points *b* and *d* are often disregarded in informal usage.)

a) **Use** *a* **before** *consonants* **and** *consonant sounds;* **use** *an* **before** *vowels* (*a, e, i, o, u*) **and** *vowel sounds.*

I ate *an* orange and *a* banana.   Wait *an* hour longer.

b) **Say** *this kind* (or *sort*) *of,* **not** *this kind* (or *sort*) *of a.*

I like *this kind of* [not *kind of a*] day.

c) **Repeat the article before** *separate items.*

She wore *a* pink and white dress. (*one item*)
She has *a* pink and *a* white dress. (*two items*)

An exception is any case in which meaning is perfectly clear without repeating the article: *A knife and fork* lay on the table.

d) **Avoid repeating** *a* **or** *an* **unnecessarily.**

WRONG: I canned *a* half *a* bushel of peaches.
RIGHT: I canned *a* half bushel of peaches.
         I canned half *a* bushel of peaches.

RULE 6. **Do not put** *and* **or** *but* **before a relative pronoun connecting an adjective clause to a main clause.**

WRONG: I'd like you to meet Joe Smith, *and who* will go with us.
RIGHT: I'd like you to meet Joe Smith, *who* will go with us.

LEARNING ACTIVITIES IN USING ADJECTIVE MODIFIERS CORRECTLY: I

A. Correct any of the following sentences that contain errors. Indicate the rule that governs each usage. If you write this exercise, exchange papers for checking as the sentences are read aloud.

1. Rhode Island is smaller than any state in this country.
2. She has a more disdainfuler look than anyone's.
3. Mother set out less tomato plants this year than last.

4. I'd like you to meet Ernie Bates, and who is our neighbor.
5. What sort of a person is he? He has a honest face.
6. Of the three, which do you think is newer?
7. Give me a half minute to decide which is best, this one or that one.
8. He is a gentleman and scholar, the kind of a man to be trusted.
9. This is the colorfulest room in the house.
10. Emily is a better organizer than any girl in the group.

B. Write sentences illustrating the rules in this lesson. Use them for oral drill.

THE RULES—Continued

RULE 7. **Place adjective modifiers to give the meaning that you intend.**

   a) **Misplaced participial modifier**

   FAULTY: A **book** was wanted by the boy *containing pictures of airplanes.*
   CORRECT: A **book** *containing pictures of airplanes* was wanted by the boy.
   The boy wanted a **book** *containing pictures of airplanes.*

   b) **Misplaced prepositional phrase**

   FAULTY: There is a new **student** in the class *from a foreign country.*
   CORRECT: In the class there is a new **student** *from a foreign country.*

   c) **Misplaced adjective clause**

   FAULTY: He gave my **aunt** a pass *who lives in Brooklyn.*
   CORRECT: He gave my **aunt** *who lives in Brooklyn* a pass.

   d) **Misplaced single-word modifier**

   FAULTY: A *feathered* woman's **hat** was left in the theater.
   CORRECT: A woman's *feathered* **hat** was left in the theater.

RULE 8. **Avoid a** *dangling participial modifier.**

   FAULTY: *Opening the window,* a cool breeze was felt. (*Who* felt it?)
   CORRECT: *Opening the window,* **he** felt a cool breeze.

RULE 9.   **Use** *singular* **demonstrative adjectives with** *kind* **or** *sort.*
   I like *this kind* [not *these kind*] of apples.

RULE 10.   **Never use** *them* **as a demonstrative adjective.**
   Those [not *Them*] papers belong in the notebook.

RULE 11.   **Do not omit the** *ed* **from a past participle used as an adjective.**
   The floor was covered with *mottled* [not *mottle*] linoleum.

RULE 12.   **Avoid the expression** *complected* **for** *complexioned.*
   Jim is the light-*complexioned* [not *complected*] boy at the left.

RULE 13.   **Do not use** *a great deal of* **for** *many.*
   We saw *many* [not *a great deal of*] friends there.

* Do not confuse dangling participles with the useful construction known as
the *nominative absolute,* explained on page 400.

LEARNING ACTIVITIES IN USING ADJECTIVE MODIFIERS CORRECTLY: II

A. Rewrite the following sentences so that the modifiers are closely related to the words that they modify. *Be sure to proofread.* Go over your work orally.

1. We saw many people begging on the streets with haggard faces.
2. I found a package on the table from Mother.
3. I'm looking for a plaid man's sport shirt.
4. Singing in the treetops, the hikers listened to the birds.
5. He threw the letter into the fire which his brother had written.
6. Swinging from tree to tree in the jungle, we saw many monkeys.
7. The man ran past the deserted house that was afraid of ghosts.
8. Hanging from the light fixture, I noticed the mobile.
9. Do you have any tortoise-shell ladies' handbags?

B. In an oral activity, rephrase these sentences to eliminate dangling participles. Place the participle as near as possible to the word modified.

1. Having eaten lunch, the picnic baskets were put away.
2. Feeling lonesome, the afternoon seemed long.
3. Frightened by the darkness, not a sound was made.
4. Waiting on the icy corner, my feet grew cold.
5. Having made up my mind, the matter is settled.
6. Beaten in every other game, an upset was scored tonight.
7. Having said good-by to our hosts, the journey was begun.
8. Accompanied by friends, the trip was most enjoyable.
9. Driving along the mountain road, many antelope were seen.
10. Having torn the dress, it was thrown away.
11. Seated in the open-air theater, the concert was very enjoyable.
12. Coiled for the strike, a hissing sound was heard.
13. Flying high over the city, the pedestrians looked like ants.

C. Choose the correct form from each pair in parentheses. Make this either a written or an oral activity but explain orally each choice.

1. (These, This) kind of earrings can be worn with many costumes.
2. A dark- (complected, complexioned) person can wear that color well.
3. I have never cared for (those, that) sort of fish.
4. Isn't that light- (complected, complexioned) man a stranger here?
5. You will need (a great deal of, many) helpers.
6. Are (them, those) boys in your home room?
7. A (wax, waxed) floor can be dangerous.
8. (This, These) sort of shoes can be worn anywhere.
9. (A great deal of, Many) people agree with me.
10. (Whip, Whipped) cream and (mashed, mash) potatoes are fattening.

FOLLOW-UP ACTIVITY

If any of the errors covered by rules 1–13 are habitual with you, work with a partner to correct each wrong use in your daily speech.

6. Distinguishing between Colloquial and Standard English

Most of the "errors" in the following rules deal with usages generally acceptable at the colloquial (informal) level but not yet considered standard English; that is, they are not suited to formal expression.

THE RULES

RULE 1. **Avoid using** *funny* **as a catch-all substitute for** *strange, odd, queer, or unusual.*

POOR: I have a *funny* feeling.   BETTER: I have a *strange* feeling.

RULE 2. **Avoid using** *said* **as an adjective except in legal documents.**

POOR: You will find *said* letter on the mantel.
BETTER: You will find *the* letter on the mantel.

RULE 3. **Avoid use of** *poorly* **in reference to health. Say that someone** *does not feel well,* **not that someone** *feels poorly.*

RULE 4. **Avoid use of** *a lot of* **or** *lots of* **for** *many, much,* **or** *a great deal of.*

On the beach I found *many* [not *a lot of*] seashells.
We have wasted *a great deal of* [not *lots of*] time.

RULE 5. **Distinguish between** *healthy* **and** *healthful. Healthy* **means "possessing health";** *healthful* **means "giving health."**

Susan is a *healthy* baby.   This climate is *healthful.*

RULE 6. **Distinguish between** *last* **and** *latest. Last* **means "final";** *latest* **means "most recent."**

This is your *last* chance. (There will not be another.)
Here is the *latest* copy of the *Post.* (There will be others.)

RULE 7. **Distinguish between** *anxious* **and** *eager. Anxious* **implies a state of** *worry* **or** *fearfulness; eager,* **one of** *keen desire.*

With *anxious* eyes, we watched the rising water.   Joe is *eager* to see you.

RULE 8. **Distinguish between** *continual* **and** *continuous. Continual* **means "at closely recurrent intervals";** *continuous* **means "without interruption."**

The *continuous* rush of the water over the dam is deafening.
My rest was disturbed by *continual* telephone calls.

RULE 9. **Use** *likely, liable,* **and** *apt* **accurately.** *Likely* **implies a** *favorable* **possibility.** *Liable* **implies an** *unfavorable* **possibility; it also means** *legally responsible. Apt* **implies a** *natural fitness or tendency.*

We are *likely* to win.   You are *liable* for the debt.
He is *liable* to fall.   Jean is an *apt* pupil.

Likely **and** *apt* **are interchangeable colloquially.**

Change any colloquial or faulty expressions to standard English. If you make this a written exercise, go over the sentences orally.

1. Don't climb to the top of the tree. You are liable to fall.
2. On the table is Dobson's last book. He is now writing a new one.
3. Too much candy is not healthy for a child.
4. Clothes that have been stored for a while have a funny smell.
5. A continual stretch of desert lay ahead of us.
6. If you will refer to said chapter, you will find the quotation.
7. I have a lot of Indian-head pennies.
8. The minister has felt poorly all winter.
9. Lots of women attended the convention.
10. I am anxious to see your new dress.
11. I have a funny feeling that we are apt to have a storm tonight.
12. Grandmother Rankin has been looking poorly.
13. Johnny's continuous questions are a nuisance.
14. Yes, we are liable to have pleasant weather tomorrow.

USING ENGLISH IN ALL CLASSES

In English class, examine any papers that you have written recently. Correct or improve any faulty adjective usage.

7. USING ADJECTIVE MODIFIERS TO EXPRESS IDEAS VIVIDLY AND EXACTLY

READ AND DISCUSS

In their commonest use, that of making ideas clearer and more definite, adjectives have a very practical value. Read this sentence:

Mr. Todd lives in a house on a hill.

That sentence lacks definiteness. "Which Mr. Todd? What kind of house? Which hill?" one may wonder. Now read this sentence:

The elder Mr. Todd lives in the colonial brick house on the second hill east of the city limits.

That sentence is an example of clear, exact description. It is the *elder* Mr. Todd. There may be other brick houses on the same hill, but his is the *colonial brick house*. Which hill is also specified: *the second hill east of the city limits*.

Aside from their practical use in giving exact definitions, directions, and descriptions, many adjectives have high picture-making qualities. Their use will bring life to your expression.

GUIDES FOR CHOOSING EFFECTIVE ADJECTIVE MODIFIERS

1. Use the exact adjective. Study the shades of meaning that the dictionary makes between synonyms. (The "Be word-wise!" activities scattered through the book give practice in making such distinctions.)
2. Use the vivid adjective or phrase. "Fiery hair," for example, is more vivid than "red hair."
3. To obtain a clear, unblurred picture, avoid piling on too many adjectives.
4. Find new adjectives for overworked ones. Look for the unusual expression, but be sure that it fits and does not sound stiff and unnatural.

Be word-wise!

Skim the guides for these words: *example, obtain, stiff.* Which of their synonyms would not be good substitutes for the words as used in this lesson? Which synonym of *example* does the drawing illustrate?

LEARNING ACTIVITIES IN EFFECTIVE USE OF ADJECTIVE MODIFIERS

A. Here are poetic lines, all found in Bartlett's *Famous Quotations.* The blanks indicate missing adjectives. Decide what words you think might be the ones chosen by the authors; then find out how close you came. Make this an oral activity. In supplying adjectives, try to keep the author's rhythm.

1. The ·········· earth soaks up the rain.—ABRAHAM COWLEY
2. Like ·········· guests a sitting audience looks.—GEORGE FARQUAHAR
3. Two ·········· men set out from Lynn through the ·········· and ·········· mist.—HOOD
4. Fame is the ·········· sunflower, with gaudy crown of gold.—HOLMES
5. The ·········· flower of battle blooms,
   And ·········· marches fill the night.—JULIA WARD HOWE
6. I know a lake where the ·········· waves break
   And softly fall on the ·········· sand.—FITZ-JAMES O'BRIEN

B. Write a paragraph or a poem in which you make good use of descriptive adjectives. Apply the Guides to Good Description, page 261. (See *Topics for speech and writing* in the Index to help you find a subject.) Use your Writing Score Card, page 197. Read paragraphs aloud for practice in critical listening.

C. Have some fun with yourself by making a list of adjective modifiers that describe you. You may enjoy reading your lists in class or in your small groups.

D. Sometimes the repetition of an adjective gives force and vividness to a description. Study this example from *A Tale of Two Cities;* then try writing a paragraph around one adjective. Exchange papers for critical evaluation; read good work aloud. Apply the Guides to Effective Oral Reading, page 41.

> It was a heavy mass of building, that chateau of Monsieur the Marquis, with a large stone courtyard before it, and two stone sweeps of staircase meeting in a stone terrace before the principal door. A stony business altogether, with heavy stone balustrades, and stone urns, and stone flowers, and stone faces of men, and stone heads of lions, in all directions. . . .
>
> —DICKENS

RELATED ACTIVITIES

A. Give a brief talk to the class, using a few definite adjectives to make your talk effective. Check the talks by your Speech Score Card, page 31.

B. Bring to class descriptive terms that you find in advertisements. Put them on the board. Discuss their effectiveness as adjective modifiers.

REVIEW · *Just to make sure!* *

Directions: As you do these activities, refer to the definitions and rules in this chapter. Go over orally any activities that you write.

A. Decide whether the clauses in the following sentences are *restrictive* or *nonrestrictive*. Punctuate accordingly.

1. The colors that she selected for her kitchen harmonize beautifully.
2. The *Silver Streak* which is a fast train does not stop here.
3. My oldest sister who is a student at Purdue is a piano major.

B. Copy the following sentences; underline one-word adjectives; draw a circle around adjective phrases; enclose adjective clauses in parentheses. Ignore one-word adjectives within phrases, and phrases within phrases or clauses.

1. Loud, boisterous behavior on the part of a girl is unbecoming.
2. The swaying of the boat is one thing that I do not like.
3. Cards to be filed are in that stack lying on the table.

C. Find each wrong or doubtful usage. Supply the needed changes.

1. I enjoy ice tea, and which is my favorite summer drink.
2. A leather man's brief case was open on the table.
3. A potato was served by the maid half baked.
4. Lee's costume was the cleverest of the two, but yours was more funnier.
5. She is reading a ode. She likes those kind of poems.
6. He has the dejectedest look on his face that you could possibly imagine.

---

* Check Test 6 should be given at this point. If the results show need for further study, pupils should do this review practice. They should then take Mastery Test 6.

D. Change colloquial forms to standard English.

1. Said issue of *Good Housekeeping* has a lot of candy recipes.
2. You are liable to hurt yourself if you walk the balcony railing.
3. A great deal of people had been waiting for a half an hour.
4. The continuous banging of the shutter gave me a funny feeling.

To keep you in practice

CAPITALIZATION AND PUNCTUATION

Copy these sentences, supplying needed capitalization and punctuation.

1. My history book says that the whigs supported the american revolution
2. Mrs baird a well to do farmers wife was born in the far west on may 6 1920
3. The american elk the wapiti is found in this region isnt it
4. Yes april 19 is patriots day a legal holiday in massachusetts
5. the sacrament of the lords supper partaken of by jesus on the night before his crucifixion was observed last sunday in the united baptist church.
6. john bull personifies britain uncle sam the united states

CASE

Choose the correct form of each pronoun in parentheses.

1. It was (I, me), not Bill, who called. Did you think it was (him, he)?
2. If I were (she, her), I'd have waited for you and (I, me).
3. (We, Us) two, Hazel and (I, me), study Latin together.
4. Mrs. Slocum gave (we, us) girls a ride to school.

AGREEMENT

Correct any errors that you find in agreement.

1. Each of the girls have their own costume to make.
2. If anyone asks for my address, give it to them.
3. Sue is one of those girls who has her own ideas about clothes.
4. Maud, not you, were asked to serve.
5. Every glass in these boxes was broken. Neither he nor she was responsible.

VERBS

Number your paper from 1 to 7. Determine the correct form of the verbs in parentheses. Write your choices after the corresponding numbers.

1. That day we (swim) to the dock and (lie) there for an hour.
2. That apple should be (throw) away. Someone has (bite) into it.
3. I (see) that many plums had been (shake) from the trees.
4. I had (begin) to think that the cake never would be (eat).
5. When we had (climb) up to the spring, we (drink) our fill.
6. The sun (shine) brightly, and the birds (burst) into song.
7. After he had (write) the letter, Grant (run) out to the mailbox.

371

Know How to Use Adverb Modifiers*

1. RECOGNIZING ADVERBS

Arbee is teasing Doretta, of course. However, though they can be over-used, adverbs, like adjectives, are useful aids in building good sentences.

1. They add movement, life, and activity to sentence ideas.
2. They make sentence ideas clearer and more definite.
3. They aid in condensing long-drawn-out ideas.
4. They help to combine short, choppy sentences.

* Pretest 7 should be given at this point.

● WHAT TO REMEMBER ABOUT ADVERBS

1. (DEFINITION) *Adverbs* are words that *modify* or *limit* the meaning of *verbs, adjectives,* or *other adverbs.*
   James walks *slowly.* A *very* sleepy voice replied. John walks *too* fast.
2. Adverbs tell *manner, place, time, degree,* and sometimes *cause;* that is, they tell *how, where, when, how much,* or *why.*
3. Many adverbs are made from descriptive adjectives by adding *ly:* sure–surely, real–really, pretty–prettily, able–ably.* *Ally* is added to most adjectives ending in *ic:* basic–basically, realistic–realistically.
4. Not all adverbs end in *ly.* Exceptions include such adverbs as *then, there, so, soon, ever, often, not, never, seldom, rather, very, always.*
5. Many adverbs have the same form as adjectives.

LEARNING ACTIVITIES IN RECOGNIZING ADVERBS

A. (1) Copy these sentences. (2) Underline each adverb. (3) Draw an arrow to the word that it modifies. (4) Above that word, label it *v., adj.,* or *adv.* to indicate the part of speech.

1. I haven't been here very often.
2. You have driven too far.
3. I have looked nearly everywhere.
4. You have come too soon.
5. The work is rather easy.
6. I am not quite ready.
7. Just then she screamed loudly.
8. I almost never see Emily.

B. Copy the following list of adjectives. Beside each adjective, write the adverb formed from it.* Go over your lists in class, spelling each adverb.

1. dull	3. dramatic	5. rare	7. busy	9. drastic	11. artistic
2. witty	4. gay	6. critical	8. loyal	10. noble	12. capable

C. Name the part of speech of each italicized word in these sentences. If you write the sentences, exchange papers and go over them orally.

1. Jim flied *out* on a *fast* ball, which actually was an *outside* pitch.
2. Try to come *back* in time for the *last* quarter.
3. *Today* will soon be in the *past.*
4. At *last* the team made its third *out.*
5. We waited *outside* until Tom had gone *past.*
6. *Just* now he is feeling *well.* I hope that the improvement will *last.*
7. Don't *back* up too *fast.*
8. You did *well* to make that large *down* payment.
9. Looking *down,* I saw only the *still* waters of the lake.
10. Joe deserves a pat on the *back today.*
11. His *past* actions show that he is a *just* man.
12. I *still* think that we should have kicked on third *down.*

D. Write sentences using *right* as (1) noun, (2) adverb, (3) adjective, and (4) verb. Compare sentences in class or in your small groups.

---

* Rules 1 and 2, page 187, and Rule 6, page 190, cover spelling changes that may occur.

2. Forming Adverb Comparisons

Like adjectives, most adverbs can be compared. If necessary, review the definitions of the three degrees of comparison, page 355.

● **WHAT TO REMEMBER ABOUT COMPARING ADVERBS**

1. **Adverbs ending in *ly* add *more* to form the *comparative degree* and *most* to form the *superlative degree*.**

POSITIVE:	quickly	emphatically
COMPARATIVE:	more quickly	more emphatically
SUPERLATIVE:	most quickly	most emphatically

2. **A few adverbs not formed from adjectives add *er* and *est* to form the comparative and the superlative:** *fast, faster, fastest; high, higher, highest; soon, sooner, soonest.*

3. **Like adjectives, some adverbs may be compared in both ways:** *often, oftener, oftenest; often, more often, most often.*

4. **Certain adverbs are compared irregularly:** *badly, worse, worst; well, better, best; far, farther, farthest.*

5. **Adverbs that cannot be compared are** *now, then, not, too, already, again, always, yesterday, almost, why, yes, no.*

LEARNING ACTIVITY

Select the fitting degree of each adverb shown in parentheses below. Make this either an oral or a written activity.

1. Of all the entrants in the race, Archie ran (fast).
2. At our house we eat oranges (often) than grapefruit.
3. Which of you two boys can leave (soon)?
4. Of the four tires, this one is (badly) worn.
5. Of those twins, the smaller one swims (well).

3. Using Phrases as Adverbial Modifiers

INTRODUCTORY ACTIVITY

Examine these sentences. Decide what each italicized phrase tells; then try to substitute a one-word adverb for the phrase. Which phrase cannot be turned into a one-word adverb?

1. You have behaved *in a thoughtless manner.*
2. He answered me *with a laugh.*
3. I have come *for the rent.*
4. We plan to leave *at an early hour.*

● WHAT TO REMEMBER ABOUT PHRASES USED AS ADVERB MODIFIERS

1. *Prepositional phrases* **may be used as adverbs.**

   We went to the park.   The problems were easy for you.

2. **Adverbs and adverbial prepositional phrases may modify** *participles* **or** *infinitives.*

   I heard Mrs. Linn **moving** quietly in the kitchen.

   He waited to speak to the manager.

3. **An** *infinitive* **or an** *infinitive phrase* **may be used as an adverb.**

   We came to investigate the strange noise.

4. *Indirect objects* **and** *adverbial objectives* **can be thought of as** *objects in adverbial prepositional phrases having the preposition understood.*

   Tom gave [to] *me* a smile.   James waited [for] *two weeks.*

5. **The object in an adverbial prepositional phrase may be a** *gerund* **(or a** *gerund phrase***), an** *infinitive* **(or an** *infinitive phrase***), or a** *noun clause.*

   This knife is useful *for* **cutting** linoleum.
   He waited *for* **you to help him.**
   I recognized him *by* **what he was wearing.**

LEARNING ACTIVITIES

A. The following sentences contain prepositional phrases used as adverbs. Copy each phrase and indicate the word that it modifies. Before any indirect object or adverbial objective, write the omitted preposition and place parentheses around it. Exchange papers for checking.

1. Harold held his breath one minute.
2. I walked slowly down the path.
3. Are you ready for the trip?
4. I am very fond of apple pie.
5. Is the day too cool for you?
6. I asked Tom a question.
7. He gave me a good answer.
8. We shall arrive the next day.

B. These sentences contain infinitives and infinitive phrases used as adverbs. In an oral activity, locate each of them and name the word modified.

1. This problem is difficult to solve.
2. Are you ready to go?
3. I am here to help you.
4. The explorers returned to find their camp deserted.
5. Is Tom prepared to defend his position?
6. I paused to enjoy the beauty of the scene.
7. Elmer has come to rake the lawn.
8. Jane was eager to learn the results.
9. Everyone arrived early to hear the concert.

C. Write five or more sentences in which you use prepositional phrases and infinitive phrases as adverb modifiers. Use these sentences as in *A.*

4. Using Clauses as Adverbial Modifiers

You have studied the dependent clause as a noun and as an adjective. Now examine the sentence that follows.

> We met where the two roads come together.

What do the words *where the two roads come together* tell? Therefore, how are they used? Prove that those words are a clause. As what part of speech is the clause used? Then what kind of dependent clause is it?

● WHAT TO REMEMBER ABOUT ADVERB CLAUSES

1. (DEFINITION) **A dependent clause that modifies a *verb* or a *verb form*, an *adjective*, or an *adverb* in a main clause is an *adverb clause*.**

   We yelled until we were hoarse.

   You look younger since you have cut your hair.

   I can crochet better than I can knit.

   I plan to leave after I have seen Lynn.

   He strode down the street, whistling as he went.

2. **An adverb clause is joined to the word that it modifies by a *subordinate conjunction*,** such as *after, although, if, as, since, though, when, because, where, while, as if, so that, unless, before, than, until, whenever, wherever.*

3. **An *introductory adverb clause* is set off by a comma.**

   Before you go, will you sign these papers?

4. (DEFINITION) **An *elliptical clause* is an adverb clause in which certain omitted words are understood.**

   James is not so old *as his sister.*

   The complete clause is *as his sister is old.*

   The linemen will not disconnect the telephone *unless notified.*

   The complete clause is *unless they are notified.*

5. **An adverb clause may come first in the sentence, but as a rule it should do so only if the sense is the same as it would be when the sentence is in natural order.**

   As he drew near, the boy smiled. The boy smiled *as he drew near.*

   Note that the sense is the same in both sentences.

   Before John left, he burned the letter. He burned the letter before John left. The sense is not the same. "He" in the second sentence evidently refers to someone other than John.

LEARNING ACTIVITIES

A. Identify each adverb modifier in the following sentences. Tell what word each modifies. Exchange papers for checking.

1. We are surely sorry to hear this news.
2. No one ever lived here until we came.
3. If you like, you may borrow this book for a while.
4. Whenever I hear a cowbell, I am reminded of my childhood.
5. After an unusually long time, a woman came to answer my knock.
6. Many people, although they have no good reason, complain constantly.
7. We are always eager to learn of your plans.
8. As a rule, we watch the dogs while Francis feeds the cats.

B. Orally, complete these sentences with the adverbial forms indicated.

1. I was (*word*) eager (*infinitive*).
2. That clock is (*word*) slower (*adverb clause*).
3. We arrived (*prepositional phrase*) (*clause*).

Diagramming Adverbial Modifiers

The diagrams on this page and pages 378–79 show types and uses of adverb modifiers. Notice how clearly a diagram gives the sentence pattern.

One-Word Adverbs

He jumped up and down.   You are very late.   John walks too fast.

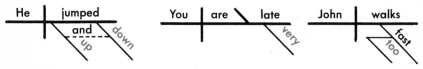

Prepositional Phrases

Wait for Ted and me in the lobby.   The suit is ready for you.

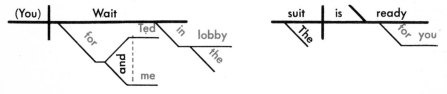

You must ask for whatever you need.

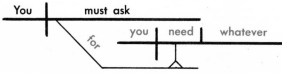

In the above example, the object of the preposition is a noun clause.

Adverb Modifying a Phrase

He returns only in the winter.

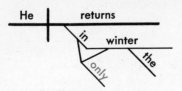

Adverb Modifying a Preposition

Fill the cup just above this line.

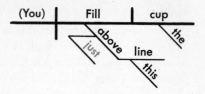

Adverbial Objective

I shall not budge an inch.

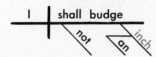

Infinitive

We are glad to help.

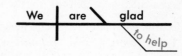

Indirect Objects

Show me the record.

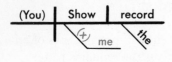

You must give whoever needs it your help.

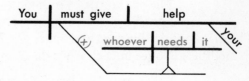

Note that in the second example the indirect object is a noun clause.

Adverbial Clauses

As we had expected, Carl was the winner

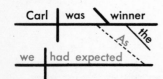

Although I like him, I see him rarely since he moved to Tryon.

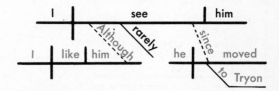

Elliptical Clauses

While standing there, I saw a friend.

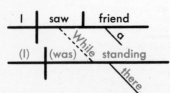

Is Don as tall as Larry?

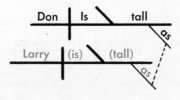

Note that the understood words are placed in parentheses.

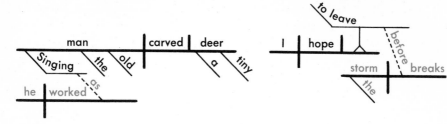

Clause Modifying a Participle

Singing as he worked, the old man carved a tiny deer.

Clause Modifying an Infinitive

I hope to leave before the storm breaks.

LEARNING ACTIVITIES IN DIAGRAMMING ADVERB MODIFIERS

Diagram the sentences in these activities: *A*, page 373; *A* and *B*, page 375; and *A*, page 377. Put diagrams on the board and analyze them orally, using a definite form in explaining them. (See the model on page 363.)

5. Using Adverb Modifiers Correctly

DISTINGUISHING BETWEEN ADJECTIVES AND ADVERBS

THE RULES

RULE 1. **Use a** *predicate adjective,* **not an** *adverb,* **to complete a linking verb.**
The food smells *delicious* [not *deliciously*].
The radio sounds *loud* [not *loudly*].

RULE 2. **Always use the adverbs** *surely* **and** *really,* **not the adjectives** *sure* **and** *real,* **to modify a predicate adjective.**
I *surely* [not *sure*] am tired.   The story is *really* [not *real*] strange.

RULE 3. **Do not confuse** *good* **and** *well.* **Use** *well* **as an** *adverb* **except in speaking of one's** *health* **or** *appearance.* **Use** *good* **only as an** *adjective.*
He works well.   Your work is good.

Mother has not felt well today.   The pie looks good to me.

RULE 4. **Do not confuse the adjective** *most* **with the adverb** *almost.*
I have *almost* [not *most*] finished reading this book about Mexico.

RULE 5. **Use** *badly* **as an** *adverb,* *bad* **as an** *adjective.*
I feel bad about my error.   He plays the violin badly.

RULE 6. **Do not use the adjective** *awful* **for the adverbs** *greatly, really, very.*
I am *really* [not *awful*] tired tonight.

LEARNING ACTIVITIES IN ADJECTIVES versus ADVERBS

A. Choose the correct form from the parentheses. If you write the exercise, go over the sentences orally in class.

1. The roses smell (sweet, sweetly). I'm (real, very) glad to have them.
2. Those clouds (sure, surely) look black.
3. That pie smells (delicious, deliciously). I'm (awful, really) hungry.
4. Don't feel (bad, badly) about breaking the cup.
5. You cannot decide (fair, fairly) until you feel (well, good).
6. His voice sounds (harsh, harshly); it's (awful, very) loud, too.
7. Help came (sudden, suddenly) after I had (most, almost) given up.

B. Write sentences similar to those in *A.* Exchange papers and read the sentences aloud, making the correct choices.

AVOIDING DANGLING MODIFIERS AND UNCLEAR MEANING

THE RULES

RULE 1. Avoid dangling adverbial constructions.

DANGLING GERUND: *After finding a seat,* the game was enjoyed.
IMPROVED WORDING: *After finding a seat,* **I enjoyed** the game.

DANGLING INFINITIVE: *To see better,* new glasses were bought.
IMPROVED WORDING: *To see better,* **I bought** new glasses.

DANGLING ELLIPTICAL CLAUSE: *While teeing off,* the rain began.
IMPROVED WORDING: *While* **I was** *teeing off,* the rain began.

RULE 2. Place modifiers so as to give your intended meaning.

a) **Let** *only, nearly,* **and similar words precede closely the words that you want them to modify.**

I only borrowed the pen. (I didn't buy it.)

I borrowed only the pen. (That is all I borrowed.)

I earned nearly a dollar. (I earned ninety cents.)

I nearly earned a dollar. (But I missed the chance.)

b) **Put prepositional phrases where they will make meaning clear.**

GOOD: *With my little sister,* I scrubbed the basement.
POOR: I scrubbed the basement *with my little sister.*

c) **Do not misplace adverb clauses.**

GOOD: *Before he left,* Bill said that the clock was slow.
POOR: Bill said that the clock was slow *before he left.*

d) **Avoid "squinting" modifiers; that is, those that can logically modify more than one sentence part.**

SQUINTING: He asked me *when I came* to make out my bill.
CLEAR: *When I came,* he asked me to make out my bill.

380

LEARNING ACTIVITY

Rewrite the following sentences, making needed corrections of dangling modifiers and of poorly placed modifiers. Explain your corrections orally.

1. This file only has two drawers.
2. While weeding the garden, the telephone rang.
3. You may use the boat by depositing five dollars for three hours.
4. Jim got up as the curtain rose and walked out.
5. To run faster, a training schedule was set up.
6. After mailing the letter, our walk was resumed.
7. Jim told me before he went into the service to write to him.
8. This is the best meal that I have almost ever eaten.
9. The generals planned how to defeat the enemy during their dinner.
10. Though feeling better, the day was spent in bed.

AVOIDING MISCELLANEOUS ADVERB ERRORS

THE RULES

RULE 1. **Avoid the** *double negative;* **that is,** *two negative words in one clause.* **Do not use** *hardly, scarcely, not* (or *n't*), **or** *never* **with one another or with** *no, nobody, none, no one, neither, nothing,* **or** *but* (meaning *only*). NOTE: An introductory *no* is not considered a part of the clause.

RIGHT: I *can hardly* decide.	WRONG: I *can't hardly* decide.
RIGHT: We *need but* one chair.	WRONG: We *don't need but* one chair.
RIGHT: She *won't* see *anyone.*	WRONG: She *won't* see *no one.*
RIGHT: *No,* I *haven't* been there. (introductory *no*)	

RULE 2. **Omit** *redundant* (unnecessary) **adverbs like** *back, up, again, with, over:* He *returned* [not *returned back*] to his home two years later.

RULE 3. **Avoid the** *singular* **form of** *adverbial objectives* **when the** *plural* **form is needed:** The storage tank holds thirty *gallons* [not *gallon*] of water.

RULE 4. **Observe the same rules for correct comparison of adverbs as for adjectives.** (Review Rule 1 and Rule 2, page 364.)

Phil certainly has grown *faster* [not *more faster*] than Perry.

RULE 5. **Do not use** *seldom ever, rarely ever.* **Say** *seldom if ever, rarely if ever;* **omit** *ever;* **or change** *seldom* **and** *rarely* **to** *hardly.*

RIGHT: I *seldom if ever* hurry. I *seldom* hurry. I *hardly ever* hurry.
WRONG: I *seldom ever* hurry.

RULE 6. **Watch the use of** *but* **in these constructions:**

a) **Avoid using** *but* **after** *negative ideas* **expressed by such words as** *doubt* or *fear:* We didn't doubt *that* [not *but that*] his plan would work.

b) **Complete** *cannot help* (or *could not help*) **by a gerund, not by** *but* **and an** *infinitive:* I *couldn't help crying* [not *couldn't help but cry*].

LEARNING ACTIVITIES

A. Using complete statements that embody the questions, answer each of the following in the negative. Make this an oral activity.

1. Were there any apples left?
2. Do you ever see Jim nowadays?
3. Have you told anyone the news?
4. Have you had much rain here?
5. Do you hear from Bill often?
6. Do you have any money left?

B. Correct any errors that you find in the following sentences. Make this a written exercise; then exchange papers for checking.

1. I seldom ever buy more than five gallon of gas.
2. I haven't no use for a bowl that holds only two cupful.
3. Jerry studies more harder than Alvin.
4. He hasn't no intention of recalling you back.
5. You haven't scarcely had time to reread over the assignment.
6. I haven't never seen a balloon ascension.
7. I have no doubt but what he can be trusted.
8. He hasn't no money to repay back what he borrowed.
9. He is so nervous that he can't hardly collect together his thoughts.
10. I don't have but one clean shirt.

AVOIDING MISCELLANEOUS ADVERB ERRORS—*Continued*

THE RULES—Continued

RULE 7. **Do not add** *s* **to** *nowhere, anywhere, somewhere, everywhere.*
Anywhere [not *Anywheres*] he goes, people honor him.

RULE 8. **Say** *anyway,* **not** *anyways: Anyway* [not *Anyways*], here we are.

RULE 9. **Do not use** *considerable* **as an adverb.**
My health is *much* [not *considerable*] better than it was.

RULE 10. **Do not use** *leave* **for the adverb** *lief:* I'd as *lief* [not *leave*] walk.

RULE 11. **Avoid using** *nowheres near* **for** *not nearly.*
There is *not nearly* [not *nowheres near*] enough money.

RULE 12. **Avoid the expression** *nohow.*
WRONG: I didn't want to go, *nohow.*   RIGHT: I didn't want to go.

RULE 13. **Do not use** *muchly* **for** *much* **or** *very much.*
She seems *very much* [not *muchly*] disturbed by the report.

RULE 14. **Do not use** *right* **as an adverb of degree.** (In certain parts of the country, however, this use is an acceptable colloquialism.)
Your suit is *very* [not *right*] smart looking, Eleanor.

RULE 15. **Do not use** *irregardless* **for** *regardless.*
I shall go *regardless* [not *irregardless*] of what you say.

RULE 16. **Do not use such expressions as** *all the farther* **or** *all the faster* **for** *as far as, as fast as:* Beloit is *as far as* [not *all the farther*] I can take you.

LEARNING ACTIVITIES

A. Correct each error in the use of adverbs. If you write this exercise, be sure to go over your papers orally.

1. Are you right sure that this is all the farther they went?
2. I need considerable more help, but I can't get it, nohow.
3. I am going, anyways, irregardless of the weather.
4. He is considerable upset because he has nowheres near finished.
5. I'd as leave not go anywheres.
6. Thank you muchly. You've been right helpful.
7. Is this all the faster we can go? I don't like it, nohow!

B. Write sentences illustrating the rules in this lesson. *Proofread for careless errors in spelling, capitalization, and punctuation.* Exchange papers for criticism.

FOLLOW-UP ACTIVITY

Concentrate on mastering your most serious adverb errors. Work on them specifically; then go on to attack other wrong usages.

DISTINGUISHING BETWEEN COLLOQUIAL AND STANDARD ENGLISH

The rules on this page and the next deal with expressions generally acceptable in colloquial (informal) use but not in standard (cultivated or formal) speech or writing.

THE RULES

RULE 1. **Avoid using** *ways* **or** *piece* **for** *distance* **or** *way.*
Aren't you a long *way* [not *ways*] from your destination?

RULE 2. **Avoid the use of** *awfully* **for** *very, very much, greatly,* **or similar intensives:** She was *very* [not *awfully*] angry.

RULE 3. **Avoid using** *worse* **to mean** *more;* **avoid using** *badly, the worst way,* **or** *in the worst way* **to mean** *very much* **or** *greatly.*
He needs help *more* [not *worse*] than ever.
I want to go *very much* [not *in the worst way*].
We miss him *greatly* [not *badly*].

RULE 4. **Use** *rather* **or** *somewhat* **in preference to** *sort of* **or** *kind of.* **Never say** *sorta* **or** *kinda:* I am *rather* [not *kind of* or *kinda*] tired.

RULE 5. **Avoid using** *someplace, anyplace, every place, no place* **for** *somewhere, anywhere, everywhere, nowhere.*
Let's go *somewhere* [not *someplace*] for dinner tonight.

RULE 6. **Avoid using** *mighty* **or** *awfully* **for** *extremely* **or** *very.*
Sam has been *very* [not *mighty*] useful during this emergency.

THE RULES—*Continued*

RULE 7. **Avoid the use of** *such* (or *such a*) **for** *very.*

Millicent has a *very* [not *such a*] sweet face!

RULE 8. **Avoid using the adjective** *some* **for the adverb** *somewhat.*

Grandfather is feeling *somewhat* [not *some*] better now.

RULE 9. **Use** *away,* **not** *way,* **as an adverb of degree.**

The baseball sailed *away* [not *way*] above my head.

RULE 10. **Use** *quite* **to mean** *entirely* **or** *completely* **and not to mean** *slightly, rather, somewhat.*

This dress is *rather* new. I bought it last month.
The room was *quite* empty. Not a soul was there.

RULE 11. **Avoid the use of** *never* **for** *did not* **in speaking of a** *one-time* **occurrence:** I *did not* sleep [not *never* slept] well last night.

RULE 12. **Avoid modifying a past participle by** *too* **or** *very.*

I am *very much* [not *very*] interested in your idea.
Don't be *too much* [not *too*] impressed by his manner.

RULE 13. **Use** *as–as* **in** *affirmative* **constructions; use** *so–as* **in** *negative* **constructions:** I am *as tall as* you are.   She is *not so old as* I.

RULE 14. **Use** *farther* **to refer to** *space;* **use** *further* **to refer to** *time, quantity,* **or** *degree:* I can walk no *farther.*   Go no *further* with this idea.

RULE 15. **Do not use** *that* **as an intensive.**

She was *so* [not *that*] highly upset that I couldn't quiet her.
Have you read *as far as that* [not *that far*]?

LEARNING ACTIVITIES IN COLLOQUIAL VERSUS STANDARD ENGLISH

A. Rewrite this paragraph from a student theme, changing each colloquial expression to standard English. Exchange papers for checking.

> I was kind of sorry when the class decided to have the picnic a long ways further from town than our committee had planned. I wanted in the worst way to tell them that I was awfully sure they would not be too pleased with the place. I was some critical of their choice, but I'm mighty glad that I was not as much so as Dick. Usually he has such a good disposition, but this time he never showed it. He snorted, "I'd rather go no place at all than there!" I was quite surprised, for I have never seen him that disagreeable before!

B. Write sentences to illustrate the rules in this lesson. Exchange papers with a partner and evaluate each other's work.

USING ENGLISH IN ALL CLASSES

Examine a report or a theme-type test that you have written recently. As a rule, such papers should be expressed in standard English. List any colloquial usages that you find; then use the list to check your next theme.

6. Using Adverb Modifiers to Express Ideas Vividly and Exactly

Like adjectives, well-chosen adverbs add vividness, force, and clarity to the sentence idea.

GUIDES FOR CHOOSING EFFECTIVE ADVERB MODIFIERS

1. Search out and use the vivid adverb, keeping in mind that the *ly* adverbs are the ones that do most to paint a vivid picture.
2. Use the *exact* adverb. For example, *sluggishly* is better than *slowly* in "The river flowed sluggishly on."
3. Avoid the use of extravagant adverbs to express ordinary ideas.
4. Avoid overworking *very*. Keep in your notebook a list of suitable substitutes. Refer to this list whenever you write a theme or plan a talk.

LEARNING ACTIVITIES IN USING EFFECTIVE ADVERBS

A. Rewrite these sentences, eliminating any extravagant adverb modifiers.

1. Louise wears the most gorgeously, perfectly beautiful clothes that I've ever seen.
2. This picture is colossally, magnificently, superbly produced.
3. He has the most devastatingly attractive smile.

B. Substitute colorful adverbs for *very* in these sentences. Compare your work.

1. His chances for recovery seem very remote.
2. The Scots are very thrifty people.
3. His answer was very abrupt.
4. Sue has very blue eyes.
5. This story has a very intriguing plot.

C. Make the following sentence ideas clearer, livelier, and more definite by adding an adverb of manner (an *ly* adverb) to the verb.

1. The policeman barked his command.
2. The eavesdropper listened at the keyhole.
3. The monkey climbed the flagpole.
4. Answer my question.
5. The Indian approached the cabin.

D. Replace each italicized adverb in the sentences below, using a vivid synonym. Read your work aloud.

1. That boy plays *well*.
2. Not everyone works *fast*.
3. John works *hard*.
4. Jean sang *happily*.

E. Bring to class printed advertisements that make good use of adverb modifiers. Point them out in a short talk. Use the Speech Score Card, page 31.

Just to make sure! *

Directions: As you do the following activities, refer to the rules and definitions in this chapter. Go over orally any activities that you write.

A. Change any colloquial expressions to standard English.

1. I am kind of glad that we didn't buy a house as large as that one.
2. That is such a pretty hat. I want it badly.
3. She was that angry that she simply refused to talk farther.
4. His timing is not too improved, but it is some better.
5. Let's go someplace tonight. I'm mighty tired of staying here.
6. We still have an awfully long ways to drive.
7. They are quite good seats, though they are way at the back.
8. I never locked the door last night.

B. Make needed corrections in the use of adverb modifiers.

1. You haven't sewed this hem very good; you'll have to resew it again.
2. Benny is sure active; he seldom ever sits still.
3. While shopping, I only looked at coats.
4. We don't have no homework assignment over vacation. I'm awful glad, because I am planning to go somewheres.
5. Most everybody felt bad because Susan forgot her lines. She must have felt muchly disappointed.
6. Irregardless of how he felt, he shouldn't have shown it nohow.
7. Bill jumped only six foot, nowheres near high enough to win.
8. I don't doubt but what we should relax more oftener.
9. I'm right sorry, but this is all the farther we can take you.
10. I'd as leave stay considerable longer.
11. While mailing a letter, a storm began.
12. To pack a bag carefully, much tissue paper should be used.
13. Anyways, hardly no one understands the questions.
14. I washed the car with my brother.
15. In grinding the corn, my mitten was cut.

C. (1) Draw a wavy line under single-word adverbs. (2) Underline all phrases that are used as adverbs, including those having understood prepositions. (3) Circle all adverb clauses. (4) Draw arrows to the words modified.

1. This morning I gave Betty the money for a new hat.
2. Before, I was not eager for the trip; now I am happy to go.
3. Frankly, I cannot help you unless you will co-operate.

---

* Check Test 7 should be given at this point. If the results show need for further study, pupils should do this review practice. They should then take Mastery Test 7.

Know How to Use Prepositions, Conjunctions, and Independent Elements*

1. USING PREPOSITIONS AS AIDS IN BUILDING SENTENCES

RECOGNIZING PREPOSITIONS

READ AND DISCUSS

As you learned in your study of adjective and adverb phrases, the preposition shows relationship between sentence parts. Notice this example:

The man walked .... the house.

The preposition has been omitted. Without it, you are unable to tell what the relationship is between *walked* and *house*. Supply prepositions to show as many different relationships as you can between *walked* and *house*.

---

* Pretest 8 should be given at this point.

WHAT TO REMEMBER ABOUT PREPOSITIONS

1. (DEFINITION) A *preposition* is a word that shows the relation between a *noun* or a *pronoun*, called its *object*, and *some other word* in the sentence: We sat *around* the blazing **campfire.**

2. Here is a list of common prepositions: *about, above, across, after, against, along, among, around, at, before, behind, below, beneath, beside, besides, between, beyond, but* (except), *by, concerning, down, during, except, for, from, in, into, like, near, of, off, on, out, outside, over, past, round, since, through, till, to, toward, under, underneath, until, up, upon, with, within, without.*

3. (DEFINITION) A preposition and its object, with or without modifiers, constitute a *prepositional phrase.* Prepositional phrases are used as *adjectives* or *adverbs.* See pages 357 and 375.

4. (DEFINITION) Sometimes two or more words are used together as a preposition to form a *phrasal preposition.* Examples are *because of, on account of, by means of, in spite of, apart from, in place of, instead of, according to, out of, as to.*

LEARNING ACTIVITIES

A. Classify the italicized words in the following sentences according to their part of speech. Each different word is used once as a *preposition;* in other places, it may be a *verb,* a *noun,* an *adjective,* or an *adverb.* Make this an oral activity.

1. Everyone is *about* ready to go *down* to the beach.
2. Would you *like* to come *along* with me?
3. He walked *by* without looking *up,* just as he had done *before.*
4. *Like* me, Dad refuses to stay *inside* on rainy days.
5. In the *past* twenty years, he has seen only two *near* relatives.
6. The first *round* of play was *over by* noon.
7. Watch *out below!* I'm coming *down* the rope.
8. He walked *out* the door and *up* the street, his *round* little face beaming.
9. Have I told you *about* the strange old gentleman who lives *near* me?
10. The houses *along* this street were built *before* 1900.
11. He escaped *over* the border and at dawn was *inside* our lines.
12. The man who lives on the floor *below* ours just went *past.*
13. Go *round* the block and *past* the park.
14. We gathered *round,* eager to hear the *inside* story of his *past.*

B. Exactness of expression calls for accurate use of prepositions. Fill the following blanks with suitable prepositions. Go over your sentences orally, noting how the choice of prepositions changes the meaning. *Do not write in this book.*

1. The dog lay .... the porch. (Do not use *on.*)
2. He waited .... the house. (Do not use *in.*)
3. Gary came .... his father. (Do not use *with.*)

C. *To, of, across, for, since, with,* and *without* are often mispronounced. Write and read aloud original sentences containing them. Your classmates will listen critically to detect whether your pronunciation is free of these sounds: *ter* or *tuh, uv, acrost, fer, sense, wid* or *wit, widout.*

Follow through

(*Based upon the sentences in* A, *page 388*)

1. Why is *Dad* capitalized in the fourth sentence?
2. Which sentences have their subject understood?
3. How are the infinitives in *1, 2, 4,* and *14* used?

USING PREPOSITIONS CORRECTLY

Certain common errors in the use of prepositions should be avoided. Those errors are covered in this lesson and the next.

THE RULES

RULE 1. Do not confuse certain pairs or groups of prepositions.

a) At, to. **Use** *to* **only for** *motion toward.*
I walked *to* the corner.   Were you *at* [not *to*] the game?

b) By, at, with. **Do not use** *by* **as a substitute for** *at* **or** *with.*
He stays *at* [not *by*] our house.   He walked *by* [past] our house.
The plan is satisfactory *with* [not *by*] me.

c) In, into. **Use** *in* **for** *location or motion within* **a place;** *into* **for** *motion from one place to another.*
I walked *into* the library.   Ed was there, *in* his usual corner.

d) Beside, besides. **Use** *beside* **to mean** "located next to"; *besides* **to mean** "in addition to": No one *besides* [not *beside*] us knows the secret.

e) Between, among. **Use** *between,* **as a rule, in referring to** *two* **objects or persons;** *among,* **to** *three or more.*
Between **Tim** and **me** sat Joe.   Divide the candy *among* **all three.**
Use *between,* **however, if each member of a group is being considered separately in relation to each other member.**
I have a plane ticket *between* **Chicago, Cincinnati,** and **Knoxville.**

f) On, for. **Do not use** *on* **for** *for:* If we wait *for* [not *on*] you, we'll be late.

RULE 2. Say *different from,* **not** *different than. Different* **is not a comparative form; hence it should not be followed by the conjunction** *than.*
The Keenes' house is *different from* [not *different than*] ours.

RULE 3. Never use *of* **or its corruptions as an auxiliary verb.**
If he *had* [not *had of*] played, we *could have* [not *could of* or *coulda*] won.

LEARNING ACTIVITIES IN CORRECT USE OF PREPOSITIONS

A. The following conversation contains errors in the use of prepositions. In pairs, read the conversation aloud, correcting each wrong expression. The class should listen closely to each performance.

"Hi, Elaine. How is everything by you?"

"Oh, nothing is much different than when we saw each other last week. Uncle Art is still staying by our house. He would of left yesterday, but he missed his train because he and Bill were to the baseball game. The trains don't wait even on my Uncle Art, you know! . . . What's new at your house?"

"Well, for one thing, Dad walked in the house last night with the news that the choice for the new foreman at his shop was announced yesterday. It was between him, Jake Ellis, and Steve Warren. No one beside them had a chance—and Dad won! You should of heard us!"

B. Write sentences to illustrate correct application of the rules in this lesson. Use the sentences for oral class practice in saying and hearing the right forms.

THE RULES—*Continued*

RULE 4. **Do not use** *off* **or** *off of* **as a substitute for** *from*.

I borrowed it *from* [not *off of* or *off*] my brother.

RULE 5. **Avoid using** *on account of* **to introduce a clause or to complete** "The reason was . . ." **or** "The cause was . . . ."

I left early *because* [not *on account of*] I needed sleep.
The reason was *that* [not *on account of*] I was in a hurry.

RULE 6. **Omit** *redundant* (unnecessary) **prepositions.**

RIGHT	WRONG
The bear was inside the cage.	The bear was inside *of* the cage.
Do you want me to come?	Do you want *for* me to come?
I don't know where she is.	I don't know where she is *at*.
I met a friend.	I met *up with* a friend.
Where are you going?	Where are you going *to?* *
He waited outside the house.	He waited outside *of* the house.
Is the ball game over?	Is the ball game over *with?*

RULE 7. **Do not omit a needed preposition.** The following italicized prepositions are needed in the sentences.

John has no desire *for* or interest in money.
Bob graduated *from* high school last month.
Make an appointment with Dr. Blaine *for* the same time as last week.

RULE 8. **To show** *possession by* **or** *connection with* **inanimate things, use a phrase with** *of,* **not a possessive noun, except with expressions of** *time* **or** *measurement.* (Even careful writers do not always observe this rule.)

The roof *of the house* [not The *house's* roof] leaks.
We had a *week's* vacation.   Give me a *quarter's* worth of popcorn.

---

* This is sometimes classed as a redundant adverb.

LEARNING ACTIVITIES

A. Correct the wrong usage of prepositions in these sentences. They cover the rules in this lesson as well as some of those on page 389. Make this a written exercise, but be sure to read the sentences aloud to give you practice in hearing and saying the right forms.

1. How do you like this tie's color? I borrowed it off of Joe.
2. She has no use or interest in baseball. She wouldn't spend a minute's time at a game.
3. When the play was over with, I hurried out. The reason was because Ed wanted for me to meet him as soon as I could.
4. You should have waited on me outside of the door. I'd never of walked in on you without knocking.
5. Have you met up with Tod? Did he tell you where he is moving to?
6. I graduated high school the same time as my brother.
7. I put the ticket inside of my wallet's secret pocket.
8. You must of come on account of you knew that I need you.
9. If you had of stayed, you could of met Alfred.
10. Other things beside money are important.
11. Divide the work between all of you.
12. I opened the door and tiptoed in the room.
13. My uncle stays by us when he comes to town.
14. Is it all right by you if I come tomorrow?
15. You shouldn't of waited on me. I told you that I'd be late.
16. Is your book different than mine?
17. He travels regularly between Buffalo, Syracuse, and Utica.

B. Write sentences to illustrate correct application of the rules in this lesson. Use the sentences for oral class or small-group drill.

USING ENGLISH IN ALL CLASSES

Go over papers that you are writing for other classes. Correct any errors that you find in the use of prepositions.

FOLLOW-UP ACTIVITY

Although most errors in the use of prepositions come in speech, mistakes may occur in written material, especially in informal writing such as friendly letters. Before sealing the next letter that you write, check your use of prepositions.

DISTINGUISHING BETWEEN COLLOQUIAL AND STANDARD ENGLISH

The following rules apply to the use of standard English; that is, of formal or cultivated language. Most of the "wrong" forms are acceptable colloquial expressions.

RULES FOR DISTINGUISHING COLLOQUIAL FROM STANDARD USAGE OF PREPOSITIONS

RULE 1. Avoid confusing these prepositions.

a) At, in. Say *live in,* not *at,* a certain city or town.

He lives *in* [not *at*] Cleveland, or so I have heard.

b) About, around. **Avoid using** *around* for *about* **in the meaning** *not far from:* I received the paper *about* [not *around*] four o'clock.

c) Outside of, except, except for. **Do not use** *outside of* **to mean** *with the exception of:* No one knows *except* [not *outside of*] you and me.

d) In back of, back of, behind. **Use** *behind,* **not the other two.**

He sits *behind* [not *in back of*] me in two of my classes.

e) Inside, inside of, within. **Avoid using** *inside* or *inside of* **for** *within* **in expressions of** *time:* I'll write to you *within* [not *inside of*] a week.

RULE 2. Avoid *at about* **for** *about* or *at:* I left *about* [not *at about*] noon.

RULE 3. Avoid saying *blame on* or *blame it on* **for** *blame.*

POOR: Some people *blame* everything *on* the government.

BETTER: Some people *blame* the government for everything.

RULE 4. In strict usage, avoid the expression *consensus of opinion. Consensus* **itself means** "a general agreement of feeling or opinion."

The *consensus* of the group was that a change should be made.

RULE 5. Say *try to,* **not** *try and; be sure to,* **not** *be sure and.*

Try to [not *and*] come early.   *Be sure to* [not *and*] call.

RULE 6. Avoid using *due to* **for** *because of. Due to* **may follow a linking verb and may modify a noun or a pronoun; it should not be used as the preposition in an adverb phrase:** *Because of* [not *Due to*] the rain, I was late.

RULE 7. Do not use *following* **for the preposition** *after.*

After [not *Following*] the ceremony, the couple left for Bermuda.

RULE 8. End a sentence with a preposition if it gives force or naturalness to a clause or a sentence. Be sure that the final preposition is really necessary; remember, it must have an expressed object.

AWKWARD: I wonder *about* **what** he is thinking.

BETTER: I wonder **what** he is thinking *about.*

RIGHT: We want to go *with* **you.**   WRONG: We want to go *with.*

LEARNING ACTIVITIES

A. Change all colloquial expressions to standard English. Make this a written exercise; then exchange papers for checking.

1. At about five o'clock, the train finally arrived.
2. All members outside of those that are ill should try and be here.

3. If you are going to the store, I am going with.
4. A friend who lives at Billings called around noon.
5. Due to the coughing in back of me, I could not hear the speaker.
6. The consensus of opinion is that prices will drop inside of a year.
7. You should not blame your failure on your teachers.
8. Following the fireworks, the crowd scattered.
9. Due to bad weather conditions, we waited an hour in Toledo.
10. Will you try and come early? If you can't, be sure and call me.
11. My grandparents have lived at San Antonio for around twenty-five years.

B. Make sentences similar to those in *A*. Use them for class practice.

2. Using Conjunctions as Aids
in Building Sentences

RECOGNIZING DIFFERENT TYPES OF CONJUNCTIONS

READ AND STUDY

Conjunctions are important words because they show how ideas are related. Certain conjunctions indicate ideas that are equal in importance; others indicate subordinate ideas.

Conjunctions give various shades of meaning to the relationship of the words or the ideas that they connect. You will note that in the following lists some of the conjunctions are made up of several words.

1. These conjunctions indicate an added idea: *and, in addition, likewise, moreover, besides, further, furthermore.*
2. These conjunctions indicate contrasting ideas: *but, however, still, nevertheless, yet, on the other hand, on the contrary, all the same.*
3. These pairs of conjunctions indicate pairs of words or ideas: *either–or, neither–nor, whether–or, not only–but also, both–and.*
4. These conjunctions indicate results: *accordingly, consequently, so, hence, thus, therefore, for that reason.*
5. These conjunctions indicate cause or purpose: *as, because, for, since, for the reason that, on the ground that, in order that, so that, why.*
6. These conjunctions indicate explanatory ideas: *that is, for instance, for example, such as, that is to say.*
7. These conjunctions indicate conditional ideas: *if, provided, provided that, unless, except that, on condition that.*
8. These conjunctions indicate concessions: *although, though, whether, even though, in spite of the fact that.*
9. These conjunctions indicate an alternative: *or, otherwise, else.*

1. (DEFINITION) A *conjunction* is a word used to connect *words, phrases,* or *clauses.*

   Bob *and* Beth agree. (*words*)   Watch by day *and* by night. (*phrases*)
   Bill scrubbed the floors, *and* Julie washed the dishes. (*clauses*)

2. (DEFINITION) *Co-ordinate conjunctions* are those that join words, phrases, or clauses of *equal* value.

   a) *Simple co-ordinate conjunctions* are *and, or, nor, but,* and sometimes *for:* Kathy likes pork *and* beans. (*simple*)

   b) (DEFINITION) *Correlative co-ordinate conjunctions* are those that go in pairs: *either–or, neither–nor, both–and, not only–but also.*
   Not only Ken *but also* Ian wore sports jackets. (*correlative*)

3. (DEFINITION) Clauses joined by co-ordinate conjunctions form a *compound sentence:* He came, *but* he did not stay.

4. Only *closely related* and *equally important* ideas should be combined to make a compound sentence. (For the punctuation of compound sentences, see pages 170 and 179.)

5. (DEFINITION) *Conjunctive adverbs* are adverbs used like conjunctions. Often they join the parts of a compound sentence. Conjunctive adverbs include *still, then, therefore, thus, hence, however, moreover, yet, besides, nevertheless, also, otherwise, so, likewise, consequently, furthermore:* I came early; *however,* Tim was already there.

6. (DEFINITION) *Subordinate conjunctions* join *dependent* (subordinate) *clauses* to *independent clauses.* Subordinate conjunctions introduce clauses used as *parts of speech*—as *nouns, adjectives,* or *adverbs.* They include *when, where, while, until, after, as, unless, if, because, for, although, though, than, as if, before, since, wherever, whenever.*

   I knew *when* **you were coming.** (*noun clause*)
   This is the time *when* **you should be studying.** (*adjective clause*)
   When **I came in,** Mr. Smith was speaking. (*adverb clause*)

7. (DEFINITION) An independent clause and one or more dependent clauses together form a *complex sentence.*

LEARNING ACTIVITIES IN RECOGNIZING CONJUNCTIONS

A. The italicized words are sometimes conjunctions and sometimes other parts of speech. Classify them; then go over the sentences in class.

1. *Either* process is good, *but* this one costs more.
2. *Since* little can be done in the fields *until* spring, we must be patient.
3. No one *but* you *still* wants to wait *until* he calls.
4. *Before* John could say a word, *out* the door she ran *after* me.
5. *Before,* he had an even temper and a just nature; *then* he changed.
6. *Either* be *still,* or I'll not iron your shirts.

B. The following sentences contain compound words, phrases, and clauses. Go over the sentences, naming the compound parts and telling how they are used. Make this either an oral or a written exercise.

1. Trees and shrubs need much water.
2. Either Tucker or Fred is waiting for you. (*Why is the verb singular?*)
3. We neither slept nor ate.
4. The boys roasted wieners and marshmallows over the fire.
5. Our furniture is old but comfortable.
6. The workers will be you and I.
7. The people talked about cabbages and kings.
8. The stranger asked Harriet and me a question.
9. Red and white roses grow in our garden, but we have no yellow ones.
10. Having packed our bags and having studied the maps, we set out.
11. He ran through the house and into the garden.
12. The scout advanced carefully but quickly.
13. To earn money and to save it are two different things.

C. Join the following pairs of clauses by appropriate conjunctions, punctuating the sentences correctly. (Use the list on page 393.) Perhaps in some sentences you can use a semicolon and no conjunction. (See Rule 1 for using semicolons, page 179.) Read your work in class; explain your choices.

1. Arthur is interested in his work . . . he is not easily distracted.
2. I do not have a car . . . do I expect ever to own one.
3. A cold climate invigorates . . . a warm climate enervates.
4. In America the people came from many different countries . . . other countries claim one racial or national background.
5. The mixture of races in America ought to make it the most tolerant nation on earth . . . sometimes little quarrelsome groups make it seem the most critical.
6. Nobody grows without the desire to do so . . . every young person should work toward some definite ambition.
7. I arose at four o'clock . . . I wanted to drive in the cool of the morning.
8. Velma did not contribute to the fund . . . her name would be on this list.

USING ENGLISH IN ALL CLASSES

Find examples in your own work of exact use of conjunctions. Perhaps you may find constructions that you can improve. Use them for practice work.

USING CONJUNCTIONS CORRECTLY

As you have seen, the careful use of the *exact* conjunction improves expression. The careful use of the *grammatically correct* conjunction marks you as an educated speaker or writer.

THE RULES

RULE 1. **Do not use** *being as, being that, beings as, beings that* **for** *as* **or** *since.*

WRONG: *Beings that* you are here, you may as well stay.
RIGHT: *Since* [or *As*] you are here, you may as well stay.

RULE 2. **Avoid the use of** *as, as how, where* **for** *that, who,* **or** *whether.*

Dick read in the paper *that* [not *where*] our parks are to be improved.
I don't know *whether* [not *as* or *as how*] I agree with you.
Everyone *who* [not *as*] was there agreed with me.

RULE 3. **Do not use the prepositions** *without* **or** *except* **for the conjunction** *unless:* He will not come *unless* [not *without* or *except*] you wish it.

RULE 4. **Do not use the preposition** *like* **for the conjunctions** *as* **or** *as if:* Do as [not *like*] I do.   He looks *as if* [not *like*] he were tired.
NOTE: **In informal usage, some authorities accept the use of** *like* **for** *as,* **though not for** *as if.*

RULE 5. **Avoid** *incomplete comparisons.*

RIGHT: He is as old *as,* or older than, *Jim.*   He is *as old as Jim, or older.*
WRONG: He is *as old or older than Jim.*

RULE 6. **Do not use** *where* **or** *when* **to introduce a definition.**

RIGHT: A lateral pass is a play *in which . . .*
WRONG: A lateral pass is *where* [or *when*] *. . .*

RULE 7. **Keep in parallel form items joined by co-ordinate conjunctions.**

WRONG: Tell me the place and when I should come. (*word and clause*)
RIGHT: Tell me the place and the time to come. (*two words*)

WRONG: I like swimming and to play golf. (*gerund and infinitive*)
RIGHT: I like swimming and golfing. (*two gerunds*)
RIGHT: I like to swim and to play golf. (*two infinitives*)

RULE 8. **Never say** "and etc." *And* **is superfluous, since** *etc.* **itself means "and so forth." Use** *etc.* **only to avoid unnecessary repetition.**

Count off in groups of ten: 1, 2, 3, *etc.* [not *and etc.*].

RULE 9. **Avoid** *till* **or** *until* **for** *when:* I had hardly come *when* [not *till*] he began an argument.

LEARNING ACTIVITIES IN USING CONJUNCTIONS CORRECTLY

A. In the following sentences, choose the correct form from the parentheses. Make this a written exercise; then go over your work orally in class. Be able to justify the choices that you have made.

1. I am not sure (as, that) I understand you.
2. (Except, Unless) you help me, I shall never finish in time.
3. It looks (like, as if) you'll not need me.

4. I read in a magazine (where, that) women live longer than men.
5. (Since, Being that) we are ready, why don't we leave now?
6. The little boy acts (like, as if) he might be lost.
7. I hear (as how, that) the meeting has been postponed.
8. (Being that, As) you are in a hurry, I'll not keep you.
9. I had hardly sat down (till, when) my name was called.
10. Do (like, as) the directions advise.
11. I don't know (as, that) your reasoning is sound.
12. The boy (as, who) just left is selling magazines.
13. (Without, Unless) he comes soon, it will be too late.

B. Rewrite the following sentences, correcting all errors in the usage of conjunctions. As you go over the sentences in class, tell why each change is needed.

1. My shoes are as old or older than yours.
2. A falsehood is when you say something that isn't true.
3. Beings as it's late, I'll not stay longer.
4. Ted works as hard if not harder than Bert.
5. A free throw is where you get an unguarded shot at the basket.
6. It seems as how I'm busier than ever.
7. Near the barn I saw chickens, ducks, geese, and etc.
8. Like I say, he really needs a job.

C. The following sentences contain errors in parallel structure. Determine what types of grammatical elements would best express the ideas intended. Write the sentences correctly; then compare results in class.

1. Jack always recites clearly and with intelligence.
2. All was silence except for the wind and that a dog was howling.
3. The yard is large, attractively landscaped, and of unusual beauty.
4. The nurse told me to sit down and that the doctor would see me soon.
5. He is talented in art, in sports, in music, and he also acts well.
6. Everyone was silent and in a thoughtful mood.
7. He was not only brilliant but also had a friendly nature.

USING ENGLISH IN ALL CLASSES

Go over papers written for any of your classes. If you find sentences containing errors in parallel structure or other faulty usage of conjunctions, make corrections. Go over your sentences in class; explain any changes that you made.

FOLLOW-UP ACTIVITY

From the rules for correct usage of conjunctions, select one or two that give you particular difficulty. Try deliberately to bring into your daily conversation the usages that those rules cover. Continue this practice until the right forms are habitual. Proceed in the same way with other rules, concentrating on only one or two at a time.

The following eight rules cover usages that are generally acceptable in colloquial (informal) expression but that are not considered suitable in formal language situations; that is, these expressions do not represent standard English.

THE RULES

RULE 1. **Try not to say, "The reason was** *because* **..." for "The reason was** *that* **...":** His reason for running was *that* [not *because*] he was late.

RULE 2. **Place correlative conjunctions** *directly before* **the elements joined.**

POOR: Usually I *either* choose vanilla *or* strawberry.
BETTER: Usually I choose *either* vanilla *or* strawberry.

POOR: Jane and Jim can *both* go to the game.
BETTER: *Both* Jane *and* Jim can go to the game.

RULE 3. **Avoid the use of** *but that* **and** *but what* **as conjunctions.**

He didn't doubt *that* [not *but what*] it was true.

RULE 4. **Do not use** *if* **to take the place of** *whether*. *If* **states a condition. Use** *if* **only when** *whether* **does not make sense.**

I'll go *if* [*on condition that*] I can.   I wonder *whether* [not *if*] he will come.

RULE 5. **Use** *than* **after such negative expressions as** *no sooner;* **use** *when* **after such an expression as** *hardly* **or** *scarcely*.

No sooner had we left *than* the storm began.
We had *scarcely* left *when* the storm began.

RULE 6. **Do not use** *providing* **for** *provided*.

The game will be played *provided* (not *providing*) the field is dry.

RULE 7. **Use** *while* **to denote** *duration of time,* **not to take the place of** *whereas, although,* **or** *but*.

While the storm lasted, we stayed inside.
Father is a Republican, *but* [not *while*] Mother is a Democrat.

RULE 8. **Do not use** *also* **as a conjunction.**

Leona has offered to bring sandwiches *and* [not *also*] milk.

LEARNING ACTIVITIES

A. Change any colloquial expressions to standard English. Make this a written exercise, but go over the sentences orally in class.

1. Tomorrow I should either write to Milly or Betty.
2. I don't doubt but that we shall enjoy our trip.
3. Tom doesn't know if his father will accept the nomination.

4. We'll be there providing the car has been repaired.
5. The reason that I fell is because I slipped, also turned my ankle.
6. No sooner had we stepped inside when the lights went out.
7. I wonder whether we shall have rain today.
8. While I don't know him very well, I believe that he is sincere.

B. For additional practice, write pairs of sentences for each rule in this lesson, one sentence that illustrates colloquial usage; the other, standard English. *Be sure to proofread.* Go over your work in class or in your small groups.

3. USING INDEPENDENT ELEMENTS AS AIDS IN BUILDING SENTENCES

The *interjection,* the *expletive,* and the *nominative absolute* are considered independent sentence elements because they have no grammatical relationship to the rest of the sentence. Interjections are usually classed as the eighth part of speech.

● WHAT TO REMEMBER ABOUT INDEPENDENT SENTENCE ELEMENTS

1. **(DEFINITION)** *Interjections* **are** *exclamatory* **words that express emotion or feeling:** *Oh! Whew! Good heavens! Boy! Wow!*

2. **Since it has no grammatical relation to the rest of the sentence, an interjection showing** *strong emotion* **is followed by an** *exclamation point;* **one showing** *mild emotion,* **by a** *comma.*

   Wow! That was close! (*strong*)   *Oh,* it doesn't matter. (*mild*)

3. **(DEFINITION) The expletive** *there* **is purely** *introductory;* **it has no relation to others parts of the sentence:** *There* is no other way to do this.

4. **The expletive is** *not* **to be confused with either the** *subject* **of the sentence or the adverb** *there.*

   There is no money here. (*expletive*)   *There* he goes. (*adverb*)

5. **(DEFINITION) The** *nominative absolute* **consists of a** *nominative noun or pronoun* **followed by a** *participial expression.* **Usually, though not always, it begins a sentence and is set off by a comma.**

   Time running short, we revised our plans.

6. **The nominative absolute is actually a** *remnant of an adverb clause.* **It is therefore useful in** *condensing* **sentences and in securing** *variety.*

   After the debts were paid, the family prospered. (*adverb clause*)
   The debts paid, the family prospered. (*nominative absolute*)

7. **The nominative absolute is** *not* **to be confused with a** *participial modifier;* **it has the** *force* **of an adverb modifier but** *does not modify* **any word in the sentence. A participial modifier must modify a noun or a pronoun.**

   The house being vacant, we rented it. (*nominative absolute*)
   Feeling chilly, we went into the house. (*participial phrase*)

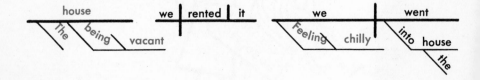

LEARNING ACTIVITIES

A. Make this activity a small-group discussion, being careful to apply the Guides to Good Discussion Habits, page 73.

Give examples of interjections currently popular with young people. What explanations can you suggest of how these expressions might have originated? What interjections can you think of that have lost their popularity? As you will discover, many interjections are slang expressions. The section "How to Choose the Suitable Word," pages 105–7, will help you if you want to eliminate overused expressions from your vocabulary.

B. Condense or vary the following sentences by changing the opening clause to a nominative absolute.

1. Because the roads were rough, we had a tiresome trip.
2. After the dishes had been washed, we went for a walk.
3. Because the house had long been vacant, many repairs were needed.
4. When the bell had rung, we trooped into the schoolhouse.
5. As the rain continued to fall, we gave up hope of going farther that night.

C. In an oral activity, distinguish between participial phrases and nominative absolutes in these sentences. Explain.

1. Having forgotten his key, Phil found himself locked out.
2. Crops being poor that year, we had a hard winter.
3. The moon having come out, the boys could see the path.
4. Closed for so many years, the mines at last were reopened.
5. The starting signal given, the final race began.

Just to make sure!*

Directions: As you do these activities, refer to the rules in this chapter. Go over orally any activities that you write.

A. Choose the correct form from the pairs in parentheses.

1. Did George stop (at, by) your house? I don't know where he has (gone, gone to). I can't wait (on, for) him any longer.
2. (Because, On account of) you are the secretary, you are just the person for whom I am (looking, looking for). I'm not sure (as, that) you know me.
3. Who left the receiver (off, off of) the hook while I was (to, at) the store? Could it (of, have) been you? You came (in, into) the room just as I left.
4. I can't imagine where (my suit's jacket, the jacket of my suit) (is, is at).
5. I have no (interest, interest in) or hope for his return.
6. Is it all right (by, with) you if I step (inside, inside of) the house?
7. No one (beside, besides) Nancy borrows anything (from, off) Terry.
8. Is there trouble (between, among) you three boys again?
9. Perjury is (when you swear falsely, false swearing) on the witness stand.
10. (Being as, Since) supplies like canned goods, coffee, sugar, (and etc., and the like) were in the cabin, we cooked our supper.
11. Those (who, as) know Dick say that he is different (than, from) Ted.
12. Henry is (as tall or taller than Ed; as tall as Ed, or taller).
13. He is (old, poor, and without friends; old, poor, and friendless).
14. (Like, As) I say, I can't go (without, unless) I get paid today.
15. I read (where, that) (a hydrogen and an atomic bomb both, both a hydrogen and an atomic bomb) had been exploded in the Pacific.

---

* Check Test 8 should be given at this point. If the results show need for further study, pupils should do this review practice. They should then take Mastery Test 8.

B. Change all colloquial expressions to standard English.

1. While there is much activity at Chicago, I prefer a small town.
2. I wonder if you will be at home around five o'clock.
3. The consensus of opinion is that we should stand in back of the club.
4. Due to a feeling of inferiority, Jim is boastful, also stubborn.
5. No sooner had I sat down than Dan called to say that he would arrive inside of an hour. Following his call, I prepared lunch.
6. I don't doubt but what he'll try and put the blame on us.
7. I had hardly fed the baby till he was crying again.
8. Everyone outside of me was there at about six o'clock. The reason that I was late was because a caller stayed too long.
9. Providing nothing happens, I'll either come at noon or at 1:30.

REVIEW *To keep you in practice*

VERBS AND AGREEMENT

Make needed corrections; change colloquial expressions to standard English.

1. Say, have you contacted the travel bureau about our reservations?
2. Lately John don't look the same as he always has. Have you saw him?
3. I'd not have got aggravated if he had proven his point.
4. I was so enthused that I would have liked to have seen the show again.
5. I should of suspicioned that one of the bolts were missing.
6. If you take sick again, you better call the doctor.
7. I set down on Tim's model airplane and busted one of the wings.
8. If Amy would have helped me, I coulda gone to the skating rink.
9. I used to could swim to the raft, but I reckon I can't now.
10. Every home in these two blocks have their special problems.

PRONOUNS, ADJECTIVES, AND ADVERBS

Correct any errors. Change all colloquial forms to standard English.

1. I am real glad that Mr. Briggs asked you and I to help him.
2. Mr. Reed's shaggy eyebrows give him a kind of a funny look.
3. Them cherries are sure tart.
4. That there old jalopy is more gaudier than any car on the campus.
5. My paper was not as interesting as your's nor typed as good.
6. Hasn't no one a extra pen? I never brought mine today.
7. Warm up the meat and the potatoes. I and Lou haven't had no dinner.
8. These kind of fish should have less bones than trout.
9. Us boys found some pudding in the refrigerator which we ate.

Know How to Use Sentences as to Structure*

1. FORMING SIMPLE, COMPOUND, COMPLEX, AND COMPOUND-COMPLEX SENTENCES

Chapters 20–25 have taught you how to use the various parts of speech to build sentences and clauses. This chapter deals specifically with the structure of the sentence as a whole.

* Pretest 9 should be given at this point.

WHAT TO REMEMBER ABOUT SENTENCE STRUCTURE

1. (DEFINITION) A *clause* is a group of words containing a *subject* and a *predicate*.

2. (DEFINITION) An *independent clause* expresses a *complete* idea. The independent clause can stand alone.

3. (DEFINITION) A *dependent*, or *subordinate*, *clause* does *not* express a complete idea. Dependent clauses are used as *nouns, adjectives,* or *adverbs*.

    INDEPENDENT: I am late.   DEPENDENT: If I am late.

4. (DEFINITION) A *simple sentence* contains a *subject* and a *predicate*, either or both of which may be compound; it expresses a *complete thought*. A simple sentence contains *one independent clause*.

    (DEFINITIONS) The *simple subject* is the subject *without* any *modifiers;* the *simple predicate* is the verb *without complements* or *modifiers*.

5. (DEFINITION) A *compound sentence* consists of *two or more independent clauses* connected (*a*) by a co-ordinate conjunction, (*b*) by correlative conjunctions, (*c*) by a semicolon, or (*d*) by a semicolon and a conjunctive adverb. Note the punctuation in the examples.
    a) This road leads to the city, **and** we shall take it.
    b) **Either** this road leads to the city, **or** we are lost.
    c) This road leads to the city; we shall take it.
    d) This road leads to the city; **therefore** we shall take it.

6. (DEFINITION) A *complex sentence* consists of an *independent clause* and *at least one dependent* (subordinate) *clause*.
    Take the highway *that leads to the city*.

7. (DEFINITION) A *compound-complex sentence* contains *two or more independent clauses* and *one or more dependent clauses*.

        dep.   *ind.*   *ind.*
    If you want my advice, do nothing; you will soon hear from me.

8. **Often expression can be improved if** *compound sentences* are changed to *complex sentences* or to *simple sentences* containing *compound parts, prepositional phrases,* or *verbals*.

    POOR: My uncle moved here a year ago, and he likes our town.
    BETTER: My uncle, *who moved here a year ago,* likes our town.
    POOR: This book belongs to me, and the cover is torn.
    BETTER: This book *with the torn cover* belongs to me.

LEARNING ACTIVITIES

A. Tell whether the following sentences are *simple, compound, complex,* or *compound-complex*. Justify your classifications.

1. Whenever I see penguins, I want to laugh.
2. They stand and strut about like men in formal dress.

3. They are trustful birds; therefore some people take advantage of them.
4. Many of the forms of life brought to the United States are accustomed to climatic conditions different from those which this country offers; consequently, temperatures are adjusted to them in their new homes.
5. In spite of careful attention, many rare creatures do not live.

B. In a class discussion or in your small groups, decide how you can improve the following sentences. Name the parts that you substituted.

1. Snow began falling at dusk, and it fell all through the night.
2. Alfred lingered on the corner and he watched the hurrying crowds.
3. The batter hit a home run to left field, and he crossed the plate standing.
4. The plans had been changed, and George gave us our new orders.
5. This is a picture of my brother, and everyone thinks that he looks like me.
6. Last year our section had sufficient moisture, and we had a good corn yield, and it was the first good crop in four years.

DIAGRAMMING COMPOUND AND COMPOUND-COMPLEX SENTENCES

The longer and more highly involved a sentence is, the more useful you will find the ability to diagram its parts, because a diagram reveals faulty sentence construction. The following diagrams show how to diagram *compound* and *compound-complex* sentences.

Compound Sentences

Either my watch is fast, or Tom is late.

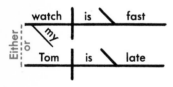

The sun had set, and the stars were shining, but the moon had not risen.

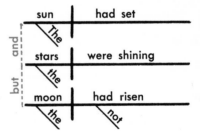

The matter is serious; what shall we do?

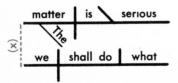

I know him; however, we rarely see each other.

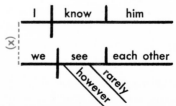

Note: The (x) indicates an understood conjunction.

405

When the half ended, our team had possession of the ball, but we were deep in our own territory.

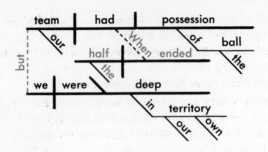

LEARNING ACTIVITIES

A. Diagram the following sentences. Put diagrams upon the board, and go over them orally. Begin by telling whether a sentence is *compound, complex,* or *compound-complex.* Then explain the parts of the independent clause or clauses. Follow with the explanation of any dependent clauses.

1. Because I was early, I thought that the hall would be empty, but John had come before me.
2. The game ended in a tie; there will be a play-off.
3. I resemble my mother, but Don is the image of Uncle Will.
4. As I had feared, he had locked the door; therefore I sat down to wait.
5. Either Lawrence is late, or I am early.
6. Business is better; a good crop of corn is expected; and everything in our little town is humming.

B. For more practice, use the sentences in *A,* page 404.

2. AVOIDING SENTENCE FRAGMENTS AND RUN-ON SENTENCES

Now that you have completed a study of the grammatical structure of sentences, you should have no difficulty in avoiding the use of sentence fragments and run-on sentences. Your knowledge of appositives and the different kinds of phrases and dependent clauses should prevent your punctuating fragments as complete sentences. It should prevent you from stringing sentences together with *and*'s and *so*'s (or with no connectives at all) or from tying sentences together with commas.

1. (DEFINITION) A *sentence fragment* is a group of words that make an *incomplete assertion or statement* about something or someone. Here are common types of fragments.

   a) **A group of words without a subject:** *Just looked at me.*

   b) **A group of words without a verb:** *The girl nextdoor.*

   c) **A group of words with neither subject nor verb:** *After the first quarter of the game.*

   d) **A dependent clause:** *Which she gave to me.*

2. **To determine whether a group of words punctuated as a sentence really is one, read the group of words aloud. If it makes an *understandable statement*, it is probably a *sentence*; if not, it is a *fragment*.**

3. **Sentence fragments are not always bad. Casual conversation contains many *elliptical sentences* that are actually fragments.** Skilled writers often use them deliberately. In your own writing, the use of an occasional fragment doubtless will have your teacher's approval if you label it as such to show that you are using it knowingly.

4. (DEFINITION) A *run-on sentence* incorrectly joins two or more sentences.

   a) **Those joined by** *and* **or** *and so*
   I was tired *and so* I lay down *and* I slept for two hours.

   b) **Those joined by** *commas*
   Tom is visiting me now, he used to live here.

   c) **Those having no connecting words or punctuation**
   I could not sleep last night I was thinking about our trip.

5. **Run-on sentences can be improved by changing them to** *complex sentences, compound-complex sentences,* **or** *simple sentences containing phrases, modifiers, verbals.*

   Poor: The door banged shut and I was left outside, finally I climbed through the kitchen window.

   Better: When the door banged shut, I was left outside; finally, however, I climbed through the kitchen window.

LEARNING ACTIVITIES

A. In class, find any fragments in these word groups; make them into good sentences. Notice the many ideas that result.

1. What I told you yesterday is true.
2. A lone survivor clinging to a piece of wreckage.
3. Leaped to his horse and galloped away, while we just stood there.
4. Just as the final whistle blew.
5. In the very spot where I had looked so carefully.
6. Praised by everyone, both young and old, with whom he worked.
7. Trust me.
8. Waiting for the bell to ring.

B. Rewrite the following paragraph, eliminating the many sentence fragments. Exchange papers. Have the paragraph put on the board correctly; then go over it in class, checking all capitalization and punctuation.

In the music festival last Friday, four hundred students participated. Coming from eight different schools in the county. Top honors in the vocal solo section went to Marion High School. Which was the smallest school represented. But which nevertheless won three of the six first places. On the other hand, in the choral competition, Mills High School, the largest school entered in the contest, winning first ranking in boys' chorus and in mixed chorus. And placing second in girls' chorus. Honors in the small-group sections were divided. No school placing first in more than two of the twelve contests.

C. Rewrite the following run-on sentences so that you make them into good sentences. In some cases, you may do this by taking out an *and* or an *and so.* In others, you may want to make use of a *dependent clause,* an *infinitive,* a *participial expression,* or some other construction. Word your sentences to make them effective as well as correct. Compare work in class, noting variations.

1. The annual football banquet will take place on Saturday, all plans are now complete, and Phil Langley, backfield star of the 1953 championship team, is coming from Chicago and he will give the main address.
2. At the next meeting of the Dramatic Club, six new students will be initiated into the organization, four of them are seniors and two are juniors, and so the total membership in the club will be increased to twenty.
3. Two new sports have been added to the school athletic program, they are tennis and golf, great interest is being shown and so it is hoped that next year there can be an intramural tournament in each of these sports.
4. Fifteen students are working in downtown stores and offices this week, they are seniors in the advanced commercial course and this activity is intended to give them a chance to apply in the business world what they have been learning at school.

D. The following paragraph contains both fragments and run-on sentences. Rewrite it, aiming not only to correct it but also to achieve a smooth, forceful style. *Proofread carefully.* Compare work in class or in your small groups.

Many people claim that they are not superstitious, nevertheless they have certain little habits, and these habits cause one to wonder. Whether they are as free from superstitions as they claim. For instance, such a person will walk around a ladder rather than under it. Saying that he is not superstitious but that there is no sense in taking chances. Another may see a black cat and so he will turn around and go back the way that he has come. His reason being to avoid having the cat cross his path, and yet he will tell you that he doesn't really believe that black cats can bring bad luck. A woman will refuse to cut out a new dress on Friday. Even though she says that she knows that she is being silly. The actions of many a person who insists that he doesn't seriously believe in good-luck charms seem to belie his words, he will hang a horseshoe over the door. Or he will carry a lucky coin, a rabbit-foot, or a four-leaf clover in his pocket. No, such people are not superstitious, they just act that way!

Go over papers that you have written for any class. If you find fragments or run-on sentences, correct those faulty constructions. You may want to offer some of the faulty sentences as practice material for those who need it.

Just to make sure! *

Directions: As you do these activities, refer to the definitions and explanations in this chapter. If you write the activities, go over your papers orally.

A. Classify these sentences as *simple, complex, compound, compound-complex.*

1. The boys studied the lesson, but neither of them understood it.
2. We encourage students to come to the conference, but no one may attend unless he brings a signed permit from his parents.
3. You may write on the back of the page if you wish.
4. Hidden almost entirely from view, the house gives us real privacy.

B. Label these word groups as *sentences, fragments,* or *run-on sentences.* Use the symbols *S, F,* and *RO.*

1. Something that was supposed to be crossed out.
2. I borrowed this book from the library I have read only a few pages.
3. Near the front of the room hangs the clock.
4. The ladies looking verv pretty in their new Easter bonnets.

C. Distinguish between *nominative absolutes* and *participial phrases.*

1. Tomorrow being Good Friday, there will be no school.
2. Having completed his basic training, Gordon was sent overseas.
3. Bruce was unable to write, both wrists being broken.
4. The tests being written now will be graded tomorrow.

D. In these sentences, underline the subject *once* and the predicate *twice.* Label the word *there* as (1) an expletive or (2) an adverb.

1. There are no extra copies of the rules.
2. There on the couch lay my dog Pepper, sound asleep.
3. There were one hundred students on the absentee list today.

E. Vary the following sentences by changing the opening clause to a nominative absolute.

1. Since the price of beef has dropped, we shall dine on steak.
2. After the meeting had ended, we adjourned to the dining room.
3. Because the day was warm, crowds thronged the beaches.

---

*Check Test 9 should be given at this point. If the results show need for further study, pupils should do this review practice. They should then take Mastery Test 9.

Know How to Improve Your Writing Style

1. USING VARIED SENTENCE TYPES

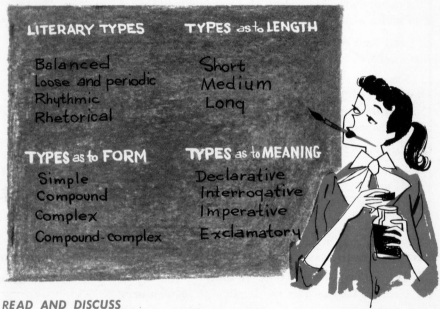

LITERARY TYPES

Balanced
Loose and periodic
Rhythmic
Rhetorical

TYPES as to LENGTH

Short
Medium
Long

TYPES as to FORM

Simple
Compound
Complex
Compound-complex

TYPES as to MEANING

Declarative
Interrogative
Imperative
Exclamatory

READ AND DISCUSS

You have studied sentences from the standpoint of grammatical structure and use. Always remember that a knowledge of grammatical forms is valuable only as it helps you to express your ideas clearly.

In addition to being familiar with sentences according to their grammatical forms, you should learn how to vary sentence length and how to use special literary sentence types. Only as you make use, consciously or unconsciously, of such devices as are explained in this chapter, can you achieve that individuality of expression known as an author's "style."

GUIDES FOR GAINING VARIETY BY USING MANY SENTENCE TYPES

1. Use balanced sentences occasionally. (DEFINITION) A *balanced sentence* is one in which two ideas are set in *contrast* or in *parallel* form.

   As a child, he was noisy and insolent; as a man, he is quiet and meek.

2. Use a mixture of *loose* and *periodic* sentences. (DEFINITIONS) A *loose sentence* is one that can end at one point or more besides the actual ending and still make sense. A *periodic sentence* is one that withholds important information and therefore makes incomplete sense unless read to the end.

   LOOSE: He tipped his hat and departed, leaving Fae standing there, alone and afraid. (The sentence could end also after *hat, departed, Fae, there, alone.*)
   PERIODIC: Suddenly, out of the dark night, floated an eerie cry. (The sentence can end only after *cry.*)

3. Use rhetorical questions now and then. (DEFINITION) A *rhetorical question* is one asked for effect only; no actual answer is expected from the reader or listener: *Where are the heroes of the past?*

4. Use rhythmic sentences for lofty or musical expression. (DEFINITION) A *rhythmic sentence* is one with a smooth, poetic-like pattern.

   If we could first know where we are, and whither we are going, we could better judge what to do and how to do it.—LINCOLN *

5. Use sentences of varying length to match ideas and mood.
   a) Use *short* sentences to show excitement, anger, haste; or to show a close-mouthed or lazy personality.
   b) Use *medium-length* sentences for ordinary ideas.
   c) Use *long* sentences for unhurried, dignified, or deep thoughts.

6. Use a mixture of sentences according to structure; that is, avoid using only simple sentences or simple and compound.

7. Use a mixture of declarative, interrogative, imperative, and exclamatory sentences. Dull writers usually fail to do so.

LEARNING ACTIVITIES

A. Change each loose sentence into a periodic sentence and each periodic sentence into a loose sentence. Make this an oral exercise.

1. With the existing colonies or dependencies of any European power, we ... shall not interfere.—MONROE

---

* Carl Sandburg has arranged the preceding sentence as free verse, making it look like poetry:
> "If we could first know where we are,
> And whither we are tending,
> We could better judge
> What to do and how to do it."

2. But with the morning cool reflection came.—Scott
3. On the right, and stretching for several miles to the north, lay a narrow plain . . . —Cooper
4. We join ourselves to no party that does not carry the flag and keep step to the music of the Union.—Rufus Choate
5. Eliza made her desperate retreat across the river just in the dusk of twilight.—Stowe
6. A troop of strange children ran at his heels, hooting after him, and pointing at his gray beard.—Irving

B. Study the following paragraphs. They illustrate the ways in which paragraphs can be built by stressing one particular type or length of sentence. In a class discussion, decide which types (*balanced, rhetorical, rhythmical; simple, compound, complex,* or *compound-complex*) each paragraph illustrates. Discuss also the effectiveness of the sentences or of sentence length.

So at last I was going to America! Really, really going at last! The boundaries burst. The arch of heaven soared. A million suns shone out for every star. The winds rushed in from outer space, roaring in my ears, "America! America!" *

When I hear people say they have not found the world and life so interesting as to be in love with it, or that they look with equanimity to its end, I am apt to think they have never been properly alive nor seen with clear vision the world they think so meanly of, or anything in it—not a blade of grass. Only I know that mine is an exceptional case, that the visible world is to me more beautiful and interesting than to most persons, that the delight I experienced in my communings with Nature did not pass away, leaving nothing but a recollection of vanished happiness to intensify a present pain. . . .†

Alone? Is he alone at whose right side rides Courage, with Skill within the cockpit and Faith upon the left? Does solitude surround the brave when Adventure leads the way and Ambition reads the dials? Is there no company with him for whom the air is cleft by Daring and the darkness is made light by Emprise? ‡

It was the best of times; it was the worst of times. It was the age of wisdom; it was the age of foolishness. It was the epoch of belief; it was the epoch of incredulity. It was the season of Light; it was the season of Darkness. It was the spring of hope; it was the winter of despair.§

I would rather have been a French peasant and worn wooden shoes. I would rather have lived in a hut with a vine growing over the door and the grapes growing purple in the kisses of the autumn sun. I would rather have been that poor peasant with my loving wife by my side, knitting as the day

* From *The Promised Land* by Mary Antin. Used by permission of Houghton Mifflin Company.
† From *Far Away and Long Ago* by W. H. Hudson. Used by permission of E. P. Dutton and Company, Inc.
‡ From "Lindbergh Flies Alone," an editorial by Harold M. Anderson. First printed in the *New York Sun* for May 21, 1927. Used by permission.
§ From *A Tale of Two Cities* by Charles Dickens.

died out of the sky, with my children upon my knee and their arms about me. I would rather have been that man and gone down to the tongueless silence of the dreamless dust than to have been that imperial impersonation of force and murder known as Napoleon the Great.*

C. In your reading, find and bring to class for analysis examples of loose and periodic sentences.

D. Let one member of the class volunteer to copy on the board several of the balanced sentences from Francis Bacon's essay "Of Studies." Let another give examples of rhetorical questions from Patrick Henry's famous speech at the Virginia Convention.

E. In a literature book or elsewhere, find a paragraph that you think has pleasing rhythm. Prepare and read it in class, being careful to apply the Guides to Effective Oral Reading, page 41.

F. Imagine yourself a sports announcer or a fashion commentator. Compose an oral paragraph in which you describe an exciting sports event or a fashion show. Use the Speech Score Card, page 31. Let your classmates or small discussion groups judge your work. Listen thoughtfully to one another's paragraphs.

USING ENGLISH IN ALL CLASSES

Which is your most difficult subject? In class, study the sentences used in the textbook. How may the purpose for which a textbook is written influence sentence types and length? Try rewriting a typical paragraph in a style that seems to you more understandable. Exchange papers for criticism.

FOLLOW-UP ACTIVITY

Examine an old theme. Select a paragraph and improve it by applying the guides on page 411. Read aloud both the original and the revised paragraph. Do not tell the class which is which. Their comments should help you to decide whether you have done an effective piece of rewriting.

Whenever you plan and write a theme, refer to the guides on page 411 for help in the best expression of the ideas that you want to convey.

2. USING VARIED SENTENCE BEGINNINGS

The loose sentence (defined on page 411) is the natural, easy type to write. If used exclusively, however, loose sentences become monotonous to the reader. Every effective writer uses a variety of sentence beginnings to eliminate monotony of expression.

* From "At the Tomb of Napoleon" by Robert H. Ingersoll.

GUIDES FOR VARYING SENTENCE BEGINNINGS

1. Begin with a *prepositional phrase,* or with more than one.

   After lunch I took a nap.   On the word of this man rests our case.

2. Begin with a *single-word adjective* or *adverb,* or with a *compound adjective* or *adverb.*

   Then a shot rang out.   Neat and efficient, the typist sat at her desk.

3. Begin with a *participial phrase.*

   Carrying its pathetic freight, the steamer drifted along.

4. Begin with a *predicate adjective*: Better than wealth or power is a healthy conscience.

5. Begin with an *adverb clause.*

   As soon as Charles came into sight, Grandfather became excited.

6. Begin with a *modifying infinitive phrase.*

   To judge by that old man, you would think that life is one long picnic.

7. Begin with an *appositive.*

   A veteran of two wars, Wilkins again answered his country's call.

8. Begin with a word or a clause used as a *direct object.*

   That favor I cannot grant. Where he came from, nobody knew.

9. Begin with a *nominative absolute:* The sky having cleared, we set out.

LEARNING ACTIVITIES

A. Write an original sentence to illustrate each type of sentence beginning given in the guides. Put sentences on the board for class evaluation.

B. In a literature book or a magazine, find sentences that illustrate varied sentence beginnings. Read them in class.

C. As an individual or a group project, prepare a chart to show each guide and an illustration of it. Put the chart on the bulletin board.

D. Write a paragraph containing various types of sentence beginnings. Apply the paragraph guides on page 199. (For theme topics, see the Index.) *Proofread for careless errors in form.* Read your paragraph to the class.

E. Give a brief talk to the class or to your group. Plan it with the help of the guides on this page. Use your Speech Score Card, page 31.

USING ENGLISH IN ALL CLASSES

Bring to class a theme or a report that you have written for any of your classes. Improve one paragraph or more by varying the sentence beginnings. Present the result for evaluation by your small group.

3. USING VARIED TYPES OF SENTENCE ELEMENTS

Pleasing variety in expression can be obtained by making full use of such sentence elements as *dependent clauses, participial and infinitive phrases,* and *independent sentence elements.*

GUIDES FOR USING VARIED SENTENCE ELEMENTS

1. Use appositives to combine two short sentences into one longer, smoother sentence or to reduce complex sentences to simple sentences. If one idea is less important, make it the appositive.

   I like Mr. Burt. He is our mailman.   I like Mr. Burt, *our mailman.*
   Arbee, *who is our captain,* won the toss.   Arbee, *our captain,* won the toss.

2. Where it is effective, turn two or more simple sentences into one good complex sentence. Place the important information in the independent clause. Remember that nonrestrictive clauses and introductory adverbial clauses require commas.

   Fritz will lead the way. He knows the neighborhood.
   Fritz, *who knows the neighborhood,* will lead the way.
   Because he knows the neighborhood, Fritz will lead the way.

3. Reduce some adjective clauses to participial phrases.

   Mother, *who dislikes clutter,* almost despairs of my improving.
   Mother, *disliking clutter,* almost despairs of my improving.

4. Use the nominative absolute to combine short sentences or to reduce adverb clauses.

   The sun had set. Darkness crept slowly upon us.
   The sun having set, darkness crept slowly upon us.
   Because everyone was ready, Phil gave the signal to set out.
   Everyone being ready, Phil gave the signal to set out.

5. Combine choppy sentences by using a variety of elements.

   The game began. The first five minutes were slow. Neither team scored.
   The game began *slowly, neither team scoring in the first five minutes.*

6. Change compound sentences to complex sentences or to simple sentences with compound parts, prepositional phrases, or verbals.

   The bell rang and we took our places.
   When the bell had rung, we took our places.
   At the sound of the bell, we took our places.
   Hearing the bell, we took our places.

7. Vary the sentence pattern by inserting parenthetical words, phrases, or clauses between subject and predicate.

   This remark, *unfortunately,* reached the wrong ears. (*word*)
   His attitude, *to be frank,* is unfriendly. (*phrase*)
   Gene, *as I have often said,* is impulsive. (*clause*)

LEARNING ACTIVITIES IN USING VARIED SENTENCE ELEMENTS

A. Applying the preceding guides, improve these student-written paragraphs. *Be sure to proofread.* Compare work in your small groups.

My father did not have a good education. He lived on a prairie during his youth. School was held only during the three most suitable months of the year. The schoolhouse was very poorly built. For this reason there was no school in the winter. The boys were needed on the farm during the summer. The only time left for school was in early spring and late autumn.

One night my mother went to her club. I did not want to stay home. She let me go to the movies. I did not know what was playing, and when I reached the theater, I found that it was a play called *Frankenstein*. I was only nine years old. I didn't know what it would be like. In the middle of the movie, several women screamed, and children down in the front seats came up and sat with their parents. I was frightened and excited after the show was over. I was four dark blocks from home. I ran all the way. I imagined that I could see monsters behind every tree. I was shaking with fear by the time that I reached home.

Three other boys and I once decided that we would visit the old mill. It was a Friday night. This old mill was on the edge of town. We entered through a window. The first thing that we came to was a stairway. It led downward. We started slowly down it. The steps creaked under our weight. At last we reached the bottom. There were large barrels and other odd objects. There were cobwebs everywhere. The wind whistled through the windows. They were broken. It gave us the creeps. We went back up the stairs. We regained our courage when we were back on the main floor. Then we climbed to the top floor. Just then we heard footsteps. We went down the ladder in a hurry. We climbed out the window fast. We resolved not to go into the old mill at night again.

B. Paraphrase (see pages 114–15) the following quotations so that you make clear the ideas that the authors are trying to express. Point out the different types of sentence elements that the quotations contain. Make this a class or a small-group exercise.

1. Not many sounds in life, and I include all urban and all rural sounds, exceed in interest a knock at the door.—LAMB
2. The greatest of faults, I should say, is to be conscious of none.—CARLYLE
3. Nothing that was worthy in the past departs; no truth or goodness realized by man ever dies, or can die; all is still here, and, recognized or not, lives and works through endless changes.—CARLYLE
4. It is as fatal as it is cowardly to blink facts because they are not to our taste.—JOHN TYNDALL
5. If one advances confidently in the direction of his dreams and endeavors to live the life which he has imagined, he will meet with success unimagined in common hours.—THOREAU
6. There are a thousand hacking at the branches of evil to one who is striking at its roots.—THOREAU

7. Let us be of good cheer, however, remembering that the misfortunes hardest to bear are those which never come.—LOWELL

8. Thank God every morning when you get up that you have something to do that day which must be done, whether you like it or not.—KINGSLEY

9. Nobody, I think, ought to read poetry or look at pictures or statues who cannot find a great deal more in them than the poet or artist has actually expressed.—HAWTHORNE

C. Write a paragraph or more in which you make your ideas forceful by the inclusion of varied elements. Write your ideas first in whatever form they come to you; then achieve the form that best conveys what you have to say. Use your Writing Score Card, page 197. *Be sure to proofread.* Read your work to the class, being careful to apply the Guides to Effective Oral Reading, page 41.

USING ENGLISH IN ALL CLASSES

Find in your old themes examples of paragraphs in which you have used some of the forms of sentence variation suggested in the guides on page 415. You may find also sentences that will serve as exercises for improvement.

To keep you in practice

REVIEW

CAPITALIZATION AND PUNCTUATION

Place needed capitalization and punctuation in the following sentences.

1. A fine piece of sculpture is tafts solitude of the soul
2. Have you read that article passers and punters
3. James 1 8 was the preachers text A double minded man is unstable in all his ways
4. From mary jane in my opinion received helpful advice
5. No sayre i was not in macon georgia in june 1953 nor was i there during the winter of 1954
6. Brooks our star forward scored thirty points in last nights game and davis his closest competitor scored twenty two
7. My favorite desserts pie cake and ice cream are fattening
8. The scene was oh words cant describe it
9. After a long hard day at the office father is ready for relaxation
10. The coloradoan a burlington train stops at creston doesnt it

THE USE OF NOUNS, PRONOUNS, AND VERBALS

List all *nouns, pronouns,* and *verbals* in these sentences; give their use.

1. Mark's decision to withdraw was a disappointment to us; but, having determined his course, he resigned nevertheless.
2. Fishing interests Jim, my oldest brother, above all other pastimes.

RECOGNITION OF PREPOSITIONAL PHRASES AND SUBORDINATE CLAUSES

List all prepositional phrases and all subordinate, or dependent, clauses in the sentences that follow. Beside each phrase or clause, write its use in the sentence.

1. What you decide about that affair may change the procedures that we have followed in the past.
2. The man at the right of the desk will speak after several members have talked on this topic.
3. Father thinks that he will take a trip where he took one last year.

PREPOSITIONS AND CONJUNCTIONS

Choose the correct forms from the parentheses. When there is a choice between colloquial and standard English, choose the standard form.

1. (Being that, Since) you have known Ellen for so long, I have no doubts (but what, that) your recommendation will be helpful.
2. No one from our room was (to, at) the game (outside of, except) us.
3. It looks (like, as if) I ought to go, but I'd rather not (without, unless) you go, too. I don't know (as, whether) it matters, though.
4. The man whose house is just (in back of, behind) ours divided his property (between, among) his many cousins.
5. The reason for my coming is (that, because) I saw in the paper (where, that) extra help is needed here.
6. He lives (at, in) Denver, just (inside, inside of) the city limits.

PRONOUNS, ADJECTIVES, AND ADVERBS

Make needed corrections in the usage of adjectives and adverbs in these sentences. Change colloquial forms to standard English.

1. Fred he showed me a airplane which he had made hisself.
2. The pole was sort of slippery, but me and Jack climbed up it, anyways.
3. Finishing his work, Phil put it carefully on a empty shelf.
4. I'm sure sorry that Jane is not too satisfied with this kind of a job.
5. Don't feel badly. Us girls thought your speech was real good.
6. Mother never realized that you are most as tall as myself.
7. The weather is some warmer today, but I haven't scarcely been outside.

VERBS AND AGREEMENT

Correct all errors in verb forms and in agreement.

1. When the sun shined on me too fiercely, I laid down under a tree to rest.
2. Have you did anything with the money that Dad give you?
3. Have either of you took my pen? Alec says that he don't have it.
4. If I had knowed that you was going, I'd have went with you.
5. You would have shaken with laughter if you had saw that program.
6. I'd have swore that she had sang that song before.
7. Some one had tore up their paper and throwed it all over the room.
8. If he had blowed harder, he might have broke the balloon.

APPENDIX

VERB CONJUGATIONS

Conjugation of TO GIVE

Principal Parts

Present: give   *Present Participle:* giving
Past: gave   *Past Participle:* given

Indicative Mood

ACTIVE VOICE		PASSIVE VOICE	

Present Tense

SINGULAR	PLURAL	SINGULAR	PLURAL
1. I give	we give	I *am* given	we *are* given
2. you give	you give	you *are* given	you *are* given
3. he * gives	they give	he *is* given	they *are* given

Past Tense

SINGULAR	PLURAL	SINGULAR	PLURAL
1. I gave	we gave	I *was* given	we *were* given
2. you gave	you gave	you *were* given	you *were* given
3. he gave	they gave	he *was* given	they *were* given

Future Tense

SINGULAR	PLURAL	SINGULAR	PLURAL
1. I *shall* give	we *shall* give	I *shall be* given	we *shall be* given
2. you *will* give	you *will* give	you *will be* given	you *will be* given
3. he *will* give	they *will* give	he *will be* given	they *will be* given

Present Perfect Tense

SINGULAR	PLURAL	SINGULAR	PLURAL
1. I *have* given	we *have* given	I *have been* given	we *have been* given
2. you *have* given	you *have* given	you *have been* given	you *have been* given
3. he *has* given	they *have* given	he *has been* given	they *have been* given

Past Perfect Tense

SINGULAR	PLURAL	SINGULAR	PLURAL
1. I *had* given	we *had* given	I *had been* given	we *had been* given
2. you *had* given	you *had* given	you *had been* given	you *had been* given
3. he *had* given	they *had* given	he *had been* given	they *had been* given

Future Perfect Tense

SINGULAR	PLURAL	SINGULAR	PLURAL
1. I *shall have* given	we *shall have* given	I *shall have been* given	we *shall have been* given
2. you *will have* given	you *will have* given	you *will have been* given	you *will have been* given
3. he *will have* given	they *will have* given	he *will have been* given	they *will have been* given

* *She* and *it* and *singular nouns* are used just as *he* is.

Subjunctive Mood

<table>
<tr><td>ACTIVE VOICE</td><td>PASSIVE VOICE</td></tr>
</table>

Present Tense

ACTIVE VOICE	PASSIVE VOICE
if I, you, he give	if I, you, he *be* given
if we, you, they give	if we, you, they *be* given

Past Tense

if I, you, he gave	if I, you, he *were* given
if we, you, they gave	if we, you, they *were* given

Present Perfect Tense

if I, you, he *have* given	if I, you, he *have been* given
if we, you, they *have* given	if we, you, they *have been* given

Past Perfect Tense

if I, you, he *had* given	if I, you, he *had been* given
if we, you, they *had* given	if we, you, they *had been* given

Imperative Mood

give	*be* given

Infinitives

Present: to give	to *be* given
Perfect: to *have* given	to *have been* given

Participles

Present: giving	*being* given
Past:	given
Perfect: having given	*having been* given

Gerunds

Present: giving	*being* given
Perfect: having given	*having been* given

Conjugation of TO BE

Principal Parts

Present: be	*Present Participle:* being
Past: was	*Past Participle:* been

Indicative Mood

Present Tense

SINGULAR	PLURAL
1. I am	we are
2. you are	you are
3. he is	they are

Present Perfect Tense

SINGULAR	PLURAL
I have been	we have been
you have been	you have been
he has been	they have been

Past Tense

SINGULAR	PLURAL
1. I was	we were
2. you were	you were
3. he was	they were

Past Perfect Tense

SINGULAR	PLURAL
I had been	we had been
you had been	you had been
he had been	they had been

Future Tense		Future Perfect Tense	
1. I shall be	we shall be	I shall have been	we shall have been
2. you will be	you will be	you will have been	you will have been
3. he will be	they will be	he will have been	they will have been

SUBJUNCTIVE MOOD

SINGULAR   PLURAL

Present Tense

if I, you, he *be*   if we, you, they *be*

Past Tense

if I, you, he *were*   if we, you, they *were*

Present Perfect Tense

if I, you, he *have been*   if we, you, they *have been*

Past Perfect Tense

if I, you, he *had been*   if we, you, they *had been*

IMPERATIVE MOOD

The imperative mood has only one form: *be,* and one person: *second.*

INFINITIVES	PARTICIPLES	GERUNDS
Present: to be	*Present:* being	*Present:* being
Perfect: to have been	*Past:* been	*Perfect:* having been
	Perfect: having been	

DECLENSION OF PRONOUNS

PERSONAL PRONOUNS

	Nominative Case	Possessive Case	Objective Case
First person, singular	I	my, mine	me
First person, plural	we	our, ours	us
Second person, singular	you	your, yours	you
Second person, plural	you	your, yours	you
Third person, singular	he, she, it	his, her, hers, its	him, her, it
Third person, plural	they	their, theirs	them.

RELATIVE AND INTERROGATIVE PRONOUNS

	Nominative Case	Possessive Case	Objective Case
Singular	who	whose	whom
Plural	who	whose	whom
Singular	which	whose	which
Plural	which	whose	which
Singular	what	.....	what
Plural	what	.....	what

PRINCIPAL PARTS OF TROUBLESOME VERBS

Present Tense	Past Tense	Past Participle	Present Tense	Past Tense	Past Participle
attack *	attacked	attacked	raise *	raised	raised
beat	beat	beaten	ride	rode	ridden
become	became	become	ring	rang,	
begin	began	begun		rung †	rung
bite	bit	bitten	rise	rose	risen
blow	blew	blown	run	ran	run
break	broke	broken	say	said	said
bring	brought	brought	see	saw	seen
burst	burst	burst	set	set	set
buy	bought	bought	shake	shook	shaken
choose	chose	chosen	shine ‡	shone	shone
climb *	climbed	climbed	show	showed	shown,
come	came	come			showed †
do	did	done	shrink	shrank,	
drag *	dragged	dragged		shrunk †	shrunk
draw	drew	drawn	sing	sang,	
drink	drank	drunk		sung †	sung
drive	drove	driven	sink	sank,	
drown *	drowned	drowned		sunk †	sunk
eat	ate	eaten	sit	sat	sat
fall	fell	fallen	sneak *	sneaked	sneaked
fly	flew	flown	speak	spoke	spoken
forget	forgot	forgotten,	spring	sprang,	
		forgot †		sprung †	sprung
freeze	froze	frozen	steal	stole	stolen
get	got	got,	swear	swore	sworn
		gotten †	swim	swam	swum
give	gave	given	take	took	taken
go	went	gone	tear	tore	torn
grow	grew	grown	throw	threw	thrown
know	knew	known	wake	waked, woke †	waked
lay	laid	laid	wear	wore	worn
lie	lay	lain	write	wrote	written

* This verb is regular, but wrong forms are frequently used in the past and the past participle.

† The first form is preferred.

‡ When *shine* means "polish," the parts are *shine, shined, shined.*

INDEX

A

A, an, the (articles), 354
  using correctly, 364
  when to capitalize, 160
Abbreviations, 165, 167; capitalizing, 162
  used in business, 229
About, not *around,* 392
Abstract noun, 316
Accent marks, 95; in poetry, 283–85
Acceptance speech, 50
Accusative case. *See* Objective case
Action verb, 294
Active voice, 297
Address, commas in, 167
  envelope, 223; inside, 224
Adjective, 353–71
  classified by position, 354
  colloquial *vs.* standard usage of, 367–68, 371, 402, 418
  comparison, 355
  correct usage, rules, 364, 365, 367
  effective, choosing, 259–60, 368–70
  infinitive as, 295, 356–58
  kinds, 354
  participial phrase as, 356–58
  participle as, 295, 354
  possessive noun as, 361
  predicate adjective, 354, 361, 379
  pronominal, 339, 354
Adjective clause, 359–60
  restrictive and nonrestrictive, 170–71, 359, 415
Adjective phrase, 356–58, 388
Adverb, 372–86
  colloquial *vs.* standard usage of, 382–84, 386, 402, 418
  comparison, 374
  conjunctive, 179, 394, 404
  correct usage, rules, 379, 380, 381, 382, 383, 384
  distinguished from adjective, 379

Adverb—*Continued*
  effective, choosing, 259–60, 385–86
  formation and kinds, 373–74
  infinitive as, 295, 374–75, 378
Adverb clause, 376–77; misplaced, 380
Adverbial objective, 327–28, 375, 381
Adverb phrase, 374–75, 388
Advertisements, writing, 239–40
Aggravate, misused, 310
Agreement
  pronoun with antecedent, 344–46
  verb with subject, 320–22, 346–48
Ain't, avoiding, 309
Alliteration, in poetry, 285
All the farther, misused for *as far as,* 382
Almost and *most,* 379
Also, avoiding as conjunction, 398
Among and *between,* 389
Anachronism, 272
And, and etc., but, 396
And, and so, avoiding, 407
Antecedent of pronoun, 340, 344–46
Antiphonal reading, 44
Antonyms, 99–100
Anxious and *eager,* 367
Any, any one, misused in comparisons, 364
Any one or *either* (*neither*), 350
Anyplace, misused for *anywhere,* 383
Anyways, misused for *anyway,* 382
Anywheres, misused for *anywhere,* 382
Apology, letter of, 235–36
Apostrophe, 173–75; rules, 174
Apostrophe, figure of speech, 284–86
Application blanks, filling, 219
Application letter, 228
Appositive, 329, 339; adjective, 354
  case of, 329, 342
  dependent clause as, 334–35
  intensive pronoun as, 340–41
Appraisal chart, letter writing, 221
Appraisal record for writing reports, 213–14
Appreciation, letter of, 234

N

Narrative, writing, 267–77
  character, creating, 270–71
  classifying ideas, 268
  dialogue, using, 273–74
  endings, story, 275
  guides, 276
  openings, story, 274–75
  plot, developing, 269–70
  setting, how to use, 272–73
  short story, essentials of, 267
  title, choosing, 275
Near-homonyms, 191
Nearly, placing near word modified, 380
Neuter gender, 316
Never, in double negative, 381
Never, misused for *did not,* 384
Newspapers, 145–53; writing for, 215–16
News story, 147–48
Nohow, avoiding, 382
Nominative absolute, 399–401, 415
Nominative case, 316, 318, 323, 342
Nonrestrictive clause, 170–71, 359, 415
No or *yes,* comma after, 167
No place, misused for *nowhere,* 383
Notes, taking, 39, 54, 212, 213, 245–47
  guides, 212, 246
Noun, 315–38
  adverbial objective, 327–28
  appositive, 328–30
  case, 316
  classification, 316
  compound, 182, 188, 316
  direct object, 324–26
  exact and vivid, using, 259–60, 336–37
  gender, 316
  gerund, 331–33
  indirect object, 327–28
  infinitive, 331–33
  noun of address, 328–30
  number, 316, 321
  objective complement, 324–26
  object of preposition, 327–28
  person, 316
  possessive noun as adjective, 345, 361
  predicate nominative, 323–24
  subject, 317–20
  we and *us,* used with, 343
Noun clause, 333–36, 357

Noun (nominative) of address, 167, 328–30
Nowheres near, misused for *not nearly,* 382
Number, 298, 316, 345

O

Object of preposition, 327–28, 339
  dependent clause as, 334, 357, 375
  gerund and infinitive as, 331, 357, 375
Object of verb. *See* Direct object
Objective case, 316, 342
Objective complement, 324–26
  adjective as, 354; dependent clause as, 334
Of, misused as auxiliary, 307, 389
Off, off of, misused for *from,* 390
On account of, avoiding, 390
On and *for,* 389
One another or *each other,* 350
One's or *his,* to refer to *one,* 345
Only, placed near word modified, 380
Onomatopoeia, 285
Oral reading, 40–43; guides, 41
Order letter, 225–26
Ordinal numbers, 354
Ought, using correctly, 307
Ourself, avoiding, 348
Outlining, 117–21; guides, 118
  working outline. 245
Outside of, except, except for, 392

P

Panel discussion, 74
Pantomime, 22–23
Paragraph
  central ideas in, 5, 110–12, 199, 206
  coherence, 199, 248
  development, types, 199–206; guides, 199
  emphasis, 199, 248
  for each change of speaker, 176
  introductory, 206–8
  key words in, 110–12, 206
  summary (conclusion), 206–8
  theme, building paragraphs into, 206–7
  topic sentence, 5, 199
  transition, 206–8
  unity, 199, 248
Parallel structure, 396
Paraphrasing, 114–17, 136, 140, 248
Parentheses, 181–84; rules, 183
Parenthetical expressions
  comma with, 170; dashes with, 183

431

Sentence; *see also* Simple, compound, etc.
  classified as to form, 404
    complex, 394, 404–5, 415
    compound, 394, 404–5, 415
    compound-complex, 404–6
    simple, 404–5, 415
  classified as to meaning
    declarative, 165, 411
    exclamatory, 165, 411
    imperative, 165, 411
    interrogative, 165, 411
  classified as to rhetoric
    balanced, 411
    loose, 411
    periodic, 411
    rhetorical question, 411
  clincher, 199
  elliptical, 407
  fragment and run-on, 406–9
  topic, 5–6, 110, 122–24, 199, 201, 204, 206
Sentence outline, 117–21
Sentence variety, ways of securing, 410–17
Series, items in, punctuating, 168, 179
Set and *sit,* 302–4
Shall and *will,* 310
Short story. *See* Narrative, writing
Should and *would,* 310
Should of, shoulda, avoiding, 389
Signature of letter, 224–25
Simile, 257
Simple predicate, 294, 404
Simple sentence, 404
Simple subject, 404
Skeleton, sentence, 323, 326
Skimming, 113–14, 136, 245–46
  practice in, 4, 9, 16, 21, 25, 33, 38, 62, 80, 114, 140, 141, 145, 186, 206, 241, 246, 254, 369
Slang, 57, 105–7
Slogans, 105–7
So-as, in negative constructions, 384
Social letters, 231–39
  acceptance, 238
  addressing the envelope, 231
  apology, 235–36
  appreciation, 234
  condolence, 236
  congratulatory, 235
  family, 233
  formal invitation, 237–38

Social letters—*Continued*
  friendly, 232
  guides, 231
  indented form, 231
  invitations and replies, 237–38
  regret, 238
  thanks, 234
Some, misused for *somewhat,* 384
Someplace, misused for *somewhere,* 383
Somewheres, misused for *somewhere,* 382
Sonnet, 289–90
Sort of, sorta, avoiding, 383
Sort of a, misused for *sort of,* 364
Speech
  analyzing, 19–20
  bodily ease, acquiring, 21–23
  choral reading, 44–47
  conversationalist, becoming a good, 58–60
  courtesy in, 56–58
  developing oral paragraph, 6
  directions, giving and following, 36–38
  discussions, special types of, 73–76
  enunciation and pronunciation, 26–30
  explanations, clear, 34–36
  for special occasions, 49–52
  improving speech habits and voice, 20–23
  interviews, taking part in, 53–55
  introductions, making and recognizing, 47–49
  oral reading, 40–43
  parliamentary practice, 61–72
  practice, 5, 6, 21, 22–23, 25–26, 27–30, 33, 35–36, 37–38, 39–40, 42–43, 44–47, 49, 50–52, 53, 55, 57–58, 59–60, 62, 78–79, 112, 114, 121, 132–33, 135, 143, 152, 153, 154, 156, 175, 200, 204, 212, 258–59, 273, 275, 370, 386, 413, 414
  progress, analyzing, 30
  questions, asking and answering, 32–34
  reporting experiences and observations, 38–40
  score card, 31
  telephone, using, 52–53
  topics, 5, 6, 7–8, 12, 35–36, 38, 39, 40, 46, 55, 58, 59–60, 74, 78–79, 82–83, 143, 152
  vocal factors, 23–26
Speech score card, 31; how to mark, 30
  practice in using. *See* Maintenance practice, speech score card

Vocabulary; *see also* Words
 building, practice in, 92–93, 96–97, 98–99,
  100, 103–4, 106–8; *see also* Maintenance practice
 improving
  dictionary, using, 93–97
  growth, evaluating, 108–9
  guides, 91
  new words, attacking, 91–93
  related words, understanding, 99–101
  suitable words, choosing, 105–8, 400
  word elements, analyzing, 101–4
  word meanings, evaluating, 98–99
 terms to avoid in writing verse, 284
Voice of verb, 297, 307
Voice, use of, 23–26, 43, 44
Volume of voice, 24

W

Want in (*out, off, through*), avoiding, 309
Way, misused for *away,* 384
Ways, misused for *way, distance,* 383
We, used with noun, 343
Well and *good,* 379
What, avoiding as relative pronoun, 348
When, after *scarcely, hardly,* 398
Where, misused for *that,* 396
Where, when, misused in definition, 396
Whether and *if,* 398
Which, faulty reference of, 345
While, to denote duration of time, 398
Who, using correct case of, 342
Who, which, that, 348
Will and *shall,* 310
With, by, at, 389
Within and *inside of,* 392
Without, misused for *unless,* 396
Words; *see also* Vocabulary
 antonyms, 99–100
 choosing wisely, 259–60
 colloquialisms, 91, 97, 105–7
 derivation, 101–4
 dialectal, 308
 dictionary information on, 93–97
 "high-brow" language, 105–7
 homonyms, 99–100, 191–92
 illiterate, 308
 key words, 91, 109–12
 literal *vs.* connotative, 98–99, 108
 mispronounced often, 29, 108, 389

Words—*Continued*
 origins, 107
 slang, 105–7
 slogans, 105–7
 specific, 311–12, 336–37, 369, 385
 synonyms, 99–100, 108
 trite, 105–7
Worse, misused for *more,* 383
Would and *should,* 310
Would have, misused for *had,* 307
Writing, mechanics of
 appraisal chart for letters, 221
 capitalization, 159–64
 correction marks, 198
 punctuation, 164–84
 score card, 197
 spelling, 185–94
 standards, setting, 195–98
Writing, original
 description, 250–61
 essays, 262–66
 letters, social, 231–39
 narration, 267–77
 paragraphs and themes, 199–208
 school publications, 215–16
 topics, 196, 200, 201, 202, 203, 204, 206,
  208, 242, 252, 255, 261, 266, 268, 270,
  274, 276–77, 280–81, 290
 verse, 278–90
Writing, practical types of
 advertisements, 239–40
 business forms and letters, 216–30
 directions and explanations, 212
 notes, taking, 212
 parliamentary forms, 215
 records, keeping, 211
 reports, 213–14
 telegrams, 239–40
 term paper, 241–49
 tests, taking, 209–10
Writing score card, 197
 practice in using. *See* Maintenance practice
  writing score card
W's, the five, in news story, 147, 216

Y

Yearbooks, 130–31
Yes or *no,* comma after, 167
You, as subject, agreement with verb, 347
You, avoiding as indefinite pronoun, 350